Message To The Blackman In America

By
Elijah Muhammad
Messenger of Allah
Leader and Teacher to the American So-called Negro

Published by
Secretarius MEMPS Publications
5025 N. Central Ave. #415
Phoenix, Arizona 85012
Phone & Fax (602) 466-7347
Email: secmemps@gmail.com
Web: www.memps.com

Call or Write For FREE Book & Audio Catalog

ISBN-13: 978-1-884855-14-6
ISBN-10: 1-884855-14-8

**Visit our website for
The Largest selection of Standard as well as
unpublished rare books by Elijah Muhammad. Also,
the largest audio research library available.**

Dedication

... To My People,

The So-called American Negro. Freedom, Justice, Equality; Happiness, Peace of Mind, Contentment, Money, Good Jobs, Decent Homes—all these can be yours if you accept your God, Allah, now and return to His (and your original) religion, Islam.

Preface

As we near the exhaustion of the Wisdom of this world which has not been able to shed enough light on our path in search for that Supreme Wisdom to keep us from stumbling and falling, we now seek the wisdom of Allah, The Best Knower and Guide in the Person of Master Fard Muhammad (to Whom be praised forever). The reader will find that light in this book.

Elijah Muhammad,
Messenger of Allah

OTHER BOOKS BY ELIJAH MUHAMMAD

MESSAGE TO THE BLACKMAN IN AMERICA (SB) & (HB)
OUR SAVIOUR HAS ARRIVED (SB) & (HB)
HOW TO EAT TO LIVE - BOOK 1 (SB) & (HB)
HOW TO EAT TO LIVE - BOOK 2 (SB) & (HB)
THE FLAG OF ISLAM (SB)
SUPREME WISDOM VOL. 1 (SB) - SUPREME WISDOM VOL. 2 (SB)
THE THEOLOGY OF TIME: UNABRIDGED DIRECT
TRANSCRIPTION EDITION (SB) & (HB)
THE THEOLOGY OF TIME: SUBJECT INDEXED ABRIDGED VER-
SION (SB)
TRUE HISTORY OF MASTER FARD MUHAMMAD,
ALLAH (GOD) IN PERSON (SB) & (HB)
FALL OF AMERICA (SB) & (HB)
GOD-SCIENCE OF BLACK POWER (SB)
BLACK STONE: THE TRUE HISTORY OF ELIJAH MUHAMMAD (SB)
BLOOD BATH: THE TRUE TEACHINGS OF MALCOLM X (SB)
CHRISTIANITY VERSUS ISLAM (SB)
DIVINE SAYINGS OF ELIJAH MUHAMMAD - VOL. 1-3 (SB)
A PLAIN UNDERSTANDING OF THE RED DRAGON (SB)
GENESIS YEARS: UNPUBLISHED-RARE WRITINGS OF ELIJAH MU-
HAMMAD (SB)
HISTORY OF JESUS' BIRTH & DEATH &
WHAT IT MEANS TO YOU AND ME (SB)
HISTORY OF THE NATION OF ISLAM (SB)
JESUS: ONLY A PROPHET (SB)
MOTHER PLANE (SB) L POLICE BRUTALITY (SB)
MY PEOPLE ARE DESTROYED: PROPER
INSTRUCTIONS IN THE TIME OF JUDGMENT (SB)
SCIENCE OF TIME (SB) L SECRETS OF FREEMASONRY (SB)
TRUE HISTORY OF ELIJAH MUHAMMAD - (HARDCOVER)
(SAME AS BLACK STONE)
YAKUB (JACOB): THE FATHER OF MANKIND (SB)

CONTENTS

ix

FOREWORD

THE TRUTH
ABOUT MUHAMMAD

It has been more than 40 years since a Negro has appeared on the national horizon of racial leadership with a program for his people as controversial and as clear-cut as that of Elijah Muhammad. Not since the days of Marcus Garvey, the West Indian visionary back in 1920, has an "either or else" plan of Negro salvation been placed before the people that is as sharply outlined as to consequences as that of Muhammad.

Garvey's "Back to Africa" slogan, based solely on vivid black nationalism, electrified Negroes to the point where more than 5 million joined his ranks and defied the pudgy black man whom they worshiped with their love and their loyalty.

His Universal Negro Improvement Association, that eventually spread throughout the world wherever black people are found, was primarily a mass movement designed to absorb the "Little Man."

This is also true of Elijah Muhammad's Temples of Islam. His movement is based solidly on awakening the great masses of America's 20 million Negroes to the truth of their racial heritage and destiny.

Like Marcus Garvey, Muhammad is building his Religious group on a nonwhite basis and like Garvey has irrefutable reasons for excluding whites.

Muhammad was born the son of a rural Georgia minister. He learned only the bare rudiments of reading, writing, and arithmetic before he had to go to the fields to help his family earn a living.

But Muhammad, born Elijah Poole under the slave name of his parents, as Garvey had been before him, was particularly fitted to be a teacher of men. Not in the sense of the popular conception of classroom teachers of rote and dogma, but in the classic molds of the great teachers of history—Socrates, Aristotle, Siddhartha Gautama [The Buddha], Guru Nanak, K'ung Fu-tze [Confucius], Zoroaster, Moses, Mohammed and Jesus Christ, most of whom were largely unlettered men.

xiii

They taught the truth of life in its practical essence, taking the torch of mental freedom among the great masses of mankind and thus enlightening the world of their day. They persisted in spreading their momentary glimpses of the Truth to all mankind in the face of the murderous opposition of the priesthood, the hostility of kings and the general unwillingness of men to hear the error of their ways.

These men were known as priests, as rabbis, as teachers; some were believed to be gods in disguise. Whatever the popular thinking about their true identity, what they taught and the good they brought to the world was of greater import and impact.

The dramatic spectacular climb of Muhammad from a sharecropper's cotton patch in Sandersville, Georgia, to national and international eminence as a leader of his people is one that must be told at another time. The Muslim name, Muhammad, was given him over 30 years ago by his own teacher in the Islamic faith. Today, Muhammad says God's goal is to give "all my people holy names to replace those given them by the slavemaster (whites) while they were in physical and mental bondage in America."

He points out that the names his followers are known by are just as legal as those given them by the white man or adopted by the descendants of former slaves. Muhammad, himself, was known as "Karriem" before he was called Muhammad. "Karriem," he says, is the original name the Prophet Mohammed was known by 1,400 years ago.

There are more than 100 praiseworthy "holy names" for God or good which people in Islam are known by, he says. "But white people frequently take the names of beasts, such as Bear, Hogg, Fox or Bull, or of marine creatures such as Fish, Salmon, and so forth. By giving Negroes such names, the white man perpetuates his rule of the black man."

A characteristic of Muhammad's teachings is that he never, as Garvey and others did before him, preached "Back to Africa" doctrines as the salvation of the American "so-called Negro." Muhammad says America is not the white man's home; he belongs in Europe and by force took America from "our Asiatic brother, the Indian. We have as much right to this soil as the white man. Why should we claim the land of our black brother in Africa for which he has given his life and labor? It belongs to him. Our destiny, he points out, "is right here in America."

Right now Muhammad is nearing that crossroad of all leaders where the value and extent of his teachings are on trial. Is Golgatha his destination? Will his own people sell him out as they sold out Marcus Garvey and Booker T. Washington?

Can he be destroyed, toppled by jealous rivals, picked to pieces by other enemies bent on reducing him to size?

These are explosive questions that should be examined in the light of the consistent drive to discredit the mild-mannered, soft-spoken, slightly built little man who directs an unprecedented nationwide all-Negro movement based on the teachings of Islam (submission to the commands of Allah, the God of the Muslims).

Wherever black men and women are found in the United States, his followers point out, there are followers of Elijah Muhammad, the "Messenger of Allah." Branch Mosques of Islam are flourishing in Detroit, Boston, New York, Baltimore, Washington, Philadelphia, St. Louis, Pittsburgh, Norfolk, Winston-Salem, Newark, Cleveland, Indianapolis, Milwaukee, Chicago, Atlanta, Houston, Birmingham, Los Angeles, San Francisco, Miami, Jacksonville, Macon and perhaps another hundred cities, towns and villages.

As one Muhammad official in Detroit said recently, "Every time a Negro is beaten by white mobs or police, a Negro's home is burned, a cross is planted on a Negro's lawn or a black man is refused service at a lunch counter, gas station or hotel, you can count on a minimum of 200 Negroes joining our movement the next day. Among us they finally find refuge and the company of people their own kind who know where they are going!"

With membership swelling in such proportions, respect and alarm is growing over the Muhammad movement among both upper level whites and Negroes.

The Negroes opposing Muhammad are mostly those egged on to it by personal jealousy or motivated by their own white "sponsors" who must not be offended or denied unless they have the ground cut from under them in politics, business or social circles. The Negro preachers, while privately agreeing with Muhammad's teachings, are almost to a man afraid to speak up and be identified. They use the traditional ideological opposition of Christianity o Islam as their escape hatch. Yet, in spite of this vast chasm so far not spanned by followers of either faith, some Negro ministers are speaking up in defense of their convictions that Muhammad deserves to be heard.

These are those courageous ministers who have not been afraid to make available their church auditoriums for Muhammad rallies and conventions in Chicago, Detroit, Cleveland, Philadelphia, Los Angeles and elsewhere.

"The man is teaching the truth, whether he says he gets it from the Christian God or the Moslem Allah." One minister said this in Cleveland, where a recent Muhammad rally attracted 3,000 persons in a heavy rain to the Cory Methodist Church to hear the fiery leader of America's Muslims speak.

To a man, however, Negro ministers, social agency leaders and politicians will assure you there is nothing communistic about the Muhammad phenomenon.

But most of them are prone to label the spread of the Islamic doctrine as espoused by Muhammad as a form of extreme "black nationalism."

Others call it "black supremacy."

Actually, Muhammad is exposing Negroes for the first time to a brutal appraisal of their actual standing in the American community and what they can expect in the future from a system that under various disguises still grips them in mental, physical and moral slavery and after 100 years of alleged freedom from the clanking shackles of southern plantation servitude continues to lull them to sleep with false promises of a bright tomorrow which never comes.

The fight against Muhammad has united Negro and white in a bond of common unity seldom achieved in the past—most certainly not against the Ku Klux Klan, the White Citizens Councils, the avowed proponents of White Supremacy and the State's Rights and Conservatives who, ever since Abraham Lincoln issued his Emancipation Proclamation freeing the slaves, have labored without letup to return the black man to actual physical slavery in the South and then deny him the meager, hard-earned and costly freedoms he has won in the courts.

Through the Christian Church, these bitter foes of Muhammad and the Negro have established as a disgraceful world-wide criterion of Christianity the saying, "Eleven o'clock on Sunday is America's most segregated hour."

To change this, Negroes are being egged into pitiful "Kneel-in" demonstrations at lily-white churches in both the North and South, making such debasing spectacles of themselves in order

xvi

to be admitted to a House of Worship to bow down to the same God the white man claims has ordered him to keep black people out.

But Muhammad, who doesn't admit whites to his spiritual meetings in his Mosque on Sunday, is bitterly accused of practicing race hatred because he does not believe it helps the Negro's cause to let the white man in on everything he does or thinks.

Compounding this unreasoning hatred and opposition to Muhammad is the fact that so many Negro so-called leaders have jumped on the white band wagon. Trying to drown out Muhammad's bitter truths, they speak at every rally and meeting in which he appears.

Actually, the fight on Muhammad and his program can be summed up on the issues listed here. They oppose him BECAUSE:

1. The truth he teaches is too unpleasant to hear, and the complacent, both Negro and white, don't want to hear it, nor do they want anyone else to hear it.

2. He stirs up the masses of Negroes in a way no one since the heyday of Marcus Garvey has done in telling them to stand up and be men!

3. They cannot break up his evergrowing following without starting major race riots and other outbreaks which would be political suicide for any official to attempt at this time or at any time in the future.

4. Muhammad is independent. No white money backs him. No white man calls the shots as to what his organization can demand from him as an accounting of his stewardship. This, he says simply, he owes only to his own people.

5. He teaches race solidarity and unity. He preaches that the Number One motto of black people everywhere must be "all for one and one for all" if the race is to lift itself by its own bootstraps from the mess of ignorance and slavery it is in today.

6. He sees what others cannot see. Unlettered as he is, Elijah Muhammad has the uncanny but God-given ability to accurately prophesy about the future. His knowledge of the true history of the world's black people is awesome and comes from years of concentrated study and research. That is why he is called the "Messenger of Allah."

7. He steps on too many toes. Truth is impersonal and a two-edged sword cutting down the lies, deceits and half-truths

with equally emphatic swipes on all sides. Muhammad tears the veil of falsehood aside and exposes the phonies, the fearful and the mountebanks among both Negroes and whites.

8. He teaches Negroes to first love one another. This perhaps is the phase of his teachings that has aroused such widespread criticism that he teaches his people to hate the white man. Muhammad says "you won't have the capacity to love anybody else if you concentrate all your love on your fellow black man." If the white man shows so little love or even respect for the black man, he points out, why should Negroes spend so much time running around begging their brothers to love those who do not have the same measure of regard or love for blacks?

9. He gives the little Negro true leadership. This tenet of Muhammad's credo is also widely seen as a source of the general jealousy of him held by Negro politicians, social workers and some ministers. For until Muhammad came along, only an isolated few Negro organizations, including churches, had the time of day for the largely illiterate, poverty-stricken, superstitious, exploited masses.

Instead, the concentration was on improving the conditions of living of the high school and college educated middle-class Negro; the well-to-do policy kings and real estate insurance and funeral tycoons were wooed and the "nickel and dime" Negroes shooed away to the tender mercies of store-front church preachers or sidewalk soapbox orators.

10. He has had the courage to open schools of his own in order to prepare young Negroes for what they must face and cope with in making a better world for themselves and their descendants.

Up to the day he opened his first University of Islam, in Detroit, the only Negro owned and operated schools and colleges were backed by such church groups as the African Methodist Episcopals, the Baptists and a few other denominations.

Muhammad's Universities in Detroit, Chicago and elsewhere have highly trained faculties and are distinguished by the fact that children in the third grade are speaking Arabic fluently and working difficult problems in Algebra!

11. He lifts up Negro women and removes them from the status of being prostitutes for white men. This startling development in the Muhammad program is unprecedented, for "Scarlet" women "saved" by the churches always carry the stinging dis-

tinction of their former lives. Muhammad relieves them of all disgrace and gives them a new life based on purity and self respect. At the same time, he makes it mandatory that his male followers honor their own women as individual examples of virtue.

12. He goes among the fallen of his people and redeems the wino, the alcoholic, the narcotics addict, the prostitute, the sidewalk hoodlum, the thief and the profane.

A visit to any Muhammad Mosque of Islam will reward the student seeking to see for himself. Calm, quiet, self-contained efficiency and pride is seen on every hand. No singing of spirituals and gospel songs or loud shouting or "amens!" and groans disturb his service. His followers acknowledge his or his assistants' scoring of points with hand applause only.

More white writers, authors and journalists are writing about Elijah Muhammad and his Mosque of Islam movement who have never met, heard or talked to him than any black man in recent history. Because they have never met or talked in person with the man, most of these writers for national magazines and newspapers take a hostile attitude toward him. Almost to a man they accuse Muhammad of teaching his followers to hate the white man, condemn him severely for "racism," and allege he is teaching "Black Supremacy."

Few write that Muhammad is teaching black people to love themselves and their race, first; nor do they point out that any person or people thus engaged have little or no time to go around loving everybody, turning the other cheek and otherwise wasting valuable effort and time that today keeps the black man on the bottom rung of the ladder. They fail to point out that Jesus Christ failed to teach humanity to love the man or men who beat, kill or enslave it or to hop spryly about with grinning lips when the enslaver heaves into view, anxious to serve and make him happy, even though the slave is still in chains—economic, political and social.

These writers view with alarm and seem perturbed that Muhammad's irrefutable logic tells his followers the truth that as a race they are third class in the white man's political and economic system and not to be content with "partial freedom"—with the gloomy promise that "some distant day in the future" the so-called Negro will be completely free at last. None has the courage to ask why this "freedom" isn't given the black man now from fear of life, limb, property and mind, since the dominant whites have the power to give or withhold it.

They never say much about the fact that White Supremacy has been and still is the basis of western world power politics or that it is present in all phases of American and European life. Yet Muhammad is condemned and looked upon as some kind of social criminal because he has the rare courage to tell his people and the world that there is such a thing as a Supreme Black man. To these writers, Black Supremacy sounds like a foul sinister plot to liberate some fierce ferocious black animals on an unsuspecting innocent white world.

They assert that this Black Supremacy doctrine Muhammad teaches is all wrong. But they themselves never put the white man in a secondary position—that is reserved for the blacks. The black man, they imply, could never make it alone without the support and help of the white man. As an example of this type of thinking, the late syndicate columnist Robert Ruark said darkly that the new black African nations will fall apart in internecine and tribal wars, petty jealousies, ignorance and "primitive passions" because they are chasing the white man out after all these centuries of colonial exploitation. One can detect in reports from South Africa in the daily papers and magazines the natural fears of the Western world that the blacks will at last gain their freedom and take over the rulership of their own land.

This, many writers describe in left-handed terms, will be an awful calamity, and as soon as the whites leave their modern structures and the ever-stocked trough at which they have been stuffing themselves ever since they subjected Africa, the whole house will come tumbling down. Such thinking argues that black men need the White Supremacy symbol even if it is only to save them from themselves.

But for Elijah Muhammad to spell out the facts of the matter, and arouse his people to glowing pride in their newly given knowledge that there can be such a creature as a Supreme Black man or Black race, is akin to treason in the eyes of these self-appointed "guardians" of the black man's thoughts and racial destiny.

What strikes me as most encouraging is the fact that Muhammad's aloofness and unavailability to these white writers, authors and radio and television commentators has for the first time presented to America a black leader who has the ability, the power and desire to stay out of their clutches.

So-called Negro leaders, the Negro press and others who have been brainwashed for so many centuries, think it a high crime that Muhammad doesn't run and tell the whites what he is doing every day or let them infiltrate his meetings and conferences where he is carrying on his work of trying to teach his people self-respect and self-reliance and point out the pitfalls around them, whether physical or mental.

When Raymond Moley, Harry Ashmore, the editors of *Time* magazine and the stooge Negro reporters for white papers sent into Muhammad meetings to "stool pigeon" for the whites who are not admitted, try to compare the Mosque of Islam movement with the white supremacy Ku Klux Klan or the White Councils of both the South and North, they do not explain why they are not campaigning as assiduously to break up the Klan and Councils in their writings as they are in seeking the disintegration of the movement started by Muhammad.

Meanwhile, in spite of all attempts by police and federal authorities to block the growth of the Mosque of Islam or to shut Muhammad's mouth, the religion is rapidly mushrooming into perhaps the largest all-black movement on the North American continent. Wherever the brilliant, sincere, dedicated, mild-mannered little man is heard or people read his writings, new converts are coming forth to be counted among the Chosen. They have learned that there is no white man alive who can and will tell the so-called Negro what he actually wants, and none will tell him truthfully how to get it. But Muhammad not only knows the aims and desires of his people but he also knows the means to get it and the quickest way to come into possession of this fundamental Truth about the black man's true self and destiny.

For most persons the general conception of a Negro leader runs something like this:

In size, he is big and imposing and has a fat well-fed appearance; he wears expensive clothes and is always immaculate; he smokes big fat cigars and makes it part of his daily routine to be seen dining in the more popular restaurants and cafes; he is typed by the costly liquors he orders, the make of automobile he drives, and the wide swath he cuts at interracial parties and affairs where the black and white sit down to "talk this thing over."

Whenever he is mentioned in the newspapers, the writer has to include much of his biography to inform readers who he is and what he means, such biographical material detailing his school and college background, his employment record (especially in government or social work or teaching) and the various honors he has received, such as awards and honorary appointments since he first entered public life.

On the other hand, you don't read biographical stuff on Elijah Muhammad as a means of introducing him to readers. That is, unless the story is printed in a white paper, which generally goes out of its way to reiterate the paper's view of the spiritual leader of America's 250,000 Muslims as being head of a "black supremacy cult that preaches hate the white man doctrine to its Negro followers."

You won't find any newspaper recording the presence of Elijah Muhammad at any kind of cocktail party because he preaches against the use of liquor in any form. He does not participate in interracial socializing because he believes the Negro weakens himself morally as well as spiritually by breaking his neck to get into the company of white persons. And Muhammad does not smoke; instead he admonishes his followers against the use of tobacco or any narcotics.

In size, Elijah Muhammad stands a "12 foot" 5 feet 6 inches. For what he might lack in height, he makes up in inner power and dedication to what to him is a twentieth century "holy crusade" to deliver the black man from his present economic, political and social shackles. He weighs a modest 150 pounds and in his mid-sixties is in consistently perfect physical condition.

Those who have had the rare privilege of visiting him at his home in Hyde Park agree that he presents the picture of a sober noble father of a well-beloved family. It is the dwelling of a dedicated man surrounded by a family also dedicated to the salvation of a race of people.

In an atmosphere of profound quiet, Mr. Muhammad's day begins at 7:30 a.m. Until late at night he dictates letters, speeches, newspaper columns and articles to his four highly competent young secretaries. During his day, starting at the breakfast table, he opens and reads every one of the more than 300 letters he receives daily from Muslim leaders in Europe, Asia, Africa and South America. All mail is answered.

Mr. Muhammad's speeches are prepared for personal delivery

in his weekly speaking engagements in cities around the nation or for his program on radio stations all over the country. His busy day also includes conferences with Negro businessmen and ministers and with officials of his various Mosques, who fly in and out of Chicago seven days of the week to take counsel with him.

Very unique in the history of American Negro leadership is the origination of a program that is established on a premise of what Negroes can do for themselves without support from white people—a program that fires the latent embers of intense black nationalism with a clear-cut glorious goal as its ultimate objective.

Accordingly, Marcus Garvey, with his "Back to Africa" exhortations during the early 1920's and his nationwide phalanx of 5 million black followers in his Universal Negro Improvement Association, electrified the black world of America's Negro masses as no other movement up to his time.

The same results have been evident since Elijah Muhammad introduced his beneficial Temples of Islam. His bold demands that black folk "throw off the shackles of the white man's Christianity and return to Islam, the religion of our ancestors," has brought Negroes from all levels swarming to his banner.

Admittedly an "unlettered man," the tiny spiritual leader of the fast-growing Muslim movement in the western hemisphere, nonetheless has self-authored more literature of his own views of his program than any of his predecessors in Negro leadership.

Week after week his flaming controversial newspaper columns in prominent Negro weeklies and his own newspaper, *Muhammad Speaks,* and thousands of sermons recorded for radio delivery on miles of tape are unprecedented in Negro organizational literature.

Not even Garvey, with his giant weekly newspaper, the *Negro World,* with a peak circulation in 1921 of more than 800,000 copies, comes close to the personal output of words of the indefatigable Mr. Muhammad. For most of the *Negro World* was devoted to articles, editorials and news stories written by others, with comparatively very little from the pen of Garvey himself. If ever correlated and put into book form, the writings of Elijah Muhammad to date would at conservative estimate make a minimum of two dozen of volumes.

And Muhammad's writings, despite his lack of formal education, are built on separate words designed for permanency. Every word in his writings is fashioned with loving care and a supreme regard for truth.

What he writes is told in the language of the little fellow so there can be no mistake or confusion of purpose or shades of meaning. This phase of his writing habits is undertaken daily with the help of highly trained and dedicated young women secretaries.

The "Messenger of Allah" is meticulous about what he writes and insists that not a word be changed when his final drafts are completed.

The result is that what he says is unmistakable, for what he puts on paper is exactly what he wants to convey, and there is the core of what makes his program for the salvation of the American black man so comprehensible and beneficial. Readers, whether or not they agree with him, are forced to admit "that man is telling us the truth."

Daniel Burley

OBEY DIVINE MESSENGERS

"And we sent no Messenger but that he should be obeyed by Allah's command" (Holy Qur-an 4:64)

The so-called American Negroes have never had a Divine Messenger sent to them before the Honorable Elijah Muhammad.

Therefore, there will be much opposition to him from his people who want to lead and not be followers of others. Especially the middle class, the black Christian preachers, and the college and university students who feel so proud of their worldly education and positions.

They think their worldly learning and high positions with the enemies of God will protect them against following the Divine Messenger of God. Wait and see.

The so-called Negroes should not be this type of people, since they have the Bible, which is full of prophecies concerning the fate of those who rejected and opposed God's prophets. Allah's warning in the Holy Qur-an is very plain against the disobedient and opposers to His Last Apostle.

And he whom God has caused to arise among the so-called Negroes to be His Apostle is most surely the last Apostle and the last person to whom the Divine Revelation and guidance is to come.

THIS IS the time the Bible and Holy Qur-an refer to as the "resurrection of the dead" (mentally dead or ignorant people) whom God wishes to make wise and set over the nations by His guidance and His infinite wisdom. After listening to what the Honorable Elijah Muhammad was taught by Allah, there is nothing left for another Messenger to teach us of self, God and the devil. Messenger Elijah Muhammad's message to us fulfills the Bible and Holy Qur-an for the last Messenger's message is to bring us face to face with the knowledge of God and the devils, that we may make our choice as to whom we shall serve.

The other Divine teaching, the Messenger says, is that which guides us into the Hereafter. I say anyone who ignores Messenger Elijah Muhammad's teaching is in danger of hell fire. The Holy Qur-an warns us against imputing sin to Allah's Messengers, though the Bible and Holy Qur-an hold no one sinless.

But the Holy Qur-an teaches us that Allah is sufficient as a judge for His Apostles, and the Bible verifies this. We just cannot be the judges of Divine Messengers. Obeying them is what Allah warns us to do.

The Messenger teaches us that Allah warned him against taking up the enemy's arms against the enemy.

Allah's orders to Messenger Elijah Muhammad are the same as those given to the prophets of old. Moses had only a rod; Noah had nothing but the word; Lot had nothing but the word; and Messenger Elijah Muhammad has nothing but word of Allah against the arms of the police. In Detroit, in April, 1934, and in Chicago, on April 2, 1935, Allah slew the police captain in the police courtroom who was trying one of Messenger Muhammad's followers. There was a display of firearms by the police against the unarmed group of Muslim men and women. Allah showed who should be killed.

Messenger Elijah Muhammad puts his trust in Allah. I am sorry for the poor fools who refuse to trust the God of the Honorable Elijah Muhammad.

Messenger Muhammad teaches us to follow the way of Allah. Some may think that Messenger Elijah Muhammad may be jealous. But this he cannot be; for no one can take the place of a Divine Messenger. They are chosen by God and not by the people.

We just cannot take a Messenger's place unless God makes us as He did them; for such a one is made of God and not of himself or the world. Regardless as to how much worldly education one may have, he cannot make himself the Messenger of God unless God wants him to be and reeducates him Divinely.

If Allah has chosen the Honorable Elijah Muhammad to be His Apostle, there is not another so-called Negro in the world who can take his place, regardless of what we may think of him. You cannot force yourself on God for such office.

The Holy Qur-an teaches us that the angels cannot say anything after Allah makes His choice of an Apostle. We may say that he is not fit for a Messenger. In the Holy Qur-an 75:37-40; 76:1-3 Moses complained of not being able to speak plainly or eloquently.

But that did not make God choose Aaron for His Apostle because Aaron was a better speaker than Moses. God told Moses he could use his brother for his prophet if he wanted to, but Allah said to Moses, YOU are my prophet and I am going to send you to Pharaoh.

There are many people, especially among the so-called Negroes, who want certain ones that we like to lead us. But God has His choice and we can like His choice or not. It makes no difference with God. There is not a prophet of the past that the people in his time did not have something to say against. But whatever the people said, it did not change God's choice.

What so-called Negro has been able to stop us from our evil ways and make us love each other so much that we will hug and kiss each other anywhere and not be ashamed.

This love of the brotherhood makes us love and respect our women, makes them go modestly dressed; we can hold 10,000 people—white and black—spellbound for 2 or 3 hours at any time.

The person who leaves the teachings of the Honorable Elijah Muhammad makes himself a fool. The advice to all our people is Get On To Your Own Kind, this world is at hand!

Minister James Shabazz
Muhammad's Temple of Islam No. 2
Chicago, Illinois

ALLAH IS GOD

WHO IS THAT MYSTERY GOD?
PART I

For thousands of years, the people who did not have the knowledge of the person, or reality, of God worshiped their own ideas of God. He has been made like many things other than what He really is. The Christians refer to God as a "Mystery" and a "Spirit" and divide Him into thirds. One part they call the Father, another part the Son, and the third part they call the Holy Ghost—which makes the three, one. This is contrary to both nature and mathematics. The law of mathematics will not allow us to put three into one. Our nature rebels against such a belief of God being a mystery and yet the Father of a son and a Holy Ghost without a wife or without being something in reality. We wonder how can the son be human, and the father a mystery (unknown), or a spirit? Who is this Holy Ghost that is classified as being the equal of the father and the son?

The Christians do not believe in God as being a human being, yet they believe in Him as being the Father of all human beings. They also refer to God as He, Him, Man, King and The Ruler. They teach that God sees, hears, talks, walks, stands, sits, rides and flies; that He grieves or sorrows; and that He is interested in the affairs of human beings. They also teach that once upon a time He made the first man like Himself, in the image and likeness of Himself, but yet they believe that He, Himself, is not a man or human. They preach and prophesy of His coming and that He will be seen on the Judgment Day but is not man. They cannot tell us what He looks like, yet man is made like Him and in the image of God, and yet they still say that He is a mystery (unknown).

How can one teach the people to know God if He, himself, does not know God? If you try teaching the Christians that God is also a human being, they will say that you are crazy, that you do not believe in God and that you are an infidel. In the meantime, while they admit that He is a Mystery God (unknown), they teach not to make any likeness of Him; yet they adorn their walls and churches with pictures, images and statues like human beings.

Can God be a Mystery God and yet send prophets to represent Himself? Have the prophets been representing a God that is not known (Mystery)? They tell us that they heard God's voice speaking to them in their own language. Can a spirit speak a language while being an immaterial something? If God is not material, what pleasure would He get out of material beings and the material universe? What is the basis of spirit? Is the spirit independent of material?

Actually, who is that Mystery God? We should take time and study what has and is being taught to us. Study the word and examine it, and if it be the Truth, lay hold to it. To teach people that God is a Mystery God is to teach them that God is unknown. There is no truth in such teaching. Can one teach that which he himself does not know?

If one teaches a thing that he himself does not know, he can be charged with lying to the people. The word "mystery," according to the English dictionaries, is something that has not been or cannot be—something beyond human comprehension. The unintelligent, or rather ones without divine knowledge, seem to delight themselves in representing the God as something mysterious, unknown.

Such teaching (a mystery God) that God is a mystery makes the prophets' teachings of God all false. There should be a law made and enforced upon such teachers until they have been removed from the public.

According to Allah, the origin of such teachings as a Mystery God is from the devils! It was taught to them by their father, Yakub, 6,000 years ago. They know today that God is not a mystery but will not teach it. He (devil), the god of evil, was made to rule the nations of earth for 6,000 years, and naturally he would not teach obedience to a God other than himself.

So, a knowledge of the true God of Righteousness was not represented by the devils. The true God was not to be made manifest to the people until the god of evil (devil) has finished or lived out his time, which was allowed to deceive the nations (read Thess. 2:9-10, Rev. 20:3, 8-10).

The shutting up and loosing of the devil mentioned in Rev. 20:7 could refer to the time between the A.D. 570-1555 which is nearly 1,000 years that they and Christianity were bottled up in Europe by the spread of Islam by Muhammad (May the peace of Allah be upon him) and his successors.

Their being loose to deceive the nations of the earth would refer to the time (A.D. 1555 to 1955) when they (John Hawkins) deceived our fathers and brought them into slavery in America and were loose (free) to travel over the earth and deceive the people."

Now their freedom is being interfered with, by the Order and Power of the God of Righteousness through the Nation of Righteousness.

For the past 6,000 years, the prophets have been predicting the coming of God who would be just and righteous. This righteous God would appear at the end of the world (the world of the white race).

Today, the God of Truth and Righteousness is making Himself manifest, that He is not any more a mystery (unknown), but is known and can be seen and heard the earth over.

This teaching of a mystery God enslaves the minds of the ignorant. My poor people are the victims of every robber. They are so pitifully blind, deaf, and dumb that it hurts, but I am going to prove to them that I am with Allah (God) and that Allah is with me, in spite of their ignorance of Allah and myself, whom He has sent. For I am not self-sent, and the world shall soon know who it is that has sent me.

Allah (God) loves us, the so-called Negroes (Tribe of Shabazz,) so that He will give lives for our sake today. Fear not, you are no more forsaken. God is in person, and stop looking for a dead Jesus for help, but pray to Him whom Jesus prophesied would come after Him. He who is alive and not a spook.

Do you hate me because I represent Allah, the Living God, your Lord and my Lord? Can you, who believe in a mystery God (unknown), trust your Mystery to bring you bread or to defend you against your open enemies? If so, on what occasion did He help you? If God is a mystery, you are lying to the world when you say that you know Him.

He wants to be known, it is His enemy (the devil) who does not want God to be known to you and me. Do you refer to God as He, Him! These pronouns refer to a man. Do you say that you want to be like Him. Surely, you don't want to be a spirit without form, as spirits have no material form. Your God and my God is a material Being—the Supreme of Beings.

WHO IS THAT MYSTERY GOD?
PART II

Did God say that He was a Mystery God, or did someone say it of Him? Did God say that He was only a Spirit, or did someone say it of Him?

The most important question of all questions that one could ask is, "Who is God?" It is like a child who does not know his father asking his mother to tell him the name of his father, wanting to know what his father looks like and if he favors his father. Can we not ask the same question who are seeking the knowledge of Our Father, God? Should we be called disbelievers or infidels just because we seek the truth or knowledge of Our Father, God? The mother may, in some cases, think it best to keep the name of her child a secret, as it was in the case of Mary and Joseph, 2,000 years ago. But, in the case of God, one would say that we all should know Him, but at the proper time.

It has been for the past 6,000 years that we had to wait for the proper time to learn just who is Our Father, for the false god (the devil) would not dare tell us lest he lose his followers. Naturally, the child will leave a foster father for his real father, especially when he is a good father. The real father by nature loves his own flesh and blood regardless of how it looks or acts, for it is his own child.

So it is with us, the so-called Negroes, "lost-found members of the Asiatic nation." He who has found us is Our Father, the God of love, light, life, freedom, justice, and equality. He has found his own, though His own does not know Him. They (the so-called Negroes) are following and loving a foster father (the devil) who has no love for him nor their real father but seek to persecute and kill them daily. He (the devil) makes the lost and found children (the American so-called Negroes) think that their real father (God) is a mystery (unknown) or is some invisible spook somewhere in space.

The only chance that the children have to know their real father is that He must come and make Himself known by overpowering and freeing them from Him whom they fear.

The devils reared the poor so-called Negroes for 400 years and put fear in them when they were babies. They (the devils) kept them apart from their own kind coming in from abroad, so as to deprive them of any knowledge other than what he (the devil) has taught them. As soon as they hear of a so-called Negro learning and teaching his own people that which they (the devils) would not teach them, the devils then seek to kill that one or trail him wherever he goes, threatening those who would listen to him, believe him and follow him. Knowing that their very presence and inquiries might frighten or scare Negroes they ask, "What is this you are listening to and believing in?" This will frighten most of them away from accepting his or her own salvation and keep them from returning to their own God, religion and people.

My people, if you only knew the time and presence of your God, Allah, there should be no fear for you nor grief. But, you are deceived in the knowledge of your God. If your God were a mystery, you and I would be a mystery people. If He were a Spirit and not a man, we would all be spirits and not human beings! If He were a mystery or only a Spirit, the prophets could not have predicted the coming of that which no one has knowledge of or of a spirit which cannot be seen, only felt.

Because of the false teaching of our enemies (the devils), God has made Himself known; for I teach not the coming of God but the presence of God, in person. This kind of teaching hurts the false teachings of the devils, for they knew that God would come in person after you. They (the devils) also are aware that God is present among us, but those of you who are asleep they desire to keep asleep.

The enemies of God today are the same as they were thousands of years ago—thinking that they will be the winner against Him. America, for her evil done to me and my people, shall be isolated and deceived by her friends. The heavens shall withhold their blessing until America is brought to a disgraceful ruin.

IS GOD A SPIRIT OR A MAN?

God is a man and we just cannot make Him other than man, lest we make Him an inferior one; for man's intelligence has no equal in other than man. His wisdom is infinite; capable of accomplishing anything that His brain can conceive. A spirit is subjected to us and not we to the spirit.

Habakkuk uses the pronoun "He" in reference to God. This pronoun "He" is only used in the case when we refer to a man or boy or something of the male sex. Are we living in a material universe or a "spirit" universe? We are material beings and live in a material universe. Would not we be making ourselves fools to be looking forward to see that which cannot be seen, only felt? Where is our proof for such a God (spirit) to teach that God is other than man? It is due to your ignorance of God, or you are one deceived by the devil, whose nature is to mislead you in the knowledge of God. You originally came from the God of Righteousness and have the opportunity to return, while the devils are from the man devil (Yakub) who has ruled the world for the past 6,000 years under falsehood, labeled under the name of God and His prophets.

The worst thing to ever happen to the devils is: The truth of them made manifest that they are really the devils whom the righteous (all members of the black nation) should shun and never accept as truthful guides of God! This is why the devils have always persecuted and killed the righteous. But the time has at last arrived that Allah (God) will put an end to their persecuting and killing the righteous (the black nation).

I and my followers have been suffering cruel persecution—police brutality—for the past 34 years; but have patience, my dear followers, for release is in sight. Even those who made mockery of you shall be paid fully for his or her mockery; for the prophesy of Habakkuk is true if understood; wherein he says: *"Thou wentest forth for the salvation of Thy people"* [*the so-called Negroes*] (3:13).

Never before this time did anyone come for the salvation of the so-called Negroes in America, whose rights have been ignored by their enemies (the white race) for 400 years. Now it is incumbent upon Allah to defend the rights of His lost-found helpless people, called Negroes by their enemies.

The whole of the third chapter of Habakkuk is devoted to the coming and work of God against our enemies and our deliverance. We must not take our enemies for our spiritual guides lest we regret it. You are already deceived by them. Why seek to follow them and their evil doings; if I would say that God is not man, I would be a liar before Him and stand to be condemned. Remember! You look forward to seeing God or the coming of the "Son of Man" (a man from a man) and not the coming of a "spirit." Let that one among you who believes God is other than man prove it!

THE COMING OF GOD: IS HE A MAN OR A SPIRIT?

According to the dictionary of the Bible: Teman, a son of Esau by Adah, (Gen. 36:11, 15, 42) and in I Chron. 1:36, now if Habakkuk saw God come or coming from the sons of Esau (Eliphaz), then God must be a man and not a spook. If Habakkuk's (3:3) prophecy refers to some country, town, or city, if there be any truth at all in this prophecy, then we can say that this prophet saw God as a material being belonging to the human family of the earth—and not to a spirit (ghost). In the same chapter and verse, Habakkuk saw the Holy One from Mount Paran. This is also earthly, somewhere in Arabia. Here the Bible makes a difference between God and another person who is called the Holy One. Which one should we take for our God? For one is called God, while another One is called Holy One. The Holy One: His glory covered the heavens and the earth was full of His praise.

It has been a long time since the earth was full of praise for a Holy One. Even to this hour, the people do not care for Holy People and will persecute and kill the Holy One, if God does not intervene. In the fourth verse of the above chapter, it says, *"He had horns coming out of his hands; and there was the hiding of His power."* Such science to represent the God's power could confuse the ignorant masses of the world. Two gods are here represented at the same time. (It is good that God makes Himself manifest to the ignorant world today.)

"The burning coals went forth at His feet," has a meaning, but what is the meaning? The ignorant do not know. "The burning coals" could refer to the anger and war among the people where His foot trod within the borders of the wicked. (Here God has feet—Spirits do not have feet and hands.) This Holy One does not refer to anyone of the past—not Moses, Jesus, nor Mohammed of the past 1,300 years. "For this Holy One the perpetual hills did bow, Cushan in affliction; the curtains of the land of Midian did tremble." (What is meant by the curtains trembling?) (Who is Cushan?) "The mountains saw thee, they trembled." (Who does this mean?) "The sun and moon stood still in their habitation." (What does this mean?) The answers to the above questions are easy when we understand who this God called the Holy One coming from Mount Paran is.

The 13th verse should clear the way for such undertaking; for it tells us why all these great things took place on the coming of the Holy One from Mount Paran. It says: "Thou wentest forth for the salvation of thy people (not for all people) for the salvation with thine annointed (His Apostle). He wounded the head out of the house of the wicked by discovering the foundation unto the neck (by exposing the truth and ruling powers of the wicked race of devils)." "Cushan" represents the Black Nation which is afflicted by the white race. "The curtains of the land of Midian" could mean the falsehood spread over the people by the white race and their leaders trembling from being exposed by the truth. "The mountains" represent the great, rich and powerful political men of the wicked; they also are trembling and being divided and scattered over the earth. "The Holy One" is God in person and not a spirit!

THE ORIGIN OF GOD
AS A SPIRIT AND NOT A MAN

"Take heed to yourselves that your hearts be not deceived and you turn aside, and serve other gods; worship them".
(Deut. 11:16)

The American so-called Negroes are gravely deceived by their slave-masters' teaching of God and the true religion of God. They do not know that they are deceived and do earnestly believe that they are taught right regardless of how evil the white race may be. Not knowing "self" or anyone else, they are a prey in the hands of the white race, the world's archdeceivers (the real devils in person). You are made to believe that you worship the true God, but you do not! God is unknown to you in that which the white race teaches you (a mystery God).

The great archdeceivers (the white race) were taught by their father, Yakub, 6,000 years ago, how to teach that God is a spirit (spook) and not a man. In the grafting of his people (the white race), Mr. Yakub taught his people to contend with us over the reality of God by asking us of the whereabouts of that first One (God) who created the heavens and the earth, and that, Yakub said, we cannot do. Well, we all know that there was a God in the beginning that created all these things and do know that He does not exist today. But we know again that from that God the person of God continued until today in His people, and today a Supreme One (God) has appeared among us with the same infinite wisdom to bring about a complete change.

This is He whom I preach and teach you to believe and obey. The devil calls Him a Mystery God but yet claims that He begot a son by Mary. They call on you and me to take this Son of Mary for a God, who was a man before and after His death. Yet they deny the coming of God to be a man. If Jesus were a Son of God, what about Moses and the other prophets? Were they not His Sons since they were His prophets?

The belief in a God other than man (a spirit) Allah has taught me goes back into the millions of years—long before Yakub (the father of the devils)—because the knowledge of God was kept as a secret from the public. This is the first time that it has ever been revealed, and we, the poor rejected and despised people, are blessed to be the first of all the people of earth to receive this secret knowledge of God. If this people (the white race) would teach you truth which has been revealed to me, they would be hastening their own doom—for they were not created to teach us the truth but rather to teach us falsehood (just contrary to the truth).

It stands true that they are enemies of the truth by their ever warring against the truth. They know that Islam is the truth; they know that the history of them that God has revealed to me is the truth but do not like for you to know such truth of them. Therefore, they seek every means to oppose this teaching. They try everyone of you that say that you believe it and are my followers. They are watching you and me, seeking a chance to do us harm. They are so upset and afraid that they visit you at your homes to question you of your sincerity to Islam.

As David said in his Psalms (37:32): *"The wicked watcheth the righteous and seeketh to slay him."* Also, Psalms (37:30): *"The mouth of the righteous speaketh wisdom, and his tongue talketh of judgment."* And in another place (Psa. 94:16): *"Who will rise up for me against the workers of iniquity?"* I have answered Him and said, "Here I am, take me." For the evil done against my people (the so-called Negroes) I will not keep silent until He executes judgment and defends my cause. Fear not my life, for He is well able to defend it. Know that God is a man and not a spook!

THE COMING OF THE SON OF MAN, THE GREAT MAHDI

"For as the lightning cometh out of the East, and shineth even unto the West, so shall also the coming of the Son of Man be." (Matt. 24:27)

My greatest and only desire is to bring true understanding of the word of God, His prophets and the scriptures, which the prophets were sent with, pertaining to the lost-found people (the American so-called Negroes) of God and the judgment of the world.

You must forget about ever seeing the return of Jesus, Who was here 2,000 years ago. Set your heart on seeing the One that He prophesied would come at the end of the present world's time (the white race's time).

He is called the "Son of Man," the "Christ," the "Comforter." You are really foolish to be looking to see the return of the Prophet Jesus. It is the same as looking for the return of Abraham, Moses and Muhammad. All of these prophets prophesied the coming of Allah or one with equal power, under many names. You must remember that Jesus could not have been referring to himself as returning to the people in the last days.

He prophesied of another's coming who was much greater than He. Jesus even acknowledged that He did not know when the hour would come in these words: *"But of that day and hour knoweth no man, no, not the angels of heaven, but my Father only."* (Matt. 24:36)

If He were the one to return at the end of the world, surely He would have had knowledge of the time of His return—the knowledge of the hour. But He left Himself out of that knowledge and placed it where it belonged, as all the others—prophets—had done. No prophet has been able to tell us the hour of the judgment. No one but He, the great all wise God, Allah. He is called the "Son of Man," the "Mahdi," the "Christ." The prophets, Jesus included, could only foretell those things which would serve as signs—signs that would precede such a great one's coming to judge the world. The knowledge of the hour of judgment is with the Executor only.

The prophets teach us to let the past judgments of people, their cities, and their warners serve as a lesson, or sign, of the last judgment and its warners. Noah did not know the hour of the flood. Lot did not know the Hour of Sodom and Gomorrah until the Executors had arrived, and Jesus prophesied (Matt. 24:37 -39): *"It will be the same in the last judgment of the world of Satan."* You have gone astray because of your misunderstanding of the scripture, the Prophet Jesus, and the coming of God to judge the world. My corrections are not accepted.

Your misunderstanding and misinterpretation of it is really the joy of devils. For it is the devils' desire to keep the so-called Negroes ignorant of the truth of God until they see it with their eyes. The truth of God is the salvation and freedom of the so-called Negroes from the devils' power.

Can you blame them? No! Blame yourself for being so foolish as to allow the devils to fool you in not accepting the truth after it comes to you. The devils have tried to deceive the people all over the earth with Christianity; that is, God the Father, Jesus the Son, the Holy Ghost—three Gods into One God—the resurrection of the Son and His return to judge the world; or that the Son is in some place above the earth, sitting on the right-hand side of the Father, waiting until the Father makes His enemies His footstool. The period of waiting is 2,000 years. Yet, He died for the Father to save His enemies (the whole world of sinners).

My friends, use a bit of common sense. First, could a wonderful flesh and blood body, made of the essence of our earth, last 2,000 years on the earth, or off the earth, without being healed! Second, where exists such a heaven, of the earth, that flesh and blood of the earth can exist, since the Bible teaches that flesh and blood cannot enter heaven? (Cor. 15:50)

Flesh and blood cannot survive without that of which it is made—the earth. Jesus' prophesy of the coming of the Son of Man is very clear, if you rightly understand. First, this removes all doubts about who we should expect to execute judgment, for if man is to be judged and rewarded according to his actions, who could be justified in sitting as judge of man's doings but another man? How could a spirit be our judge when we cannot see a spirit? And, ever since life was created, life has had spirit. But the Bible teaches that God will be seen on the Day of Judgment. Not only the righteous will see Him, but even His enemies shall see Him.

On that day, a Son of a Man will sit to judge men according to their works. Who is the Father of this Son, coming to judge the world? Is His Father of flesh and blood or is He a "spirit"? Where is this Son coming from? Prophet Jesus said: *"He will come from the East."* (Matt. 24:27)—from the land and people of Islam, where all of the former prophets came from. Jesus compared His coming as "the lightning." Of course, lightning cannot be seen or heard at a great distance.

The actual light (the Truth) which "shineth even unto the West," is our day sun. But the Son of Man's coming is like *both* the lightning and our day sun. His work of the resurrection of the mentally dead so-called Negroes, and judgment between truth and falsehood, is compared with lightning—on an instant. His swiftness in condeming the falsehood is like the sudden flash of lightning in a dark place. America is that dark place, where the darkness has blinded the people so that they cannot find the "right way" out. The sudden "flash of lightning" enables them to see that they are off from the "right path." They walk a few steps toward the "right way" but soon have to stop and wait for another bright flash. What they actually need is the light of the Sun (God in Person), that they may clearly see their way. The lightning does more than flash a light. It is also destructive, striking whom Allah pleases, or taking property as well as lives. The brightness of its flashes almost blinds the eyes.

So it is with the coming of the Son of Man, with the truth, to cast it against falsehood—that it breaks the head. Just a little hint of it makes the falsehood begin looking guilty and seeking cover from the brightness of the truth. Sometimes lightning serves as a warning of an approaching storm. So does Allah warn us by sending His Messengers with the truth, before the approaching destruction of a people to whom chastisement is justly due. They come flashing the truth in the midst of the spiritually darkened people. Those who love spiritual darkness will close their eyes to the flash of truth—like lightning, pointing out to them the "right way," thus blinding themselves from the knowledge of the approaching destruction of the storm of Allah—and are destroyed. "As the lightning cometh out of the East, so shall the coming of the Son of Man be."

Let us reflect on this prophecy from the direction in which this Son shall come, "out of the East." If He is to come from the East, to chastise or destroy that of the West, then He must be pleased with the East. The dominant religion of the East is Islam. The holy religious teachings of all the prophets, from Adam to Muhammad, was none other than Islam (Holy Qur-an 4:163). They all were of the East and came from that direction with the light of the Truth and shone toward the old wicked darkness of the West. But the West has ever closed its eyes and thus making it necessary for the coming of the Son of Man, the Great Mahdi, God in person.

Being the end of the signs, in His person, He dispels falsehood with the truth—as the sun dispels night on its rising from the East. Why should the tribes of the earth mourn because of the coming of the Son of Man, instead of rejoicing?

THE COMING OF ALLAH (GOD)

The reality of God. I have been and am still trying to make clear to you how important it is. This knowledge of the True God, the reality of God has been and is even now a mystery to the world of mankind with a few exceptions. The day has come that all mankind MUST know the reality of Allah (God).

"There can be no judgment of the people until this knowledge has been given to the people." How can we serve a God without knowledge of Him? My people, the so-called Negroes (the Tribe of Shabazz), are the worst off when it comes to the reality of God.

The whole world has been and is looking for the coming of God. Several places in both the Bible and the Holy Qur-an refer to the coming of Allah (God)—"The Coming of the Son of Man." Referring to God as the Son of Man should remove all doubts as to his being anything other than a man.

The Bible mentions Him as the Son of Man and also mentions Him as not being a man but a spirit. On one side He is made clear and on the other He is made a mystery. Representation such as this causes confusion in understanding. We are blind to the knowledge of God when we make Him a mystery and unreal.

Anyone so blind to the reality of God is the servant of the devil, until he or she sees God as a reality. Thousands of years the devil has been blinding man to God's reality, and that is the reason why God had to come in person (and He has), to clear us of such ignorance and blindness to the knowledge of Him.

Therefore, we have the "Coming of Allah (God)." He is referred to as the Son of Man because, first, He is the Son of Man and gotten for a special purpose, which is to return the lost back to their own and to punish and destroy the wicked for their destruction of the righteous, that the righteous may live in peace and do the will of the God of righteousness, free from trouble and interference. Second, He must be a man to deal with a man, and we cannot receive or respect other than man.

Since His work is to destroy the wicked, He must remain hidden from the eyes of the world until the time is ripe (the end), for the two (God and devil) cannot rule together.

The Son of man (Allah) must wait until His time, after the works of the devil. II Thessalonians 2:8-9; Holy Qur-an 7:14-18 and another place in the Holy Qur-an describes them as the people with the blue eyes (Holy Qur-an 20:102).

Third, the reality of God is as clear as the reality of the devil, but we did not know it until His coming to judge the world. For instance, if we take God for something other than a man (not the man devil), we cannot prove it. If we believe that He is a spirit and not a man, then we can never expect to have any knowledge of Him except by the sense of feel.

We cannot see a spirit; therefore, the teachings of His coming would be false. The spirit of life is and has been with us all of our lives. God is in person among us today. He is a man, He is in His time. God sees, hears, knows, wills, acts and is a person (man). The evil workings of the devil MUST come to an end.

THE COMING OF GOD
AND
THE GATHERING TOGETHER
OF HIS PEOPLE

The prophets have warned us of a time that would come when God would judge the wicked and punish, or rather destroy, the wicked and give the earth over to the rule of a righteous people. So many of us have misunderstood just what we should expect. What will God look like? If we expect the destruction of the devil, what will the devil look like? How will I distinguish him? If the devil should be destroyed, what does that devil look like? In order not to follow him to his destruction I must be able to recognize him so that he won't be able to deceive me. What world's end will come, and what is that world that is going to end? Does that include everything that makes up the solar system? The planet earth? If so, what shall we expect? What kind of solar system will we have after the destruction of the present one? Think over these things. We must get down to the facts so that we can recognize them when they are presented to us. But you never questioned the first teacher. Shouldn't we be fair about this? Let us go after the thing right!

If we want to give each teacher justice, we should start with the first one. When Moses began to preach to the Hebrews to make themselves ready to go out to another country that God had promised their fathers on the condition that they believe and obey, here was the reply: "Who made you a judge over us?"

Let us question this as they questioned Moses. Why didn't you question Pharaoh, "Who made you a judge over us?" Question me with facts. If they did not question Pharaoh, why should they question Moses since Pharaoh didn't say that a God sent him? They should have made Pharaoh answer the question, "Who made you God over us!?" They were born under Pharaoh's teaching; therefore, from their early existence, they believed in Pharaoh, right or wrong. They worshiped Pharaoh's God and when Moses made himself present, they wanted Moses to give them a good knowledge of who had sent him and made him such a man. If today a Moses were in your midst and he said, "The God of your fathers has sent me" and "the Government of America has deceived you as to the knowledge of God and has you indirectly worshiping them," wouldn't your reply be the same as the one given to Moses? That is right. You are asking me that. A man questioned me the other day when he said, "You mean to say that you talked to God face to face?"

Where was Moses, and what time was that? What did the God have in mind? If no one has gone to heaven or seen the face of God, then all of these prophets, are liars. You must think these things over. You have a lot to learn if you understand it; otherwise, you are still in the dark as to the Truth. We are here to know whether God has visited America or whether He is yet to come. The hour can come at any day, because it is prophesied that it will come in any hour that you think not. Naturally, I had expected it to come at a certain day but the book said you won't know the day nor the hour. If all of these signs of His coming are exhausted and I don't see any end to the World, that is to show me that it could take place at any time. If there is such a thing as a Judgment of the World, as you and I believe, if there are signs that will be produced before that particular destruction of the old world, how many signs do you know of today that have not been fulfilled that must now be fulfilled? If you know one sign that the Bible refers to that has not as yet taken place, point it out to me.

Allah came to us from the Holy City Mecca, Arabia, in 1930. He used the name Wallace D. Fard, often signing it W. D. Fard. In the third year (1933), He signed his name W. F. Muhammad which stands for Wallace Fard Muhammad. He came alone. He began teaching us the knowledge of ourselves, of God and the devil, of the measurement of the earth, of other planets, and of the civilization of some of the planets other than earth.

He measured and weighed the earth and its water; the history of the moon; the history of the two nations, black and white, that dominate the earth. He gave the exact birth of the white race; the name of their God who made them and how; and the end of their time, the judgment, how it will begin and end.

He taught us the truth of how we were made "slaves" and how we are kept in slavery by the "slave-masters" children. He declared the doom of America, for her evils to us was past due. And that she is number one to be destroyed. Her judgment could not take place until we hear the truth.

He declared that we were without the knowledge of self or anyone else. How we had been made blind, deaf and dumb by this white race of people and how we must return to our people, our God and His religion of peace (Islam), the religion of the prophets. We must give up the slave names of our slave-masters and accept the name of Allah (God) or one of His divine attributes. He also taught us to give up all evil doings and practices and do righteousness or be destroyed from the face of the earth.

He taught us that the slave-masters had taught us to eat the wrong food and that this wrong food is the cause of our sickness and short span of life. He declared that he would heal us and set us in heaven at once, if we would submit to Him. Otherwise he would chastise us with a severe chastisement until we did submit. And that He was able to force the whole world into submission to his will. He said that he loved us (the so-called Negroes), his lost and found, so well that he would eat rattle-snakes to free us if necessary, for he has power over all things.

I asked him, "Who are you, and what is your real name?" He said, "I am the one that the world has been expecting for the past 2,000 years." I said to Him again, "What is your name?" He said, "My name is Mahdi; I am God, I came to guide you into the right path that you may be successful and see the here-after." He described the destruction of the world with bombs, poison gas, and finally with fire that would consume and destroy everything of the present world.

Nothing of the present world of white mankind would be left. Those escaping the destruction would not be allowed to carry anything out with them.

He pointed out a destructive dreadful-looking plane that is

made like a wheel in the sky today. It is a half-mile by a half-mile square; it is a humanly built planet. It is up there and can be seen twice a week; it is no secret.

Ezekiel saw it a long time ago. It was built for the purpose of destroying the present world. He also hinted at plaguing the world with rain, snow, hail, and earthquakes.

He spoke with authority, not as one who is under authority but as one independent. He said the world's time was out in 1914, but people could get an extension of time, depending upon their treatment of the righteous. He declared that there can be no judgment until we (the so-called Negroes) hear Islam, whether we accept it or not.

This includes the history of the world and a knowledge of God and the devil. He condemned the teachings of God not being a man as a lie from the devils for the past 6,000 years; he said that Christianity was a religion organized and backed by the devils for the purpose of making slaves of black mankind.

I also bear witness that it certainly has enslaved my people here in America, 100 per cent. He chose me to bear the message of life (Islam) to my people here. Islam is our salvation. It removes fear, grief, and sorrow from any believer, and it brings to us peace of mind of contentment.

The greatest hindrance to the truth of our people is the preacher of Christianity. He will not accept it, nor is he content to let others alone who are trying to accept the truth. He is the man who stands in the way of the salvation of his people, and as soon as the people awaken to the knowledge of this man in their way to God, freedom, justice and equality and stop following him, the sooner they will be in heaven while they live.

THE COMING OF THE SON OF MAN

"And then shall appear the sign of the Son of Man in heaven; and then shall all of the tribes of the earth mourn, and they shall see the Son of Man coming in the clouds of heaven with power and great glory." [Matt. 24:30].

Here in the plainest words is the Son of Man on the Judgment Day. We are not told by either Moses or Jesus to look for God on Judgment Day to be anything other than man. Spirits and spooks cannot be the judge of man's affairs. Man is material, of the earth. How long will you be ignorant of the reality of God? You are poisoned by the devil's touch. Why are you looking for a God that is not flesh and blood as you are? Spirits can only be found in another being like yourself. What pleasure would you have in an invisible world? And on the other hand what pleasure would spirits have in this material universe of ours? Your very nature is against your being anything other than a human being.

These are the days of the resurrection of the mentally dead so-called Negroes. The Son of Man is here. His coming has been fulfilled. He seeks that which was lost (the so-called Negroes). Many now are receiving His name, and that name alone will save you. The wicked nations of the earth are sorry and angry to see the Son of Man set up a government of justice and peace over this, their wicked world. They see signs in the heavens (sky) of great power to execute judgment on the world of the wicked, and they mourn.

We must have a new ruler and a new government, where the people can enjoy freedom, justice, and equality. Let the so-called Negroes rejoice, for Allah has prepared for them what the eye has not seen, the ear has not heard, and the heart has not been able to conceive. The enemy knows this to be true and is now doing everything to prevent the so-called Negroes from seeing the hereafter.

THE COMING OF THE
SON OF MAN
THE INFIDELS ARE ANGRY

Who is His father if God is not His Father? God is His Father, but the Father is also a man. You have heard of old that God prepared a body, or the expected Son of Man; Jesus is a specially prepared man to do a work of redeeming the lost sheep (the so-called Negro). He had to have a body that would be part of each side (black and white), half and half. Therefore, being born or made from both people, He is able to go among both black and white without being discovered or recognized. This He has done in the person of Master W.F. Muhammad, the man who was made by His Father to go and search for the lost members of the Tribe of Shabazz. Master W.F. Muhammad is that Son of Man whom the world has been expecting to come for 2,000 years, seeking to save that which was lost. There are no historical records that there was ever a people lost from each other for 400 years other than we, the so-called Negroes. We have been so long separated from each other that we have lost the knowledge of each other. Even today the white American slave-masters are ever on the watch to keep out any Asiatic influence that might come among the so-called Negroes to teach them the truth. They are our real open enemies. This is no secret. The Son of Man is after the so-called Negroes to set them in Heaven and His enemies in hell. After His conquest of the black nation's enemies, the world will know and recognize Him (Allah) to be God alone. There is no problem today that is as hard to solve as the problem of uniting the American so-called Negroes. They are like a dead man totally without life. They have lost all love of self and kind and have gone all out in loving their enemies. They do not seem to want any God to do anything like blessing them unless that God blesses their enemies too. Fear of their enemies is the real cause. The time is now ripe that they should have no fear, only the fear of Allah, Who is in person among them to save them from their enemies. By all means, they must be separated from the white race, in order that the scripture might be fulfilled. *"For I will take you from among the heathen and gather you out of all countries and will bring you into your own land."* (Ezek. 36:24)

The so-called Negroes have no home that they can call their own. They have helped the white race to own a free country, but they have nothing for themselves. This is the purpose of His coming, to give everyone that which is rightfully theirs. The Son of Man has power over all things. You cannot find a defense against Him in a war. Your weapons mean nothing. The powers of heaven and earth today will be ordered to fight on the side of the Mahdi against His enemies. He is the friend of the so-called Negroes and not of the white people. His purpose is to take the so-called Negroes and kill their enemies; although many of us will suffer from persecution and hunger. But the good end is for those of you who will hold fast to Allah and His religion, Islam. They (the devils) are now planning many tricks to keep the so-called Negroes here with them to suffer the fire of hell which they (the devils) cannot escape. Fly to Allah! Come, follow me. Although I may look insignificant to you, you will find salvation with us. The white race is excited and cannot think rightly for themselves. The so-called Negroes, Muslims, in their midst, are a shelter, but little do they know it.

ALLAH, THE BEST KNOWER

There are many others chapters of the Holy Qur-an Sharrieff that open with the above words, "Allah is The Best Knower." The beautiful teachings of the Holy Qur-an have no equal in other scriptures.

All so-called Negro preachers should have one, but be sure it is the one translated by Yusuf Ali, or Maulvi Muhammad Ali. Any other translation of the Holy Qur-an, by Christian authors, is as poisonous to the reader as a rattlesnake.

What I am trying to make clear is that white people do not believe in Allah and Islam or the prophets of Allah. Why then, should you seek the truth of it from them? You will soon come to know that you should not seek any truth from them. They have you following in the wrong direction and hope to keep you like that; but by my Allah's power and wisdom, and my life's blood, you shall know the Truth even against your own will.

They (white people) have nearly all of the poor black preachers on their side to oppose Allah, myself and Islam, the religion of righteous. They will fail and be brought to disgrace as Pharaoh's magicians and he himself were by Allah (God), for you have not known Him, or His religion, as Israel had not known God by His name Jehovah (Exod. 6:3).

They felt that they should not believe Moses' representation of God by any other name than God Almighty, regardless of Moses' stress upon Jehovah as being the God of their Fathers. Pharaoh had not used that name (Jehovah); so Israel would not accept it until a showdown between Jehovah and Pharaoh. I would not like to have you wait until a showdown between Allah and the modern Pharaoh's people; therefore I come to you with the truth, verifying that which is before it, and giving good news to the believers that they most certainly shall have Heaven in this life. I also come to you with a warning to those who disbelieve that you most certainly shall have hell in this life, and in the hereafter you most certainly will be among the losers, or do they say, "He has forged it?" Nay, it is the truth from the Lord, that you may warn a people to whom no warning has come before, that they may follow the right direction (Holy Qur-an 32-3).

You say, "Who is this Allah, and this religion Islam?" Know my people, the Divine Supreme Being, has 99 attributes that make up His name, and Allah is the 100th. Surely His are the most beautiful names. He will make Himself known to the world that He is God and besides Him there is no God and that I am His Messenger, that Islam is a religion backed by the Power of Allah (God) to free you from the hands of your merciless enemies (the slave masters) once and forever.

Allah, your God, will grant you power to overcome your enemies though their power may look as endurable as the mountains. Fear not! Allah is the Best Knower. Armageddon has started, and after it there will be no Christian religion or churches. Jesus was a Muslim, not a Christian.

THE DAYS OF ALLAH

"Say to those who believe that they forgive those who do not fear the days of Allah, that He may reward a people for what they earn" [Holy Qur-an 45:14]

What is meant by "Days of Allah" are the battles between right and wrong. They are often mentioned as follows: the Days of Judgment, the Days of the Resurrection, the Days of the Son of Man, and the Days of Allah. These days must not be mistaken for the regular 24 hour day. No, the Days of Allah, the Days of the Resurrection, the Days of Judgment, and the Days of the Son of Man mean years; not the common 24 hour day.

What will make us know when we are living in the Days of Allah? It is by the fulfilling of the predictions made by the Prophets of Allah, long before they come to pass. I quote Maulvi Muhammad Ali's footnote 2276 on this verse, in which he says: "The Days of Allah are the contests in which the righteous shall be made successful." That no one can deny for this is a sign for the disbelievers who have enjoyed great temporary prosperity and who thought that they were too rich and powerful to be brought into a state of helplessness. Although they had the histories of those who were before them, there is no difference between the disbelievers today or the past.

We are living in the Days of Allah. The earth and its people have been ruled by the evil race known as the white race. In these days of Allah, the righteous (the Muslims) are now gaining power over the wicked and will soon rule the earth again as they did before the creation of the white race.

Take notice of my followers who have given up the wicked ways of the white race and their self-styled Christianity and have accepted the Truth. They are gradually becoming the most successful people in the world. Allah has chosen us; we have chosen Allah.

Who can successfully oppose Allah in His Days and time of rule? It is easy for a weak and poverty-stricken people to give up, but it is not so easy when they are powerful and wealthy. They think there will be no end to their power and wealth which is made to deceive them.

IF GOD WAS YOUR FATHER, YOU WOULD LOVE ME

"If God was your Father, you would love me"
[John 8:42:]

Read and study the above chapter of John 8:42, all of you, who are Christians, believers in the Bible and Jesus, as you say. If you understand it right, you will agree with me that the whole Caucasian race is a race of devils. They have proved to be devils in the Garden of Paradise and were condemned 4,000 years later by Jesus.

Likewise, they are condemned today, by the Great Mahdi Muhammad, as being nothing but devils in the plainest language. The so-called American Negroes have been deceived and blinded by their unlikeness, soft-smooth buttered words, eye-winking, back-patting, a false show of friendship and handshaking.

The above-mentioned acts, with the exception of handshaking, by men are a disgrace to any decent intelligent person. Know the truth and be free of such disgrace.

Surely, if the Father of the two peoples, black and white, were the same, the two would love each other because they are of the same flesh and blood.

It is natural then for them to love each other. Again, it is not unnatural then for a member or members of a different race or nation not to love the nonmember of their race or nation as their own.

The nature in which we are created will not allow us to be like that, and it works the same in all things living that have a bit of intelligence, including the birds and beasts.

The argument here between Jesus and the Jews in that the Jews claim they all were the same people (children) of one God or Father, but this Jesus disagreed with and proved they were not from the same Father.

He, having a knowledge of both Fathers, knew their Father (devil) before his fall and before he had produced his children (the white race), of whom the Jews are members. Here, in this chapter (John: 8), it shows there was no love in the Jews for Jesus.

PERSECUTION FOLLOWS
THE COMING OF GOD

He (Mr. W.F. Muhammad, God in person) chose to suffer 3½ years to show his love for his people, who have suffered over 300 years at the hands of a people who by nature are evil and wicked and have no good in them. He was persecuted, sent to jail in 1932, and ordered out of Detroit, on May 26, 1933. He came to Chicago in the same year and was arrested almost immediately on his arrival and placed behind prison bars.

He submitted himself with all humbleness to his persecutors. Each time he was arrested, he sent for me so that I might see and learn the price of Truth for us, the so-called American Negroes (members of the Asiatic nation).

He was well able to save himself from such suffering, but how else was the scripture to be fulfilled? We followed in his footsteps, suffering the same persecution.

My people are yet sound asleep to the knowledge of the good that is being carried on for their deliverance. The whole world of our kind awaits the awakening, and our awakening is the last step in the Resurrection and Judgment of the world. It is a sin that we were put so soundly to sleep. The end of the world has arrived, and most of us know it not. Our enemies' greatest desire is that we remain asleep. My people fight and oppose the God of our own salvation.

Allah chose for us Islam as a religion. He desires to set us in Heaven at once, on condition that we submit to Him and accept the religion of Islam, the religion of God and His prophets. In this religion (Islam), He offers us universal friendship, and we who have submitted to Him know this to be true.

We know white people have and will continue to persecute anyone who offers help to us, the so-called American Negroes (Asiatics). Should persecution or even death stop the worthy help that will save the lives of the so-called Negroes? No, it shall not.

The so-called Negroes are absolutely friendless and have sought in vain friendship from their enemies, due to the ignorance of self and their enemies. Now they are offered universal friendship if they will only accept their own (Allah and Islam).

Seek first the friendship of your own people and then the friendship of others (if there is any friendship in the others).

We have made the grave mistake of Lazarus and the Prodigal Son, (St. Luke: Chapter 15), the one who was so charmed over the wealth and food of the rich man that he could not leave his gate to seek the same for himself,—regardless of the disgraceful condition in which the rich man puts him, even to sending his dogs to attack him. The angels had to come and take him away.

The other (Prodigal Son), being tempted by the loose life of strange women, drinking, gambling, and adultery, caused him to love the stranger's way of life so much so that it cost him all that he originally possessed (self-independence and Divine Guidance). His Father (God in person) had to come and be his representative to again meet his brothers, family, and friends.

Nothing fits the description of us better, the so-called Negroes (Asiatics). Many of us today are so lazy that we are willing to suffer anything rather than go for self. It is true that our God has come to set us in Heaven, but not a Heaven wherein we will not have to work.

Fear is the worst enemy that we have, but entire submission to Allah (God) and His Messenger will remove this fear. The white race put fear in our foreparents when they were babies, so says the word of Allah.

We must have for our peace and happiness (the 17,000,000 so-called Negroes) that which other nations have.

This beforementioned peace and happiness cannot come under any other flag but our own. If God desires for us such joy, why shouldn't we give up begging and be real men and sit with the rulers of the earth, ruling our own?

Our first step is to give back to the white man his religion (Christianity), his church, and his names. These three are chains of slavery that hold us in bondage to them. We are free when we give up the above three.

The so-called Negroes must know that they have been deceived and must be brought face to face with God and the devil. They must get away from the old slavery teaching that Jesus, who was killed 2,000 years ago, is still alive somewhere waiting and listening to their prayers.

He was only a prophet like Moses and the other prophets and had the same religion (Islam). He did His work and is dead like others of His time and has no knowledge of their prayers to Him.

Since Islam overran mankind in the seventh century after Jesus and is still a power over man, why did not the translators of the Bible mention it? Why didn't they give us the name of the religions of the prophets, since they claim a religion for Jesus?

THE SO-CALLED NEGROES SALVATION

The number one principle of belief is that your God is One

God and beside Him you have no other god that can help you. I shall begin with this, the most important of all principles of belief.

How many non-Muslims will we find who do not believe in God as being One God? Regardless of the trinity belief preached by the Christians, they (the Christians) claim and agree that Allah (God) is One God. They make fools of themselves when they reject Islam and the Muslims five principles of belief: One God, His Prophets, His Books, the Resurrection, The Judgment. How, then, did they (the Christians) go astray believing in three Gods? Nevertheless, they make one of the three the Father of the other two—and these remaining two the equal of the Father.

The so-called Negroes have been led into the gravest of errors in the knowledge of God (Allah) and the true religion (Islam) by their white slave-masters. They (the so-called Negroes) have been robbed more than any other people on the planet Earth. If they will only read and listen to the simplest of truths of which I write and speak have three essentials in it: power, light and life.

"I am a mortal like you—it is revealed to me that your God is One God (18:110)." Will you not bear witness with Muhammad in the above quoted chapter and verse of the Holy Qur-an?

The white race will not agree with Muhammad and the true religion of God (Allah), which is Islam because of the nature in which they were created,—as they are the opposers of Allah and the Truth. They (white people) know that the so-called Negroes believe in them, but with the help of my God (Allah)—who came in the person of Master W.F. Muhammad we will show up the false with the truth in its plainest simplest form.

It is foolish to believe in three gods—foolish to make Jesus the Son and the equal of his Father (the one of 2,000 years ago). If Jesus said in his suffering "My God, My God, why hast Thou forsaken me?" (Matt. 27:46) then most surely he did not recognize himself as being the equal of God, and no other scripture shows Jesus as the equal of God.

If Jesus said that He was sent (Matt. 15:24 and John 4:34), then he cannot claim to be equal of his sender. God is not sent by anyone; He is a self-sender. He says in Isaiah (44:08-45:22): "Is there a god besides Me? I know not any." In another place He states, "I am God, there is none else." (Isaiah 46:9). Also, "One God and none other." (Mark 12:32).

ALLAH IS JUDGING TODAY

Today is the day in which the God of Justice (Allah) is judging between man and man and nation and nation.

To understand the present, we must learn of the past.

We are 4,000 years from Moses and Moses was 2,000 years after the creation of the Caucasian race, or 2,000 years after the fathers of the Caucasian, or white race of Europe.

This makes 6,000 years from the time of the birth or grafting of the Caucasian race.

In 4,000 years of the white man's rule they have practiced and exercised their power and authority over us as was divinely given to them.

The trouble is going on between the so-called Negroes and the American white people, who have always shown themselves to be the enemies and haters of their slaves, the so-called Negroes. This thing must come to an end.

So God, Himself, intervenes to make manifest the two peoples. Everything that is of good, according to recorded history, has trouble in its infancy, but as it grows, it triumphs in the end.

The so-called Negroes must know the truth. This is the only way to bring them into the light of truth as they are spiritually blind to the knowledge of themselves but God, Himself.

Prophets of God can only deliver the truth to the people. But to make them to believe, see, and understand it and accept or reject it this must come from God.

It took the destruction of the people of Korah by Almighty God to make Israel understand that it was God who had appointed Moses to lead them and that self-made leaders such as Korah would not work in the way of delivering Israel another country.

Because Allah had chosen Moses to act as a guide for Israel, and all other self-made leaders would be failures.

He sent poisonous and fiery serpents against them to bite and kill those who rebelled. So this is a warning and a sign for us today: That when God intends to separate a people, or remove a people and put another in their stead, it is His work and the people who rebel against His work who will come to naught.

The so-called American Negroes must learn these truths today. That they cannot deliver themselves from the evils they are suffering from the white race without the help of Allah.

You see the trouble that our people and the American whites are suffering from the struggle of our people with a few whites on their side to bring about integration between the two races, of which is opposed by God, Himself. It is the time that the two people should separate.

SUBMIT TO ALLAH (GOD) AND FEAR NOT

Islam, the religion of entire submission to the Will of Allah (God). "Nay, whoever submits his whole self to Allah and is a doer of good, he will get his regard with his Lord, on such shall be no fear, nor shall they grieve." (Holy Qur-an 2:112).

That and that alone is Salvation according to the Holy Qur-an. Fear is the number one enemy that is blocking progress and success from coming to the so-called Negroes of America. This fear causes them to grieve. The whole world knows the poor so-called Negroes of America have suffered and still suffer more grief and sorrow than any people on the earth! This fear is the fear of the slave-masters (white man) and what the slave-masters dislike. Let the so-called Negroes submit to Allah (God) and they will not fear anymore, nor will they grieve. As it is written: "The fear of man bringeth a snare." (Proverbs: 29). It has surely snared the so-called Negroes.

The Lord of the world's Finder of we the lost members of the Asiatic Black Nation for 400 years said that the slave-masters put fear in our Fathers when they were babies. Allah is the only one that can remove this fear from us, but he will not remove it from us until we submit to His will, not our will, and fear Him and Him alone. Then, as it is written, "And it shall come to pass in the day that the Lord shall give thee rest from sorrow and from thy fear, and from the hard bondage wherein thou wast made to serve" (Isaiah 14:3). There are so many places that I could point out in the Bible and Holy Qur-an that warn us of fearing our enemies above or equal to the fear of Allah (God). It is a fool who has greater fear of the devils (white man) than Allah who has the power to destroy the devils and their followers

(Rev. 21:8; Holy Qur-an 7:18 and 15:43).

We must remember that if Islam means entire submission to the will of Allah, that and that alone is the True religion of Allah. Do not you and your religious teachers and the Prophets of old teach that the only way to receive God's help or Guidance is to submit to His will!—then WHY NOT ISLAM! It (Islam) is the true religion of Allah and the ONLY way to success.

ORIGINAL MAN

KNOW THYSELF

It is knowledge of self that the so-called Negroes lack which keeps them from enjoying freedom, justice and equality. This belongs to them divinely as much as it does to other nations of the earth.

It is Allah's (God's) will and purpose that we shall know ourselves. Therefore He came Himself to teach us the knowledge of self. Who is better knowing of who we are than God, Himself? He has declared that we are descendants of the Asian black nation and of the tribe of Shabazz.

You might ask, who is this tribe of Shabazz? Originally, they were the tribe that came with the earth (or this part) 66 trillion years ago when a great explosion on our planet divided it into two parts. One we call earth and the other moon.

This was done by one of our scientists, God, who wanted the people to speak one language, one dialect for all, but was unable to bring this about. He decided to kill us by destroying our planet, but still He failed. We were lucky to be on this part, earth, which did not lose its water in the mighty blasting away of the part called moon.

We, the tribe of Shabazz, says Allah (God), were the first to discover the best part of our planet to live on. The rich Nile Valley of Egypt and the present seat of the Holy City, Mecca, Arabia.

The origin of our kinky hair, says Allah, came from one of our dissatisfied scientists, 50,000 years ago, who wanted to make all of us tough and hard in order to endure the life of the jungles of East Asia (Africa) and to overcome the beasts there. But he failed to get the others to agree with him.

He took his family and moved into the jungle to prove to us that we could live there and conquer the wild beasts, and we have. So, being the first and the smartest scientist on the deportation of our moon and the one who suffered most of all, Allah (God) has decided to place us on the top with a thorough knowledge of self and his guidance.

We are the mighty, the wise, the best, but do not know it. Being without the knowledge, we disgrace ourselves, subjecting ourselves to suffering and shame. We could not get the knowledge of self until the coming of Allah. To know thyself is to know all men, as from us came all and to us all will return.

I must keep warning you that you should give up the white race's names and religion in order to gain success. Their days of success are over. Their rule will last only as long as you remain asleep to the knowledge of self.

Awake and know that Allah has revealed the truth. Stop believing in something coming to you after you are physically dead. That is untrue, and no one can show any proof of such belief.

Again, know that Jesus was only a prophet and cannot hear you pray any more than Moses or any other dead prophet. Know too, that this white race was created to be the enemy of black mankind for 6,000 years, which makes their number to be six. That is not your number or mine. We do not have a number, because we have no birth record. Do not let anyone fool you. This is the separation and the War of Armageddon.

FIRST, LOVE YOURSELF

One of the gravest handicaps among the so-called Negroes is that there is no love for self, nor love for his or her own kind. This not having love for self is the root cause of hate (dislike), disunity, disagreement, quarreling, betraying, stool pigeons and fighting and killing one another. How can you be loved, if you have not love for self? And your own nation and dislike being a member of your own, then what nation will trust your love and membership.

You say of yourself, "I love everybody." This cannot be true. Love for self comes first. The Bible, the book that you claim to believe says, "Love the brotherhood" (I Peter 2:17). "Love one another" (John 15:17). Love of self comes first. The one who loves everybody is the one who does not love anyone. This is the false teaching of the Christians for the Christians war against Christians. They have the Bible so twisted by adding in and taking out of the truth that it takes only God or one whom God has given the knowledge of the Book to understand it.

The Bible puts more stress upon the "love for thy neighbor" than the "love for the brother." When asked "Who is my neighbor?" the answer was contrary and incorrect. Jesus' answer was that of two men who were on a journey. They were not from the same place. One was from Jerusalem, the other one was a Samaritan. The Samaritan came to where the man from Jerusalem lay wounded by the robbers who had stripped him of his possessions. The Samaritan showed sympathy for the fellow traveler. (He was not a neighbor in the sense of the word. A neighbor can be an enemy.) Many enemies live in the same neighborhood of a good neighbor. But, the answer that Jesus gave was a futile one which could be classified as a parable of the so-called Negroes and their slave-masters.

The so-called Negroes fell into the hands of the slave-masters, who have robbed, spoiled, wounded and killed them. The Good Samaritan here would be the Mahdi (Allah)—God in Person, as He is often referred to by the Christians as the "the second coming of Jesus, or the Son of Man to judge man." This one will befriend the poor (the so-called Negroes) and heal their wounds by pouring into their heads knowledge of self and others and free them of the yoke of slavery and kill the slave-masters, as Jehovah did in the case of Pharaoh and his people to free Israel from bondage and the false religion and gods of Pharaoh.

There are many other proofs in the Bible which agree with the above answer.

Love yourself and your kind. Let us refrain from doing evil to each other, and let us love each other as brothers, as we are the same flesh and blood. In this way, you and I will not have any trouble in uniting. It is a fool who does not love himself and his people. Your black skin is the best, and never try changing its color. Stay away from intermixing with your slave-masters' children. Love yourself and your kind.

UNDERSTAND SELF

There are some efforts to celebrate a so-called "Negro History Week," and some of my people will participate. The planning of that week to teach the slave a knowledge of his past is not complete, sufficient or comprehensive enough to enable my people to learn the true knowledge of themselves. It is important that my people learn the true knowledge of self, as it means their salvation.

We are not Negroes, because God, whose proper name is Allah, has taught me who we are. We are not "colored " people because God has taught me who the colored people are. The American Negro is without a knowledge of self. You are a so-called Negro because you are "not" a Negro. Allah has given to me our proper names, the people from whom we were taken and brought here to the shores of North America and the history of our forefathers. Allah has taught me and today I do not fear to tell you, that you can discard that name "Negro." We are not "Negroes." We are not colored! Those are some of the main things which we should remember.

We must become aware of the knowledge of self and the time in which we are living. You must know these things whether you agree that Elijah Muhammad is on time or out of time. If what I say is out of season, it goes for nothing. If I am on time or in season, then all I say will bear fruit.

There is much misunderstanding among us because of our inferior knowledge of self. We have been to schools where they do not teach us the knowledge of self. We have been to the schools of our slave-master children. We have been to their schools and gone as far as they allowed us to go. That was not far enough for us to learn a knowledge of self. The lack of knowledge of self is one of our main handicaps. It blocks us throughout the world. If you were the world and you were a part of the world, you would also turn a man down if he did not know who he actually was. If we, the so-called Negroes, do not know our own selves, how can we be accepted by a people who have a knowledge of self?

Are we representing ourselves as Negroes and "colored" people in the ancient history of black men? Our search of the ancient history of the black man of the earth will prove that not once in time were Negroes or "colored" people living in Asia or Africa. How did we come by those names? The names are from the slave-masters. They have called us by their names and the nick-names used among themselves.

It even seems that we like being called by the slave-masters' name. After nearly a hundred years of freedom, we are still repre-senting ourselves by the names our slave-masters called us! We must learn that the slave-master's names are not accepted by God or by the righteous people of God.

It is time for us to learn who we really are, and it is time for us to understand ourselves. That true knowledge is here for you today whether you accept it or reject it. God has said that we are members of the original people or black nation of the earth. Original means first. Historian J. A. Rogers points out in his book that beyond the cotton fields of the South and long before the white man himself was a part of our planet, we were the original people ruling the earth, and according to the Holy Qur-an, we had governments superior to any we are experiencing today. Trace over the earth. Check back 5,000, 10,000 or 20,000 years ago. Look at history. Who were those people? They were our people. Today, we are confronted with proof of who the original people are and who shall live on this earth and call it their own.

HELP SELF
BEFORE HELPING OTHERS

Many of my people, the so-called Negroes, say we should help the nations of Africa which are awakening. This has been said as if we owned America. We are so foolish! What part of America do you have that you can offer toward helping Africa? Who is independent, the nations of Africa or we? The best act would be to request the independent governments of Africa and Asia to help us. We are the ones who need help. We have little or nothing to offer as help to others. We should begin to help at home first.

We are 20 million strong. Many of the nations today that have their independence, and those who are getting their indepen-dence, are much smaller in number than my people in America. We are dependent on the slave-master. We do not have 2 feet of earth for our nation of people. You and I, here in America, are licking the boots of the slave-master, begging him for the right of independent people. Yes, we are licking his boots. "Sir, let me shine your shoes?" You have been doing that for approximately 400 years. Today, if one rises up in your midst and says, "We should not lick the slave-master's boots, we should lick our own boots," you would say, "He should be killed! He should be killed because he is teaching us to hate." My people, you are in a dangerous position. Get that fear out of you and stand up for your people! Who are you not to die for your people? Who am I not to die for my people! If I am shot down or cut down today, who is little Elijah Muhammad to 20 million of you! If a million of us throw ourselves in the fire for the benefit of the 20 million, the loss will be small compared to the great gain our people will make as a result of that sacrifice. Hundreds of thousands of Muslims gave their lives in Pakistan to get their nation's independence. They were successful. The black men in Africa are fighting and dying today in unity for their independence.

We sit here like pampered babies. We cannot even stand up on the floor, not to mention taking a chance of crawling out of the door. We are too careful of shedding blood for ourselves. We are willing to shed all of it for the benefit of others. I am not trying to get you to fight. That is not even necessary; our unity will win the battle! Not one of us will have to raise a sword. Not one gun would we need to fire. The great cannon that will be fired is our unity. Our unity is the best. Why are you afraid to unite? Why are you afraid to accept Allah and Islam?

It is only because the slave-master did not teach you of this! We must unite to ourselves as a nation of people.

Separation of the so-called Negroes from their slave-masters' children is a MUST. It is the only solution to our problem.

You must know that this is the time of our separation and the judgment of this world (the Caucasian), which you and I have known. Therefore, Allah has said to me that the time is ripe for you and me to accept our own, the whole planet earth. Are you waiting for the Divine Destruction? Come! Let us reason together. First, in order for us to reason, you must have a thorough knowledge of self. Who is going to teach you that knowledge of self? Who are you waiting for to teach you the knowledge of self? Surely, not your slave-master, who blinded you to that knowledge of self. The slave-master will not teach you the knowledge of self, as there would not be a master-slave relationship any longer.

WHAT THE
SO-CALLED NEGRO
MUST DO FOR HIMSELF

Men everywhere are seeking unity among themselves. Every race of people want unity with their own kind first, except my people, the so-called Negro in America. Our condition and lack of love for ourselves must be attributed to the slave-master. He has been our teacher until the coming of Almighty God, Allah. The slave-master has robbed my people of their God, religion, name, language and culture.

The worst kind of crime has been committed against us, for we were robbed of our desire to even want to think and do for ourselves. We are often pictured by the slave-master as a lazy and trifling people who are without thoughts of advancement. I say, this is a condition which the slave-master very cleverly wanted and created within and among the so-called Negroes.

Robert H. Kinzer and Edward Sagarin, in their book, "The Negro in American Business" (page 81), states that the history of America would be different today if the slaves freed from bondage had been given, in addition to the three amendments to the Constitution, the famous "forty acres and a mule."

The slaves instead started not only without land and the money to purchase it but with few avenues open to earn and save money. Ownership of producing land is a prime and necessary part of freedom. A people cannot exist freely without land, and the so-called Negro in America is evidence of that fact. The slave-master passed laws limiting the so-called Negro in land ownership or limiting the areas in which such purchases or even rentals could be made. Are you not left restricted to the poorer sections the slave-master is abandoning throughout America?

Again, Mr. Kinzer and Mr. Sagarin gave a hint in their book of the great psychological strategy of the slave-master on his slave—that is the original brainwash. On page 84, the authors state that the land sold to the ex-slave was of poor quality and in an inferior location. They state the so-called Negro faced pressure against his becoming a farm owner and pressure from the white community that he remain a tenant. We encountered credit difficulties, hardships of repayment of loans and hardship with white executives from whom the loans must be asked.

All of this is part of the clever plan to discourage my people from wanting to own producing land for themselves and to cause a great dislike within them for having anything to do with tilling, cultivating, extracting and producing for themselves as other free and independent people. It is a shame! This shows you and I what white America is to us and just why we have not been able to do anything worthwhile for self. They want us to be helpless so they can mistreat us as always. We must come together and unite. It is time.

I think it is a disgrace for us to be satisfied with only a servant's part. We should and must, as other people, want for ourselves what other civilized nations have! Let us do for ourselves that which we are begging the slave-master to do for us. Do not be fooled by the false promise of civil rights and the softening of their language. It is offered to you now to keep you from becoming free of their evil plans of depriving you of the offer made to us by Allah—if we would submit to Him, He will set us in heaven at once. It is only justice that we be given land and provisions for a start so we may do for ourselves. This what the other new emerging nations are given. We want good productive land, not earth that is scorched but land that will produce crops and hold foundations for structures.

Let us make this clear. I am not begging. For, it pleases Allah, He will give us a home, and I am with Him. Today, according to Allah's Word, we are living in a time of the great separation of the blacks and the whites. The prophecy—400 years of slavery—as to the time the so-called Negroes would serve white people ended in 1955. The so-called Negroes must return to their own. The separation would be a blessing for both sides. It was the only solution, according to the Bible, for Israel and the Egyptians. It will prove to be the only solution for America and her slaves.

GET KNOWLEDGE
TO BENEFIT SELF

I am for the acquiring of knowledge or the accumulating of knowledge—as we now call it; education. First, my people must be taught the knowledge of self. Then and only then will they be able to understand others and that which surrounds them. Anyone who does not have a knowledge of self is considered a victim of either amnesia or unconsciousness and is not very competent. The lack of knowledge of self is a prevailing condition among my people here in America. Gaining the knowledge of self makes us unite into a great unity. Knowledge of self makes you take on the great virtue of learning.

Many people have attempted to belittle or degrade my followers by referring to them as unlettered or unschooled. They do this to imply that the believers in Islam are ignorant. If such a claim were so, then all the more credit should be given for our striving for self-elevation with so little. But truth represents itself and stands by itself. No followers, nor any other people are more zealous about the acquiring of knowledge than my followers. Throughout the Holy Qur-an, the duty of a Muslim to acquire knowledge is spelled out.

My people should get an education which will benefit their own people and not an education adding to the "storehouse" of their teacher. We need education, but an education which removes us from the shackles of slavery and servitude. Get an education, but not an education which leaves us in an inferior position and without a future. Get an education, but not an education that leaves us looking to the slave-master for a job.

Education for my people should be where our children are off to themselves for the first 15 or 16 years in classes separated by sex. Then they could and should seek higher education without the danger of losing respect for self or seeking to lose their identity. No people strive to lose themselves among other people except the so-called American Negroes. This they do because of their lack of knowledge of self.

We should acquire an education where our people will become better students than their teachers. Get an education which will make our people produce jobs for self and will make our people willing and able to go and do for self. Is this not the goal and aim of the many foreign students who are studying in this country? Will not these students return to their own nations and give their people the benefit of their learning? Did not Nkrumah return to Ghana to lead his people to independence with the benefit of learning he acquired here in America and elsewhere? Did not Dr. Hastings Banda return to give the benefit of his education to his people who are striving toward freedom and independence in Nyasaland? Did not Nnamdi Azikiwe of Nigeria give the benefit of his education to the upliftment and independence of his people. Does not America offer exchange scholarships to smaller, weaker and dependent foreign governments so their students will acquire knowledge to aid the people of those countries? Then why shouldn't the goal in education be the same for you and me? Why is scorn and abuse directed toward my followers and myself when we say our people should get an education which will aid, benefit and uplift our people? Any other people would consider it a lasting insult, of the worst type, to ask them to refrain from helping their people to be independent by contributing the benefit of their knowledge.

Get an education, but one which will instill the idea and desire to get something of your own, a country of your own and jobs of your own.

I recall, in 1922 or 1923, when a debate was taking place in Congress concerning appropriation of funds for Howard University, a school set aside to train my people, in the nation's capital. A senator said this, and it is in the records to be examined in effect: What would be the need of the government appropriating money to educate Negroes? He said that they would not teach our people the science of modern warfare (defense), birth control or chemistry. He knew these were things free people must know in order to protect, preserve and advance themselves. We have not been able to protect, preserve and advance ourselves. This shows the slave-master has been very successful in dominating us with an education beneficial to him. There is a saying among us, "Mother may have, father may have, but God blesses the child who has its own." It is time we had our own.

I want an education for my people that will let them exercise the right of freedom. We are 100 years up from slavery. We are constantly told that we are free. Why can't we take advantage of that freedom? I want an education for my people that will elevate them. Why should we always be lying at the gate begging for bread, shelter, clothing and jobs if we are free and educated? Do not get an education just to set it up as some useless symbolic monument to the black man in the Western Hemisphere. We need an education that eliminates division among us. Acquire an education that creates unity and makes us desire to be with our own.

The acquiring of knowledge for our children and ourselves must not be limited to the three R's '—reading, 'riting and 'rithemetic. It should instead include the history of the black nation, the knowledge of civilization of man and the universe and all the sciences. It will make us a greater people of tomorrow.

We must instill within our people the desire to learn and then use that learning for self. We must be obsessed with getting the type of education we may use toward the elevation and benefit of our people—when we have such people among us, we must make it possible for them to acquire this wealth which will be beneficial and useful to us.

One of the attributes of Allah, The All-Wise God, Who is the Supreme Being, is knowledge. Knowledge is the result of learning and is a force or energy that makes its bearer accomplish or overcome obstacles, barriers and resistance. In fact, God means possessor of power and force. The education my people need is that knowledge, the attribute of God, which creates power to accomplish and make progress in the good things or the righteous things. We have tried other means and ways and we have failed. Why not try Islam? It is our only salvation. It is the religion of Allah, His prophets and our forefathers.

KNOWLEDGE
OF
YOURSELF

You are ever making mistakes which will prove fatal to you and others of your own. If you could only recognize the time and knowledge of yourself and kind, the knowledge of the others who are on the same planet rotating around the sun daily, you would know who you are. And you should know who you are, as well as know your planet and its consistency and remember at all times how you were brought here through our parents 400 years ago and how our parents were mercilessly brought here against their will. They did not ask to come but were forced and were used for merchandise to be sold and resold for 300 long years like livestock and wild beasts.

You do not have a second thought about this, because you have your mind, eyes and heart filled with hopes that you may become one of those who did this evil against your parents and be recognized as a great admirer and lover of these same people who now rehearse the same evil with a little addition, the fire hose and the dogs, the burning and the lynching of you and your women. You are not able—at this day and time—100 years a free slave, to protect yourself and your women from the murderous hands of the children of the murderers of your fathers and mothers 400 years ago.

Today, God, in the Person of Master Fard Muhammad, is asking you and me to "Accept our own and return to our own kind on some of this earth, that we can call our own," and you are rejecting this offer to return to your own unless you can carry the same enemy along who has destroyed your fathers and is now destroying you. They were not bought and sold as you were; they did not come from Africa but from Europe. You are so blinded that you cannot see them and so deaf that you cannot hear the truth of them and desire to be one of them and mix into their blood and have them mix into your blood. This is like Sodom and Gomorrah before God.

You should remember that you have a great offer made to you in the words, "Accept Your Own." To accept your own means yourself and your kind, your God Who is of you and you are of Him. It was your fathers who created the heavens and the earth, while there is nothing that the white man has created independently. He did not even create himself. The Black Nation is self-created, while the white race is made by one of the gods and scientists of the Black Nation. Their time on our planet is nothing compared to the time that we have been in the universe on this planet. It is hardly a fraction of a minute if we divide their 6,000 years into our billions and trillions of years. It would run into little or no time at all.

We are the originals, so Almighty God Allah has revealed. He has asked you who belong to the original people of the earth to accept your place among them, since you have been robbed of knowledge and your place on this planet that you can call your own and your place among your own. You must remember that this is a wonderful offer, and it is a wonderful knowledge to know the truth, and it is even more wonderful to know that the truth is in your favor and the earth as well as the heavens above belong to you. Accept your own, that which you have been dead to the knowledge of, now that God has come in your midst to resurrect you and put you in your place of authority. You are ignorant enough to put yourself in the place of a dog at the feet of the white race, begging them to accept you as their brother, when they could not do this if they tried. They would still be deceiving you, and their efforts would end in the manifest truth that it was only false of them to try to establish brotherhood among you. Their time of ruling the people of earth is up. Accept your place in the sun as it was originally before the creation of this world.

You must remember that slave-names will keep you a slave in the eyes of the civilized world today. You have seen, and recently, that Africa and Asia will not honor you or give you any respect as long as you are called by the white man's name. The example was evident when I took Muhammad Ali (the World's Heavyweight Champion) out of the white man's name (the name itself made him a servant and slave to the white man). All Africa and Asia then acclaimed him as also being their champion. This shows you that all previous black men of America who were bestowed with the title of the world's heavyweight champion were only exalting the white man of America, Europe and Australia. Their people said nothing because they were not theirs and were not enhancing their honor among the people of the world. Just a change of name has given Brother Muhammad Ali a name of honor and a name of praise that will live forever (its meaning). His people of the near and far East acclaimed him and laid the red carpet for him to come among them as a prince.

I warn you to wake up and accept your own or go to the doom with other than your own.

IF THE CIVILIZED MAN FAILS TO PERFORM HIS DUTY WHAT MUST BE DONE?

The duty of the civilized man is to teach civilization to the un-civilized—the arts and sciences of civilized people and countries of advanced civilization.

A Divine Messenger of God (Allah), raised among His people with the Divine Message, is held responsible for its delivery. His message teaches spiritual civilization, which is important to the success of a nation and society. According to history, the people who refuse to accept Divine Guidance or His Message sent by His Messengers are classified as uncivilized or savages.

A well-educated, cultured and courteous people make a beauti-ful society when it is spiritual. Good manners come from the civilized man who does not fail to perform his duty.

There are several civilizations. We have a wicked one and a righteous one. It is a righteous civilization that is in the workings now. We all have been well trained into the wicked civilization. Now we must be trained into the knowledge of the righteous one. We must have a righteous, trained civilized man who will not fail to perform his duty to us in guiding and teaching us.

My people in America are under the searchlight of the right-eous, who are offering to them the right guidance to a supreme civilization of righteousness never witnessed before on earth. The white race has failed to perform its duty of civilizing the Ameri-can so-called Negroes. Of course,they have been their slaves for many centuries, and the slave-masters have rights over them as long as they are slaves. However, if the slave-masters free their slaves, not in words but in deeds, the slave-masters should pro-vide the once-slaves with the right civilization and with every-thing necessary for them to start an independent life as their slave-masters have.

Certainly the so-called Negroes are being schooled, but is this education the equal of that of their slave-masters? No; the so-called Negroes are still begging for equal education. After blind-ing them to the knowledge of self and their own kind for 400 years, the slave-masters refuse to civilize the so-called Negroes into the knowledge of themselves of which they were robbed. The slave-masters also persecute and hinder anyone who tries to perform this most rightful duty.

I will continue to say that as long as the so-called Negroes do not know who they really are and do not have the knowledge to free themselves from their slave-masters' names and religion, they cannot be considered free or civilized. To this their slave-masters will agree. Some of the so-called Negroes are ignorant of this important advantage of having their own nations' names. They think there is nothing to a name (and there is not to the ones they are using), but the Bible says "a good name is better than gold." To continue to bear the slave-masters' names makes my people the property of their slave-masters or their children and we can never hope to receive equal recognition in the civilized world.

Will a free people accept slaves as their equal? The so-called Negroes must be truly civilized, and the right civilized man has not performed his duty until this is accomplished. However, the so-called Negro is free to receive his or her own if they just will not allow fear and ignorance to stand in their way.

It has been seen from the little chance they have had to get a little education—they have shown and proved that they are the original people who are only asleep and in great need of the right civilized man who will perform his duty of awakening them. The so-called Negroes' fear of being deprived of food, clothing and shelter, and also the usual smile of the white slave-masters' children, prevents them from seeking the true knowledge of their own nation's civilization. They must drop the slave-masters' names and religion, which both they have and do not understand. This means nothing but slavery. Of course, some preachers and politicians who live off the ignorance of their people are opposed to the right civilization of our people.

You must know that you have not been rightly civilized. No one can enslave another who has equal education (knowledge). My people lack science of the right kind. Allah is here to give you and me a superior knowledge of things and a country to ourselves. Separation of the so-called Negroes from their slave-masters' children is a must. It is the only solution to our problem. It was the only solution, according to the Bible, for Israel and the Egyptians, and it will prove to be the only solution for America and her slaves, whom she mockingly calls her citizens without granting citizenship. We must keep this in our minds at all times; we are actually being mocked.

I think it is a disgrace to us for ever being satisfied with only a servant's part. Should not we, as a people, want for ourselves what other civilized nations have? It takes a true friend or friends to help another or others to enjoy equal freedom, justice and equality. Today for the first time in our history we have that true friend in Allah (who came in the person of Master Fard Muhammad) and the nation of Islam, if we only would submit and accept Him.

It is written (Rev. 14:1) that 144,000 of us will accept and return to our God and people and the rest of my people will go down with the enemies of Allah. For this sad prophecy of the loss of my people I write what I am writing, hoping perhaps that you may be able to beat the old prophets' predictions by making the truth so simple that a fool can understand it. You must be rightly civilized. You must go back to your own people and country, but not one of you can return with what you have. You must know that this is the time of our separation and the judgment of this world (the Caucasian race) that you and I have known. Therefore, Allah has said to me that the time is ripe for you and me to accept our own (the whole planet earth). What are you waiting for? The destruction? Come, let us reason together, but you cannot until you have a thorough knowledge of self. Who are you waiting for to teach you the knowledge of self? Surely not your slave-masters who blinded you to the knowledge. The white race's civilization will never work for us.

ACCEPT YOUR OWN

America has been number one on the list of God for total destruction for a long time; even in the prophecy of Moses, Isaac, Habakkub and Jesus. Her (America) destruction has been coming gradually for the past 34 years.

The nations of the earth are becoming her enemies because

of her evils and the murders of the so-called American Negroes, who now could choose to build the kingdom of heaven. There is no let-up in her evil, brutality and murder of her once slaves (the Negro) who are still her slaves mentally. She would not like you to know that the doom is because of the way she treated her slaves. She has deceived everyone who deals with her, as recorded in the Revelations of John of the Bible. Today, she has, as the Revelation of John prophesied, the head of the church (the Pope of Rome) helping her deceive Negroes and keep them in the church so that they may be destroyed with her.

The only thing that will hold the Negro is his belief in whites as a people of divinity. They hold to his religion (Christianity), which they use to deceive everyone they possibly can. It was through Christianity that they got their authority over the black, brown, yellow and red races.

The holding to the white man's name is another chain that carries the Negro down with his enemies. It is laughable and saddening to see the so-called Negro preachers reading and preaching from the Bible while they do not understand it. Negro professionals, scholars and scientists are still ignorant of the fact that as long as they are in the white man's name, they are his slaves. In every nation, as soon as he presents himself in the name of the white man of America or Europe, they know that he is dumb to the fact that he cannot be free until he breaks his slave-master's hold on him—his name, his religion, his way of living and his evil practices. These must be given up before any nation or even God can help or even aid the Negro in becoming a free people recognized by other nations.

Proof has been offered in the name of the present heavyweight champion of the world, Muhammad Ali. It is a' divine name—both Muhammad and Ali are the names of God. Quickly the nations of his kind held out their hands and called to him Christian black preachers have never been so recognized because of their ignorance in holding the name and religion of their slave-master.

The Revelation of John in the Bible (the Revelator represents them spiritually as beasts because of their savage way of dealing with and murdering black people) and even Isaiah warn you who hold to the white man's names and his religion.

This is your America. We have proven this to you, not your slave-master, that you will get respect and honor throughout the world if you accept your own and take on the names of the divine supreme being. It is in your Bible, and now it has been made manifest to you.

Watch how anxious the white man is to hold you and call you by his name. He still would like to call the champion, Cassius Clay, after himself, and he would like to call me Poole, after himself. This is to keep the blind, blind; the deaf, deaf and the dumb, dumb to the knowledge that even the name alone is sufficient to free you of this evil people.

I have offered America a solution to her problems with her slaves. But because she knows that you are dumb enough not to want to accept it, she is condemning herself to an early doom by rejecting it. The only way out is to separate the two people despite the foolish Negroes' cry that they love white people and want to remain with them.

The time has arrived. The only way to put off for a few more years the total destruction America is to deal fairly with the Negro. But, nevertheless, one day it will come, unless she would like to return to Europe instead of sending the Negro back to Africa.

The whole Western Hemisphere belongs to the darker people, and Europe was given to the white people. Your anger against the Negro getting a just deal has hastened your doom. America will suffer some of the worst calamities within the next year or two—calamities worse than any nation has endured since man has been on earth—that is, if she does not make the right move.

Square up with justice for the slave, and do not try to deceive him through intermarrying your women. Give him up and let him go, or suffer death and destruction.

WE MUST TEACH OUR OWN

Today with all of our white civilized schooling, we have not been taught of our own. They will never teach us of our own.

Since the coming of Allah, their reason for not teaching us of our own is made crystal clear. The knowledge that Allah has given us gives the knowledge of our own. Being the first people of the earth, we are destined to be the last; we are the creators and the makers. This limited civilization of the white man and his rule is now terminating, never to be brought into existence again. This makes it absolutely against the will of the white man to honor and respect you and me and our Nation as being the first people and the makers of the universe.

Why so much teaching and warning given to the American so-called Negro and so little or no teaching of the kind being given to the African and Asian Black Nation? It is due to the fact that we are living in the midst of a people whom Allah (God) will destroy in the very near future. We are on the brink of fire and must be removed to a zone of safety. The ignoring of such warnings and of the time of the Judgment of this world (the Caucasian world with their great universal power that they have exercised over the Black Nation) makes it very hard for the average black person to conceive of the idea of such a strong race of people being removed. This is a very small thing in the eyes and power of Allah, removing and destroying people who have brought His anger against them for their neglect of worship and respect of Him as the Supreme Being, who do not even respect His representatives but prosecute and kill them.

These people have been the worst people to us (the Black Nation) since they have been on the face of the earth. They were created and made for just the purpose of destroying our peace as well as our lives. They have destroyed 600 million of the Black Nation since they have been on our planet. This averages 100 million every thousand years of their rule. They have affected nine-tenths of the total population of the Black Man under their rule, including the brown, red and yellow races. They have deceived—as the Bible (Revelation of John) says—the whole world, and now they are being made manifest as the deceivers and adversaries of Allah and His true religion of entire submission to His will (Islam).

This black people of America, who have been swallowed symbolically by the white slave-master and his children, must now be brought out of this race of people and be taught the knowledge of their own. Allah is holding the affair in person under the name of Master Fard Muhammad. He has chosen us today to be His people and means to take us and build and establish forever a people of righteousness and a people with unlimited knowledge of the Divine Supreme Being. The very last of one of these will become greater than the greatest of this world.

The Orthodox Muslims will have to bow to the choice of

Allah. Allah will bring about a new Islam. As for the Principles of Belief, they remain the same. There will be no more signs to be watched for the coming of God and the setting up of a new world of Islam. We are seeing this change now and entering into it. The devils oppose this change, and the Orthodox join them in opposing us because of their desire to carry on the old way of Islam.

Allah will place those of His choice in authority in the making of the new world, and others must obey whomever He puts in authority or find themselves fighting against the power of whomever they hold to be on their side and in their favor. We must have a new world. We accept for a new nation completely.

As Yakub brought about a people (the present white race) who were a completely new people made out of the original of us, another new people must be made to be the ruling voice of tomorrow out of this old world that is now living her last days. They will be completely new people. The Holy Qur-an and Bible refer to them as being brought about by the power and will of God in Person in the resurrection of the mentally dead, lost-found original people in America. We may not seem to please you or to be pleasing to Allah, but it is written in the Bible that He will give to whom He pleases and chastise whom He pleases.

This is to warn us that we have no choice in the matter. Whatever Allah desires, He will bring into being, whether we like it or not.

BLACKMAN,
ACCEPT YOUR OWN

(God said: *Accept your own*)

It is an act of intelligence and love for us to accept our own.

One will say, "What is our own?" No. 1, our own people—our own earth, God and His religion, Islam (the religion of peace) and our own place in the sun. This Divine call to us to accept our own makes sense. Everything of life will accept its kind as its own.

Why the so-called Negroes (members of the Great Asiatic Nation of the Tribe of Shabazz) refuses to accept his own is because of being made blind, deaf and dumb to the knowledge of self and kind by the devils when they were babies under slavery.

Today, they cling to this same enemy of their fathers and the enemies of all Black people upon the face of the earth because they cannot see any hope for a future for themselves in their own kind and self, due to the lack of knowledge of self.

They beg the enemy even for friendship, which is like the frog pleading to the snake not to swallow him after the snake has gotten him in his mouth.

The Black people of America have been swallowed by the slave-masters, who are a race of devils, says all-wise God, Allah, and now refuse to let us go free without hinderance and hold us a prey against the will of Allah in the person of Master Fard Muhammad, who now seeks our deliverance, since our people love the enemy more than God.

For God to fulfill His promises to deliver us from our enemies, He must go to war against the enemy and break the enemy's power of resistance to free us. War is inevitable. The so-called Negroes must come to the knowledge of Truth, that they have no future in their enemies who are the enemies of Almighty God, Allah. God must come to put an end to war and, that is to say, destroy those who love to make war and delight in making mischief.

The American white people delight in mistreating us, their former slaves.

There is no justice for us among such people, the devils in person. They hate us if we try being good; they have turned upon us, who have turned to Allah and have accepted His true religion, Islam, and are persecuting and killing some of us just because we are Muslims and they fear the teachings of Islam and the history and knowledge of the devils and that All of our people will believe in Allah and His true religion, Islam.

They hate unity among the so-called Negroes. A continued war is made upon us by the white devils of America.

Why shouldn't we accept our own and return to our own? There is no future in this people for us. They have hundreds and thousands of my followers in jails and state and government penitentiaries and are falsely accusing many more and putting them under unjust heavy penalties and long terms of imprisonment just because they want to be Muslims.

The refusal of the Supreme Court to hear the unjust judges' decisions against my followers (the Muslims) in Louisiana and the killing and the wicked unjust plan that the Los Angeles Court seeks to place against the poor innocent Muslims that Allah saved from the police guns last April 27, 1962, is enough for the unintelligent animal world to shudder and weep.

Shouldn't Allah destroy such an unjust people as our slave-masters' children? The day of visitation has come. She shall reap what she has sown.

WHO IS THE ORIGINAL MAN?

The above question is now answered from the mouth of Allah to us, the so-called Negroes, for the first time since our straying away from our own nation.

This secret of who is God and who is the devil has been a mystery to the average one of mankind, to be revealed in all of its clearness to one who was so ignorant that he know not even himself—born blind, deaf and dumb in the wilderness of North America.

All praise is due to the Great Mahdi, who was to come and has come, the sole master of the worlds. I ask myself at times, "What can I do to repay Allah (the Great Mahdi, Fard Muhammad) for His coming, wisdom, knowledge and understanding?"

Most of us having been born in the southern part of this wilderness of sin, where the member of white race (man of sin) has always manifested himself to us (the so-called Negroes), should have known that he was really the evil one by the way he treated us. Yet, we were made so dumb that we still could not recognize him.

The truth of him is now being told and taught throughout the world, to his anger and sorrow. He is losing no time trying to hinder the truth of the above question, who is the original man?

He is setting watchers and listeners around me and my followers to see if he can find some other charge to put against us to
satisfy his anger of the truth that we preach from the mouth of
Allah, who is with us in person.

The original man, Allah has declared, is none other than the
black man. The black man is the first and last, maker and owner of the universe. From him came all brown, yellow, red and
white people. By using a special method of birth control law
the black man was able to produce the white race.

The true knowledge of the black and white mankind should
be enough to awaken the so-called Negroes and put them on
their feet and on the road to self-independence. Yet, they are so
afraid of the slave-masters that they even love them to their
destruction and wish that the bearer of truth would not tell the
truth even if he knows it.

The time has arrived when it must be told the world over.
There are millions who do not know who is the original man.
Why should this question be put before the world today? Because it is the time of judgment between the black and white
and the knowledge of the rightful owners of the earth.

Allah is now pointing out to the nations of earth their rightful places, and this judgment will bring an end to war over it.
Now it is so easy to recognize the original man, the real owner
of the earth, by the history of the two (black and white). We
have an unending past history of the black nation and a limited
one of the white race.

We find that history teaches that the earth was populated by
the black nation ever since it was created, but the history of
the white race does not take us beyond 6,000 years.

Everywhere the white race has gone on our planet they have
either found the original man or a sign that he had been there
previously. Allah is proving to the world of black men that the
white race actually does not own any part of our planet.

The Bible and Holy Qur-an bears witness to the above, if
you are able to understand it. The Holy Qur-an, the beauty
of Scriptures, repeatedly challenges the white race to point out
the part of the heavens and earth that they created.

It further teaches that they are not even their own creators.
We created white man from a small life germ, the soft pronoun
"we" used nearly throughout the Holy Qur-an makes the knowledge of the original man much clearer and more intelligent of

how the white race's creation took place.

In the Bible, referring to their creation, we have US (Gen. 1:26) creating, or rather making, the race; the US and WE used show beyond a shadow of a doubt that they came from another people.

A knowledge of the white race removes once and for all times the mistakes that would be made in dealing with them. My followers and I can and are getting along with them in a more understandable way than ever because we know them.

You cannot blame one for the way he or she was born, for they had nothing to do with that. Can we say to them why don't you do righteousness when nature did not give righteousness to them? Or say to them, why are you such a wicked devil? Who is responsible, the made or his maker? Yet we are not excused for following and practicing his evil or accepting him for a righteous guide just because he is not his maker.

A GOOD NAME IS
BETTER THAN GOLD

One of the first and most important truths that must be established in this day is our identity. This is what our God, Whose Proper Name is Allah, is guiding me to point out to you, my people, who are members of the Lost and Found Nation in North America. You, my people, who have been robbed of your complete identity for over 400 years. Is it not time for you to know who you are after 400 years of submission to the white slave-masters of American and their false religion of Christianity?

Our true God is not like the "Spook God" of Christianity who demands death for our salvation and redemption. He is offering us Freedom, Liberty and the Pursuit of Happiness on this earth while we live. First, you must be given the names of your forefathers, whose names are the most Holy and Righteous Names of Allah, Again, I repeat, that restoring to you your identity is one of the first and most important truths to be established by God, Himself.

All nations of the earth are recognized by the name by which they are called. By stating one's name, one is able to associate an entire order of a particular civilization simply by name alone. For example, if you take the name Lu Chin, we know immediately that this is a Chinese name, whose land or origin is China, a country that operates on an independent basis and is recognized through the world as a nation and whose people demand respect.

We know this and more from the name "Lu Chin." If we search among the peoples and nations of the earth, we will discover that this is an established truth from country to country and from continent to continent.

It is only when we come to America and learn the names that our people are now going by that we discover that a whole nation of 20,000,000 black people are going by the names of white people. How can a so-called Negro say that his name is "Sam Jones," a white man's name with roots in Europe, when "Sam Jones" (Black Man) comes from Africa or Asia?

My poor blind, deaf and dumb people are going by the wrong names and until you accept the truth of your true identity and accept the names of your people and nation we will never be respected because of this alone. This is one of the reasons Almighty Allah has come among us, that is, to give us His Names, the Most Holy and Righteous Names of the Planet Earth.

It is Allah who gave me my name, "Muhammad." From this name, alone, our open enemies (the white race) know that the True and Living God has come into our midst and is doing a Divine Work among the so-called Negroes of America. The white man knows that Islam was our religion, our civilization and our way of life before he made us blind, deaf and dumb to this knowledge.

It has never been the white man's intention to restore to us this knowledge. Now that he sees his formerly dead ex-slaves returning to their own religion (Islam) and worshiping their own God (Allah) and awakening to the truth of their true identity, he knows that God alone is bringing this change about.

The white race knows and admits that it is only a matter of time when all the truth will be accepted by our people (to his deepest regret). I warn you, my people, discard your former slave-master's names and be willing and ready to accept one of Allah's Pure and Righteous Names that He Alone will give our people from His Own Mouth! A good name is, indeed, better than gold. I am naught but a warner and a Messenger to you, my people, not self-sent but sent directly from Almighty God (Allah).

HELP SELF:
WHAT MUST BE DONE
WITH THE NEGROES?

Since our being brought in chains to the shores of America, our brain power, labor, skills, talent and wealth have been taken, given and spent toward building and adding to the civilization of another people. It is time for you and me, the so-called Negroes, to start doing for ourselves. We must not let our children be as are we, beggars of another man for his home, facilities, clothing, food and the means of providing a living. Man depends on land for the necessities, food, clothing and shelter for survival. A prime requisite for freedom and independence is having one's own land. There can be no freedom without a people having their own land.

The acquisition of land has been the factor for more wars than any other cause. Economists agree that in order for any type of nation or system, capitalism or communism, democracy or totalitarian or what have you, to exist and have a degree of independence there must be ownership of land. The so-called Negroes are without a state they can call their own. We have nothing to show for our more than 310 years of forced slave labor and more than 100 years of our free servitude to our slave-masters' children.

We were brought here to work. We have worked! We are still the workers. Some of us say, "What will we do if we do not work for the white man? How will we live?" I say, when you are free and independent you have a job! You have a tremendous task of doing something for self. You have the job of building a civilization for yourself as other free and independent people are doing for themselves.

As a people, we must become producers and not remain consumers and employees. We must be able to extract raw materials from the earth and manufacture them into something useful for ourselves. This would create jobs in production. We must remember that without land there is no production. The surplus of what we produce we would sell. This would develop a field of commerce and trade as other free and independent people whose population is less than that of the 20 million so-called Negroes who are dependent in America.

We must begin at the cradle and teach our babies that they must do something for self. They must not be like we, their fathers, who look to the slave-makers' and slave-masters' children for all. We must teach our children now with an enthusiasm exceeding that which our slave-masters used in having our fore-fathers imbed the seed of dependency within us. We must stop the process of giving our brain power, labor and wealth to our slave-masters' children. We must eliminate the master-slave relationship.

We must educate ourselves and our children into the rich power of knowledge which has elevated every people who have sought and used it. We must give the benefit of our knowledge to the elevation of our own people.

Presently in this country, in almost all of the major universities and colleges, there are thousands of young students from Africa and Asia. Yet, as young, primitive and backward as we say these countries of Africa and Asia might be, their students here are returning to their shores. Their intent and purpose is to give their people the benefit of their learning. All civilized people give the benefit of their knowledge, skill and wealth to their own people. Those who do not are called traitors, defectors, spies, tools and Toms.

Why should we spend 12 and 16 years seeking an education only to give the benefit of our knowledge back to the one we sought it from? It is time for us to wake up! Why should we work to give the meager earnings of our labor back to our slave-masters' children? Why can't we have our own? Why can't we do for our own? Why can't we learn to spend with and sup-port our own? Why can't we strive toward keeping our brain power, labor and wealth within and among and elevating our own?

We must have that which will make us want to do for our-selves as other people want and do for themselves. You ask, "How can this be done?" The so-called Negroes must be taught and given Islam. Why Islam? Islam, because it teaches first the knowledge of self. It gives us the knowledge of our own. Then and only then are we able to understand that which surrounds us. "Know thyself" is the doctrine Socrates espoused, and this is the base of the educational system in America. The religion of

Islam makes the so-called Negroes think in terms of self and their own kind. Thus, this kind of thinking produces an industrious people who are self-independent. Islam is actually our religion by nature. Allah is the proper name for God. Islam is not a European-organized white man's religion. It is time for the so-called Negroes to help their own kind and be benefited by Islam.

THE BLACK WOMAN

The woman is man's field to produce his nation. If he does not keep the enemy out of his field, he won't produce a good nation. If we love our vegetable crops we will go out and turn up the leaves on that vegetable stalk and look carefully for worms that are eating and destroying the vegetables. We will kill that worm—right?

Again, we will go out into the cotton field and look for the enemies of our cotton and try to kill that enemy. We study poisons and chemicals of the earth and we pour these chemicals on the enemies of our crops to keep the enemies from destroying them. We love a crop that we can produce every year, every season, so well that we will kill every enemy that we find seeking to destroy it.

We will even kill one another if we find the other one out there trying to steal that crop.

Is not your woman more valuable than that crop of corn, that crop of cotton, that crop of cabbage, potatoes, beans, tomatoes? How much more valuable is your woman than these crops that you should keep the enemies from destroying the crops. Yet you are not careful about your women. You don't love them. Why? It is because you have allowed visitors to run in and out of your house, thus they have destroyed your love for your woman and your woman has not the love for you that she should.

That is a good sign. Until we learn to love and protect our woman, we will never be a fit and recognized people on the earth. The white people here among you will never recognize you until you protect your woman.

The brown man will never recognize you until you protect your woman. The yellow man will never recognize you until you protect your woman. The white man will never recognize you until you protect your woman.

You and I may go to Harvard, we may go to York of England, or go to Al Ahzar in Cairo and get degrees from all of these great seats of learning. But we will never be recognized until we recognize our women.

On visiting with a couple of my sons in what they call the Near East, in 1959, I began in Turkey. We traveled from Turkey down to Africa to Ethiopia and the Sudan. We visited Arabia (Mecca and Medina), and we visited Pakistan. We returned home from Lahore, Pakistan, on about the 6th of January, 1960. We didn't even find on that entire tour such a thing as not recognizing the black woman.

Everywhere we went, the Black man recognized his woman. He had great respect for her. We dined in many of the "top (as you say in slang) homes." We dined with some of the most influential people of these countries—government people. In some of their homes, we never did see any of their family, only men.

The waiter was a man or boy, not any woman. My beloved brothers in America, you have lost the respect for your woman and therefore you have lost the respect for yourself. You won't protect her; therefore you can't protect yourself.

She is your first nurse. She is your teacher. Your first lesson comes from your mother. If you don't protect your mother, how do you think you look in the eyes of other fellow human beings?

PROTECT AND ELEVATE YOUR WOMAN

Allah, Himself, has said that we cannot return to our land until we have a thorough knowledge of our own selves. This first step is the control and the protection of our own women. There is no nation on earth that has less respect for and as little control of their woman as we so-called Negroes here in America. Even animals and beasts, the fowls of the air, have more love and respect for their females than have the so-called Negroes of America.

Our women are allowed to walk or ride the streets all night long, with any strange men they desire. They are allowed to frequent any tavern or dance hall that they like, whenever they like. They are allowed to fill our homes with children other than our own. Children that are often fathered by the very devil himself. Then, when the devil man decides to marry her, the so-called Negro press and magazines will make it front page news. The daily press will not print a so-called Negro man marrying into their race, but you seem to think it is an honor to your own nation when your daughter goes over to your enemies, the devils.

Our women have been and are still being used by the devil white race, ever since we were first brought here to these States as slaves. They cannot go without being winked at, whistled at, yelled at, slapped, patted, kicked and driven around in the streets by your devil enemies right under your nose. Yet you do nothing about it, nor do you even protest.

You cannot control or protect your women as long as you are in the white race's false religion called Christianity. This religion of theirs gives you no desire or power to resist them. The only way and place to solve this problem is in the Religion of Islam.

It is a pleasure to Allah to defend us from our enemies. In the religion of Christianity the white race has had us worshiping and praying to something that actually did not even exist.

Islam will not only elevate your women but will also give you the power to control and protect them. We protect ours against all their enemies.

We protect our farms by pulling up our weeds and grass by the roots, by killing animals and birds, and by poisoning the insects that destroy our crops in order that we may produce a good crop. How much more valuable are our women, who are our fields through whom we produce our nation.

The white race does not want us to destroy their race by inter-marrying with them. They will even kill you to protect their women. Can you blame them? No, blame your foolish self for not having enough respect for your own self and your own nation to do likewise. Stop our women from trying to look like them. By bleaching, powdering, ironing and coloring their hair; painting their lips, cheeks and eyebrows; wearing shorts; going half-nude in public places; going swimming with them and lying on beaches with men.

Have private pools for your women and guard them from all men. Stop them from going into bars and taverns and sitting and drinking with men and strangers. Stop them from sitting in those places with anyone. Stop them from using unclean language in public (and at home), from smoking and drug addiction habits.

Nothing but Islam will make you a respectable people. We Muslims are your example, living here in your midst.

There is no delinquency in Islam. Are you with us to put our people on top of the world?

THE SO-CALLED NEGRO MUST DO SOMETHING FOR HIMSELF

In unity, we can accomplish much. Think of the 20 million of your and my kind putting one dollar a year aside for ourselves in a national treasury toward the day of want. Suppose we laid aside one dollar every month against the day of want. Look at the millions that we could build up for ourselves within a few years. Suppose all of you who are wealthy would spend your wealth to build up a better and more economic system among your own people. It would do much to aid our people. Do not put your wealth in the taverns and gambling houses and on race horses and other sports. Then, you would not be so easy to push over when the day of want arrives.

There is no need for us, millions through the country, spending our money for the joy and happiness of others. As a result, as soon as they throw us out of a job we are back at their doors begging for bread and soup. How many clothing shops do we operate in the country? Very few! Yet, all of us wear clothes. Who made our clothes for us? Who sold them to us? We have thousands of grocery stores, but what about our naked bodies? Should we not have more stores to sell our people clothes? Should we not sell our people everything they want or need? But no, we give all the money out of our pockets to the slave-master. We are satisfied in doing so. There are millions of us. We do not have enough factories to weave clothes for our people here in America. Think over that. Where is our shoe factory? Where are our cattle that we are skinning to make shoes for our people? These are small things, but we want equality with a nation that is doing these things.

We boast that we should be recognized as equals. Let us make ourselves equals. We cannot be equal with the master until we own what the master owns. We cannot be equal with the master until we have the freedom the master enjoys. We cannot be equal with the master until we have the education the master has. Then, we can say "Master, recognize us as your equal."

Today you are begging the master, the slave-masters' children for what? You are begging them for a job. You are begging for complete recognition as their equals. Let us be honest with ourselves. According to history, we cannot find where the master made his slave equal until the slave made himself worthy of equality.

I am with you to go on top. We cannot go on top with weight that is hanging on us. We cannot charge the white man with all our faults. We are supposed to be, according to his own teachings, free. We are supposed to have been freed from him approximately 100 years ago. Have we exercised that freedom? We must answer that we have not availed ourselves of that freedom. If we have not availed ourselves of that freedom which he says he gave us, why should we think hard of him about the way he treats us? This may be a little hard to swallow.

Our fathers, in the days they were set free by the slave-master, had no knowledge of how to go for self. Today, you are educated. You claim that you have equal education. Then, why don't you take a walk? Before we can be justified in accusing the other man, let us examine ourselves first. I do not say that our fathers are the ones to blame for their ignorance, and neither are you. Neither they nor you are at fault. The root of the cause can be placed back into the laps of the slave-masters. When the slave-masters say we are free and continue to say that we are free, should we not take a free step? We charge the slave-masters' children with mistreating us. Suppose you tell a man that he is free. "Get out of our house and go into your own house." But the freed slave says, "No, no, I'll work for you. I'll serve you as a servant if you will allow me to remain in your house." The man of that house tells you, "I will not give you a new suit this year. I'll not pay you today for any work. Go home and sit down." Why should you say that man is not treating you right? Why say to that man, "I have to have a job the same as you." Has not he offered the door to you?

If the slave-master did not mean that you and I were free, we should have them admit it. You remain as a free slave to your slave-master. You demand that he recognize you as his equal. You are making yourself look small in the eyes of the world. If every so-called Negro were fired, what would you do? Would you unite and go to Washington and demand that the government give you a job? You would be foolish enough to do that! If they beat you by the thousands, what right have you to say that he should not lash you? You have made yourself his slave. You continue to preach a doctrine of remaining with the slave-master. You are still called by your slave-masters' names. By rights, by international rights, you belong to the white man of America. He knows that. You have never gotten out of the shackles of slavery. You are still in them. You are still in authority over your wife as long as she goes in your name, regardless of her separating herself from you. If she has not gotten a legal divorce and freed herself from your name, you are still in authority over her by law. Likewise, you are still under authority of the chains of your slave-masters. You have not tried to free yourself from them. You have not exercised the freedom that they claim to have given you.

Today is the day of decision. We have lived here more than 400 years. That, you know according to prophecy, is the prediction of our stay among these people. That time has expired. The time is up. The decision is being made for your departure and mine. It is most important to God Almighty, Whose proper name is Allah, that I speak to you according to the time that we are living in now. Today you are standing face to face with the alternative of accepting your own or forever being erased from the earth as a people. No one is trying to make you see this importance but your own. Why do you not see? You are blindly looking toward the slave-master to tell you this. How can the master tell the slave, "Look, slave, your day has arrived. You should sit in the seat of authority." We cannot beg for jobs anymore. We cannot build a future on a job that was given to us by the slave-master 400 years ago. The day has arrived. He has no more work for us to do. He is not willing to tell us that. The time has arrived when deep within his own heart he desires that you go out and find a job for yourself. He will forever be burdened. The burden will get greater and greater as long as he tries to carry you and me. It is time for a separation of the two—black and white. Allah, God, is calling for a separation!

BIRTH CONTROL DEATH PLAN!

To the Lost-Found members of the tribe of Shabazz (the so-called Negroes), I warn you my people and especially the women. Be aware of the tricks the devils are using to instill the idea of a false birth control in their clinics and hospitals.

STERILIZATION IS NOT BIRTH CONTROL, BUT THE END OF ALL POSSIBILITY TO BEAR CHILDREN.

The example of the clinic in Fauquier County, Virginia, where poor and helpless black mothers are pressured into accepting sterilization is certainly not confined to that clinic alone.

It would be better to do as many African and Asian husbands and wives have done, to take care of these matters yourselves rather than rely on such treachery and deceitful counsel.

I say beware of being trapped into the kind of disgraceful birth control laws now aimed almost exclusively at poor, helpless black peoples who have no one to rely on.

Who wants a sterile woman?

No man wants a non-productive woman. Though he may not want children for a time, he does want a woman who can produce a child if he changes his mind. Using birth control for a social purpose is a sin.

Using the birth control law against production of human beings is a sin that Allah (God) is against and for which he will punish the guilty on the Day of Judgment. Both the Bible and Holy Qur-an's teachings are against birth control.

So you and I, too, should be against it.

The white race is a race that was produced by using the birth control law, says God to me.

Do not accept this death plan of the devils to destroy, and keep from being a people.

There is no people on earth (even the little savage Pygmie of Africa and the Malayan Islands of the Pacific love their own) who will let anyone change or destroy their identity and culture without a fight. The American black women are ignorant of the real motive behind the so-called birth control schemes proposed and demanded by white officials.

The motive behind these schemes is not designed to promote the welfare of black families, but to eliminate these families in the future.

Our enemies, the devils, know and now seek to prevent us from being a nation through our women, as Pharaoh attempted to destroy Israel by killing off the male babies of Israel at birth.

The thousand years before Moses, Yakub killed off the black babies at birth to produce this present white race.

Pharaoh was envious of Israel's future of becoming a great nation, beloved of Allah which would overcome Egypt and her future as a world power.

The same goes for the so-called Negroes and the slave-masters' children. The slave-masters envy their once-slaves' future and want to destroy it.

So the best thing to do is to tell you the truth whether you care for it or not. I will feel, then, that I have done my duty as a member of the same Nation as you.

My love for you and your future is the same as that for myself. The life of this world and its sport and play is only temporary.

PLAN TO DESTROY OUR RACE

The American so-called Negroes are gravely deceived by the slave-masters' teaching of God and the true religion of God. They do not know they are deceived and earnestly believe they are right regardless of how vile the white race may be.

My poor people are mentally blind, deaf and dumb and full of fear. Blind because they do not see the light of truth after being shown it for over thirty years. Deaf because they will not hear the truth, Islam that has come to them from Allah through the Messenger (myself).

They are dumb because they will not see or open their ears and hearts after the light has shown clear for many years. You are full of the fear that was instilled in you when you were babies, so Allah told. This fear was put in you by the white slave-masters through tortures, lynchings, burnings, rapings and killings and has caused you to be blind, deaf and dumb.

This fear of the white slave-master has caused you to love them in a crazy kind of way. You, my dear people, are like a woman desperately in love with a man who does not love her. Therefore, this love is blind. This man can beat, torture, ravage, humiliate, shame and mock, but she will yet love him. And even when someone tries to tell her that this man is no good for her and certainly does not love her, she will yet love him, and will become angered and defend such a man. This is a very sad thing, but a very true picture of the so-called Negroes. They love their tormentors.

Beware, they do not love you, they are like dogs with a bone. They do not want you to be taken by Allah's messenger to your salvation. They want to carry you with them to their doom. The wicked white devils are by no means asleep to the knowledge of the time. They are really on the job trying to keep all of those who are blind, deaf and dumb to what is going on in this day and time mentally dead. They watch every step of the righteous Muslims, seeking to do them harm in their endeavor to spread the truth (Islam).

The people of Allah (so-called Negroes) are dumb to the time as the people were in the days when Moses was sent to Pharaoh to bring his people out of bondage into a land wherein they could enjoy independence. Instead of the Israelites being joyful to hear that Allah was ready to deliver them from Pharaoh and give them land of their own, they set out to contend with Moses and to help Pharaoh not God (Jehovah).

The government of Pharaoh had no love for Israel, just as America has no love for the so-called Negroes. Pharaoh became afraid of the truth that Moses was teaching his people in the midst of his country.

So Pharaoh began to plan the death of Moses and the future of Israel by killing off the babies. Pharaoh wanted Moses put to death because he was teaching his people the truth of Pharaoh and his government of wickedness. Today, America is afraid of the power our great number presents. She fears that if we ever unite we would, overnight become independent.

America desires to keep us a subjected people. So she, therefore, wants to stop our birth (as Pharaoh did). The Birth Control Law or Act of today is directed directly at the so-called Negroes and not at the American whites. The story of Moses and the Pharaoh is a warning to you today. They are seeking to destroy our race by the birth control law, just as Pharaoh sought to stop Moses' race by killing off all the male babies at birth. They are seeking to destroy our race through our women. DO NOT LET THEM TRICK YOU.

Follow me and we will, with the help of Allah, stop this most wicked sin against our people.

ISLAM

WHAT IS ISLAM?

While teaching and representing a religion called "Islam" to you, the first important thing to do is to answer the questions: What is Islam? Who is the author? Who are its prophets and people? Such questions could be answered in a few words or one could make books out of the answers. Briefly, "Islam" means entire submission to the Will of Allah (God). It is, moreover, a significant name. Its primary significance is the making of peace, and the idea of "Peace" is the dominant idea in Islam.

The author of Islam is Allah (God). We just cannot imagine God being the author of any other religion but one of peace. Since peace is the very nature of Allah (God), and peace He seeks for His people and peace is the nature of the righteous, most surely Islam is the religion of peace. It is the religion offered to the people to bring about a peace of mind and contentment after the destroyers of peace with falsehoods have been destroyed. The entire creation of Allah (God) is of peace, not including the devils who are not the creation of Allah (God) but a race created by an enemy (Yakub) of Allah. Yakub rebelled against Allah and the righteous people and was cast out of the homes of the righteous into the worst part of our planet to live their way of life until the fixed day of their doom.

These enemies of Allah (God) are known at the present as the white race or European race, who are the sole people responsible for misleading nine-tenths of the total population of the black nation.

The prophets of Islam include: Noah, Abraham, Moses, Jesus, Job, David, Solomon, and Jonah. The people of Islam are the black people, and their numbers are made up of the brown, yellow and red people, called races. The Book of Islam is the Holy Qur-an Sharrieff, and the scriptures that were brought by the above-mentioned prophets were of Islam.

The Bible does not mention Islam by name as the religion of the prophets, nor does it give us the name of any of the divine prophets' religions. By not teaching the reader the name of the former prophets' religions, yet giving the name of Christianity to what Jesus taught, it leaves the reader to seek the name of the religion of the former prophets from Adam to Muhammad. The followers or believers of Islam are over one-half billion people. Even among the infidels you will find many who confess Islam, although by nature they are against Islam. If I teach or preach a religion claiming its origin is from Allah (God), I must prove it, and if you oppose it with another religion which you claim has God as its author, then you must prove your claim. A religion whose origin or roots cannot be found in the universal order of God cannot be said to be the religion of God. The first prophet of God and His scripture must be that of the true religion of God.

Islam has five beautiful fundamental principles of belief. The most essential of them all is "The belief in One God." This was the belief (Oneness of God) and preachings of the prophets of God from Noah to Muhammad (the last). As I have said, if your religion's roots are not found in the universal order of things, it is not from Allah (God). I defy any opposer to prove the religion (as we know it today) called Christianity to be the religion of God and his prophets Noah, Abraham, Lot, Moses, David and Jesus.

What is Islam? It can be answered in one word—righteousness. Briefly, it is the religion of Allah (God) and His Prophets. Islam is as old as Allah (God) Himself and is the religion of which Allah (God) is the author. Islam is the religion of Adam, Noah, Moses, Jesus, and Muhammad (the last). Islam is the religion of entire submission to the will of Allah (God). Islam is the religion which the Holy Qur-an teaches.

Allah (God) says, "This day I have perfected for you your religion, completed my favor on you and chosen for you Islam as a religion" (Chapter 5:3). Allah (God) also says in another chapter of the Holy Qur-an, "Surely the true religion with Allah is Islam" (Chapter 3:18).

The significance of the name "Islam" is peace, the true religion. It is a religion of eternal peace. We cannot imagine Allah (God) offering to us a religion other than one of peace. A religion of peace coming to the righteous after the destruction of the wicked is also mentioned in several places in the Bible: "The Lord will bless His people with peace." (Psa. 29:11): also, "He will speak peace unto His people and to His saints" Psa 35:8) and "the Lord of Peace give you peace always" (II Thess. 3:16).

Islam is the religion referred to in the above-mentioned Biblical verses. It is the only religion that gives the believer a peace of mind and contentment. It removes grief and fear at once on believing: "Yea, whoever submits himself entirely to Allah and he is the doer of good to others, he has his reward from his Lord and there is no fear for him, nor shall he grieve" (Holy Qur-an 2:112).

Allah invites to the abode of peace (Holy Qur-an 10:25). Can you imagine a divine prophet being sent with anything other than a religion of peace to his people?

Our people, the so-called American Negroes, will love Islam when they learn more of it. For it is the religion of their fathers, and it is the last of the three great religions on earth. The other two, Buddhism and Christianity, cannot give us a lasting peace. We have tried them to our disappointment.

Christianity is one of the most perfect black-slave-making religions on our planet. It has completely killed the so-called Negroes mentally.

Now it takes Allah (God) Himself to revive and restore our people back into their own. Though I am His Messenger, and Allah can use my life as He pleases for them, they are my people and many—while I am only one.

Islam will give them the heaven while they live. Islam has more to offer than the white-controlled Christianity. Islam is universal. The true believers of Islam are equal in number to the total population of the whites on our planet (400 million).

By nature, all members of the black nation are Muslims (lovers of peace), whose number is over the billion mark.

We must have Islam as our religion to restore our peace after suffering under the slavery, the persecutors, and the grief of wars for 6,000 years. The so-called Negroes of America, who have never known the way of peace, who have never had love or mercy shown to them, today have Allah (God).

The God of mercy is on their side in the religion of Islam. But they are so dumb about it that it hurts my very heart. I am not surprised at what disbelievers think and say of me, but when a supposed brother Muslim joins the disbelievers against what I write, then I am surprised. For no true Muslim will speak against another Muslim to the delight of the disbelieving people of Allah and His prophets and the religion of Islam.

MEANING OF ISLAM

E ntire submission to the Will of Allah (God), the religion of Allah (God), and His prophets is the natural religion of the righteous (Holy Qur-an 30:30), which will dominate all other religions (Holy Qur-an 61:8-9). "Surely the true religion of Allah (God) is Islam" (Holy Qur-an 3:18). Can we say this of other religions? Does the Bible give us any prophecy that Christianity will finally rule and dominate the whole world? Islam is the religion which the Holy Qur-an teaches. The Holy Qur-an is a book which white Christianity never has and probably never will introduce to the so-called Negroes. They love for you to read the book (Bible) which they have fixed for you and desire that you never be able to understand it (though the original of the Bible was true). The Jews are charged with tampering with the original scripture (adding to and taking from it). The Christians are charged with poisoning the original scripture, called the Gospel of Jesus.

Islam means salvation to each and every one who believes in it. To the American so-called Negroes, it is the master key which opens wide every door locked against them. The door of universal friendship with the Creator and His Creatures swings wide open to you and the doors of freedom, justice, and equality. All the believers of Islam are the brothers of the others, unlike Christianity, where the white Christians are too proud to make the black people their equal.

Since the American so-called Negroes never were recognized by white Protestant Christianity as equal members, they flocked to the Catholic church to join it, running from a garter snake to a rattlesnake. The garter snake runs from them, the rattlesnake swallows them. They know nothing of the true religion (Islam) of God and care very little, because their minds are to be whatever the white race's minds are.

Christianity has no power for the Negroes against their enemies. Islam is a powerful religion. If the so-called Negroes of the South, or America in general, would accept Allah and His religion, Islam, their dreaded fear of the white man's brutality and murder would be over. Allah will defend the believers of Islam. The believers are united against their enemies. For every Islamic believing so-called Negro in America, there are 100 Muslim brothers on his or her side. This means if the whole 17 million so-called Negroes were believers in Islam, there would be 17 million of their people with them as brothers and sisters.

Allah's (God) finding of the lost members of the black nation is more valuable in His eyes than the whole world of mankind, and even they are very valuable in the eyes of any Asiatic Muslim. The finding of the so-called Negroes by Allah (God) means the end of the present world and the beginning of a new world under the guidance of Allah (God).

THE PRINCIPLES OF ISLAM

The number one principle of Islam is a belief in Allah (God); the belief in a power higher than man. Although man may be ignorant of just who it is who has such supreme power, it can be traced back to the beginning of the civilization of the human race and to the beginning of the writing of history. Regardless of tribes and national gods, there still exists the belief in a greater God that was more powerful than their national gods or those who were molded by their own hands out of clay, wood, iron, silver, gold and stone. Some of these gods were the leaders of their tribes or people. There were fire gods and birds, animals, snakes, beasts and even trees were worshiped as God.

The God in Islam is not a national or tribal god, but, as the Holy Qur-an describes Him in the opening words, "He is the Lord of the Worlds." This conception of God is best, since man's belief is by nature, that there must exist somewhere in the universe one who has and can exercise a greater power than can he or the object that he is bowing to as his god. The Islam God is One of Whom there is no equal! One to Whom whatsoever is in the heavens and whatsoever is in the earth submits willingly or unwillingly. He is the Lord of the Creation of the Universe, and since He has no equal, He demands universal recognition and complete submission to His will.

All religions, directly or indirectly, recognize and preach the Oneness of God. The conception of a Divine Supreme Being is accepted by all intelligent human beings—even savages recognize a power that is supreme. Islam rejects the belief in the plurality of persons in the Godhead. Say, "He Allah is one, Allah is He of Whom nothing is independent but upon Whom we all depend. He begets not, nor is He begotten and there is none like Him."

In another place it reads: "And my mercy encompasses all things" (Holy Qur-an 7:156). Muhammad Ali says: "The great Apostle of the Unity of God could not conceive of a god who was not the author of all that existed. Such detraction from His power and knowledge would have given a death blow to the very loftiness and sublimity of the conception of the Divine Supreme Being." But, until today, the true knowledge of the One, Divine Supreme Being, is known only to a few. We are daily coming into the knowledge of this One God. There are some people who think that God is something that cannot be seen or felt. A belief in God is the first principle of Islam.

ISLAM,
ONLY TRUE RELIGION OF GOD

Say: *"He, Allah, is one. Allah is He on whom all depend. He begets not, nor is He begotten and none is like Him"* (Holy Qur-an 114: 1-4)

A Muslim is one who believes in One God. It is forbidden by Allah (God) for us to believe in or serve anyone other than Himself as a god. He warns us not to set up an equal with Him, as He was the One in the beginning from whom everything had its beginning and will be the One God from which everything will end. He is independent, having no need of anyone's help, but on the other hand, upon Him we all depend. It is the highest of ignorance for us to choose a God or attempt to make something as an equal to Him. Foolish people all over the earth have been for the past 6,000 years, and still are, trying to make an equal to Allah (God). He has no beginning, nor is there any end of Him. How, O foolish man, can you make an equal for such a One? How foolish we make ourselves, serving and worshiping gods other than the One God, Allah.

The foolish become rich and highly educated in their way and not in the way of Allah and then begin making and worshiping gods of their own, the work of their own hands—then comes the end of them as it is of today.

It is the fundamental principle of the religion of Islam to believe in Allah, the One God. According to the belief, the teaching and preaching of the prophets of Allah is of One God. Noah, Abraham, Moses, and Jesus—all believed in One God (Allah). The Christians claim a belief in the above named prophets—then how do they make Jesus the equal of Allah (God)? The Bible says, and God spoke all these words saying: "I am the Lord, thy God, thou shalt have no other gods before Me. Thou shalt not make unto thee any graven image, or any likeness of anything that is in the heavens above, or that is in the earth beneath, or that is in the water under the earth; thou shalt not bow down thyself to them, nor serve them, for I, the Lord Thy God, am a jealous God."

Both Jews and Christians are guilty of setting up rivals to Allah (God). Adam and Eve accepted the guidance of the serpent instead of that of Allah (Gen. 3:6). They made a golden calf and took it for their god and bowed down to it (Exod. 32:4). This was the work of their own hands to guide them and fight their wars. The Christians have made imaginary pictures and statues of wood, silver and gold—calling them pictures and statues of God. They bow down to pictures and statues alleged to be of Jesus, His mother, and his disciples as though they could see and hear them. They (the Christians) claim sonship to Allah (God) and take the Son to be the equal of the Father, though they say "that they killed the Son." Today they take the weapons of war for their gods and put their trust in the work of their own hands.

Muhammad took hold of the best, the belief in one God (Allah), and was successful. Fourteen hundred years after him, we are successful, that is, we who will not set up another god with Allah. The fools who refuse to believe in Allah alone as the One God, if asked who made heaven and earth, most surely would say God and would not say God, the Son and the Holy Ghost. Then why do they not serve and obey Allah (God)?

It is a perfect insult to Allah (God) who made heaven and earth and makes the earth to produce everything for our service and even the sun, moon, and stars—they serve our needs—for us to bow down and worship anything other than Allah as a god. The Great Mahdi, Allah in person, who is in our midst today, will put a stop once and forever to the serving and worshiping of other gods besides Himself.

It is the devil's way of bringing the people (so-called Negroes) of Allah (God) in opposition to Him by teaching the people to believe and do just the thing that God forbids. Muhammad did not try making a likeness of God, nor have his followers done that. He and his followers obey the law of (the one God) Allah, while the Jews and the Christians preach it and do otherwise. We are now being brought face to face with Allah (God) for a showdown between Him and that which we have served as God besides Him. The lost and found members of the Asiatic nation are especially warned in the 112th chapter of the Holy Qur-an against the worship of any other God than Allah, for it is Allah in person who has found them among the worshipers of gods other than Allah.

ISLAM, THE
TRUE RELIGION OF GOD

PART I

"He it is Who sent His Apostle with the Guidance and the true religion, that he make it overcome

*the religions—all of them, though the polytheists
may be averse."* According to the Holy Qur-an
61:9 (the right Scripture for the Time).

In the above verse Allah (God) in the last days of this present
world (wicked and infidel) states that he must destroy false religions with the true religion (Islam). It (Islam) must overcome all
other religions. The verse also teaches us that Allah in the judgment of the world will not recognize any religion other than
Islam.

Take to task all the learned teachers of religions, and they
will admit that God is One and that He will have only one
religion in the hereafter.

Search the Scriptures of the Bible and Holy Qur-an and be
convinced. There are two other religions today that oppose the
religion of peace (Islam) namely, Buddhism and Christianity.
These two opposing forces will be removed from the people
completely by the light of Islam, Truth, guided by Allah in the
person of the Great Mahdi, Fard Muhammad. I am His apostle.
It will come to pass that you will not even find a trace of them.
Christianity is already dying a natural death. We want a religion
of peace, freedom, justice and equality. We want it from the
Divine Supreme Being Allah and not a religion prepared by the
hand of His (Allah's) enemies.

They desire to put out the light of Allah with their mouths,
but Allah will perfect His light though the unbelievers may be
averse (Holy Qur-an 61:8). Regardless of the opponents' efforts
to put out the light of truth (Islam) today, their efforts will be
a complete failure. Think over the slavery teachings of Christianity—the three gods, the worship of Mary, the disciples of Jesus,
the many gods of Buddhism, the incarnation taught by both and
other ignorant practices. Islam teaches an eternal heaven for the
righteous, for hell is not eternal.

These (heaven and hell) are not necessary places but conditions.

Islam teaches that if a brother kills a brother, the murderer must be killed, or anyone that murders a Muslim.

The Christians go to war against each other daily, killing their own brothers and others. The righteous must be rid of such people. Make Islam to overcome all other religions whether the disbelievers like it or not. Our God is One God. Can One God believe in more than one religion and be true to Himself and others?

If the other religions were true religions, surely Allah (God) would not send an apostle to overcome them with another religion. "Is it other than Allah's religion that they seek to follow and to Him submit whoever is in the heavens and earth, willingly or unwillingly" (Holy Qur-an 3:82). We all bear witness to the truth that everything of Allah's creation obeys Him, regardless of size or numbers.

But the proud, wicked man of sin refuses to submit and goes about teaching ignorant people not to believe in Allah and His religion, Islam.

The true religion of Allah (God) is Islam (Holy Qur-an 3:18). The emblem of Islam represents the sun, moon and stars; the meaning is Freedom (Sun), Justice (Star), and Equality (Moon).

No other nation's religion has the sun, moon, and stars as its emblem. No religion is worthwhile if its roots are not found in the universal order of things. No nation can use the sun, moon, and stars to represent their government or religion but the nation that owns it (the nation of Islam).

We are the sole owners of the earth. It was our father who made it. The prayer service of Islam is not equaled by any other religion—five prayers a day made with the face turned in the direction of the sunrise.

Prayer is at sunrise, noon, mid-afternoon, sundown and before retiring. On awakening during the night, another prayer is made. In fact, two prayers should be said during the night, making a total of seven prayers a day. There is no worship of a Sunday or Sabbath in Islam. All the days are worship days. The Muslims wash and clean all exposed parts of their bodies before prayer early at the gray dawn of day.

ISLAM, THE
TRUE RELIGION OF GOD

PART II

*"Set yourself upright to the right religion before
there comes from Allah the day which cannot be
averted; on that day they shall become separated"*
(Holy Qur-an 30:43)

We are now living in the time mentioned above according to
the Holy Qur-an. When we as a people should begin setting our
faces upright to the religion in the right state and stop believing
in the slave-master's slavery religious teachings, which are not in
the right state, then we shall be successful and the world will
respect us.

Which one of these emblems represent a good religion, the
cross or the Star and Crescent? To attract one to do good, you
must have something of good. Our religion, Islam, has the best
sign (the Crescent). There is no doubt about it. We have taken
the best of everything for our own (the Sun, Moon and Stars);
ever since it was created by our Father, we know the best. What
can be more essential to our well-being than the Sun, Moon,
and Stars?

The spiritual meaning of our emblem (the Crescent) is Freedom, Justice, and Equality, not that we "say" one thing and do
otherwise; a Muslim tries to carry into practice what he preaches;
not so the Christians. They "say" and do not. But after all,
their religious emblem (the cross) and its meaning compare with
the nature of the so-called Christians. By nature they are murderers. By nature they love to make slaves of others. By nature
they are haters of the Black Nation, which loves freedom, justice and equality. It looks strange to see people accepting the
cross as a sign of good religion.

The Ten Commandments which Moses gave to them (the
white race) have never been practiced by them or those whom
they teach. They (the white race) were condemned by Jesus as

not obeying. Why should we be looking and begging for that which is good (freedom, justice and equality)! Islam is that right religion (which by nature they cannot give us).

According to the Holy Qur-an (30:30), one of the greatest teachings of brotherhood is laid down by us by the Prophet Muhammad in these words: "A Muslim is not a Muslim until he loves for his brother what he loves for himself." The old Christian religion has been the white man's whip to lash the black man ever since it was organized. My people here in America are fast awakening to the slavery teachings of Christianity to the dislike of their enemies.

A few years ago the so-called Negroes could easily be frightened and worked up into emotion by the preacher, yelling and spitting out foam all over the pulpit, preaching hellfire after death and the dying of Jesus on the cross. He would paint an imaginary picture in the minds of the listeners—of meeting some dead relative up in the heavens (sky) after death or mourn them into grief and sorrow. My people are leaving and rejecting such nonsense as they advance more and more educationally. After they have heard the truth of it all, that Allah has and is teaching me, they will not go near that slavery teaching. Their eyes must be opened to the truth at any price.

EVERYTHING HAS FAILED

Islam comes after everything else fails. Its significance is the making of Peace. The Muslim's greeting to each other is "Peace." What better religion could we desire after being divided and made enemies of each other? Do not tell us that you have "unity and peace" in the white race's religion called Christianity. The white race does not like Islam, because it is truth and entire submission to the will of Allah, and this is against their nature. They cannot live the life of freedom, justice and equality—not even among themselves.

Many of you sing that old song, "Give Me That Old Time

Religion." Islam is that "old time religion." It is as old as God Himself, and God is the Author of Islam. Islam was not invented as is the case of Christianity and other religions. Islam came with Allah (God) and the universe. In the Holy Qur-an it says: "This day I have perfected for you, your religion and completed my favour on you; and have chosen for you, Islam as a religion" Holy Qur-an (5:3).

Here, Islam claims to be a perfect religion and its author, the Perfect One (God). What can be imperfect about Islam when it means "Entire submission to the Will of God?" What can be wrong or imperfect about this religion Islam, which was the religion of Noah, Abraham, Moses, Jesus and all the Prophets of God, to Muhammad, the last of the Prophets? Islam proves that its author is God, inasmuch as Allah (God) is on the side of every true Muslim. This is easy to see today. Every one of you who are accepting Islam can bear witness that, for the first time in your life, you feel the power and help of Almighty Allah (God) on your side. Your whole life becomes changed for the better. Your fear is removed. Your grief is gone. Your desire to continue to do evil things is leaving you for good. Love for your brother (your people) for the first time is now becoming a reality. It is the aim of Allah (God) in giving Islam to you and me; to unite us; to remove fear, sorrow, sickness; and to bring us into that heavenly life, peace of mind and contentment.

Do you mean to say that you do not need such religion? Or do you say that the white race's manufactured Christianity is giving you peace and contentment—whose world recognized Father is the Pope of Rome? Not Jesus, nor Allah (God), is the Father of the Christian religion, as practiced by the white race and those who believe in it.

Islam is the natural religion of the Black Nation. It is the nature in which we are made. We are called to return to Islam in these words from the Holy Qur-an: "Set your face upright for religion in the right state. The nature made by Allah in which He has made men: there is no altering of Allah's Creation. That is the right religion, but most people do not know" Holy Qur-an (30:30).

The devils know the true religion of Allah and have always known it. But they will not teach it because it is against their nature to believe and teach the true religion of God, which would upset his chances of ruling the people under falsehood.

ISLAM
FOR SO-CALLED NEGROES

Say: *"O people, if you are in doubt as to my religion, (Islam) then know that I do not serve those whom you serve besides Allah, Who will cause you to die"* (Holy Qur-an 10:104)

According to the past histories of prophets and reformers, the very people to whom they were sent with the light of truth were their rejectors and even their enemies. When the time comes for a change in the life of a people, there are those who will not appreciate a change. They are suspicious and doubt that which is other than what they have been believing all their lives. The people of Noah, Abraham, Moses and Jesus doubted that which these prophets brought to them from Allah (God) until Allah brought about a showdown between the two.

The so-called American Negroes have been so gravely deceived by the white man's Christianity and Bible that they doubt everything that does not have the white man's approval. Again, the time has arrived for a change. This time is universal, and the great problem now is to awaken the American so-called Negroes.

The so-called Negroes are made to believe that all religions other than the Christian religion are false and idol worship, while the Christians worship idol gods in their churches and religious literature. They bow in reverence to statues and imaginary pictures of God, the angels, the prophets and the disciples as if they could speak. Worst of all, the pictures and statues are not of God, His angels, the Prophets, or the disciples of Jesus. Therefore, they are false worshippers and ignorant enough to love the falsehood. Isaiah and Ezekiel have well described them. The Christian believers claim to believe in One God. Should not the Divine Supreme Being destroy those who serve and worship gods other than He? Allah (God) does not approve of you and me worshipping His angels and prophets as His equal. It is a disgrace.

The religion of Islam teaches that Allah is One God, and the Holy Qur-an teaches that what you worship besides Allah is the firewood of hell. You doubt the Truth of Islam, while it is the religion of Allah (God) and the prophets whom you claim to believe in.

Again, the principles of belief in Islam are: One God, His Prophets, His Scriptures, His Judgment, His Resurrection (of the mentally dead). The main principles of action in Islam: keeping up prayer, spending in the cause of truth, fasting especially during the month of Ramadan, pilgrimage to Mecca, speaking the truth regardless of to whom or what, being clean internally, loving your brother believers as yourself, doing good to all, killing no one whom Allah has ordered not to be killed, setting at liberty the captured believer, worshiping no god but Allah, and fearing no one but Allah. These are the teachings of the prophets.

MAKE ALL THINGS NEW

"Behold I, [Allah], make all things new and He said unto Me, write: For these words are true and faithful" (Bible, Rev. 21:5)

It is necessary for me to consult or refer to the Bible for this subject. It can be found in the Holy Qur-an, but not in the exact words as are found in the Bible. So, because of the truth of it, and because my people do not know any Scripture or ever read any Scripture other than the Bible (which they do not understand), I thought it best to make them understand the book which they read and believe in, since the Bible is their graveyard and they must be awakened from it. There are many Muslims who do not care to read anything in the Bible. But those Muslims have not been given my job.

Therefore, I ignore what they say and write! By all means, we must get the "truth" to our people (the so-called Negroes), for the time is limited. The coming of a "New World," or a new order of things, is very hard for the people of the Old World to believe. Therefore, they are opposed to the New World.

It does not take a wise man to see the necessity of a new order or a new world, since the old one has fulfilled its purpose. Let the Christians' preachers and scientists ponder over the above prophecy of their Bible. If the time comes when Allah (God) will make all things NEW, will the Christians as we see them today be in that which Allah (God) will make NEW? When should we expect Allah (God) to make all things NEW? After the destruction of the wicked, their king and world. Just when should the end of the old world be? The exact day is known only to Allah, but many think that they know the year. But we all know that 1914 was the end of the 6,000 years that was given to the old world of the devils to rule. A religion used by the devils to convert people cannot be accepted by Allah, especially when it did not come from Him.

We all know that Christianity is from the white race. Should we be surprised at this late day to see it come to pass? Think over the saying of your own Bible. "The great deceiver of the nations?" (Rev. 20:3-8). Of course, he deceived them (the so-called Negroes) that had received his mark (the mark of Christianity, the cross).

More than anyone else, those who worship his image (the so-called Negroes) are guilty of loving the white race and all that race stands for. One can even find the pictures of white people on the walls, mantel, shelves, dressers and tables of their homes. Some carry them on their person. The so-called Negroes go to church and bow down to their statues under the name of Jesus and Mary and some under the name of Jesus' disciples, which are only the images of the white race, their arch-deceiver.

They even worship the white race's names, which will not exist among the people of the new world, for they are not the names of God.

The so-called Negroes would greatly benefit themselves if they would seek their places in "that" which Allah (God) makes new by giving back to the great deceiver his religion (Christianity), churches and names and accept the religion of their righteous nation, Islam, a name of their God, which is unlimited in the eyes of any white person.

There is no end to the black nation. That nation will live forever. The so-called Negroes do not know it, and their slave-masters know that they do not know. Therefore, they have the so-called Negroes deceived 100 per cent. It is really pitiful to see how the poor black preachers are blinded and chained by the slave-masters hand and foot. They could not speak or agree with truth even if they wanted to. Come to me, brother preachers, and believe in Allah, the true God and the true religion, Islam! Free yourselves from such chained slavery.

I am very insignificant in your eyes, but I have the keys of God to your problems. You should not fear. The day has come that you will have to seek refuge in (the new world) something better and more enduring than the white race's Christianity. It is not your religion.

ISLAM DIGNIFIES

Why do I stress the religion of Islam for my people, the so-called American Negroes.

First, and most important, Islam is actually our religion by nature. It is the religion of Allah (God), not a European organized white man's religion.

Second, it is the original, the only religion of Allah (God) and His prophets. It is the only religion that will save the lives of my people and give them divine protection against our enemies.

Third, it dignifies the black man and gives us the desire to be clean internally and externally and for the first time to have a sense of dignity.

Fourth, it removes fear and makes one fearless. It educates us to the knowledge of God and the devil, which is so necessary for my people.

Fifth, it makes us to know and love one another as never before.

Sixth, it destroys superstition and removes the veil of falsehood. It heals both physical and spiritual ills by teaching what to eat, when to eat, what to think, and how to act.

Seventh, it is the only religion that has the divine power to unite us and save us from the destruction of the War of Armageddon, which is now. It is also the only religion in which the believer is really divinely protected. It is the only religion that will survive the Great Holy war, or the final war between Allah (God) and the devil.

Islam will put the black man of America on top of the civilization. So, why not Islam? Some people say, "Why so much religion?" It is very necessary for me to teach the knowledge of that which is the only key to the hereafter for his brother. I will say here that this alone is salvation to you and me, just learning to love each other as brothers. Islam, unlike Christianity, is doing this right in your midst.

Regardless as to how long and how hard you try to be a good Christian, you never have a sincere true love for your own black brother and sister as you should. Islam will give you true brothers and sisters the world over. This is what you need.

A people subjected to all kinds of injustice need to join Islam. You are sure of Allah's (God) help in Islam. Why don't the preachers of my people preach Islam? If they would, overnight they would be on top.

Are you too proud to submit to Allah and sit in heaven while you live and have His protection against your open enemy? Take it or leave it. You will soon wish you had taken Islam. God is drying America up by degrees. The time is at hand, and hell is kindling up. Islam is the right way.

THE BIBLE
AND
HOLY QUR-AN

THE BIBLE AND HOLY QUR-AN: WHICH ONE CONTAINS WORDS OF GOD?

Both books are called holy. The word of Allah (God) is holy, and His word is true. Therefore, all truth is holy; for Allah (God) is holy and is the author of truth, without the shadow of a doubt! Allah is the representative of the Holy Qur-an (not a prophet) in these words: "This book, there is no doubt of it, is a guide to those who guard against evil" (2:2), translated by Maulvi Muhammad Ali. Abdullah Yusuf Ali's translation of the same verse reads nearly the same: "This is the book; in it is guidance, sure, without doubt, to those who fear Allah (God)" (2:2).

The Bible does not claim God to be its author. Jehovah calls to Moses out of the burning bush to go to Pharaoh (Ex.3:9). There is no mention of a book or Bible that is found that Jehovah gave to Moses in the first five books of the Bible, which are claimed to be Moses' books. Moses' rod is the only thing used against Pharaoh and the land of Egypt; and tables of stone in the mountains of Sinai. The miraculous rod of Moses, and not a book, brought Pharaoh and his people to their doom. The Ten Commandments served as a guide for the Jews in the Promised Land. Where do we find in the Bible that it was given to Moses by Jehovah under such name as Bible or the Book?

But, on the other hand, Allah (God) tells that He gave the Book, the Holy Qur-an, to Muhammad. "I am Allah, the best knower, the revelation of the book there is no doubt in it, it is from the Lord of the worlds" (Sura 32:1, 2). Allah says to Muhammad in the same above (Sura 32:23): "We gave the Book to Moses, and be not in doubt in receiving it, we made it a guide for the children of Israel."

(If Moses' rod and book were given as a guide for Israel, and the gospel God gave to Jesus as a guide and warning to the Christians, and the Holy Qur-an to Muhammad for the Arab world, will God give us (the so-called Negroes) a book as a guide for us? Will He bring it or send it? For those books were for other people and not for us.)

If we are in the change of the two worlds (Christianity and Islam), then surely we need a "new book" for our guidance; for those books have served the people to whom they were given. But all or both books are guidance for us all. Yet we must have a new book for the "new change"; that which no eye has seen nor ear has heard, nor has entered into our hearts what it is like. We know these books, they have been seen and handled by both the good and no good. Certainly the Holy Qur-an is from the Lord of the Worlds, there can be no doubt in the word of Allah (God). But if the book or books have the words of someone else other than Allah's words in it or them, there is no doubt in our hearts concerning the receivings of such book or books!

THE BIBLE

The original scripture called "The Torah"--revealed to Musa (Moses) — was Holy until the Jews and the Christian scholars started tampering with it. Today, the Bible has become a "commercialized book," therefore, many are allowed to rewrite or revise it. I think when it comes to the word of Allah (God) or a book revealed by Him, that word or book is sacred and should be protected from corruption by the hands of people who care nothing for its sacredness. It is like a "rattlesnake" in the hands of my people, for they (most of them) do not understand it.

Some believe (in that story of the Bible) that the black people are a curse of Noah on one of his sons (Ham) because this son laughed at his father's nakedness while being drunk from

wine (Genesis 9:21-25). The black nation has no birth record.
There were as many or more black people on our planet in the
days of Noah as there are today. The Bible's record of the flood
is 2,348 years before Christ, and if the records are true, we are
nearly 4,500 years from Noah's flood. If there were no black people before Noah, then that wicked people who were destroyed
in the flood were white people. And again, if those were of that
race, the warning of the destruction of the wicked world by fire
the next time is made clearer to those whom that fire will destroy.

The black people, and especially the so-called Negroes, are
now in the very area where God has said to me that the fire
(often referred to as the "fire of hell" or "hell fire") will begin
which will destroy the present wicked white race of America first.
The sins of the white race are far worse and more pungent to
the nostril of God than the sins of Sodom and Gomorrah! The
fire of hell is not intended for the so-called Negroes: only those
who, after hearing this teaching of the truth which I am giving
to you and the warnings of Allah (God), will wilfully hold on to
the white race and their religion, Christianity.

The so-called Negroes are made so poisoned by this wicked
race of devils that they love them more than they love their
own people. It is really because of the evil done to them by
the American white race that Allah (God) has put them on His
list, as the first to be destroyed. The others will be given a little
longer to live, as the prophet Daniel says (7:11, 19 and Rev.
19:20). Believe it, or let it alone, the above refers to America.
She is the only white government out of the European race that
answers the description of the symbolic Fourth Beast. The so-
called Negroes are warned to come out of her (America) (Rev.
18:4), though the truth of Daniel and Revelations could not be
told until the time of the end of this prophecy.

The Bible means good if you can rightly understand it. My
interpretation of it is given to me from the Lord of the Worlds.
Yours is your own and from the enemies of the truth. The so-
called Negroes will be the lucky ones, that is, if they stop following and practicing the evils and indecent doings of this wicked
and doomed race of devils (whose true self has been a secret for
6,000 years.)

So-called Negroes, accept your own God, religion and people
so that you may be successful in escaping the fire!

TRUE KNOWLEDGE OF
BIBLE AND HOLY QUR-AN

If we have the true knowledge of the Bible and Holy Qur-an, we could agree on the truth of God, devil, religion and the people of Allah. We cannot say and prove that the Bible is all the word of Allah. The Bible is nearly two-thirds prophecy— What some others say that God said.

It is originally referred to as the "Book," I suppose because of the compilation of the book which contains the books of many others on histories, predictions, stories of rulers, people and nations, poems, parables, rules and laws.

The First Book called "Genesis" consists of an attempt at describing the creation and the history of the Old World; and steps taken by God towards the formation of the theocracy. The Second Book called "Exodus" – the history of Israel's departure from Egypt; the giving of the law. The Third Book called "Leviticus," contains ceremonial laws. The Fourth Book is called "Numbers"--the census of the people; the story of the wanderings in the wilderness. The Last Book, called "Revelations," contains very interesting symbolic predictions.

The English translators of the Bible dedicated the Book to one of their kings--James of England. The first half of the Book is often referred to as the Torah. The second half is called the Gospel of New Testament.

The Bible is called holy, and the word of God. Some of you go too far in such belief. The Bible is not all holy, nor is it all the word of God! I hope that you who believe that it is all the word of God and holy will read my proofs as taken from the Bible, which show that it is not all holy and all the word of God.

The preachers of the Bible should know that it is not all holy without being told or proved that it is not. But, most of these preachers' mouths and tongues are controlled by the enemy of truth for the sake of certain privileges; just as the false prophets of Baal and magicians of Pharaoh wanted to please the enemies of God!

If we should set ourselves aside to preach the truth, then we must be sure that we have and know the truth ourselves. If we preach it from a book, we must make certain that the book is true and that it is from the author of Truth. The Bible and Holy Qur-an are filled with truth that leads us up to the judgment, and some of their prophecies refer to the hereafter. Since these prophecies are a small percentage of the whole, it makes it necessary for a new scripture (or guidance) for the hereafter.

The enemy has tampered with the truth in both books: for he has been permitted to handle both books. Neither the Holy Qur-an nor the Bible was revealed with the intention of converting the white race into truth and righteousness; for God knew that there was no good in them the day they were created. But they are capable of deceiving you in regard to Allah and the righteous.

If you desire to preach or teach that a certain religion is true or right, you should know all religions and their scriptures. The man that God chooseth for Himself from among the people as a warner to them, such a one does not need previous training and knowledge, for Allah is his teacher and trainer.

The white man does not have knowledge of the Book that he is preaching.

The Bible's first five books (or Old Testament) are said to be Moses' Books. But it only mentions the giving of the Ten Commandments, and not a Book (Exodus 20:1-18).

I hope that you will not misunderstand me and think that I do not believe in Moses receiving the Torah. Nor does the New Testament open by saying: "This is a book or scripture revealed to Jesus," nor does Jesus tell us that He received a book. But yet the New Testament was revealed to Jesus, and the Revelation (the last Book of the Bible) was revealed to Yakub (titled John).

The Bible being tampered with by the Jews and the Christians has caused many divisions among the people because of their not understanding it. Since the creation of the white race, scripture after scripture, along with many prophets, have been given to the people of this world for the purpose of guiding and warning the righteous of their enemies, the devils.

The Holy Qur-an and Bible warn us of a day of judgment of this world — a day of total destruction — that none shall be left from that destruction but the righteous, or the original owners. The black nation are the original owners and makers.

The Holy Qur-an Sharrieff is a revealed book (scripture) given to Muhammad, like the prophets before him. This Book contains the last warnings, and makes clear to us that which we did not understand to the Torah and the Gospel. It also gives to us the perfect rule and guidance.

One of its names is, "That Which Makes A Distinction," and another, "That Light" or "The Truth." It is the Book for the American so-called Negroes; and it is best that they throw the Bible in the waste pail since they cannot understand it. There is another Book that none has been able to see or read, its contents coming soon from Allah—the "Last Book," which takes us into the hereafter.

The so-called American Negroes are great disputers of the Bible without half knowing its true meaning. The wise scholars even of Christianity have very little respect for the way in which the Bible is written up.

According to the Bible, "Adam's sins meant the death of all of the human family." As Mr. Naseem Saifi says in his book entitled, *"This is Christianity,"* pp. 10 and 11: — "Why should everyone die for the wrong done by one person?"

Some, according to the Bible, were even taken to heaven whole soul and body. And what is worst, Jesus, a righteous man, had to be murdered to pay the price of the sin of the murderer (Adam) in order to free the people who were under a death penalty for the sin of Adam — while yet the Book teaches that God is a just God.

No common father of a son would like to kill his own son for the wrong of a man who lived 4,000 years before his son was born. Yet his son's death did not pay the price; nor did it stop the people from sinning. And, yet the father has to kill that same people (the Adamic) in order to get rid of sin.

"Is God justified in condemning the whole of mankind for the sin of one man?" (Mr. Naseem Saifi says on the same page 10).

Another error was made: Jesus is supposed to have given His life for the sins of the people, and after three days He took it back. Well, this just does not make sense! If a man pays a certain amount of money to redeem some property held in pawn by the pawnbroker, and the next few days he returns and demands his money without returning the property, we call such a man a robber.

It cannot be said that Jesus gave His life to the world as a ransom for the sins of the world and then later took it back!

We can only say that someone has made a very bad job of the Bible. No wonder the slave-masters were so careful of their slaves reading it.

THE GLORIOUS
HOLY QUR-AN SHARRIEFF

The book that the so-called American Negroes (Tribe of Shabazz) should own and read, the book that the slave-masters have, but have not represented it to their slaves, is a book that will heal their sin-sick souls that were made sick and sorrowful by the slave-masters. The book will open their blinded eyes and open their deaf ears. The book that will purify them, the book that makes a distinction between the God of righteousness and the god of evil, the book of guidance, the book of light and truth, the book of wisdom and judgment.

But the average one should first be taught how to respect such a book, how to read it, how to understand it, how to teach it. The Holy Qur-an Sharrieff contains some of the most beautiful prayers that one ever heard recited or read. It is called the Glorious Qur-an and without mistake that is just what it is. This book is not from a prophet, but direct from Allah to Muhammad, not by an angel, but from the mouth of Allah (God). The great distinguisher between truth and falsehood in the judgment of the world, of whom the enemy of truth has ruled the nation of black mankind with falsehood for the past six thousand years.

This book pulls the cover off the covered and shows the nation for the first time that which deceived 90 per cent of the people of the earth without the knowledge of the deceiver. The revelation of the book is from Allah, The Mighty, The Knowing (Chap. 40:2), according to the above chapter and second verse. Allah is the Mighty One over all other beings, and is the Knowing One. Therefore He knows what is best for every living thing. And the book (Qur-an) that he has revealed there is no doubt about it, for the All Knowing One, the Best Knower has revealed it: One who has no equal, the All Wise.

Man makes himself a fool to try attacking Him in arguments. So, we have no doubt the Holy Qur-an is from the Lord of the Worlds. It is one of the cleanest reading books you ever read. The God that revealed the Holy Qur-an Sharrieff to Muhammad is the same that revealed the scriptures to the other prophets according to the Holy Qur-an Sharrieff, "Surely we have revealed to you as we revealed to Noah and the prophets after him, we revealed to Abraham, Ishmael, Isaac, Jacob, the Tribes, Jesus, Job, Jonah, Aaron, Solomon and we gave to David a scripture, and Moses Allah addressed His words speaking to Him. And we sent Apostles we have mentioned to you before, and Apostles we have not mentioned to you" (4:163, 164). Some people whom the devils have deceived in regard to the Holy Qur-an call it the work of Muhammad.

Some call the religion Islam a dream of Muhammad, though the Bible doesn't say it is from God, but from prophets, and is dedicated to King James of England. The white race does not like to worship a black god and his prophets. They are too proud to recognize a black prophet or god. The so-called Negroes should know this by this time. The Holy Qur-an's readings are not the kind that will lull one to sleep, but to get a real Qur-an one should know the Arabic language in which it is written. However, you can find a good translation of it by Yusuf Ali and Muhammad Ali.

THE BIBLE AND HOLY QUR-AN: WHICH ONE IS RIGHT?

Which one is right? I don't know of any scriptural book of religion that doesn't contain some good. What Allah (God) demands today is a book or religion that is all good, not a mixture of truth and false, not a book or religion that is or has been tampered with by His enemies.

The Bible is called a Holy Book, and is often referred to as the Word of God. The present English Bible is said to be translated out of the original tongues, into the present English language by the authority of one King James in 1611.

What is the original tongue or language that the Bible was written in? What language did Moses speak? Originally, the Torah (old Testament) was given in 2,000 B.C. to Musa (Moses) who spoke ancient Egyptian Arabic; and the second half (the New Testament) was revealed to Isa (Jesus) who spoke both Arabic and Hebrew, 2,000 years ago.

The Holy Qur-an was revealed to Muhammad, who spoke

Arabic, in the seventh century A.D., over 1300 years ago. The believers and followers of these three Scriptures are referred to as follows: (1) Hebrews or Jews, believers in Musa (Moses) and the Torah; (2) Christians, followers of Isa (Jesus) and the Injil or gospel revealed to Isa (Jesus); (3) Muslims, believers in all of the Prophets of God and the Scriptures revealed to His Prophets, The Torah, Injil, Qur-an. The Muslims, make no difference in any of them, as long as it is from Allah (God).

The Jews or Hebrews believe that Musa (Moses) was a Jew, who brought them the Torah. The Christians believe that both Musa (Moses) and Isa (Jesus) were Jews. Muhammad, an Arab, was a member of the black nation. The Jews and Christians are of the white race, and they don't believe in the Scriptures (Holy Qur-an) that Allah (God) revealed to Muhammad. Muhammad and his followers believe in Moses and Jesus and also the true Scriptures that these two prophets brought to their people.

The Arabs or Muslims have tried and are still trying to get the white race to believe and recognize Muhammad as a Divine Prophet of Allah (God) and the Qur-an, a Divine revelation, as they recognize Musa (Moses) and Isa (Jesus) and the Bible as coming from Allah (God). This is sufficient proof to the worship of Allah (God) Himself; if Allah desires to make the black nation the equal or superior of the white race. Again their objection proves beyond a shadow of a doubt that there is no such thing as a divine relation of brotherhood between the black nation and white race. God forbid. The history of the two people is a proof; for 6,000 years the two (black and white) have been and still are unable to get along together in peace. This is due to the fact that the God of the two people is not the same.

The Bible is now being called the Poison Book by God Himself, and who can deny that it is not poison? It has poisoned the very hearts and minds of the so-called Negroes so much that they can't agree with each other. From the first day that the white race received the Divine Scripture they started tampering with its truth to make it suit themselves, and blind the black man. It is their nature to do evil, and the Book can't be recognized as the pure and Holy Word of God. It opens with the words of someone other than God trying to represent God and His Creation to us. This is called the Book of Moses and reads as follows: *"In the beginning God created the Heaven and Earth"* [Gen. 1:1]. When was this beginning? There in the Genesis the writer tells us that is was 4,004 B.C. This we know, now, that it refers to the making of the white race, and not the heavens and earth. The second verse of the first chapter of Genesis reads: *"And the earth was without form and void; darkness was upon the deep and the spirit of God moved upon the face of the waters."* What was the water on, since there was no form of earth? As I see it, the Bible is very questionable. After God had created everything without asking anyone for help then comes His weakness in the 26th verse of the same chapter (Gen. 1:26). He invites us to help Him make a man. Allah has revealed "the us" that was invited to make a man (white race). A man is far more easy to make than the heavens and earth. We can't charge these questionable readings of the Bible to Musa because he was a prophet of God, and they don't lie.

If the present Bible is the direct Word of God, why isn't God speaking rather than His Prophet Musa (Moses)? Neither does Moses tell us here in the first chapter of Genesis that it is from God. No, we don't find the name Moses mentioned in the chapter. The Bible is the graveyard of my poor people (the so-called Negroes) and I would like to dwell upon this book until I am sure that they understand that it is not quite as holy as they thought it was. I don't mean to say that there is no truth in it; certainly there is plenty of truth, if understood. Will you accept the understanding of it? The Bible charges all of its Great Prophets with evil, it makes God guilty of an act of adultery by charging Him with being the father of Mary's baby (Jesus), again it charges Noah and Lot with drunkenness, and Lot with getting children by his daughter. What a Poison Book.

The Holy Qur-an, is holy because it is the Word of Allah (God) speaking Himself directly to His servant. Holy means something that is perfectly pure and we just can't say that of the Poison Bible Al-Qur-an the Qur-an means, according to the Arabic scholars of the language in which it is written, that which should be read, which was revealed to Muhammad in the month of Ramadan 2:185.

We, the so-called American Negroes, are mentioned in the New Testament under several names and parables. I will name two, the parable of the Lost Sheep and the Prodigal Son (Luke 15:1,11); we could not be described better.

Before the coming of Allah (God), we, being blind, deaf and dumb, had mistaken the true meanings of these parables as referring to the Jews. Now, thanks to Almighty God Allah, Who came in the person of Master Fard Muhammad (who be praised forever), who has opened my blinded eyes, and unstopped my ears, loosen the knot in my tongue, and has made us to understand these Bible parables are referring to us, the so-called Negroes and our slave-masters.

The answer (Luke 15:4, 6) to the charges made by the proud and unholy Pharisees against Him (God in Person) for eating with His lost-found people whom the Pharisees and their people had made sinners, can't be better. It defends Him and His people (lost and found sheep). He proved their wicked hatred for His love for His people who were lost and He (God) has found them. They (the Pharisees and their people) had more love for a lost and found animal of theirs than they did for the lost and found people of Allah (God).

Regardless of our sins that we have committed in following and obeying our slave-masters, Allah (God) forgives it all today, if we, the so-called Negroes, will turn to Him and our own kind. If the wicked can rejoice over the finding of his lost and strayed animal, or a piece of silver, or a son who had a desire to leave home and practice the evil habits of strangers, how much more should Allah and the nation of Islam rejoice over finding us, their people, who have been lost from them for 400 years following other than our own kind? We, being robbed so thoroughly of the knowledge of self and kind, are opposed to our own salvation in favor of our enemies, and I here quote another poison addition of the slavery teachings of the Bible: "Love your enemies, bless them who curse you, pray for those who spitefully use you, him that smiteth thee on one cheek offer the other cheek, him that taketh (rob) away thy cloak, forbid not to take (away) thy coat also." (Luke 6:27-28-29). The slave-masters couldn't have found a better teaching for their protection against the slaves' possible dissatisfaction of their masters' brutal treatment.

It is against the very nature of God and man, and other life, to love their enemies. Would God ask us to do that which He, Himself, can't do? He hates His enemies so much that He tells us that He is going to destroy them in hell fire, along with those of us who follow His enemies.

The misunderstanding of the Old and New Testaments by the so-called Negro preachers makes it our graveyard and must be resurrected therefrom. Moses didn't teach a resurrection of the

dead nor did Noah, who was a prophet before Moses. The New
Testament and Holy Qur-an's teaching of a resurrection of the
dead can't mean the people who have died physically and returned to the earth, but rather a mental resurrection of us, the black
nation, who are mentally dead to the knowledge of truth; the
truth of self, God and the arch-enemy of God and His people.

That is that Truth (John 8:32) that will make us free, where-
of John (8:32) doesn't say what truth shall make you free; therefore leaving it questionable and to the advantage of the enemy.
Oh, that my poor people, the so-called Negroes could understand,
they would sit in heaven at once. The enemy is alert, wide-awake
and ever on the job to prevent the so-called Negroes from believing Allah and the true religion of Allah (God) and His Prophets, the Religion of Islam. The enemy is well aware that Allah
(God) is the Rock of our Defense and Islam the House of our
Salvation. Woe to you who try to hinder the teachings of Islam
and the truth of God and the devil, also ever planning the death
of the Messenger of Allah and His followers. It would have been
better that you were not born. The chastisement of Allah shall
abide upon you until you are brought to shame and disgrace.

Remember the disgrace suffered by Pharaoh and his people for
their opposition to Moses and his followers, just because Pharaoh
feared that Moses would teach this people the true religion, Islam!
Pharaoh set his whole army against Moses only to be brought
to naught. Pharaoh had deceived his slaves in the knowledge of
Allah and the true religion Islam, and indirectly had them worshiping him and his people as God.

The poor so-called Negroes are so filled with fear of their
enemy that they stoop to helping the enemy, against their own
salvation. Be aware of what you are doing lest you be the worst
loser. If they had only been taught the truth, they would act
differently. The Bible, church and Christianity have deceived
them. I pray Allah to give them life and light of understanding.

The Holy Qur-an, the Glory Books, should be read and studied
by us, the so-called American Negroes. Both the present Bible
and Holy Qur-an must soon give way to that Holy Book which
no man as yet but Allah has seen. The teachings (prophesies) of
the present Bible and Qur-an takes us up to the resurrection and
judgment of this world, but not into the next life. That which
is in that Holy Book is for the righteous and evil. The preparation for that unseen life is now going on in the few believers of

Islam in America. Islam, the true religion of Allah (God), makes a distinction between the lovers of righteousness and lovers of evil. It is that which Allah (God) is using today to separate the righteous from the evil-doers.

Let us take a look at the opening of the second chapter of the Holy Qur-an. Here Allah addresses Himself to us as being the Best Knower and says that we must not entertain any doubts about the purity of His Book (the Holy Qur-an).

"The apostle believes in what has been revealed to him from His Lord, and so do the believers. They all believe in Allah, His angels, His books and His apostles. We made no difference between any of His apostles; and they say, We hear and obey, our Lord, Thy forgiveness do we crave, and to Thee is the eventual course" (Verse 2:285).

Can the proud Christian say with truth the same? No, they don't believe in Allah not to mention His prophets and the scriptures of the prophets; but they like to make a difference in the prophets. All the old prophets are condemned as being other than good, but Jesus they go to the extreme in making Him a Son and finally God. Yet they say that they killed Jesus, the Son of God, because He made Himself the Son of God.

The history of this man Jesus has been gravely misunderstood by us, the American so-called Negroes.

TRUTH

"And mix not up the Truth with falsehood, nor hide the Truth while you know" [*Holy Qur-an* 2:42].

The Holy Qur-an is a great book when it is understood. The above verse warns against mixing Truth with falsehood, as it is the policy of the devils. But nearly all the religious leaders of Christianity are guilty of mixing up the Divine Truth with falsehood. Now they don't know which is Truth and which is falsehood. They are really confused, thinking and planning against the Truth, trying to hide falsehood. They mixed up the Truth of the Bible so much that today they admit someone has tampered with the book. The Bible now teaches against evil and for evil. For instance, it says that we should not drink strong drinks; wine is prohibited in some places and in others it says that it is good for us.

The Truth must triumph over falsehood, as day triumphs over night. When we deny the truth it shows that we love falsehood more than truth. If we fear to speak the truth for the sake of falsehood, this is not only hiding the truth, but is actually showing fear and distrust in the Divine Surpeme Being, His wisdom and His power.

This hiding and mixing the truth with falsehood because of fear of the enemy (devils) is taking a great number of our people to hell with the devils.

It is natural for one to fear that of which he has no knowledge. However, when Truth and Knowledge are made clear to you, you have no cloak for your fear. Your mixing up Truth with falsehood is only because you fear your enemy (the devils).

Allah (God) doesn't care for us when our fear is greater for our enemies than for Him Allah says: "I and I alone, should you fear. Believe in that which I have revealed, verifying that which is with you, and be not the first to deny it; neither take a mean price for my message; and keep your duty to Me, and to Me alone" (Holy Qur-an 2:40-41).

Once the so-called Negroes drop slavery (Christianity), and accept Allah for their God, and His religion (Islam) Allah will remove their fear and grief, and they will not fear nor grieve any more.

It is a shame to see our people in such fearful condition. "The fearful and the unbelieving shall have their part in the lake which burns with fire and brimstone which is the second death" (Rev. 21:8).

The devil whom they fear more than Allah (God) was not able to protect himself against Allah; therefore his followers shared with him the fire of hell. They had suffered one death (mental), and by fearing the devils and rejecting the Truth, they suffered a physical death, which was the final death.

The devils know that they have deceived the world with their false religion (Christianity). The devils are so afraid that Islam is going to give life and light to the so-called Negroes that they sit and watch over them day and night.

THE DEVIL

DEVILS FOOL AND DISGRACE YOU

Almighty Allah (God) and the Nation of Islam elsewhere (Asia and Africa, the Islands) are grieved and hurt to the heart to see you walking into the trap your enemies (the devils) have and still are setting for you.

I am your sincere brother with the truth from your God and mine, which means your very life and the future of your children and nations of black men and women. The truth being that you should know your enemies and their tricks being played on the world of our kind. Will you listen or read the truth?

Do not take what I am teaching and writing lightly. It is the truth from your God and you shall soon bear me witness that it is the truth. Allah has said to me that we are living in the end of the world of white rule, a race whom Allah has made manifest to you and me as being real devils.

They were created to rule us for 6,000 years, and then Allah (God) will destroy them from the earth and give the earth back to its original owners—the Black Nation.

The time has arrived, and you must know the truth of this race and yourself and nation. You must be reunited to your own Nation. The time is ripe for your return. You will never again be slaves to any other nation. Allah will make you the head and not the tail. Accept your own! Stop destroying yourself trying to be other than your own kind and patterning after a doomed race of devils. You may say, "How am I to live without going along with my enemies' desires?" They did not create themselves —we are their creators—our father, the Black man, feeds them. Is it not our God who created food for all?

He raises the clouds from the earth and causes them to pour their water on the thirsty parts and causes the seeds to germinate and grow for your food. Can this devil whom you trust do these things? And is it not Allah (God) who has made the earth to rotate on her axis in such a way that she causes changes in seasons four times a year to satisfy life and vegetation in all parts of the earth?

You are letting the devils fool and disgrace you and are taking you to hell with them! Your God, Allah, will be happy and will rejoice in feeding, clothing and sheltering you if you believe. The Bible teaches you that He fed and sheltered Israel in the desert (Exod. 16:12-15). Fear not, Allah (God) is with us. The enemies of Allah and the righteous are leading you only to evil and indecency, as the Holy Qur-an teaches you and me.

They are pulling off your clothes and showing the world your shame, and you think it is right. They are used to going nude. They have nudist colonies here in America to prove it. Four thousand years ago all of Europe was a nudist colony. And your little daughters are being brought up to not be shy of indecency.

You have them stripped to their trunks, all because the devils invited you to wear such styles of theirs, and you are obeying. This is to tempt the black people in becoming sharers in their doom.

Your common sense teaches you that God does not approve of such filth. This should also bring you into the knowledge that the religion (Christianity) so talked and preached of by the white race is only a bait for you to swallow to become the followers of them (the enemies of God). Your loving and sweethearting with them only means that you are in love with the devils in person, and you are courting death and hell fire. Believe this or leave it. Read Holy Qur-an 7:27, "O children of Adam, let not the devil seduce you, as he expelled your parents from the garden (this was done by the father of this race, Yakub, 6,000 years ago) pulling off their clothing that he might show them their shame, he surely sees you as his host.

They make fools of you and then laugh at you for being dumb enough for them to trick. (The devil scientists and rulers prepare the trap for you and the others spring it on you.) The above verse you are now fulfilling by going partly nude. You have confidence in the devils because you do not know them to be devils. You are now being taught, and there will be no excuse for your taking them for friends instead of Allah.

The clothing that guards against evil is the knowledge of good and evil, the reward of good and the consequences of doing evil and the good of both. Again, the above verses (26,27) answer the lie (that you are not able to feed and clothe your children and that you should not have many children) that the devils are tricking you into birth control in order to sterilize the so-called Negroes of America.

Beware, my dear sister, the tricks of your enemies and mine, the devils.

TRUTH OF GUILTY
MADE KNOWN

What can the guilty say when the truth of their guilt is made known? I have been teaching for over 35 years what Almighty Allah (God) has revealed to me of the truth of this subject. The origin of sin, the origin of murder, the origin of lying are deceptions originated with the creators of evil and injustice—the white race.

I am sick, tired and worn out with suffering from the persecutions cast against me and my people by the hands of the most wicked and deceiving race that ever lived on our planet.

I say as David in his Psalms, "Oh Lord, persecute them and take them." None of them are righteous—no not one—they are ever seeking to do harm to you and me every second of the day and night.

They (white race) are not hostile toward me because I am a Muslim and because I am teaching the true religion, Islam, to my people and the worship of the true and living God who is not a spook, but is flesh and blood (Allah).

They are hostile against me and my followers because we are of the Original Black Nation whom they were made to hate from the very beginning of their existence, 6,000 years ago.

They were not made to love or respect any member of the darker nations, for they are by nature, as Almighty Allah has taught me, incapable of loving even themselves.

They cannot produce good, for they are without the nature of good. They cannot love Allah and His religion Islam, for it is against their nature to submit to Allah, the Lord of the Worlds. All manner of evil and corruption has come from the white race.

Though we as a people have become affected by over 400

years of contact with this race of devils, we have become like them in many ways, but we are not by nature evil or unrighteous. For we are not a grafted product from any other race, so we are not weak physically nor mentally toward doing evil.

Almighty God, Allah, has appeared in the Western Hemisphere (North America) to tear off the covers of this wicked nation for their evils committed against our people, the so-called Negroes.

We have been living under the God of darkness while in the absence of the God of light. In the same way that the light of day appears to put out the black of night, so it is that Almighty Allah has come with Truth to cast out and destroy falsehood.

As long as the devil is on our planet we will continue to suffer injustice and unrest and have no peace.

The guilty who have spread evilness and corruption throughout the land must face the sentence wrought by their own hands.

I am offering you from Allah a Kingdom of righteousness that will never decay, a New World that will be based upon the principles of truth and justice while we live.

THE MAKING OF DEVIL

You have learned, from the reading of history, that a nation's permanent success depends on its obedience to Allah. We have seen the white race (devils) in heaven, among the righteous, causing trouble (making mischief and causing bloodshed), until they were discovered.

They made trouble for six months, right in heaven, deceiving the ancient original people who were holy. But, when they learned just who was causing the trouble; they, as you have learned, cast the troublemakers out into the worst and poorest part of our planet earth.

They were punished by being deprived of divine guidance, for 2,000 years which brought them almost into the family of wild beasts—going upon all fours; eating raw and unseasoned, uncooked food; living in caves and tree tops, climbing and jumping from one tree to the other.

Even today, they like climbing and jumping. The monkeys are from them. Before their time, there were no such things as monkeys, apes and swine. Read the Holy Qur-an (Chapter 18) entitled: "The Cave." The Holy Qur-an mentions them as being turned into apes and swine as a divine curse, because of their disbelief in Moses.

We do know that both of these animals are loved and be-friended by the white race, along with the dog. But, all of the divine curses sent upon the white race in these days are not enough to serve as a warning to that race. They rose up from the caves and hillsides of Europe, went back to Asia, and have ruled nine-tenths of that great continent.

Muhammad set the devils back for 1,000 years. They were released on the coming of Columbus, and his finding of this Western Hemisphere. They have been here now over 400 years. Their worst and most unpardonable sins were the bringing of the so-called Negroes here to do their labor.

The so-called Negroes have not only given free labor, but have given their lives on the soil of their masters and, all over the earth wherever his hateful and murdering slave-master wants them to go. Now, the slave wants better treatment. They are fast learning today, that these are the children of those who made merchandise out of their fathers. The devil is the "devil" regardless of place and time.

They deceived our fathers and are now deceiving the children, under many false disguises, (as though they want to be friends of the black man) such as integration and intermarriage.

The devil said to Allah: "I shall certainly come upon them from before them and from behind them; and from their right and from their left; and Thou wilt not find most of them thank-ful" (Holy Qur-an 7:17). This is being fulfilled before our very eyes today. The devils are doing both.

They come to the so-called Negroes as friends and as open enemies. They go before them, changing the truth into false; and come behind the Truth-bearer to the so-called Negroes, speaking evil of the truth. They threaten the so-called Negroes with poverty and imprisonment, and make rosy promises to them, only to deceive.

They are telling the so-called Negroes that they realized that they used to mistreat the Negroes, but now they are going to do better and forget the past. "Let us live like brothers for we are all from God."

Along with such smooth lies is an offer of one of the devils' women. The poor so-called Negroes fall victim and the devil men raid the neighborhood of the so-called Negro women, day and night, to make all desirous of hell fire.

This is the way they have planned to beat Allah to the so-called Negroes. What should you do? The answer: Stay away from sweethearting with devils. Surely this is the end of their time, on our planet. Allah said to the devil: "Get out of it despised, and driven away. Whoever of them (the Negroes) will follow you, I will certainly fill hell with you all" (7:18). So remember, your seeking friendship with this race of devils means seeking a place in their hell.

The devil swore to them that he was a sincere adviser (7:21). The Holy Qur-an further says: "Surely they took the devils for friends instead of Allah, and they think that they are right guided" (7:30). Not only the so-called Negroes are deceived by this race of devils, but even many of the Asiatic Muslims do not know that the white race are devils.

Some hate me for teaching this manifest truth of that race; but I want my people here (the so-called Negroes) to wake up and escape the fire that Allah has kindled for their enemies. For they really are not to blame and only need awakening.

Some so-called Negroes, who are in love with the devils, do not like to see nor hear it being made manifest. We could lose them without ever missing them; for all who are found believing in, and in love with, the devils will be destroyed with the devils.

Now, the world must know how to distinguish the real devils from the non-devils, for there are thousands of our peoples throughout the world who can hardly be distinguished, by color, from the real devil. There are certain climates which seem to change the white race into a "red" or "brown" color.

And where they mix freely with our own kind, their skin and eyes show a difference in color. Their eyes are brown and grayish blue. By carefully watching their behavior, you can easily distinguish them from our people (dark, brown, yellow or red).

The characteristics of their children are easily distinguished from the original children, regardless of how near in color they may be. The devil children, whenever they are around and among original children, like to show off, and love to make mockery of the original children.

They teach them evil; talk filth; sing filthy songs; filthy dancing; and games; and will not leave the original children without starting a fight. Their little mouths, like their parents' before them, are filled with cursing and swearing.

Remember the Bible's teaching of this race of devils, and especially in II Thessalonians (Chapter 2:3-12), and Revelation (12:9-17,20:10). The treatment of the so-called Negroes by the devils is sufficient proof to the so-called Negroes, that they (the white race,) are real devils.

And if this teaching, along with what they are suffering from their beloved devils, does not awaken them to the knowledge of the devils, all I can say for them, then is that they are just lost. They won't be accepted by God nor by the righteous Muslims, with even the name of the devils.

Muhammad took hold of the best, the belief in one God (Allah), and was successful, Fourteen hundred years after him we are successful. That is, we who will not set up another God with Allah. The fools who refuse to believe in Allah alone, as the one God, if asked: "Who made the heavens and earth?" most surely would say "God," and would not say: "God the Son, and the Holy Ghost." Then why don't they serve and obey Allah?

It is a perfect insult to Allah, who made the heavens and earth, and makes the earth to produce everything for our services, and even the sun, moon and stars—which serve our needs — for us to bow down and worship anything other than Allah as a God. The Great Mahdi, Allah in person, who is in our midst today, will put a stop once and forever, to the serving and worshiping of other gods beside Himself.

It is the devil's way of bringing the people (the so-called Negroes) of Allah in opposition to Him by teaching the people to believe and do just the thing that God forbids. Muhammad did not try making a likeness of God nor have his followers done so.

He and his followers obey and do the law of Allah, while the Jews and the Christians preach it and do otherwise. We are now being brought face to face with Allah, for a showdown between Him and that which we have served as god beside Him.

Whatever is in the heavens and whatever is in the earth submits to the God of black mankind — the sun, the moon, the stars and the powers that uphold them are from the original black nation. He is the first and the last.

The black man produces these four colors: brown, red, yellow and white. The original people, whom the white race found here (red people), were the brothers of the black man, they are referred to as the Red Indians.

The Indian part of the name must refer to the name of the country from which they came, India. The All-wise Allah said that they came here 16,000 years ago and that they were exiled from India for breaking the law of Islam.

All of our colors — brown, red and yellow — have ruled since the black. The white race, the most recently made color, ruled all the other colors for the past 6,000 years.

Why is the black man just coming into his own? Because he desired to try getting experience (or trying everything) himself. Today you see every color in power but the black man, yet he is the originator of all. Now the Great Mahdi (God in person) with His infinite wisdom, knowledge and understanding, is going to put the original black man in his original place as he was at first, the God and ruler of the universe.

Notice the general awakening of this number one man of these people throughout the world of mankind, the crushed ones of the five above-mentioned colors. The last 6,000 years have witnessed the most terrible blows, meant to complete the destruction of this color.

Their color is most adapted to any part of our planet under any climatic condition. The color of their eyes (black and white) is of all the others, the best — the most beautiful of all. Their black hair, white teeth are all the best for they are the best people.

They haven't had their day in many thousands of years. Fifty thousand years ago he had his complete fall. (I shouldn't use the word fall for it was not; he only allowed the weaker of himself to rule).

When he put the last color of his color into power, the white color or race became the real enemy of the father (black man) and tried and is still trying to exterminate the original color (black) by many ways and means.

Today, the white race, the blacks' worst enemies, has planned to make a last try to destroy the black man by pretending to be their friends and allow intermarriage.

Many Americans (especially the Southerners) don't like the idea, but will finally be persuaded by their more learned men when they see no other way of making a final stroke at the black man. It will be short-lived for the judgment will sit, and the agreement will be broken between the black and whites as it is written (Isaiah 29:17,18).

The original black man has been without the knowledge of himself for a long time and this one (the American so-called Negroes), of all of his kind, is the dumbest to the knowledge of self, due to the way his slave-master teaches and trains him.

But this is the time of the awakening of this poor slave and no powers on earth or in the heavens above will be able to prevent it. For it is the will and work of Allah and His choice of the people.

He has chosen the so-called Negroes, but they being blinded and made deaf and dumb, have not but a few chosen Allah to be their God; but they will, after they see more of His power displayed in the West— and they will see it. It is going on now. It is a must with Allah to restore the lost sheep.

The black people are by nature the righteous. They have love and mercy in their hearts even after trying to live the life of the devils — this is still recognized in them. When they are fully in the knowledge of self, they will do righteousness and live in peace among themselves.

One can't judge them now for they are not their own selves. We, the original nation of earth, says Allah, the Maker of everything — sun, moon and stars and the race called white race — are the writers of the Bible and Qur-an.

We make such history once every 25,000 years. When such history is written, it is done by twenty-four of our scientists. One acts as Judge or God for the others and twenty-three actually do the work of getting up the future of the nation, and all is put into one book and at intervals where such and such part or portion will come to pass, that people will be given that part of the book through one among that people from one of the Twelve (twelve major scientists) as it is then called a Scripture which actually means script of writing from something original or book.

There is a significance to the number 24 Scientists and the 25,000 years. The number twenty-four Scientists used is in accordance with the hours in our day and the measurement of the circumference of our planet around the Equator and in the region of our Poles, Arctic and Antarctic Oceans.

Our planet is not exactly 25,000 miles in circumference, it is 24,896 and we, according to astronomy, don't have a full 24-hour day but near that—23 hours, 56 minutes and 46 seconds. The change made in our planet's rotation at the Poles is about one minute a year and takes 25,000 years to bring about a complete change in the region of the Poles. The actual Poles are inclines 23½ degrees to the plane of its orbit. The original black nation used 23 scientists to write the future of that nation for the next 25,000 years, and the 24th is the Judge or the one God, Allah. Allah taught me that, once upon a time they made history to last for 35,000 years. Let me stop here and say this:

My people must know the truth, the God's truth—the time is at hand! They are reared and taught by the devils and they know it not; and being ignorant of the truth, they offer opposition to the God of their salvation, Who is the very author of Truth.

I am His Messenger. They do this because of the fear of the devils. They are made to believe that without the friendship of the devils they would perish.

The Bible warns them against the friendship of the devils (James 4:4). "Whosoever therefore will be a friend of the world is the enemy of God." The sixth verse of the same chapter reads: "Submit yourselves therefore to God. Resist the devil, and he will flee from you."

Do they dare resist the devils? No! Being without the truth of Allah and the devil, they are afraid; and that fear is the cause of their suffering and will be the cause of their destruction in hell, with the devils whom they love and fear. Preachers, who read and study to teach the Bible to your own people, get the understanding of it first before teaching it to the blind, deaf and dumb of your people lest you lead both them and yourselves to hell. Remember—your white slave-masters are your translators and teachers of the Bible. They—who will not give you justice under this law—will not give you truth and justice in the World of God! Stop being a fool for false friendships of the devils. Stop teaching your people to love their enemies, which is a lie the devils teach and claim that Jesus taught it.

We are the makers of divine histories, and who is better in knowledge than Allah?

Man is easily made, but the sun, moon and stars are much harder to make. Yet we are the makers of them. In making the moon, it was not our original father's intention to make the moon as it is. His real intention was to destroy the moon (earth) but failed and all others who make such attempts will fail.

What! You disbelieve it? Do you not see that the devils are trying to make themselves a satellite to make you believe that they are the masters of the heavens and earth, as it is written of them in the Bible and Holy Qur-an (Isaiah 14:13, 14-16th verses).

They destroyed other people, cities and opened not the house of his prisoners. None has fulfilled this prophecy better than America. She has destroyed other nations' cities while she has not suffered the loss of one of her cities by a foreign nation, while preaching the freedom of her own people from the powers of other nations.

She holds a whole nation (so-called Negroes) prisoner, and refuses to open the door of freedom, justice and equality to them. She threatens to go to war against other nations who hold any of her citizens prisoners. They now boast of building rockets to land on our moon, and to build a small contraption to try circling the earth like our moon, which we have made to revolve around the earth.

The following is from the Holy Qur-an: "And we (the devils) sought to reach heaven, but we found it filled with strong guards and flames; and we (the devils) used to sit in some of the sitting-places thereof to steal a hearing. But he who tries to listen now finds a flame lying in wait for him" (Holy Qur-an 72:8,9).

I am for the separation of my people from their enemies; that they share not in the enemies' destruction, even though I may lose my own life in this daring attempt to save them by the plain, simple truth of God and power. It must be done and will be done, regardless of whom or what. It can be done in one day, but Allah desires to make Himself known in the West, as it is written of Him.

Our 66 trillion years from the moon has proven a great and wise show of the original power, to build wonders in the heavens and earth. Six thousand years ago, or to be more exact 6,600 years ago, as Allah taught me, our nation gave birth to another God whose name was Yakub. He started studying the life germ of man to try making a new creation (new man) whom our twenty-four scientists had foretold 8,400 years before the birth of Mr. Yakub, and the Scientists were aware of his birth and work before he was born, as they are today of the intentions or ideas of the present world.

According to the word of Allah to me, "Mr. Yakub was seen by the twenty-three Scientists of the black nation, over 15,000 years ago. They predicted that in the year 8,400 (that was in

our calendar year before this world of the white race), this man
(Yakub) would be born twenty miles from the present Holy City,
Mecca, Arabia. And, that at the time of his birth, the satis-
faction and dissatisfaction of the people would be: — 70 per cent
satisfied, 30 per cent dissatisfied."

And, that when this man is born, he will change civilization
(the world), and produce a new race of people, who would rule
the original black nation for 6,000 years (from the nine thousandth year to the fifteen thousandth year).

After that time, the original black nation would give birth to
one, whose wisdom, Knowledge and power would be infinite.
One, whom the world would recognize as being the greatest and
mightiest God, since the creation of the universe. And, that He
would destroy Yakub's world and restore the original nation, or
ancient nation, into power to rule forever.

This mighty One, is known under many names. He has no
equal. There never was one like Him. He is referred to in the
Bible as God Almighty, and in some places as Jehovah, the God
of Gods, and the Lord of Lords.

The Holy Qur-an refers to Him as Allah, the One God; beside Him, there is no God and there is none like Him; the Supreme Being; the mighty, the wise; the best knower; the light;
the life giver; the Mahdi (this is He, Whom I have met and am
missioned by).

He, also, is referred to as the Christ, the second Jesus. The
Son of Man, who is wise and is all-powerful. He knows how to
reproduce the universe, and the people of His choice. He will
remove and destroy the present, old warring wicked world of
Yakub (the Caucasian world) and set up a world of peace and
righteousness, out of the present so-called Negroes, who are rejected and despised by this world.

Mr. Yakub was, naturally, born out of the 30 per cent dissatisfied. As we know, wherever there is a longing or demand
for a change, nature will produce that man, who will bring it
about.

Allah taught me that the present percentage of dissatisfaction
is 98 per cent, near 100 per cent, with the present ruling powers.
This 100 per cent dissatisfied, will bring about a 100 per cent
change. Yakub did not bring about a 100 per cent change,
but near (90 per cent). Allah said: "When Yakub was six years
old, one day, he was sitting down playing, with two pieces of

steel. He noticed the magnetic power in the steel attracting the other. He looked up at his uncle and said: "Uncle, when I get to be an old man, I am going to make a people who shall rule you." The uncle said: "What will you make; something to make mischief and cause bloodshed in the land?" Yakub said: "Nevertheless, Uncle, I know that which you do not know."

And, it was at that moment, the boy Yakub, first came into the knowledge of just who he was – born to make trouble, break peace, kill and destroy his own people with a made enemy to the black nation.

He learned his future from playing with steel. It is steel and more steel that his made race (the white race), are still playing with. Steel has become the most useful of all metal for the people. What he really saw in playing with the two pieces of steel was the magnetic power of attraction.

The one attracting and drawing the other under its power. In this, he saw an unlike human being, made to attract others, who could, with the knowledge of tricks and lies, rule the original black man – until that nation could produce one greater and capable of overcoming and making manifest his race of tricks and lies, with a nation of truth.

Yakub was the founder of unlike attracts and like repels, though Mr. Yakub was a member of the black nation. He began school at the age of four. He had an unusual size head. When he had grown up, the others referred to him as the "big head scientist."

At the age of 18 he had finished all of the colleges and universities of his nation, and was seen preaching on the streets of Mecca, making converts. He made such impressions on the people, that many began following him.

He learned, from studying the germ of the black man, under the microscope, that there were two people in him, and that one was black, the other brown.

He said if he could successfully separate the one from the other he could graft the brown germ into its last stage, which would be white. With his wisdom, he could make the white, which he discovered was the weaker of the black germ (which would be unalike) rule the black nation for a time (until a greater one than Yakub was born).

This new idea put him to work finding the necessary converts to begin grafting his new race of people. He began by teaching Islam, with promises of luxury to those who would believe and follow him.

As Mr. Yakub continued to preach for converts, he told his people that he would make the others work for them. (This promise came to pass). Naturally, there are always some people around who would like to have others do their work. Those are the ones who fell for Mr. Yakub's teaching, 100 per cent.

As he made converts in and around the Holy City of Mecca, persecutions set in. The authorities became afraid of such powerful teachings, with promises of luxury and making slaves of others. As they began making arrests of those who believed the teaching, the officers would go back and find, to their surprise, others still teaching and believing it.

Finally they arrested Mr. Yakub. But, it only increased the teachings. They kept persecuting and arresting Yakub's followers until they filled all the jails.

The officers finally reported to the King that there was no room to put a prisoner in—if arrested. "All the jails are filled; and, when we go out into the streets, we find them still teaching. What shall we do with them?" The King questioned the officers on just what the teachings were; and of the name of the leader.

The officers gave the King the answers to everything. The King said: "This is not the name of that man." On entering the prison, the King was shown Yakub's cell. "As-Salaam Alaikum." The King said: "So you are Mr. Yakub?" He said: "Yes, I am." The King said: "Yakub, I have come to see if we could work out some agreement that would bring about an end to this trouble. What would you suggest?"

Mr. Yakub told the King: "If you give me and my followers everything to start civilization as you have, and furnish us with money and other necessities of life for twenty years, I will take my followers and we will go from you."

The King was pleased with the suggestion or condition made by Yakub, and agreed to take care of them for twenty years, until Yakub's followers were able to go for themselves.

After learning who Mr. Yakub was, they all were afraid of him, and were glad to make almost any agreement with him and his followers.

The history or future of Mr. Yakub and his people was in

the Nation's Book, by the writers (23 Scientists) of our history, 8,400 years before his birth. So, the Government began to make preparation for the exiling of Mr. Yakub and His followers. The King ordered everyone rounded up who was a believer in Mr. Yakub. They took them to the seaport and loaded them on ships.

After rounding them all up into ships, they numbered 59,999. Yakub made 60,000. Their ships sailed out to an Isle in the Aegean Sea called "Pelan" (Bible "Patmos"). After they were loaded into the ships, Mr. Yakub examined each of them to see if they were 100 per cent with him; and to see if they were all healthy and productive people. If not, he would throw them off. Some were found to be unfit and overboard they went.

When they arrived at the Isle, Mr. Yakub said to them: "See how they (the Holy People) have cast us out. Now — if you will choose me to be your King, I will teach you how to go back and rule them all."

Of course, they had already chosen Yakub to be their King at the very start. So, Yakub chose doctors, ministers, nurses and a cremator for his top laborers. He called these laborers together and told them his plan for making a new people, who would rule for 6,000 years.

He called the doctor first and said: "Doctor, let all the people come to you who want to marry; and if there come to you two real black ones, take a needle and get a little of their blood and go into your room and pretend to be examining it, to see whether their blood would mix. Then, come and tell them that they will each have to find another mate, because their blood does not mix." (It was the aim of Yakub to get rid of the black and he did.) "Give them a certificate to take to the minister, warning the minister against marrying the couple because their blood does not mix. When there comes to you two browner ones, take a pretended blood test of them; but, give them a certificate saying that they are eligible to marry."

Mr. Yakub's charge to his laborers was very strict -- death if one disobeyed. They didn't know what Yakub had in mind until they were given their labor to do. He made his laborers, from the chief to the least, liars. The doctor lied about the blood of the two black people who wanted to marry, that it did not mix.

The brown and black could not be married (brown only). The

doctors of today hold the same position over the people. You go to them to get a blood test to see if you are fit to be married.

Today, they say it is done to see if there are any contagious germs in the blood. I wish that they would enforce such a law today (keep the white from mixing with black – just the opposite). Perhaps we could remain black and not be disgraced by a mixture of all colors.

In the days of Yakub's grafting of the present white race, a new and unalike race among the black nation for 600 years, his law was—that they should not allow the birth of a black baby in their family, but the white (devil) should mix their blood with the black nation, in order to help destroy black; but, they should not allow the black to mix with their blood.

His aim was to kill and destroy the black nation. He ordered the nurses to kill all black babies that were born among his people, by pricking the brains with a sharp needle as soon as the black child's head is out of the mother.

If the mother is alert (watching the nurse), then the nurse would lie and fool the mother to get possession of child to murder it, by saying that she (mother) gave birth to an "angel child." And that she (the nurse) would like to take the baby to heaven, so when the mother dies, she would have a room with her child in heaven, for her baby was an angel.

This is the beginning of the first lie or liar; and, it was so that the nurse would take the black baby away on this falsehood and claim that they were taking the poor black baby to heaven. As Yakub had taught them, they would feed it to wild beasts and if they did not a wild beast to feed the black babies to, Yakub told the nurses to give it to the cremator to burn.

Mr. Yakub warned the laborers, from the doctor down to this cremator, that if anyone of them failed to carry out his ororders, off go their heads.

When there was a birth of a brown baby, the nurse would come and make much ado over it, and, would tell the mother that she had given birth to a holy child and that she would nurse it for the next six weeks, for her child was going to be a great man (that is when it was a boy baby).

After the first 200 years, Mr. Yakub had done away with the black babies, and all were brown. After another 200 years, he had all yellow or red, which was 400 years after being on

"Pelan." Another 200 years, which brings us to the six hundredth year, Mr. Yakub had an all-pale white race of people on this Isle.

Of course, Mr. Yakub lived but 150 years; but, his ideas continued in practice. He gave his people guidance in the form of literature. What they should do and how to do it (how to rule the black nation). He said to them: "When you become unalike (white), you may return to the Holy Land and people, from whom you were exiled."

The Yakub made devils were really pale white, with really blue eyes; which we think are the ugliest of colors for a human eye. They were call Caucasian—which means, according to some of the Arab scholars, "One whose evil effect is not confined to one's self alone, but affects others."

There was no good taught to them while on the Island. By teaching the nurses to kill the black baby and save the brown baby, so as to graft the white out of it; by lying to the black mother of the baby, this lie was born into the very nature of the white baby; and, murder for the black people also born in them—or made by nature a liar and murderer.

The black nation is only fooling themselves to take the Caucasian race otherwise. This is what Jesus learned of their history, before he gave up his work of trying to convert the Jews or white race to the religion of Islam.

And, the same knowledge of them was given to Muhammad by the Imams (or scientists) of Mecca. That is why the war of the Muslims against them came to a stop.

Muhammad was told that he could not reform the devils and that the race had 1,400 more years to live; the only way to make righteous people (Muslims) out of them was to graft them back into the black nation.

This grieved Muhammad so much that it caused him heart trouble until his death (age sixty-two and one half years). The old scientists used to laugh at Muhammad for thinking that he could convert them (the devils) to Islam. This hurt his heart.

Mr. Yakub taught his made devils on Pelan: "That—when you go back to the holy black nation, rent a room in their homes. Teach your wives to go out the next morning around the neighbors of the people, and tell that you heard her talking about them last night.

"When you have gotten them fighting and killing each other,

then ask them to let you help settle their disputes, and restore peace among them. If they agree, then you will be able to rule them both." This method the white race practices on the black nation, the world over. They upset their peace by putting one against the other, and then rule them after dividing them.

This is the reason why the American so-called Negroes can never agree on unity among themselves, which would put them on top overnight. The devils keep them divided by paid informers from among themselves. They keep such fools among us. But, the real truth of the devils sometimes converts the informers, and brings them over to us as true believers. We don't bother about killing them, as I am not teaching that which I want to be kept as a secret, but that which the world has not known and should know.

After Yakub's devils were among the Holy people of Islam (the black nation) for six months, they had our people at war with each other. The holy people were unable to understand, just why they could not get along in peace with each other, until they took the matter to the King.

The King told the holy people of the black nation that the trouble they were having was caused by the white devils in their midst, and that there would be no peace among them until they drove these white made devils from among them.

The holy people prepared to drive the devils out from among them. The King said: "Gather every one of the devils up and strip them of our costume. Put an apron on them to hide their nakedness. Take all literature from them and take them by way of the desert. Send a caravan, armed with rifles, to keep the devils going westward. Don't allow one of them to turn back; and, if they are lucky enough to get across the Arabian Desert, let them go into the hills of West Asia, the place they now call Europe.

Yakub's made devils were driven out of Paradise, into the hills of West Asia (Europe), and stripped of everything but the language. They walked across that hot, sandy desert, into the land where long years of both trouble and joy awaited them; but—they finally made it. (Not all. Many died in the desert.)

Once there, they were roped in, to keep them out of Paradise. To make sure, the Muslims, who lived along the borders of East and West Asia, were ordered to patrol the border to keep Yakub's devils in West Asia (now called Europe), so that the original nation of black men could live in peace; and that the devils could be alone to themselves, to do as they pleased, as long as they didn't try crossing the East border.

The soldiers patrolled the border armed with swords, to prevent the devils from crossing. This went on for 2,000 years. After that time, Musa (Moses) was born: the man whom Allah would send to these exiled devils to bring them again into the light of civilization. Before we take up this first 2,000 years of the devils exiled on our planet, let us not lose sight of what and how they were made, and of the god who made them, Mr. Yakub.

Since we have learned that Mr. Yakub was an original man (black) the ignorant of our people may say: "If Yakub was a black man and the father of the devils, then he was a devil." That is like one saying "The horse is as much a mule as the mule."

Or, that an orange or lemon is as much grapefruit as the grapefruit: because the grapefruit is grafted from the orange and lemon. They are not alike because the grafted is no longer original.

Just what have we learned, or rather are learning from this divine revelation of our enemies, the devils? Answer: We are learning the truth, which has been kept a secret for 6,000 years concerning the white race, who have deceived us. We learn what is meant by the Bible's symbolic teachings: that they were made from dust.

This only tends to convey the idea that they were created from nothing; which means the low and humble origin of such creation.

Again, we learn who the Bible (Genesis 1:26) is referring to in the saying: "Let us make man." This "US" was fifty-nine thousand, nine hundred and ninety-nine (59,999) black men and women; making or grafting them into the likeness or image of the original man.

Not that they are the same, but have the ways of a human being they are referred to as "mankind"—not the real original man, but a being made like the original in the sense of human beings.

The Holy Qur-an throws a great light on the truth of the creation of this pale, white race of devils. "O mankind, surely we have created you from a male and a female" (Chap.49:15).

This makes it very easy to understand to whom it is referring. "What mankind?" Surely we created man from sperm mixed (with ovum) to try him, so we have made him hearing and seeing" (Chap. 76:2).

Inasmuch as these chapters have a further reference to the spiritual creation of the Last Messenger, it is equally true that they refer to the physical creation of the white race. In another place, the Holy Qur-an says: "We have created man, and now he is an open disputer."

Yakub's race of devils were exiled in the hills and caves of West Asia (now called Europe). They were without anything to start civilization and became savages. They remained in such condition for 2,000 years—no guide or literature.

They lost all knowledge of civilization. The Lord, God of Islam, taught me that some of them tried to graft themselves back into the black nation, but they had nothing to go by. A few were lucky enough to make a start, and got as far as what you call the gorilla. In fact, all of the monkey family are from this 2,000 year history of the white race in Europe.

Being deprived of divine guidance for their disobedience, the making of mischief and causing bloodshed in the holy nation of the original black people by lies, they became so savage that they lost all their sense of shame.

They started going nude as they are doing today (and leading the so-called Negroes into the very acts).

They became shameless. In the winter they wore animal skins· for clothes and grew hair all over their bodies and faces like all the other wild animals.

In those days, they made their homes in the caves on hillsides. There is a whole chapter devoted to them in the Holy Qur-an. They had it very hard, trying to save themselves from being destroyed by wild beasts which were plentiful at that time in Europe.

Being without a guide, they started walking on their hands and feet like all animals; and, learned to climb trees as well as any of the animals. At night, they would climb up into trees, carrying large stones and clubs, to fight the wild beasts that would come prowling around at night, to keep them from eating their families.

Their next and best weapons were the dogs. They tamed some of these dogs to live in the caves with their families, to help protect them from the wild beasts. After a time, the dog held a high place among the family because of his fearlessness to attack the enemies of his master. Today, the dog is still loved by the white race and is given more justice than the so-called Negroes, and, is called the white man's best friend. This comes from the cave days.

After 2,000 years of living as a savage, Allah raised up Musa (Moses) to bring the white race again into civilization: to take their place as rulers, as Yakub had intended for them. Musa (Moses) became their God and leader. He brought them out of the caves; taught them to believe in Allah; taught them to wear clothes; how to cook their food; how to season it with salt; what beef they should kill and eat; and, how to use fire for their service. Moses taught them against putting the female cow under burden.

He established for them Friday as the day to eat fish, and not to eat meat (beef) on that day. And, fish is the main menu on Fridays in many of the whites' homes today.

They were so evil (savage) that Moses had to build a ring of fire around him at night; and, he would sleep in the center of the ring to keep the devils from harming him. They were afraid of fire, and are still afraid of fire.

Allah said that: "One day, Moses told them he was going to have fish come up from the sea that so that tomorrow we will have some fish."

On the next day, the fish were there. Moses had a boat load sent up from Egypt. Moses said: "See! The sea came up last night and brought us some fish." One of the savages was a little smart and he said to Moses: "Where is the water?"

From then on, Moses recognized the fact that he could not say just anything to them. He had a hard time trying to civilize them. Once they gave Moses so much trouble that he took a few sticks of dynamite, went up on the mountainside, placed them into the ground, and went back to get those who were giving him the most trouble.

He said to them: "Stand there on the edge of this mountain and you will hear the voice of God." They stood there about 300 in number. Moses set the fuse off and it killed all of them.

The Imams got after Moses for performing this trick on the devils. Moses said to the Imams: "If you only knew how much trouble these devils give me, you would do as I do." Moses taught the devils that if they would follow him and obey him, Allah would give them a place among the holy people. Most of them believed Moses, just to get out of the caves.

The Imams recognized the tremendous job Musa (Moses) had, trying to civilize the savages. These enemies of the righteous black nation of earth now had to take the place as the rulers and conquerors of the earth. The devils were given the knowledge and power to bring every living thing, regardless of its kind of life, into subjection.

And God said: "Let us make man in our image, after our likeness: Let them have dominion. over the fish of the sea; and over the fowl of the air; and over the cattle, and over all the earth; and over every creeping thing that creepeth upon the earth:" and God said unto them: "Be fruitful and multiply; and replenish the earth, and subdue it" (Gen. 1:26, 28).

The above was all necessary if the devils were to rule as a God of the world. They must conquer, and bring into subjection, all life upon the earth — not land life alone, but they must subdue the sea and the like therein — master everything, until a greater master of God comes, which would mean the end of their power over the life of our earth.

We all bear witness that the scripture quoted above refers to the Caucasian race. They are the only people who answer that description and work for the past 4,000 years.

They have subdued the people and most every kind of living thing upon the earth. God has blessed them to exercise all their knowledge, and blessed them with guides (prophets) from among our own people; and, with the rain and seasons of the earth.

Today, their wealth is great upon the earth. Their sciences of worldly good have sent them, not only after the wealth of other than their own people, but even after the lives and property of their own kind. They have tired to re-people (replenish) the earth with their own kind, by skillfully killing off the black man and mixing their blood into the black woman.

But, the job is too big for them to ever conquer. The black nation, including its other three colors, brown, red and yellow, outnumber the Caucasian race, eleven to one.

"God created them in His image" (Gen. 1:27). They are in the image and likeness of a human being (black man), but are altogether a different kind of human being than that of the black human beings.

Their pale white skin; their blue eyes (even disliked by themselves) tells any black man or woman, that in those blue and green eyes, there just can't be any sincere love and friendship for them. They are unlike and we are like. Like repels — unlike attracts. The very characteristics of black and white are so very different.

Black people have a heart of gold, love and mercy. Such a heart, nature did not give to the white race. This is where the so-called Negroes are deceived in this devil race. They think they have the same kind of heart; but the white race knows better. They have kept it as a secret among themselves, that they may be able to deceive the black people.

They have been, and still are, successful in deceiving the black man, under the disguise of being the ones who want peace, love and friendship with the world, and with God — at the same time making war with the world, to destroy peace, love and friendship of the black nation.

A brother loves and desires for his brother what he desires for himself. So-called Negroes, do you have this kind of love and desire from the white race for you? Why? Because as I have shown to you, they are not your brothers, by nature. They are fully showing you, this day, openly, that they are different from you; and, you are different from them.

Why not try making brotherly love and friendship with your own kind first? To see you trying to integrate with the very enemy of yours, and God, shows beyond a shadow of a doubt, that you don't know yourself nor your enemies; or rather are lost in love for our enemies, I know you, who love your enemy, don't like that I tell you this truth. But, I can't help it—come what may. God has put upon me this mission, and I must do His will or burn.

Are you with me to do the will of God, or the will of the devil and the disbelieving people? I know you are, for you have learned and are learning more truth than you have ever read or ever will read. Fear not! Allah is on our side, to give you and me the Kingdom.

SERPENT

That old serpent, called the devil and Satan, which deceiveth the whole world (Rev. 12:9) is a person or persons whose characteristics are like that of a serpent (snake). Serpents or snakes of the grafted type cannot be trusted, for they will strike you when you are not expecting a strike.

Let us refer to Genesis: "Dan shall be a serpent by the way, an adder in the path that biteth the horses's heels so that his rider shall fall backward" (Gen. 49:17). Here Jacob on his deathbed foretelleth the future of his sons (Moses calls Dan a lion's whelp; he shall leap from Bashan; Deut. 33:22). That old serpent, devil and satan, the old beast, is the dragon which deceiveth the whole world of the poor ignorant darker nations and has caused them to fall off their mount of prosperity, success and independence by accepting advice, guidance and empty promises which he (the serpent-like Caucasian devil) never intended to fulfill.

How well the prophets have described the characteristics of this race of devils as corresponding to the nature of a snake (serpent). Most snakes wobble and make a crooked trail when and wherever they crawl. So it is with the white race, which goes among the black nation leaving the marks of evil and crooked dealings and doings.

In spiritual dealings, there again you will find them like a snake (serpent), following on the heels of the truthbearers (prophets and messengers of God) to bite the believers with false teachings and fear in order that he may cause them to fall off their mount of truth. Like a snake (serpent) he parks in and on the pathway of all the so-called Negroes who seek the way to freedom, truth, justice and equality (Allah and the true religion, Islam). In many instances, they threaten you with imprisonment, the loss of your jobs, hunger, lack of shelter and disrespect of human rights. On some occasions, they threaten to take away your very life! By speaking evil of the truth (Allah and His apostle and Islam), they cause fear to enter the hearts of the weak believers and they fall off the mount of the truth of God which would have saved them from fear, harm, hunger and lack of shelter. As he caused the fall of Adam and his wife from the Garden of Paradise, so they are trying to cause the fall of you and me and prevent us from entering Paradise by not believing in Allah and His religion, Islam.

Allah (God) drove out both Adam and Eve and cursed the serpent and set a day of execution upon the (human) serpent (the devil and satan) and enmity and hatred (discord, dislike, disapproval) between the apostles and prophets of God and the human serpent. "And God said unto the serpent, because thou hast done this, thou art cursed above all cattle, and above every beast of the field, and I will put enmity between thee and the woman and between thy seed and her seed, it shall bruise thy head and thou shall bruise his heel" (Gen. 3:15).

Notice that the above verse refers to the woman's seed as "it" and in the last two words of verse 15, "his heel" is used. The woman's seed and the serpent's seed are involved. Therefore, the seed of the two will settle the wrong between the woman and the serpent caused by the serpent in the Garden of Paradise 6,000 years ago. The woman's seed shall bruise the serpent's head.

What is the head of this human serpent? It is the false religious leaders of the human beast serpent. "Come hither, I will show unto thee the judgment of the great whore that sitteth upon many waters with whom kings of the earth have committed fornication and the inhabitants of the earth have been made drunk." (They are silly drunk from the false religious teachings of the head of the serpent. Under this drunkenness they war against the truth and persecute and kill the servants of truth, thinking that they are doing God's will, or they try to prevent the truth from manifesting falsehood).

In the fourth verse, the woman is arrayed in purple and scarlet color and is filthy. In the first and sixteenth verses, she is called a whore. The beast supports her.

THE BEAST   PART I

Who is like unto the beast? Who is able to make war with him?" (Rev. 13:4). This beast that is spoken of in the prophecy of the first book of the Bible called Revelations and has and still is being much misunderstood by my people. But one thing is certain, the name (beast) is believed by most all readers of the Book to refer to a person or persons, which is right. But who is the person or persons? (Note: There is mentioned in the same chapter and verse a dragon which gave power to the beast. Who can this dragon be? Is he also a person? Then how are the two related?)

The eighteenth verse of the same chapter reads: "Here is wisdom. Let him that hath understanding count the number of the beast: for it is the number of a man." Here we are told that the number of the beast referred to here is a man or people. Now the only way of knowing just what man or people is to watch and see what man or people's doings or works compare with the doings and works of the symbolic beast of the Revelation.

This name "beast," when given to a person, refers to that person's characteristics, not to an actual beast. Study the history of how America treats the freedom, justice and equality which is supposed to be given to all citizens of America (of course, the Negroes are not citizens of America). A citize.. cannot and will not allow his people and government to treat him in such way as America treats her so-called Negroes.

To call a person a "beast" is simply to say, according to the English language: Nouns—violent person, berserk or berserker, demon, fiend, shaitan or sheitan or Satan, or dragon, evil spirit, Satanas, devil, diable, Iblis, azazel, abaddon, apollyon, the prince of the devils, the prince of darkness, the prince of this world, the prince of the power of air, the wicked one, the evil one, the archenemy, the archfiend, the devil incarnate, the father of lies, the author and father of evil, the serpent, the common enemy, the angel of the bottomless pit. Adjectives— satanic, devilish, diabolic (al), hell-born, demoniac, savage, brute, fierce, vicious, wild, untamed, tameless, ungentle, barbarous, unmitigated, unsoftened, ungovernable, uncontrollable (obstinate), brute force, forcibly, by main, with might and main, by force of arms, at the point of the sword or bayonet (the devil and Satan). The above in the explanation of "beast" when applied to human beings or people in general, according to *Roget's International Thesaurus*. The so-called American Negroes have and still suffer under such brutish treatment from the American Christian white race, who call themselves followers of Jesus and his God.

The Revelator could not have better described the white race's way of dealing with the black nation. They (white race) are the people described as "beast" in the Revelation of the Bible. Study them and their history and dealings with people and you will without hesitation agree with me 100 per cent that these are the people meant by the Revelator, who foresaw their future and end and wrote it while he and his followers were in exile from the Holy Land 6,600 years ago on the Island of Pelan in the Aegean Sea, where he grafted the present white race.

The revelation is claimed by the Christians to have been given to a Saint John Divine who was a follower of Jesus, but this is erroneous and wrong. It is by the father of the white race (Mr. Yakub or Jacob). The people other than the beast are mentioned as worshipers of the beast: "And they (the people of the darker nation) worshiped the dragon which gave power unto the beast." The power given by the dragon to the beast refers to a higher wisdom and knowledge of the time and wise preparedness. The chief head and spiritual guidance of the white race is the Pope of Rome.

THE BEAST   PART II
WHO IS ABLE TO
MAKE WAR WITH HIM?

Who is able to make war with him? (Rev. 13:4)
dreadful and terrible (Dan. 7:7).

God and His Prophets could not have given the white race a better name (serpent) according to the characteristics of that race. The serpent of Genesis 3:1 was none other than the devil (white race). He deceived Adam and his wife, causing them to disobey Allah (God), which was the plan of the serpent (devil), according to the history of the devils. Their greatest desire is to make the righteous disobey the law of righteousness.

They are referred to by this name "serpent" in the Holy Qur-an (37:65) translated by Maulvi Muhammad Ali: "To a tree that grows in the bottom of hell, its produce is as the heads of serpents which the disbelievers shall eat from." In his footnote (2112), he says: "That the Arabs apply the name Shaitan to a sort of serpent having a mane, ugly or foul in the head and face." In Mr. Abdullah Yusuf Ali's translation of the Holy Qur-an in English, the same chapter and verse (37:65), it reads: "The shoots of its fruit stalks are like the heads of devils."

The Bible's forbidden tree (Gen. 2:17) was a tree of the knowledge of good and evil. This also tells us that the tree was person, for trees know nothing! This tree of knowledge was forbidden to Adam and Eve. The only one whom this tree could be is the devil. After deceiving Adam and his wife, he has been called a serpent due to his keen knowledge of tricks and his acts of shrewdness; he made his acquaintance with Adam and his wife in the absence of God. Since this is the nature of a liar, he can best lie to the people when truth is absent.

We know that there was never a time when an actual serpent (or snake) could talk and deceive people in the knowledge of God's law. This same serpent is mentioned in Revelation 12: 9 as a deceiver. There (12:9) it is made clear to us that the serpent is "the dragon, devil and satan which deceiveth the whole world." In Gen. (3:1) he appeared in the Garden of Paradise before the woman and deceived her (Rev. 12:4). He stood before the woman who was ready to be delivered to devour her child as soon as it is born.

The serpent, the devil, dragon, satan, seems to have been seeking the weaker part of man (the woman) to bring to naught the man—the Divine Man. It is his first and last trick to deceive the people of God through the woman or with the woman. He is using his woman to tempt the black man by parading her half-nude before his eyes and with public love-making, indecent kissing and dancing over radio and television screens and throughout their public papers and magazines. He is flooding the world with propaganda against God and His true religion, Islam. He stands before the so-called Negro woman to deceive her by feigning love and love-making with her, give the so-called Negro woman preference over her husband or brother in hiring.

In some cities, the Negro woman receives a much higher salary that the so-called Negro man. The devil takes the so-called Negro woman and puts his hands and arms around her body. She may be married or single, it makes no difference. Whenever he can he is making eyes at her. This is an outright destruction of the moral principles of the black man.

In some cities, we convert five to one woman. The so-called Negroes should unite and put a stop to the destruction of their women by the serpent. The woman in (Rev. 12:4) actually refers to the last Apostle of God, and her child refers to his followers, or the entire Negro race as they are called, who are not ready to be delivered (go to their own).

THE BLOOD SHEDDER

According to the word of Allah (God) and the history of the world, since the grafting of the Caucasian race 6,000 years ago, they have caused more bloodshed than any people known to the black nation. Born murderers, their very nature is to murder. The Bible and Holy Qur-an Sharrieff are full of teachings of this bloody race of devils. They shed the life blood of all life, even their own, and are scientists at deceiving the black people.

They deceived the very people of Paradise (Bible, Gen. 3:13). They killed their own brother (Gen. 4:8). The innocent earth's blood (Gen. 4:10) revealed it to its Maker (thy brother's blood cryeth unto me from the ground). The very earth, the soil of America, soaked with the innocent blood of the so-called Negroes shed by this race of devils, now crieth out to its Maker for her burden of carrying the innocent blood of the righteous slain upon her. Let us take a look at the devil's creation from the teaching of the Holy Qur-an.

"And when your Lord said to the angels, I am going to place in the earth one who shall rule, the angels said: "What will Thou place in it such as shall make mischief in it and shed blood, we celebrate Thy praise and extol Thy holiness" (Holy Qur-an Sharrieff 2:30).

This devil race has and still is doing just that—making mischief and shedding blood of the black nation whom they were grafted from. Your Lord said to the angels, "Surely I am going to create a mortal of the essence of black mud fashioned in shape" (Holy Qur-an Sharrieff, 15:28).

The essence of black mud (the black nation) mentioned is only symbolic, which actually means the sperm of the black nation, and they refused to recognize the black nation as their equal though they were made from and by a black scientist (named Yakub). They can never see their way in submitting to Allah and the religion Islam and His prophets.

The slave-masters' every cry is to beat—beat—kill—kill—the so-called Negroes. Maybe the day has arrived that Allah will return to the devils—that which they have been so anxious to pour on the poor innocent so-called Negroes. Allah will give you your own blood to drink like water and your arms and allies will not help you against him (Rev. 16:6).

The heads and bodies of the so-called Negroes are used to test the clubs and guns of the devils, and yet the poor, foolish, so-called Negroes admire the devils regardless to how they are treated.

America is now under Divine Plagues. One will come after the other until she is destroyed. Allah has said it.

NOT YOUR BROTHER

The so-called American Negroes actually believe that they have the same right as American citizens to go any place in white America they please and be accepted or allowed to enter into white society on an equal basis with the white man.

If you understood that which you are seeking to be accepted into and if you understood the nature of those whom you are seeking to integrate with you would, instead, be seeking your own people's society or building one of your own on some land or territory separate from the American whites.

We need land wherein we can build our own society free from the tension, hatred and violence that have accompanied our race relationship with the white race of America.

When you learn that the white man is not your brother, you will readily begin to see and accept the Divine Plan that Almighty Allah (God) has in the working for our people. Who has been our aggressors and murderers ever since we have been in America? Who, by nature, was made quick to shed blood— even his own?

And how much easier it is for them to shed our blood. They are heartless, merciless, when it comes to you and me we all know the true answer, whether you wish to bear witness with your tongues or with your hands, we know that the white man is our aggressor—the hater of good, justice and equality for you and me.

Do not expect your former slave-master's children to give you the privileges to do as you desire in his own house. According to the Emancipation Proclamation, we as a people were proclaimed free to go for ourselves. In other words, we were on our own to build a nation of our own regardless of our hardships and barriers.

But this we did not do because we were unable and unqualified in the knowledge of self and how to build a civilization of our own. And today our people are too afraid and doubtful even though a way is being made in this wilderness by Allah (God) in Person.

Many so-called Negroes despise and hate "Black Supremacy" without having knowledge of what this means, and yet they support and believe in "White Supremacy." If you say you do not either, then you are neutral. But nay—some must rule over the other. It is the law of nature.

The ex-slaves of America desire to go to their white masters' restaurants instead of building one for self and kind. You want to go to their schools and learn with white people who hate your very shadows.

I say to you this is a disgrace to act so dependent and loving toward a people who have been your worst enemies and who will go to war against each other before they will give you and me equal justice under their own laws.

Allah (God) is offering you heaven at once on accepting Him for your God, enjoyment and unlimited progress in the new world of universal peace and happiness, unlike anything seen, heard or imagined since the creation of the universe.

You are not American citizens or members of the white man's world. The only American citizens are the white people who are originally from Europe. So why fight a losing battle by trying to be recognized as something you are not and never will be. I am not trying to disillusion you but merely telling you the truth.

Almighty Allah came to make Himself known that He alone is God and beside Him there is no God His equal—I know of none His equal. I am going to do my part in representing Him in teaching His words of Truth.

We do not need soft talk when it comes to the truth, we need the thrust that will pull us off our knees from begging and put us on our feet as intelligent men and women no longer dependent upon the slave-master but striving to build an independent nation of our own as others have done before us.

We the black people in America have to fight against great opposition coming to us from all sides—the ignorant blacks and the wise, skillful whites who envy our progress in the way of self-support.

They hate the wide spread of the Truth that Allah has re-

vealed here in the worst part of our Planet Earth. A truck load
of our papers MUHAMMAD SPEAKS was set afire by the envious and jealous haters of the progress this paper is making
toward getting the Truth to the mentally dead of our people.
Oh seek refuge in Allah from such evil, for I know a day that
is coming to them when they will wish they, too, were Muslims.

WILL WHITE CHRISTIANS
ACCEPT ISLAM?

We have thousands of the darker people joining Islam all over
the earth, but a very few whites accept Islam. The door of Islam
has always been open to everyone who desired to accept it, but
today it is different. The door of this religion is now being
closed against the white race which has repeatedly rejected Islam,
made mockery of it, persecuted and killed the Prophets and the
believers (the followers), hid and concealed the truth of it and
its God, Allah, who is the God of the Universe, and Islam, His
only religion. They follow the poor teacher of Islam seeking a
way or an excuse to kill him. They put spies (stool pigeons)
on him to try to find a way to charge him with something other
than the truth in order to do him evil for the truth's sake that
he teaches.

As David says in his Psalms 94:20: "Shall the throne of iniquity have fellowship with thee, which frameth mischief by a
law?" The poor lost-found members of the Tribe of Shabazz
(nicknamed "Negroes" by their slave-masters) can well understand that they are the victims of such a frameup against them
throughout America when they seek truth, love and unity among
themselves. The white race does not want to see the poor black
people of America united in Islam, a religion that is of Allah
(God) backed by the spirit and power of God, to unite all of
its believers into one nation of brotherhood. It is the only uni-
fying religion known and tried by the races and nations of earth.
This the white race knows.

They were offered Islam by Musa (Moses), Jesus, Muhammad
and many other prophets, but they rejected it. "And certainly
we raised in every nation an Apostle saying serve Allah and shun
the devil. So there were others against whom error was due;
therefore, travel in the land, then see what was the end of the

rejectors" (Holy Qur-an 16:36). The prophets had delivered to them the message of truth and shown them the right way; but they chose to remain in error (evil doings). This stands true of this people today. They know the truth, and right from wrong, but they like wrong or evil better than right; therefore, they are against Islam and its truth. The Holy Qur-an says:

"Surely we have revealed to you as we revealed to Noah and the Prophets after him, and we revealed to Abraham and Ishmael and the Tribes, and Jesus, Job and Jonah, Aaron, Solomon, and we gave to David a scripture. We sent Apostles as the givers of good news and as warners, so that people should not have a plea against Allah after the coming of the Apostles" (4:163, 165). The Messengers of Allah (God) bring good news to the people, but if that good news is rejected, therefore, they are warned that bad news will come.

The Christian white world, whose leader and teacher is the Pope of Rome (the Father of the church) claims that Jesus brought a new religion to them. But the scripture of both Bible and Holy Qur-an denies such false charge, and makes Jesus' religion the same as the Prophets' who were before Him. Muhammad was also given the same religion of Jesus and the Prophets before Him.

The Holy Qur-an further says: "Surely those who believe, and those who are Jews, and the Christians, and the Sabians, whoever believes in Allah and the last day and does good, they shall have their reward from their Lord, and there is no fear for them, nor shall they grieve" (2:62). The religion of Islam is everything that we need for salvation. The poor black man is waking up to this truth and is coming into Islam by the thousands, against the wishes of the whites, because of the love and unity and universal friendship which Islam brings to the believers. This is what the poor black man of America needs more of — TRUE FRIENDS! He gets them in Islam! The white race has and still is trying to keep us from having true friends among our own kind or even among ourselves here in America. Because of the truth of Islam, they are now charging that it fans hate against them.

THE WHITE RACE'S FALSE CLAIM TO BE DIVINE, CHOSEN PEOPLE

According to the Bible (Gen. 3:20-24), Adam and his wife were the first parents of all people (white race only) and the first sinners. According to the Word of Allah, he was driven from the Garden of Paradise into the hills and caves of West Asia, or as they now call it, "Europe," to live his evil life in the West and not in the Holy Land of the East. "Therefore, the Lord God sent him (Adam) forth from the Garden of Eden, to till the ground from whence he was taken. So He drove out the man; and He placed at the east of the Garden of Eden cherubims (Muslim guards) and a flaming sword which turned every way to keep the devils out of the way of the tree of life (the nation of Islam)." The sword of Islam prevented the Adamic race from crossing the border of Europe and Asia to make trouble among the Muslims for 2,000 years after they were driven out of the Holy Land and away from the people, for their mischief-making, lying and disturbing the peace of the righteous nation of Islam.

The Holy Qur-an says: "But the devil made them both fall from it, and caused them to depart from that (state) in which they were; and we said: "Get forth, some of you being the enemies of others, and there is for you in the earth an abode and a provision for a time!" (The time here refers to the limited time of the Adamic race. The time is 6,000 years.) According to the above verse (2:36), they were driven out because they were the enemies of the people of the Garden, in these words: "Get forth, some of you being the enemies of others." The others cannot refer to any others than the people of the Garden (the Muslims.)

The Adamic race is still the enemy of the Muslims (the black man). Nevertheless, Allah did not deprive the Adamic race right guidance through His prophets, whom they persecuted and killed. The Adamic white race's history is proof that they are the enemies of God and the righteous, for they never did sincerely accept a prophet of God. Can they now claim to be the chosen race of God? Why would God limit their time of rule? Why did God send His prophets to warn them that He was going to destroy them? Holy Qur-an (7:14): "He said (the devil) respite me until the day when they are raised up." Those that are referred to as being "raised up" refer to the resurrection of the black man into the knowledge of the white race as being the devils, the enemies of Allah (God) and the black nation. "He as (*the devil*) said: Thou hast caused me to remain disappointed, I will certainly lie in wait for them in Thy straight path" (Holy Qur-an 7:16). What Allah disappointed the devils in was the limiting of their rule over the nations and making it manifest to the world of black man that they are the enemies and great deceivers of the righteous.

The white race is not, and never will be, the chosen people of Allah (God). They are the chosen people of their father Yakub, the devil.

PRAYER SERVICE

PRAYER IN ISLAM

"Surely prayer keeps [one] away from indecency and evil; and certainly the remembrance of Allah is the greatest [force] and Allah knows what you do" (Holy Qur-an 29:45).

Surely the best way to strive to be upright in a sinful world is to pray continuously to the One True God, whose proper name is Allah, for guidance.

As we are generally sinful and easily yield to temptations, it is only fitting to keep up prayer.

Allah, the One True God, has blessed us with the universe. A sun to shine and brighten up the heavens, giving light for us to see; warmth enabling us to live, and causing vegetation to grow and all life to exist. We reside on the planet through His will, so why should we not pray and continuously thank Him for this privilege?

He it is who created the atmosphere for us to breathe. He it is who created all good vegetation for us to eat, plus the fowl and other animals which we partake of daily. He it is who created the beautiful atmosphere in which we live, and which we, with our own hands, mutilate and destroy for lack of proper guidance.

We cannot improve upon the nature in which Allah (God) has created all beautiful things, yet we try. We cannot substitute the original beauty with artificial creations, yet we try. So let us realize the power of Allah, that without Him we cannot exist, and make obeisance to Allah through our prayers to Him.

Prayer is obligatory in Islam (the true religion). "And remember Allah's favor upon you and the covenant which He made with you, when you said, "We hear and we obey," and fear Allah. Surely Allah knows well what is in our minds.

"O ye who believe! Be steadfast in the cause of Allah, bearing witness in equity; and let not a people's enmity incite you to act otherwise than with justice," says the Holy Qur-an. Be always just; that is nearer righteousness. And fear Allah. Surely

Allah is aware of what you do.

Allah has promised those who believe and do good deeds that they shall have forgiveness and a great reward (Holy Quran 8:10).

We owe our very lives to Allah, the Lord of all the worlds. Why should we not thank Him? Our every good thought we owe to Allah, the beneficent, the merciful. Surely as often as we sin, we turn to Him in prayer. He is most merciful and grants us pardon and oftentimes we drift back again to some other flaw. For this we must turn to Him again, asking to be forgiven. Surely Allah knows what is in our hearts, and what is more, He is oft-forgiving.

He it is who is the All Perfect One, who knows our imperfection and pardons most through His Messenger. Remember: And the best way for remembrance of Allah (God) is through prayer.

The five prayers of the day are spiritual refreshments and he who cleanses himself in and out leaves no filthiness. It would be an insult to invite His Lord's holy spirit into a house the outside of which was filthy.

Why should we not pray five times a day to our Maker since we feed our bodies three times a day? What is so important that would keep us away from prayer to the Originator of the heavens and the earth?

Let us give praises to our God and submit ourselves to the Lord of the worlds and learn how to pray the right prayers in the right manner. Let us serve the One True God, whose proper name is Allah, in the right state.

"My Lord, make me to keep up prayer, and my offspring too. Our Lord, accept the prayer. Our Lord, grant Thy protection to me and to my parents and to the faithful on the day when the reckoning will be taken." (The prayer of the Muslims will get you an answer!)

THE SIGNIFICANCE OF PRAYER

"O you who believe, remember Allah, remembering Him frequently and glorifying Him morning and evening. He it is Who sends His blessings on you, and so do His angels, that He may bring you forth out of utter darkness into the light and

*He is merciful to the believers [Prayer is better
than sleep.]"* (Holy Qur-an 33:41-43).

This alone is salvation, just to be brought out of the darkness
of ignorance into the light of the truth. Who is in more need
of the truth than the American so-called Negroes who do not
have the knowledge of self nor of anyone else, and who love
those who hate them and spitefully use them?

"O Prophet, surely we have sent you as a witness and as a
bearer of good news and as a warner and as one inviting to
Allah by His permission and as a light-giving torch" (Holy Qur-
an 33:45, 46). Come to success; prayer and obedience to Allah
will bring you success. The prayer is recited standing erect with
face towards the east with hands raised and declaring to the one
God, Allah, that he has turned himself to Allah (God), the
originator of the heavens and earth. This prayer and positions
are especially designed and worded for those lost sheep (the
so-called Negroes) who have been lost from the knowledge of
their God and people and now declare that they are turned
again to their God, Allah, and are upright to Him.

Imagine a native Muslim who never was lost from Allah and
His people in the Holy Land or Holy City, reciting the above
prayer. The prayer has been turned into the wrong direction.
He is in the west, looking again due east, confessing his faults
for going astray from his God and people and declaring that
he has been unjust to himself. He confesses his faults and
declares that none can grant him protection from his faults but
Allah (God). He further asks that evil morals be turned away
from him and that he be guided to the best of morals. He is
now leaving the infidels of the west who brought him into darkness and pleading to be guided to better morals. Surely we, the
so-called Negroes, lost all of our good morals among the enemies
of the West. The type of the so-called Negroes is given in many
parables of the Bible. In fact, if the Bible is rightly understood,
it is referring to none other than the so-called Negroes and their
enemies, the chosen people of God to whom the God gave the
firstborn (convert), and even the (Mahdi) Christ offered His life
to restore the so-called Negroes again to their own kind.

But the so-called Negroes are blinded with a picture of the
Jews' salvation and cannot see their own selves in prophecy. They
should shout with joy over the understanding that God has and
is causing me to give them of the Book.

It is a prayer for forgiveness that Solomon advised you and me to make to Allah if we be lost from our own under the name of Israel (II Chronicles 6:36 - 39). Solomon was a Muslim prophet and king. He and his father David, were of the black nation. He advised us to pray toward our own land and toward the Holy City (Mecca) which He has chosen.

In the parables of the prodigal son (which is one of the most beautiful) and of the lost sheep it is, or should be, easier for the so-called Negroes to see that they are the ones referred to. It is with the turning toward his home and father's house to pray that the sins of the prodigal son were forgiven, and he was accepted by his father and restored to his rightful place among his brethren. It is the turning again of the lost-found so-called Negro—the tribe of Shabazz—in prayer to Allah, their true God and His true religion, Islam, that they will be seated in heaven overnight (at once). The enemy knows this as well as I.

The prayer service is divided into two parts, one to be said in private and the other to be performed in congregation, preferably in a Mosque. While the private part is meant simply for the development of the inner self of man, the public part has other ends as well in view: ends, that, indeed, make the Islamic prayer a mighty force in the unification of the human race.

In the first place, this gathering of all people living in the same vicinity five times daily in the Mosque, is a help to the establishment of healthy social relations. In the daily service these relations are limited to a narrow circle, i.e., to members of the same neighborhood. But the circle becomes wider in the weekly Friday service which gathers together all Muslim members of a particular locality and becomes still wider, in the two great "Id" gatherings.

Thus, prayer promotes social relations between the different sections of the Muslim community. Far more important than this, however, is the leveling of social differences brought about by means of congregational prayer. Once within the doors of the Mosque, every Muslim feels himself in an atmosphere of equality and love. Before their Maker they all stand shoulder to shoulder, the king along with his poorest subject, the rich arrayed in gorgeous robes, the beggar clad in rags.

Nay, the king or rich man standing in a back row will have to lay his head, prostrating himself before God, at the feet of a slave or a beggar standing in the front. There could be no more leveling influence in the world. Differences of rank, wealth and color vanish within the Mosque and quite a new atmosphere, an atmosphere of brotherhood, equality and love, totally different from the outside world, prevails within the holy precincts.

To be able to breathe, five times daily, in an atmosphere of perfect peace in a world of strife and struggle, of equality where inequality is the order of the day, and of love amid the petty jealousies and enmities of daily life, is indeed a blessing. But it is more than a blessing; for it is the great lesson of life. Man has to work amidst inequalities, amidst strife and struggle, amidst scenes of hatred and enmity, and yet he is drawn out of these five times a day and made to realize that equality, fraternity and love are the real sources of human happiness.

The time spent on prayer is not, therefore, wasted even from the point of view of active humanitarianism; on the contrary, the best use of it is made in learning those great lessons which make life worth living. And these lessons of fraternity, equality and love, when put into practice in daily life, serve as foundations for the unification of the human race and of the lasting civilization of mankind.

In fact, the five daily congregational prayers are meant, among other things, to carry into practice the theoretical lessons of equality and fraternity for which Islam stands; and, however, much Islam may have preached in words the equality of man and the fraternity of the community of Islam, all this would have remained a dead letter, had it not been translated into the everyday life of man through the institution of five daily congregational prayers.

MUSLIM PRAYER SERVICE AND ITS MEANINGS

We must study the words and the different positions taken by the Muslim in his daily prayer. This helps us to understand better the true way to worship Allah (God). The following short prayer should be said by all darker people in America, as it fits us so well.

"Our Lord, do not punish us if we forget or make a mistake. Our Lord, do not lay on us a burden as Thou didst lay on those before us. Our Lord, do not impose upon us that which we have not the strength to bear; and pardon us and grant us protection and have mercy on us. Thou art our protector, so help us against the unbelieving people."

Our prayer in the past was made to Jesus, the last prophet God sent to the Jews, according to the way we were taught. It is wrong to take Jesus or any prophet of God as His equal. We may pray to God in the names of the prophets, but not pray directly to the prophet. The Sender (God) is greater than the sent.

We have been away from our own people and native land so long that we no longer turn in the direction of home to pray. You follow the way of your enemies who are against Allah (God) and His religion (Islam) and all black mankind. You will be acting wisely to begin turning and traveling eastward, to the God of our fathers, otherwise your prayers are hopelessly made to Jesus and to a god which neither you nor your teachers know anything of.

According to the teachers of Christianity, no man has ever seen Him nor can see Him unless he dies. That is infidel teaching. Why are you representing something that no man has ever seen nor will see (a mystery god; unknown)? Why are you praying to a dead prophet who, the infidel teachers claim, is now alive in heaven, sitting on the right side of His Father, who is called a spirit, yet the Son is not for He has flesh and bones. And this flesh of the Son, wounded 2,000 years ago, does not heal nor does it decay, according to the Christians' religion?

This is the greatest falsehood ever told, or the greatest mistake ever made. Such doctrine cannot be proved true. Most of such believers will try to contend that the spirit which they feel that the Christians worship, and still there is no proof that God is something other than man, for a spirit must have a base. Let us recite another prayer of the Muslim.

"Glory to Thee, O Allah, and Thine is the praise. Blessed is Thy name and exalted is Thy majesty and there is none to be served besides Thee. I betake me for refuge to Allah against the accursed devil."

Study the words of the Muslims' prayers and try finding anything to equal them in any other religion. The Christians have no intelligent prayer service set forth in the Bible. There is no mention of God teaching Adam to pray. Jesus set forth only one prayer to His disciples and did not appoint any certain time to recite it.

The following is the oft-repeated prayer of the Muslims:

"In the name of Allah, the Beneficent, the Merciful; all praise is due to Allah, the Lord of the worlds, the Beneficent, the Merciful, Master of the day of requittal. Thee do we serve and Thee do we beseech for help. Guide us on the right path of those upon whom Thou hast bestowed favors, not of those upon whom Thy wrath is brought down, nor of those who go astray. Amen."

What a good prayer for one who is lost from the right direction as the so-called Negroes are to pray. They (the white race) cannot regain paradise because they are not members of that family. But, on the other hand, the lost-found so-called Negroes are really, by nature, members of the original family of paradise. It was by prayer and the turning in the right direction (toward the Holy Temple Mecca) that delivered Jonah from the belly of the fish (Jonah 2:2-4) which is only a type of us here in America (the anti-typical fish) who has swallowed us.

Our prayers will be speedily heard and Allah will fight our battles against our enemies and bring them to disgrace.

TIME OF PRAYER AND ITS MEANING

NOTE: *The morning prayer is of two parts, the first part called FARD in Arabic and the other part called TRADITION, and it is made obligatory. The morning prayer being obligatory is called FARD, meaning the early morning.*

The Great Mahdi has taken FARD as a name for himself corresponding with the time of His coming—which is in the early days (or years) of the seventh thousand years. The early morning is the first part of the seventh thousand years and the year under the name Millennium (which the Christians say means the 1,000 years Christ will reign on the earth).

This is the 1,000 years which it will take to restore peace and honor, after the removal of peace breakers. This time also includes the birth of a new nation from the mentally dead. However, the name FARD fits the context.

We are reminded that this prayer is made obligatory; it is also binding upon the Believers (Muslims) in Allah (God) to obey Him. For in that 1,000 years of Millennium, the disbelievers will cease to be. And to those who live in that time it shall be binding upon them to serve and obey One God: Fard Muhammad the Great Mahdi, or Allah in Person. The Mahdi must restore the Kingdom of Islam and He must weed out from the kingdom of Islam all disbelievers. This He will do in His time.

FARD is a name many of the scholars have said is not one of the 99 attributes, but still it is a name that is self-independent, and one which means that the Believers are obligated to obey. We can see clearly why He took this Name (FARD) for Himself.

We are now living in the early morning of that seventh thousand years. The world of evil was given 6,000 years to reign over the righteous. Now, since their time expired in 1914, as all the religious scientists agree, we are in the seven-thousandth year since the creation of Adam, or the Caucasian race. It shall be binding upon you to serve and obey the Great Mahdi (FARD MUHAMMAD) or else be cut off from the people of righteousness.

All praise is due to our Lord and Saviour, Master Fard Muhammad. To Him do we submit; to Him we fly for refuge from the evils of Yakub's civilization.

And remember, the time that we are living in is the end of the world we have known and the coming in of the world of Allah—the world of peace and security. Having this in mind, we must be mindful of the things that are written. The following verse warns the powers of this world that their like existed before and Allah destroyed them:

"Travel in the land, then see what was the end of those before! Most of them were polytheists" (Holy Qur-an 30:42).

We read of the history of the flood that drowned a disobedient people who refused to take warnings from Allah's prophet, Noah. The following verse warns you and me, the so-called American Negroes, that after nearly one hundred years we have not been able to see that Christianity is not an upright religion; and it further warns us that on that day we will be separated. These days now approach you and me, SO MAKE A DECISION:

"Then set thyself, being upright, to the right religion before there come from Allah the day which cannot be averted: on that day they will be separated!" (Holy Qur-an 30:43).

"Observe prayers in the early morning at the close of the day, and at the approach of the night. Prayers are good deeds which drive away the evil doing" (Holy Qur-an 11:114).

"Glorify Allah (by rendering prayers to Him) when it is evening and in the morning—praise to Him in the heavens and the earth—and in the afternoon and at noontide" (Ibid., 30:17).

"Put up then with what they say; and celebrate the praise of your Lord before sunrise, and before sun setting, and during the night do thou praise Him, and in the extreme of the day, so that thou mayest be well pleased" (Ibid. 20:130).

"Observe prayers at sunset until the first darkening of the night and observe reading (the Qur-an) at daybreak. Lo! the recital of the Qur-an (that is rendering prayer) is ever witnessed. And some part of the night awake for it, a largess for thee. It may be that your Lord will raise thee to a praised state" (Ibid., 17:78-79).

"Take aid by observing patience and prayer" (Ibid., 2:45).

"When you have fulfilled your prayer, remember Allah, standing and sitting and lying on your sides. And when you are in safety then be steadfast in prayer. Verily prayer is a timed ordinance on the believers" (Ibid., 4:103).

"That which leads man to infidelity is neglect of prayers."

"No one of you must say his prayers in a garment without covering the whole body."

"Allah accepts not the prayers of a woman arrived at puberty unless she covers her head as well as the whole body."

"The five stated prayers erase the sins which have been committed during the intervals between them, if they have not been mortal sins."

"The prayers of a person will not be accepted, who has broken his ablution until he completes another ablution."

Order your children to say the state prayers when they are seven years of age, and beat them if they do not do so when they are ten years old."

"Tell me if any one of you had a rivulet before his doors and bathed five times a day therein whether any dirt would remain on his body? The companions said, 'Nothing would remain.' The Prophet said, 'In this manner will, the five daily prayers as ordered by Allah erase all minor sins.' "

The lost-found joins the righteous in prayer for the first time upon their finding by Allah.

We see him turning himself to Allah to recite the prayer of the righteous. The presence of Allah is like the sun in all its brilliance on him in the early morning after a long dreary night and his first thought was to rise up and prepare for the day.

We see him washing his hands and all the exposed parts of his body. We see him washing his face, his eyes, ears, mouth and nose and even those wet hands go over his head to clean the very scalp because he is now turning for the first time, to His God, Allah. And looking upon the presence of God and the light which He has shone upon him makes him to feel he was unclean and that he needed to clean up. Even the outer appearance is to be cleaned in the presence of God to hear His words of guidance.

He stretches forth his hand while standing as erect as a soldier before his captain, at attention. He has said that he has surely turned himself to Allah. He has taken an oath that he will not worship any God but Allah and that his prayer, his sacrifice, his life and death are all for Allah. He has declared that Allah has no associate and he is commanded not to set up any rivals with Allah.

He is now ready to enter the prayer service of the Nation of Islam and to recite the oft-repeated prayer. He closes his eyes against looking upon the world of evils and filth. He has washed his ears from the hearing of evil. He takes no more part in listening to the conversation of the evil doers.

He has washed his nostrils from even the smell of things offensive to the intelligent and decent society of righteousness. He has washed out his mouth; cleansed it as far down his throat as water could go without strangling him.

He washes his mouth from speaking of evil and planning evil and indecent things. He takes no more part in using his mouth and his tongue for the service of evil. Now, the mouth and the language his tongue utters are saying that which he believes will please Allah and the Nation of righteousness. He has washed his hands and all exposed parts of his body. His hands are washed from taking part in evil and indecent doings. His feet are washed from the evil service of walking, standing and sitting in the presence and path of the wicked.

He cleans them to walk towards Allah and stand in His Holy presence. His body garments are no more filthy, but now made sacred to the service of Allah.

We have heard him declare that Allah is the Greatest and that there is no God but Allah. He declares none deserves to be worshiped beside Allah and that Muhammad is His last Apostle. He has declared himself to be turning to the service of Allah and not pursuing the evils of the darkened West.

He now looks eastward to behold the light of God and his people from whence he has strayed for the last 400 years. He now wishes to be guided on the right path of Allah. Thus, he now recites the following prayer that is designed especially for him who was lost in the darkness of evils in the Western World of the Shaitans (devils of European origin).

He now prays in the Name of Allah and not to a mystery God that he nor anyone else has seen, nor does such exist. Neither does he pray in the name of dead prophets. He now stands in the light and reality of Almighty God, Allah, who appeared in the Person of Master W. F. Muhammad. He recites the following:

> *"In the Name of Allah, the Most Merciful. All*
> *praise is due to Allah the Lord of the Worlds, the*
> *Most Merciful Master of the Day of Requital.*
> *Thee do we serve and Thee do we beseech for help.*
> *O Allah, guide us on the right path; the path of*
> *those upon whom Thou has bestowed favors and*
> *not of those upon whom Thy wrath is brought*
> *down, nor of those who go astray. Amen."*

As you notice in the above prayer, it is designed for one who has lost himself from the right path of Allah. He now wishes to be guided on that path the Prophets walked in; upon the path that Allah has bestowed favors for those who walk thereon.

He now desires favors, Divine favors, to be bestowed upon him after being deprived of friendship and favors from those who walk in darkness of evil and murder. He desires not to walk in the path of those whom Allah dislikes and is angry with, and whom Allah has sent His curse upon in the past and has recorded it in history for their own warning and as an example of what will befall them and those who wilfully and knowingly go astray from His (Allah's) path. He has declared Allah to be the final judge on the day of resurrection.

THE MORNING PRAYER

Surely I have turned myself, being upright, to Him who originated the heavens and the earth and I am not of the polytheists. Surely my prayer and my sacrifice and my life and my death are all for Allah, the Lord of the Worlds; no associate has He, and this am I commanded and I am of those who submit.

"O Allah! Thou art the King, there is no god but Thee; Thou art my Lord and I am Thy servant. I have been unjust to myself and I confess my faults so grant me protection against all my faults, for none grants protection against faults but Thee, and guide me to the best of morals, for none guides to the best of them but Thee, and turns away from me the evil morals but Thee."

The following brief prayer is however, the one more generally adopted.

"Glory to Thee, O Allah! Thine is the praise and blessed is Thy Name and exalted is Thy Majesty and there is none to be served beside Thee. I betake me for refuge to Allah against the accursed devil."

A Muslim must say his prayers. When we say that we are Muslims (those who have submitted to the will of Allah) and then we must give praises to the One to whom we have submitted, to do His will.

If we are believers in the Divine Supreme Being, we are always in need of His help, one way or another. Therefore, it is necessary that we give praises to Him and thanks, and ask forgiveness for any wrongdoing on our part.

Praising His name in the saying of prayers, pouring out the heart's sentiment before and to our Divine Supreme Being shows submission and proves to the world that our life and our death are all for Allah.

This above prayer is divided into two parts; one part called Fard and the other one tradition, or I should say it is tradition that the Muslim should pray and give praises to Allah. It is not something just started in the time of Mohammed, 1,400 years ago, but it has always been the righteous way to do (to pray and give praises to Allah).

Prayer is something that we must and are compelled to do if we expect guidance and mercy from Allah. And Allah's using Fard as His name here on His coming teaches us that if we expect to be successful, we must bow in submission to the will of Master Fard Muhammad; the All Wise God in Person who is worthy to be praised and praised much.

It is really the nature of the righteous to give praise and honor to Allah. The Prayer is one of the greatest prayers that we can pray. Being lost from Allah and from our people and native land or country, we now turn ourselves to Allah. We live right to Him, who originated the heavens and the earth.

But we must remember we are taking an oath in this prayer, that we will not accept any god but Allah, in the words: "My prayers, my sacrifice, my life and death are all for Allah."

We live for Allah; we die for Allah; we sacrifice all we have and our lives for Allah and His cause.

Let the Muslims and hyprocrites who read this teaching taught in the above prayer know that we have taken an oath with our life to live for Allah and sacrifice everything we have for Allah and that we will even die for Allah!

This will be held against us on the day we shall meet Allah who turns back on their heels and you who become hypocrites read, study and learn the prayer above and recite it if you are believers as often as you can and know that you have fled to Allah and have taken refuge in Him against the accursed devils.

The devils were cursed from the day they were created—or grafted—until this day and a doom was fixed for them. You are not blind to the knowledge of the devil; you know who the real devil is today.

As the Holy Qur-an gives it to you and me, they are our open enemies—that race which is called the Caucasian race, or the European white race.

THE PREPARATIONS
AND ITS MEANING

1. The washing and cleansing of all exposed parts of the body of filth and uncleanness, to stand and bow before the Lord of the Worlds.
2. The rinsing out of the mouth (the impure and evil that the mouth is guilty of speaking).

3. The washing of the hands that are subject to the handling of clean and unclean things. They are cleansed to be spread before Allah, the Lord of the Worlds.

The Holy Qur-an says that our hands will bear witness against the evil-doers on the Day of Resurrection. They will say: "O hands why hast thou borne witness against me? The hands will say: "As Allah makes everything to bear witness, so has He made us to bear witness." Whatever we do, every member of our body plays a part in it.

4. The feet are washed up to the ankles if they were exposed. The feet should be washed once every day, even though one wears shoes.

5. A total bath should be taken if there were sexual relations.

He is now ready for prayer. He stands erect with his face and body towards the rising of the sun (the East) in the direction that the earth is rotating, and all the planets.

In this direction is the Holy City of Mecca, the only Holy place on the earth. From this direction do we look for Allah (God) and His Angels to come to judge the world.

6. He lifts his opened hands with his thumbs pointing towards his ear lobes. He says, "Allah is the Greatest" (Twice). "I bear witness that none deserves to be worshiped besides Allah (repeated twice) and that Muhammad is His last Apostle" (twice).

The regular Prayer Caller in the minarets of the Mosque calls the prayer from four (4) directions: East, West, North and South. He repeats "Allah is the Greatest" four times.

7. He begins his prayer by saying: "Surely I have turned myself to Thee being upright to Him who originated the heavens and the earth and I am not of the polythesists. Surely my prayer, my sacrifices, my life and my death are all for Allah, the Lord of the Worlds. No associate has He, and this am I commanded. Oh Allah, Thou art the King, there is no God but Thee. Thou art my Lord and I am Thy servant."

THE MEANINGS:

First, the cleansing of the body before asking prayer to the Most Honored and Wisest Person in the Universe, the Lord and King over all, none is His equal, shows respect for Him. He desires to show (in words) in his prayer that his words are clean and coming from a clean heart.

Should not that clean heart be a clean body? If one is offered clean water in an unclean outer surface of a glass, will he accept it? This is so with a Muslim; he believes in cleanness internally as well as externally.

THE DIFFERENT POSITIONS TAKEN IN PRAYER

Standing erect to address our Superior is proper and again it shows respect and honor. The raising of the hands with the palms open in the same direction shows an act of surrender to the King of Kings and Lord of the Worlds and is coming before Him with clean and emptied hands.

The hands, the most active members of our bodies, play the part of evil and good for the body. They sometimes bear witness for, or against us. The Muslims declare that there is only One God, and none deserves to be worshipped except Him. This is true.

Almost all religious persons acknowledge that there is but one God who made the heavens and the earth. The Muslims declare in one of their prayers that they worship Allah (God) in the best manner, in the direction (East) in which He turns Himself—towards the holiest of places and one day the whole of the people of earth will be just as holy or holier. I would say holier.

This position also has another meaning; it refers to the lost and found people of Islam. Before their return they must turn in this direction with clean hands and hearts, bow in submission to the will of Allah alone with righteousness that they may be welcomed to take their place again among their own people. This shall soon be made clear to my people here, that if holy war be declared, no so-called Negro could return to his native land and people unless he or she accepts Allah as his God and Islam as his religion.

> "*O you who believe, enter into submission one and all, and do not follow the footsteps of the devil. Surely he is your open enemy.*" Holy Quran 2:208

Here the Muslim is about to begin his prayer. He has cleansed all the exposed parts of his body, washed out his mouth, nose and ears. Standing upright, with his face towards his Holy City

(Mecca), which is in the direction of sunrise, he lifts his cleansed hands up beside his head with the thumbs towards the lobes of his ears and declares that: "Allah is the Greatest" (four times), and that: "Nothing deserves to be worshiped but Allah."

What better preparation could have been made for the service of our God? With due respect and great honor, he is turned in the direction of sunrise in which our planet is carrying him at a speed of 1,037 1/3 miles per hour. Physically, he has turned his face in the direction in which he is traveling, and in which he looks forward to the light of day. From the same direction (sunrise) came all the spiritual light—the holy prophets, the holy land and the holy cities of the earth.

With his cleansed hands open, with the palms towards the Holy Land and cities, he signifies an open confession of his internal purity and entire submission to the will of Allah (God). Whatever evils he has committed with his hands, by washing them with the water of life he shows forth his heart's repentances for the evils that his hands have committed.

Now as the open cleansed hands show forth a sincere surrender to their Maker without concealing or hiding anything, so it is with the heart—that only Allah (God) can see into—is clear of the evils and desires forgiveness, for such evils have been washed from the heart, the ears from hearing them, and the eyes are closed to keep out the evil morals, for none can turn away from me the evil morals but Thee.

The above prayer is preferred as the morning prayer, but can be said by the individual any time that he likes. Here the prayer declares that he is strictly a believer in one God Who originated the universe (the Heavens and earth) and not in three, and further declares "that his sacrifice, life, and death are all for Allah (God) and to Him does he submit." He acknowledges his sins and asks protection against them, or rather against a future sin.

THE OPENING

The Fatiha, "Opening," is the first Chapter of the Holy Quran and constitutes the Muslim's prayer for guidance.

Here is a Prayer we shall recite.

"In the Name of Allah, the most Merciful, all praise is due Allah the Lord of the Worlds. The Most Merciful Master of the Day of Requital. Thee do we serve and Thee do we beseech for help. O Allah, guide us on the right path; the path of those upon whom Thou hast bestowed favors, and not of those upon whom thy wrath is brought down, nor of those who go astray. Amen."

This prayer is found in the first Sura (Chapter) of the Holy Qur-an, and is the opening of every Sura of the Holy Book except the ninth chapter (the chapter of the Hypocrites). He seeks the right guidance; he does not want to walk in the path of the Jews and Christians. He saw the Jews go astray from the right faith and cause the wrath of Allah to descend upon them and cause the Jews to suffer many afflictions and finally the loss of world independence. And they fell into the hands of their enemies wherever they sojourn.

And now, take notice of those who call themselves Christians going astray from the right path (Islam). Notice them going to the extreme by worshiping Jesus: first by falsely accusing Jesus of being the Son of Allah (God) born without the agency of man, thus accusing God of an act of adultery. They preach the rightful laws of God, but practice the laws of Satan and now have become the world's greatest trouble makers (war makers), and have caused the nations to deviate from the path of Allah (God). And now they are heading the entire world into total destruction.

He wants to be guided on the path of the Prophets of Allah where he can receive the favors of Allah. He has not as yet entered the congregational prayer service in the beautiful Mosques of the Holy Land of Islam to hear the caller of the faithful (early in the morning and five times a day) from the minarets of the Mosques. The caller with his hands raised to his ears goes from one door or window to the other (there are four in all); he opens it to the East, West, North and South saying; "Allah-u-Akbar" four times (which means: Allah is the Greatest regardless of what direction you may look). The beautiful words one may note from the caller at nearly the end of the call are these: "Come to prayer" (turning the face to the right, repeated twice). "Come to Success" (repeated twice). And turning the face to the left: "Prayer is better than sleep (repeated twice)."

The touch of Islam makes the lost-found have a sense of dignity and for the first time he feels that he should do something for self. And he desires to rid himself of the things that hinder him. He, therefore, now prays the following prayer:

*"O Allah! I seek Thy refuge from anxiety and
grief and I seek Thy refuge from lack of strength
and laziness and I seek Thy refuge from cowardice
and niggardliness and I seek Thy refuge from
being overpowered by debt and the oppression of
men. O Allah! Suffice Thou me with what is lawful to keep me away from what is prohibited and
with Thy grace make me free from want of what
is besides Thee."*

We, the lost-founds, should repeat the above prayer seven (7)
times a day. For it sums up our greatest hindrance to freedom
and self-independence. We must get away from the idea of depending on others to do for us what we can do for self. Fear,
cowardice and laziness are our greatest enemies. We are brave
enough to fight to preserve the white race's independence, but
not brave for self and kind. Shake such shackles off and face
the consequences like men and we all will be free!

KNOWLEDGE OF PRAYER

Since learning of the prayer service of Islam—the religion of
entire submission to the will of Allah—we see him now not only
trying to keep his internal parts clean, but the external parts too.
He washes his face, his hands, and all the exposed parts of his
body before going to prayer. Never before has he done such
under the cross (Christianity): prostrating himself with his shoes
off and his forehead kissing the rug or the bare earth in praises
and humble submission to the will of Allah (God).

He says again in the above prayer that he is thankful to Allah.
He thanks Allah for the knowledge of words to say, to know Him
to be the true God, to believe in and worship Him alone and not
to set up a rival to Him.

No more is he ungrateful to God as he declares in the following words: "We are not ungrateful to Thee." He no longer be-
friends an enemy of Allah. While under the cross (Christianity)
he befriended the enemies of God, thinking he was getting the
favor or friendship of God by loving and befriending every
creature whether of the righteous or the devils. In reading the
above prayer, we find him forsaking and casting off the ones who
do not obey Allah.

He is now in accord with the teachings of the Qur-an, the

Holy Book of Allah, and in accord with the teaching of Jesus and the Prophets. We will not find any Believers in Allah (God) who will befriend and show friendship to the enemies and disbelievers of Allah, though they be their near of kin, says the Holy Qur-an. And the Qur-an (60:4) gives us an example in Abraham, who forsook his father and declared that enmity and hatred had appeared between them until he believed in Allah alone.

The Bible again puts it in Jesus' words (Luke 14:26) as he says to the disciples that they must even hate their mothers and fathers and sisters and brothers or they could not be his followers. But here today in America, as you may know, the Christians teach that we should love everybody. This is just the deceitful way of the devils to get love and honor from the people of God under their religion (Christianity) that they organized in order to oppose the true religion of Allah, Islam.

He now further says and acknowledges that he prays to Allah alone and make obeisance as it reads in the words of the prayer as follows: "O Allah, Thee do we serve and to Thee do we pray and make obeisance."

He seeks refuge in no other God but Allah and he declares this in the following words of the prayer: "Thee do we flee and we are quick." He now hastens himself for refuge in a living God. A God that exists, a God he can depend upon for help, a God who knows and understands all of his life's trouble and woes.

He is not perfect; therefore, he hopes for mercy from the true God in the words of the prayer as follows: "We hope for Thy mercy. And fear Thy chastisement." He has learned of the suffering and chastisement of Allah upon those who disbelieve in Him.

He is no longer an unbeliever, for he has surely turned himself, being upright, to Allah, the Originator of the heavens and the earth.

PRAYERS TO PRAY

" *O Allah, we beseech Thy help and ask Thy protection and believe in Thee, and trust in Thee, and we laud Thee in the best manner and we thank Thee and we are not ungrateful to Thee, and we cast off and forsake him who disobeys Thee.*"

In the above prayer we learn that the whole of the Muslim prayer, as Maulvi Muhammad Ali says, "is only a declaration of divine majesty and glory, divine holiness and perfection and of the entire dependence of man on his Maker" (Preface of the Holy Qur-an).

If you would only adopt the saying of the Muslims' prayer, you would be helped. Of all the praying people on earth, the Muslims' worship to God is in the best manner. The words used in their prayers are the best and most humble. They cast off and forsake those who disobey Allah (God).

The Christians teach love for the enemy because of the fact that they are really the enemy and desire to mingle with you for the purpose of misleading you. It is nothing but right to sever friendly relations with those who do not care to serve and obey Allah (God).

There are many Muslims and black Christians who, for the sake of certain privileges, do not carry into practice the casting off of those who disobey Allah (God) and think it is a sin for the true righteous Muslims to do so. Today I am often asked, "Can white people attend your service?"

When told that white people are not Muslims, some of the ignorant Muslims falsely charge me in their writings and sayings as not teaching Islam. They also falsely charge that my teachings not only do not represent Islam, but that it is not recognized by the Muslim world. This is just what the enemies of Islam and the so-called Negroes of America desire that the so-called Negroes believe. They sow such lies in the hearts of the weak Muslims and the so-called Negroes in general. You are going to be greatly surprised. I have Allah (God) on my side to bring my people out of the darkness and power of our enemies; is not He (God) sufficient? And, most surely He is with me and I with Him. You most certainly will be the loser if you are not on our side.

The Lord's Prayer, as it is called, contains some words that should not have been written there, such as: "Lead us not into temptation." God will not lead us into temptation. It is the devils that tempt us to sin. The above words show a lack of confidence in God to lead us aright, that He must be reminded just how to lead us.

Another is: "Give us this day our daily bread." Here again, the words "this day" could lead one to believe that on that day the prayer was given, there was a shortage of bread, or that the Christians' prayers seek their physical bread first and spiritual bread last, even though the Bible says "You first seek the Kingdom of Heaven and all these things shall be added unto you" (Luke 12:31). In another place it says "Man shall not live by bread alone, but by every word that proceedeth out of the mouth of God" (Matthew 4:4).

These scriptures are contrary to the prayer, although it stands true of the Christians who seek bread, swine's flesh (the poison), whiskey, wine and beer first, and pray for spiritual food last.

The Bible shows (Exodus 16:2, 3, 8) that it was the want of bread and meat first of all that gave Moses and Aaron much trouble trying to lead the people into the spiritual knowledge of Jehovah and self-independence. They even said when they were hungry: "Would to God we had died by the hand of the Lord in the land of Egypt ' (Exodus 16:3).

Ofttimes, they angered Moses and Aaron by their longing for the food of their slave-masters even while on their way to freedom and self-independence.

The Muslims pray in their oft-repeated prayer to seek Allah's help in guiding them on the right path, the path of those whom God has favored and not on the path of those who have caused His anger to descend upon them (the Jews and Christians). This want of the slave-masters' bread, meat and luxuries is depriving the so-called Negroes today of their independence.

"O Allah, we beseech Thy help and ask Thy protection. We believe in Thee and trust in Thee. We worship Thee in the best manner and we thank Thee. We are not ungrateful to Thee and we cast off and forsake him who disobeys Thee. O Allah, Thee do we serve and to Thee do we pray and make obeisance. To Thee do we flee and we are quick. We hope for Thy mercy and we fear Thy chastisement, for surely Thy chastisement overtakes the unbelievers."

We now see the lost-found members of the great Black Nation, the original people of the sun, are greatly improving their prayer services and obedience to Almighty God Who, in the Person of Master Fard Muhammad, founded them and to Whom praises are due forever for bringing us Islam, the knowledge of God, our Friend, and the devil, our enemy.

To my people in America who bow in submission to Allah's will, He declares He will set us in heaven at once on our acceptance of Him as our God: money, good homes, and friendship in all walks of life. Read for yourself the promised reward and blessings prophesied in the Bible and Holy Qur-an for us who turn to Allah in the last days of the world of the infidels.

We have been looking toward the east, from the direction the light of Truth has come and we have been reading for the past few weeks of the prayers made by the lost-found members (so-called Negroes) of the great Nation of Islam and we are getting more knowledge of how to serve Allah in the best manner. As the above prayer reads, "We worship Allah in the best manner."

Remember, as we grow into the knowledge of Allah, the more we desire to serve Him faithfully and give praises to Him.

We hear the lost-found repeat the above words as follows: "O Allah, we beseech Thy help." For the first time he is calling on Allah for help. Before being found, however, he had lifted his eyes into space and called on the God that the enemy infidels had directed him, that actually does not exist. And he found no help coming to him from out of space.

But today, his prayer bears witness, since the coming of Allah in the Person of Master Fard Muhammad (to whom be given praise forever) that he receives help from God. He received no protection from the God somewhere above the sun, moon and stars that the enemy pointed out to him and the rest of the poor, lost-found members of the Asiatic Nation—the Nation of Islam. The lost-found received no help or protection until the appearance of Allah in the Person of Master Fard Muhammad to Whom praises are due forever.

We hear him say now that he "Ask Allah's protection and believe in Thee (Allah in the Person of Master Fard Muhammad to whom all praises are due forever) and trust in Thee." He is confident today. He now puts his trust in Allah who he knows will answer his prayers. As the Holy Qur-an teaches him, "Allah hears the prayers of the believers."

He worships Allah now in the best manner, as he says the following: "We laud Thee in the best manner and we thank Thee. We are not ungrateful to Thee and we cast off and forsake him who disobeys Thee." Even though they be his near of kin, a true believer will not befriend a disbeliever in Allah.

A PRAYER
FOR THE MESSENGER

The following prayer is for the Messenger of Allah: "O Allah make Muhammad successful and the true followers of Muhammad successful as Thou didst make Abraham successful and the true followers of Abraham successful. For surely Thou art praised and magnified in our midst. Allah bless Muhammad and the true followers of Muhammad as Thou didst bless Abraham and the true followers of Abraham. Surely Thou art praised and magnified in our midst."

In the above prayer, the Believers of the lost and found members of a great nation pray for the Messenger whom Allah (God) has raised among them; a guide to the lost and now found path of Allah. For 400 years they have been wandering in darkness, blinded by the touch of Satan, the devil.

But now the light of Allah has shone upon them and they have turned themselves now to Him. And they have submitted to Allah to do His will, being blessed as the Jews and the Arabs were, to have a Messenger born in their midst to teach and guide his people into the spirit and knowledge of his Teacher, Almighty God, Allah in Person.

The Believers are not satisfied with prayers and seeking refuge in Allah without asking a word of prayer for the success and blessings of Allah upon the Messenger and his followers whom Allah has so abundantly bestowed upon them; "the answer to Abraham's prayer" that he raise a Messenger from among them that he may teach the wisdom of the Book (Bible) to so many of them who do not understand the very book (Bible) in which they think they believe, but without the true knowledge or understanding of the scriptures of Moses and Jesus.

Therefore, a correction must come to them in the way of true understanding of these scriptures in which their history is constantly referred to in the mentioning of the Jews and Christians through the Prophets that were sent to them.

The Orthodox Muslims think this refers to Arabia and that Muhammad (may the peace and blessings of Allah be upon him) of nearly 1,400 years ago was the one fulfilling the answer to Abraham's prayers. But if they look at it again and ponder over it, it is like their belief in thinking that Muhammad of nearly 1,400 years ago was a prophet like Moses, that Moses prophesied in Deut. 18:18. But they forget that Moses was a man who was raised in the house of bondage under a king who held him and his people in bondage to him and to his false worship of God and religion. And he desired no one to interfere with his teachings, given to his slaves. His fear, according to the Holy Quran, was that Moses would change the religion.

The Orthodox Muslims think this was fulfilled in the Meccans' opposition to Muhammad. Not so! He does not compare with the prophecy of a man like Moses, for there was no king singled out who opposed Muhammad in Mecca. There was no separation of the Arabs from any slave-masters and a destruction of the slave-masters. It was a certain class of people of science.

The Meccans were not enslaved to any physical king and people—only to false belief. But remember that prophecy: "Like unto me." The man had to be one who received a revelation or guidance from Allah to physically liberate a people from the physical holding of a superior force or ruler. He must fight with this particular ruling class to release his people—like Moses. Then, he must give them their own religion, teach them the knowledge of the true God (Allah) and His true religion, Islam. And set up a completely new religious service, never known to his people before. He must overcome them with nothing but the Truth and the power and guidance of Allah as Moses did with Pharaoh and his well-armed army, because he is not in a position to arm himself and his followers with carnal weapons. The enemy controls the manufacture of arms.

He must be one like Moses, dependent upon Allah for the victory over his enemy. Here he shows forth, in a land where Allah has not been worshiped and where Islam has not been accepted as the true religion; the power of Allah is shown by letting Allah fight his and his people's battle against their wicked oppressors.

This is the true type of a man like Moses. If you study the prophecy concerning the last Messenger of God, according to the description given to the man by the Bible's prophecy in the Torah and Gospel, you will find that he is a man, according to the Psalms, with the name of "Muhammad" and also you will find him in the Revelations under the symbolical name, "Lamb." He gets the name (Praised) from the honor of the "twenty-four elders" or Islamic Scientists. The position that he is shown under, the symbolical "Lamb" in Revelations, is like the Holy Qur-an's teaching one who is illiterate and whom the people will find written down in the Torah and the Gospel. (The book of Isaiah; the parables of Jesus.)

This is the man the above prayer is made for because he, as one of the Islamic writers says, will be born among the infidels. The revelations of the Bible symbolically place him in the midst of "four beasts." Therefore, prayer must be made for his protection among a people without the teachings of Islam—not a country where never had any former prophets of Allah risen and set up signs of the future greatness of Islam, as had Arabia in the time of Muhammad. The signs of the future of Islam and its last Messenger, Abraham, had already been set up in the Holy City Mecca. Muhammad did not destroy these signs, but rather he repaired the sign to live until it had served its purpose.

CONFIDENCE GAINED THROUGH PRAYERS

The following prayer shows the complete confidence the Apostle and his followers have in Allah and the great praise of Allah for His protection and blessings that they enjoy from Him daily:

"I seek the protection of Allah, my Lord, from every fault, and turn to Him.

"Oh Allah, Thou art the author of peace and from Thee comes peace. Blessed art Thou, O Lord of Glory and honour.

"Nothing deserves to be worshiped except Allah. He is One and has no associate; His is the Kingdom and for Him is praise. And He has power over all things.

"O Allah, there is none who can withhold what Thou grantest and there is none who can give what Thou withholdest and greatness does not benefit any possessor of greatness as against Thee."

Let you and me who believe learn and recite this prayer for the glory and honor, praise and thanks to Allah who is blessing us, the lost-found of our people, for guiding us on the right path. That we, too, may be as successful as the Prophets and their followers before us. We must remember that we cannot be proud over greatness: only Allah.

For if Allah makes you great you are great indeed! And if Allah bring you low, none can raise you up but He.

Salvation has come to us from Allah, let us rejoice in Him and be thankful to Him for visiting us and accepting us as His own.

"O you who believe, take not the Jews and the Christians for friends. They are friends of each other And whoever amongst you takes them for friends he is indeed one of them. Surely Allah guides not the unjust people" Holy Qur-an 5:51.

"To Allah belongs whatever is in the heavens and whatever is in the earth. And whether you manifest what is in your minds or hide it, Allah will call you to account according to it. So He forgives whom He pleases and chastises whom He pleases. And Allah is Possessor of power over all things" (Holy Qur-an 2:284).

"The Messenger believes in what has been revealed to him from his Lord, and so do the believers. They all believe in Allah and His angels and His book and His messengers. We make no difference between any of His messengers. And they say: "We hear and obey; our Lord, thy forgiveness do we crave, and to Thee is the eventual course" (Holy Qur-an 2:285).

"Allah imposes not on any soul a duty beyond its scope. For it is that which it earns of good and against it that which it works of evil. Our Lord, punish us not if we forget or make a mistake. Our Lord, do not lay on us a burden as Thou didst lay on those before us.

"Our Lord, impose not on us (afflictions) which we have not the strength to bear. And pardon us! And grant us protection! And have mercy upon us! Thou art our Patron, so grant us victory over the disbelieving people" (Holy Qur-an 2:286). NOTE: The latter verse (2:286) is a prayer; let us recite it very often.

PROGRAM
AND POSITION

WHAT DO
THE MUSLIMS WANT?

This is the question asked most frequently by both the whites and the blacks. The answers to this question I shall state as simply as possible.

1. We want freedom. We want a full and complete freedom.

2. We want justice. Equal justice under the law. We want justice applied equally to all regardless of creed, class or color.

3. We want equality of opportunity. We want equal membership in society with the best in civilized society.

4. We want our people in America whose parents or grandparents were descendants from slaves to be allowed, to establish a separate state or territory of their own—either on this continent or elsewhere. We believe that our former slave-masters are obligated to provide such land and that the area must be fertile and minerally rich. We believe that our former slave-masters are obligated to maintain and supply our needs in this separate territory for the next 20 or 25 years until we are able to produce and supply our own needs.

Since we cannot get along with them in peace and equality after giving them 400 years of our sweat and blood and receiving in return some of the worst treatment human beings have ever experienced, we believe our contributions to this land and the suffering forced upon us by white America justifies our demand for complete separation in a state or territory of our own.

5. We want freedom for all Believers of Islam now held in federal prisons. We want freedom for all black men and women now under death sentence in innumerable prisons in the North

as well as the South.

We want every black man and woman to have the freedom to accept or reject being separated from the slave-masters' children and establish a land of their own.

We know that the above plan for the solution of the black and white conflict is the best and only answer to the problem between two people.

6. We want an immediate end to the police brutality and mob attacks against the so-called Negro throughout the United States.

We believe that the Federal government should intercede to see that black men and women tried in white courts receive justice in accordance with the laws of the land, or allow us to build a new nation for ourselves, dedicated to justice, freedom and liberty.

7. As long as we are not allowed to establish a state or territory of our own, we demand not only equal justice under the laws of the United States but equal employment opportunities —NOW!

We do not believe that after 400 years of free or nearly free labor, sweat and blood, which has helped America become rich and powerful, so many thousands of black people should have to subsist on relief or charity or live in poor houses.

8. We want the government of the United States to exempt our people from ALL taxation as long as we are deprived of equal justice under the laws of the land.

9. We want equal education—but separate schools up to 16 for boys and 18 for girls on the conditions that the girls be sent to women's colleges and universities. We want all black children educated, taught and trained by their own teacher.

Under such school system we believe we will make a better nation of people. The United States government should provide free all necessary text books and equipment, schools and college buildings. The Muslim teachers shall be left free to teach and train their people in the way of righteousness, decency and self respect.

10. We believe that intermarriage or race mixing should be prohibited. We want the religion of Islam taught without hindrance or suppression.

These are some of the things that we, the Muslims, want for our people in North America.

1. We believe in the One God Whose proper name is Allah.

2. We believe in the Holy Qur-an and in the Scriptures of all the Prophets of God.

3. We believe in the truth of the Bible, but we believe that it has been tampered with and must be reinterpreted so that mankind will not be snared by the falsehoods that have been added to it.

4. We believe in Allah's Prophets and the Scriptures they brought to the people.

5. We believe in the resurrection of the dead—not in physical resurrection but mental resurrection. We believe that the so-called Negroes are most in need of mental resurrection; therefore, they will be resurrected first.

Furthermore, we believe we are the people of God's choice as it has been written that God would choose the rejected and the despised. We can find no other persons fitting this description in these last days more than the so-called Negroes in America. We believe in the resurrection of the righteous.

6. We further believe in the judgment. We believe this first judgment will take place, as God revealed, in America.

7. We believe this is the time in history for the separation of the so-called Negroes and the so-called white Americans. We believe the black man should be freed in name as well as in fact. By this we mean that he should be freed from names imposed upon him by his former slave-masters. Names which identified him as being the slave of a slave-master. We believe that if we are free indeed, we should go in our own people's names—the black peoples of the earth.

8. We believe in justice for all whether in God or not. We believe as others that we are due equal justice as human beings. We believe in equality—as a nation—of equals. We do not believe that we are equal with our slave-masters in the status of "Freed slaves."

We recognize and respect American citizens as independent peoples, and we respect their laws which govern this nation.

9. We believe that the offer of integration is hypocritical and is made by those who are trying to deceive the black peoples into believing that their 400-year-old open enemies of freedom, justice and equality are, all of a sudden, their "friends." Furthermore, we believe that such deception is intended to prevent black people from realizing that the time in history has arrived

for the separation from the whites of this nation.

If the white people are truthful about their professed friendship toward the so-called Negro, they can prove it by dividing up America with their slaves.

We do not believe that America will ever be able to furnish enough jobs for her own millions of unemployed in addition to jobs for the 20,000,000 black people.

10. We believe that we who declared ourselves to be righteous Muslims should not participate in wars which take the lives of humans. We do not believe this nation should force us to take part in such wars, for we have nothing to gain from it unless America agrees to give us the necessary territory wherein we may have something to fight for.

11. We believe our women should be respected and protected as the women of other nationalities are respected and protected.

12. We believe that Allah (God) appeared in the Person of Master W. Fard Muhammad, July, 1930—the long awaited "Messiah" of the Christians and the "Mahdi" of the Muslims.

We believe further and lastly that Allah is God and besides HIM there is no God and He will bring about a universal government of peace wherein we can live in peace together.

EXPLANATION OF
WHAT MUSLIMS WANT
AND BELIEVE

I would like to put a little emphasis on some of what the Muslims want.

If we ask you (meaning the white American slave-master) for freedom in deed, I think that we are right. We use the words IN DEED, as we have been your subjects for now 400 years. That is a long time to be subject to a people or the slave of a people. Three hundred of those years we worked for you for nothing. And those 300 years we were treated like your own herd of cattle. You have no regard for our human rights, no more than you did your animals.

You slashed the backs of my fathers and my mothers without any mercy. You killed them whenever you felt you wanted to, and you sweethearted with my grandparents.

Truth hurts. You went into our grandmothers, had children by them and then put them on the block for sale, and today you are still crossing over to our women. This should show you why we want to take leave of you today. In those days you sold her children, who were your own sons and daughters. I am telling you what my own grandparents told me. My father's mother told me her father was a white man, and she looked it. Today our women are all subject to your biddings. You take their sons and bash their brains in with your club and blow their brains out with your gun—throughout the country without due process of the law that you already put here before them.

You have in words trodden us under foot in the name of civilization and now today you stand as our chief adversary to prevent us from escaping your evil and unjust doings to our people whose sweat and blood has helped to build the greatest country and government on the earth.

You are so rich today that you are able to feed almost every mouth in Europe. You are so rich that you can now give away billions of dollars to nations in order to get their friendship. You are so powerful that you can command the high seas, the air, the land, even the ice caps of the poles of the earth. All this we helped you do. Some of us went to your wars, shooting down your enemy as you pointed them out to us and we were being shot down also.

If we cry out for justice you twist it and make it look as though we are the real enemies of justice. If we say that you are evil, you want to make a case against us for "falsely" accusing you, when you know that you have never been good to us.

Today you are trying to deceive the poor once-servant slaves of yours by telling them that you will now show a little friendship. I will let you ride beside me on my best transportation; I will also allow you to work in my office. I am going to put you in the government. What is that going to do for us and our children in the future? Will this help us to make a great future for our people and own what you still own, which is a place we can call our own?

WHY HINDER US?

Your dog is more classified as a citizen in the land than we so-called Negroes. If the dog wants freedom, if the dog whines in the night because he is uncomfortable, you will get up and try to comfort it. But if you hear a million Negroes crying and suffering from the brutal treatment at your hand and the hand of your people, you will laugh.

I am here with the truth. Take the words, turn them over and examine them, put them on the scale of facts and weigh them, and if I am not teaching you the truth I say come up here and prove it and I will lay down my head on the floor and let you chop it off.

We want freedom IN DEED. Why should we not want to leave a people who have lynched and burned us. Why continue to send our own brother out there falling under the blows of so-call peace officers and falling from a bullet from his gun. I have seen police vex our people to try and make them say something so they can beat or kill them.

You say you want to help us. Help us to do what? If you do not want to help us leave you with a good sendoff, then what are you going to help us do if we stay here?

I have lived with you all my life. I was born in the South. I have looked upon the evil treatment of our people day and night. I have shed tears for you many times. No justice whatsoever. I have seen people kicked about who asked for a fair salary. I have heard it said to a brother, "You take what I say, you don't figure behind me, Nigger."

We are 20 million people who have come (according to the old prophets) through "toil and tribulations." We are here today asking for equal justice under YOUR OWN LAW. We are asking for freedom that you claim you have given to us. Freedom to do for ourselves. We do not want to be beggars. But if we are given freedom IN DEED we can build for ourselves the same things that you have.

Our people who are educated in your colleges and universities, our technicians and engineers of all kinds, why shouldn't they go and make a way for their own people as a nation, build and construct a government for their people as your fathers did for you when they crossed the Atlantic? They may be a little lazy and want to start at the top first, but you were not able to start (at the top). You have put it in their minds that they can not go for themselves.

How educated were your fathers when they crossed the Atlantic and started working for their freedom? They were not wise politicians and senators as you are today, but, nevertheless, they kept digging and turning the soil, felling trees, pacing the country for a place for themselves. Today they have made a nation. They were not satisfied with trying to do this alone, they had to go across the Atlantic and get our fathers to help them. If you wanted to be your lily-white self, why did you go and get black people to come here? Why would you mix your blood with the black people and yet deprive them of equal justice?

We built your railroads with our own sweat. We plowed your farms and plantations. We cut down the underbrush and trees, and now today you have replaced that kind of labor with mechanical labor and you do not have anything for us to do. With just two or three men you can cultivate hundreds of acres of land with machine operations. You pick your cotton with a mechanical machine. Everything is done mechanically today. Why don't you want us to leave you? Especially when you do not want us to do anything but labor. Why shouldn't we want some of this earth where we can start building a government for the future of our people so that they will not be just a people who labor, year after year, for another people and all their labor still be subject to the brutal treatment?

You should be ashamed of yourself today to lynch and kill so-called Negroes while you have an army full of Negroes helping you to fight and protect and maintain the government. You should be ashamed of it. Especially when that same man's father slaved for your fathers for nothing, and now you will go and take him before your own judges and give him an unjust judgment.

This is a sham. Do you think you are going to get away with it forever?

We say Allah is God. We say in Arabic language, Allah Oou Akbar. We say in the Arabic language, La e La ha el Allah, Muhammad rasoul Allah. We that say that in your midst today should make you tremble and go off and commit suicide.

Those babies crying in the Name of Allah (they were never taught by you to worship), you know that your time must be short. Today, I say you see all of these things, hear all of them as the Bible teaches even of being plagued with divine plagues, and you still will not worship the God of truth and justice. The white race has never believed in God—not the God of freedom, justice and equality.

The man of sin does not want to hear the poor so-called

Negroes who are under your feet—he does not want them to seek help from God because he is guilty and he knows he has mistreated us. We called on the God that you said was the right one for a long time. For a hundred years we have been calling on your God and the Son, both.

I am sure today that God and his Son that you are presenting to us have been for white people, surely they were not friends of ours. He never heard us. He must have been off somewhere in conversation over your future and did not have time to hear our prayers. But Allah hears, Allah acts. Never any more will you fool us to bow and pray to a dead Jesus any more than Moses or any other dead prophet and hope that my people believe that there is a Jesus killed and buried but still sitting receiving their prayers. I hope that they wake up and know that they haven't been heard since the day he was killed. Those who represent that Jesus to you do not wait for Jesus to answer their prayers, they answer their own prayers. Get out of that kind of stuff.

There is no such thing as dying and coming up out of the earth, meeting your friends and meeting those who died before you. I say, get out of such slavery teachings. It keeps you blind, deaf and dumb to reality. Get out of it, for if you depend on such, you will not believe in yourself. When you are dead, you are DEAD. I have proof of that. Do you have proof of that which you say—they will come back? No! I say to you my friend, the mentally dead are awakening. Your slave-masters have deceived you. They want you to remain deceived.

They hate any one of you that will try to teach facts. They hate any one of you that want to become equal. They hate any one of you that want justice. They do not want that, yet, they will tell you that they want to help you and they want to give you justice. You do not get it.

We want freedom, indeed, and we want to be human beings along with other humans. We want the world to know that we love to be respected as other people who are now being respected.

I say to you my beloved, freedom indeed is what we want. Freedom to do for ourselves as we think best. That is what they (white race) are fighting for themselves. To be free to do as they want to, and they are fighting to the death for it. You and I should fight to the death to be free to do what we want. You know and I know how much these people hate me because I am teaching the truth, and they know I am doing a better job with you than any one of those who ever appeared among you.

If the white circle leaders want to keep their circle white, I say keep it white. If the Ku Klux Klan want to keep their race white, I say, help yourself, go to it. Now when I say to keep mine black—white Circle League German Nazi—keep your mouth out of it.

We want to build a nation that will be recognized as a nation that will be self-respecting and receive respect of the other nations of the earth.

I say we have a God that will make a place here for us.

"What the Muslims want for the whole black nation of our people is freedom, justice and equality—that is what we want for you. We cannot exercise or enjoy freedom, justice and equality unless we have a home on this earth that we call our own.

A PROGRAM FOR
SELF-DEVELOPMENT

We must remember that we just cannot depend on the white race ever to do that which we can and should do for self. The American so-called Negroes are like the Bible story of Lazarus and the rich man, the story that Jesus must have forseen at the time. This Bible beggar was charmed by the wealth of the rich man to whom he was a servant, and he could not make up his mind to go seek something for self.

This beggar was offered a home in Paradise but could not make up his mind to leave the gate of his master, the rich man, wishing for that which God had in store for destruction along with its owner. The beggar's eyes could not turn from that perishable wealth. So it is with the American Negroes; they are charmed by the luxury of their slave-master, and cannot make up their minds to seek for self something of this good earth, though hated and despised by the rich man and full of sores caused by the evil treatment of the rich man. On top of that he is chased by the rich man's dogs and still remains a beggar at the gate, though the gates of Paradise were ever open to him and the gates of hell were open to receive his rich master.

The American Negroes have the same gates of Paradise open

to them but are charmed by the wealth of America and cannot
see the great opportunity that lies before them. They are suffering untold injustices at the hands of the rich; they have been
and still are being lynched and burned; they and their women
and children are beaten all over the country, by the rich slave-
masters and their children. The slaves' houses and churches are
bombed by the slave-masters; their girls are used as prostitutes
and at times are raped in public. Yet the Negroes are on their
knees begging the rich man to treat them as the rich man treats
himself and his kind. The poor beggar kindly asks for the
crumbs, a job and a house in the neighborhood of the rich man.

The Negro leaders are frightened to death and are afraid to
ask for anything other than a job. The good things of this earth
could be theirs if they would only unite and acquire wealth as
the masters and the other independent nations have. The Negroes could have all of this if they could get up and go to work
for self. They are far too lazy as a Nation—100 years up from
slavery and still looking to the master to care for them and give
them a job, bread and a house to live in on the master's land.
You should be ashamed of yourselves, surely the white race has
been very good in the way of making jobs for their willing
slaves, but this cannot go on forever; we are about at the end
of it and must do something for SELF or else.

The slave-master has given you enough education to go and
do for self, but this education is not being used for self; it is
even offered back to the slave-masters to help them to keep you
a dependent people looking to them for support. Let us unite
every good that is in us for the uplifting of the American so-
called Negroes to the equal of the world's independent nations.
Ask for a start for self and the American white people, I believe,
are willing to help give us a start if they see you and I are willing to do for self. It would remove from them not only the
worry of trying to give jobs and schools to a lazy people but
also would get them honor and sincere friendship all over the
Asiatic world and God, Himself, would prolong their time on
the earth.

We must stop relying upon the white man to care for us.
We must become an independent people. So-called Negroes
should:

1. Separate yourselves from the "slave-master."

2. Pool your resources, education and qualifications for independence.

3. Stop forcing yourselves into places where you are not wanted.

4. Make your own neighborhood a decent place to live.

5. Rid yourselves of the lust of wine and drink and learn to love self and your kind before loving others.

6. Unite to create a future for yourself.

7. Build your own homes, schools, hospitals, and factories.

8. Do not seek to mix your blood through racial integration.

9. Stop buying expensive cars, fine clothes and shoes before being able to live in a fine home.

10. Spend your money among yourselves.

11. Build an economic system among yourselves.

12. Protect your women.

Stop allowing the white men to shake hands or speak to your women anytime or anywhere. This practice has ruined us. They wink their eye at your daughter after coming into your home—but you cannot go on the North side and do the same with his women.

No black man feels good—by nature—seeing a white man with a Negro woman. We have all colors in our race—red, yellow, brown and jet black—why should we need a white person?

Africans would not dare allow their women to be the targets that we allow ours to be.

If I were not protected by Allah (God), how would I be able to stand before this white man unafraid and speak as I do.

You educators, you Christian ministers should stop preaching integration. The most foolish thing an educator can do is to preach interracial marriage. It shows the white man you want to be white.

Educators should teach our people of the great history that was theirs before they were brought to America in shackles by slave-masters.

Our children should be trained in our own schools, not dropped into the schools of the enemy where they are taught that whites have been and forever will be world rulers.

I am the first man since the death of Yakub commissioned by God directly. I say no more than what Jesus said. He said that he came from God. I say that I am missioned by God.

PUT MUSLIM PROGRAM
TO CONGRESS

Ever since the 30's America has been struck by drought and dust storms. The outlook is for hail and snow storms, great flooding rains, earthquakes, terrific cold and ice. These blasts of the elements will ruin crops, highways, railroad tracks, bridges and street pavements.

The Holy Qur-an prophesies Allah sending a calamity to destroy crops and generally plague man. It could be locusts, insects already here. If they were multiplied into unlimited numbers they would terrify man and drive him to distraction.

The members of the black nation who refused to believe and submit to the truth will be burdened with overwhelming grief and hounded by bitter regret. They will find no relief or rest day or night.

The things of which I have spoken will come upon America and its people within the next 6 years. You will separate yourselves automatically when these things come to pass before your eyes.

Who can be saved, you will ask?

The Muslim believers who have submitted to the will of Allah and His religion, Islam, and those who faithfully followed and obeyed His Messenger. Let us try to do something for ourselves.

Give praises to Allah for converting the people to me and blessing us with peace and security. Allah is one God. He is independent and has no need of us, but we have great need of Him. It is He the Prophets predicted would come in the last days of the world seeking us, the Lost People, to save us and restore us to our own.

I declare to you that He has come in the person of Master Wallace Fard Muhammad by (1) a summary of His work for the past 33 years and (2) by the Messenger, who believes in what has been revealed to him by his Lord, as do the believers. They believe in Allah and His Prophets and His books. We make no distinctions in His Messenger. We hear and we obey.

It is difficult for me to advise my followers on taking part in the corrupt politics of our enemies, who are in complete control of the political affairs.

There are many black men and women who make splendid politicians. They could accomplish considerable good if they—like the white politician and his people—were given proper and equal recognition and justice for themselves and their people.

If our politicians are to serve us, they must have no fear of the white man when they plead our case in the white courts before white judges.

The strongest politician of our kind—or the person who comes nearest as far as I know, to giving us political justice in the white courts (if he had our complete backing)—is congressman Adam Clayton Powell, Jr., though he is not a Muslim. A Muslim politician is what you need, but Congressman Powell is not afraid and would not be easily bribed, for he is not "Hungry."

There are two other good politicians, but I will not mention them by name at this time. If they could shed their fear, they would make excellent political leaders to guard our interest.

We must give good black politicians the total backing of our population.

Your program—the one I have given you which is carried in the first part of this chapter—should be put before Congress. The Civil Rights Bill and integration will not stand and can never bring independence to you and your people, no matter who is President.

The wisest and surest way to success is to unite behind me. I assure you that, with the help of Allah, you will accomplish your goals—money, good homes, and friendships in all walks of life.

AN ECONOMIC BLUEPRINT

The Black man in America faces a serious economic problem today and the white race's Christianity cannot solve it. You, the so-called American Negro, with the help of Allah can solve your own problem. The truth must be recognized by the black man. He, himself, has assisted greatly in creating this serious problem of unemployment, insecurity and lack. Before the black man can begin to gain economic security, he must be awakened from the dead and gain knowledge, understanding and wisdom which will enable him to follow my teachings. Islam and only Islam will point the way out of the entanglement of "want in the midst of plenty" for the followers of Islam, the true religion of the black nation.

Know thyself and be yourself. Islam makes a true brother to brother. If this be true, how can a believer (Muslim) be a true brother to another believer and boycott his brother and support the enemy? The believers in truth, Islam, must stop looking up to the white race for justice and take the following steps to correct this problem.

Acknowledge and recognize that you are a member of the Creator's nation and act accordingly. This action, in the name of Allah, requires you, as a Muslim, to set an example for the lost-found, your brothers in the wilderness in North America. This requires action and deeds, not words and lip service.

The following blueprint shows the way:

1.   Recognize the necessity for unity and group operation (activities).
2.   Pool your resources, physically as well as financially.
3.   Stop wanton criticisms of everything that is black-owned and black-operated.
4.   Keep in mind—jealousy destroys from within.
5.   Observe the operations of the white man. He is successful. He makes no excuses for his failures. He works hard in a collective manner. You do the same.

If there are six or eight Muslims with knowledge and experience of the grocery business—pool your knowledge, open a grocery store—and you work collectively and harmoniously, Allah will bless you with success.

If there are those with knowledge of dressmaking, merchandising, trades, maintenance—pool such knowledge. Do not be ashamed to seek guidance and instructions from the brother or sister who has more experience, education and training than you have had. Accept his or her assistance.

The white man spends his money with his own kind, which is natural. You, too, must do this. Help to make jobs for your own kind. Take a lesson from the Chinese and Japanese and go give employment and assistance to your own kind when they are in need. This is the first law of nature. Defend and support your own kind. True Muslims do this.

Because the so-called American Negro has been deceived and misled, he has become a victim of deception. He is today in the worst economic condition of North America. Unemployment is mounting, and he feels it most. He assisted in reducing himself to his present insecure economic condition. You, the black man, are the only members of the human race that deliberately walk past the place of business of one of your own kind—a black man—and spend your dollars with your natural enemy. The so-called American Negro has never in the history of America been known to boycott or criticize the white man as he does his own kind. He thus shows love for his enemy and hatred for his own kind.

A true Muslim would never boycott the place of business of his fellow Muslim or black brother. A true Muslim is proud of the success of his black sisters and brothers. He recognizes that their success is his success. He recognizes the law of Islam. If one brother has a bowl of soup you have half of that soup.

TO GAIN

A PLACE IN THE SUN

In this perilous and evil time, with the confusion of the people, government, leaders and rulers, the poor lost-found members of the Black Nation who are called Negroes, and their enemies, must know that the truth is their salvation and their greatest weapon at this time. The preachings and teachings of the true knowledge of God and the devil, which Allah (God) has mission-ed me to do—and I am doing for you—are beyond value. It is your life and the light of your life. It will bring you out of the spiritual darkness and ignorance into which you have been placed by the enemy of the God of truth and light and understanding.

The rising of opposition against divine truth, revealed in the last days (years), also has been told by the prophets of old, and we have it in writing that this opposition against the truth is not to be feared by you who believe and have understanding. The truth will be attacked by the disbeliever and hypocrite in the last days.

A champion without an opponent cannot be recognized as the champion. Since the making of the devil, he has been the chief opponent, and he will continue to be until he is destroyed by God. He (the devil) teaches and trains others of all races, or-ganizations and religions.

His world has created various religions in opposition to the true religion, and he prepared them for a final attack on the

God of truth and His word—which is truth—as well as His representatives, who are called apostles, messengers and prophets. This is a last attempt to defend falsehood and mislead the people, who otherwise would have followed and believed in the God of truth and His messengers and prophets.

No. 1. You should know that this is the time in which such war has begun. Without the knowledge of the time, you are still the loser. Allah (God) has revealed the time, and it is verified by the prophecy of the Bible and Qur-an.

No. 2. Your place in such times is with your own. Why should you join your own? The answer is because of the divine judgment destruction and doom of other than your own. The most hated and despised thing today in this, the devil's wicked world, is the truth or true knowledge of God and the devil. This truth must come to you today. If not, there can't be any justification of the teachings and prophecy of the prophets. However, it will stand and be fulfilled to the very letter and spirit.

The heavens and earth were created, according to the Holy Qur-an, in truth. Therefore, since the foundation of our universe was created and built in truth, falsehood cannot survive in it. The average lost-found member of the original Black Nation is afraid to accept his own or his salvation because of the dislike of his enemies.

No. 3. We must forget about trying to do for others before doing that which we have not done for ourselves, which is to establish love and unity in our brotherhood. You rise up and yell out in ignorance against yourself when you say that you want unity, love and brotherhood of the nations. Those nations look at you—where disunity is the order of the day—and see your dislike of self and kind.

You are an ignorant and foolish people. Your first desire should be love of self instead of love for those other than of your own. If you do not love your own brother—who is of your flesh and blood—how can other than your own flesh and blood accept your love and brotherhood? First, love thyself and thy own brother as thyself, and others will love you.

I advised you to accept our 3 Year Economic Plan, which will work a miracle for you. Unite and stop your extravagant spending, trying to live on the level with millionaires, and you will make a heaven for yourselves like others nations have done. My followers and I are doing just that and will continue to do so. You are invited to join us and contribute to our program.

The preaching that we should have some of this earth we can call our own is far from being an ignorant teaching that cannot be accomplished. This is wisdom you should know in these days and times. Without some of this earth of our own, we will never be a people to produce for ourselves.

We cannot continue to increase our population in hope that the white man will continue to create employment for us. I warn you daily that there will come a time when they probably will drop you and you will have to do for yourself. Start practicing the art of doing for self now. It is only laziness for you and your children to want to be servants for another nation.

How can self-independence be accomplished? Israel, with her disbelieving people, said the same thing. But God knew how to make a way for Israel to have something to call her own. He had too many people who did not believe in Him. So, He destroyed them and gave Israel a house. If you will believe in Allah and in His revelation that He has given to me, he is well able to do the same for you.

We must give up trying to live in peace with a people with whom we have spent 400 years without peace. Even today, they stand ready to slaughter you just because they hate you.

WHAT IS UN-AMERICAN?

My followers and I are being accused of being un-American. We actually do not know what is American and what is un-American, as the United States of America has not instructed us as to what constitutes an American or an un-American.

Recently, the California State Senate Fact-Finding Subcommittee on Un-American Activities, in their "Eleventh Report" to the 1961 Regular California Legislature, in Sacramento, California, on pages 131-138 under the heading "THE NEGRO MUSLIMS," are charging us with being un-American, that we now operate a school for the indoctrination of young Negroes with race hatred. (This is untrue, for we only teach them who YOU really are. They can hate or love you, it is up to them.)

You have always had private schools. First, your students

not only learn to hate Negroes but are the number one murderers of Negroes. Second, we do not teach them to disregard their
family names—they do NOT KNOW them.

We teach them to discard YOUR family NAMES and get
their real Nation's names, for your names are not our legal
names!

On page 136, we are classified along with the Communist
Party. For 34 years we have not been anything other than a
peaceful people who have never carried weapons, nor have we
made any aggressive moves or attacks on anyone.

The Negro Muslims! Of course, Muslims or Moslems means
the same, as Mohammed and Muhammad, only one is common
in English (Moslem and Mohammed). In Arabic, Muslim and
Muhammad are scholarly. The so-called "Fact-Finding Committee," we are not surprised to hear, read false statements
against us, the Muslims, by the American white people. This is
only their nature. They were not created to tell, teach, preach
or represent the truth when it comes to the Negroes, God and
the Righteous.

Usually, I do not waste my time on the untrue things that
I hear or read about me and my followers, stated by our open
enemies (the white people), and those of my people whom they
have poisoned against self and their kind (the black race).

It is written in the scriptures of truth that the devils would
put out such evil and false accusations against the Messenger
of Allah and his followers in these last days of their evil, bloody
world. I think Allah (God) will not allow falsehood to triumph
over truth in His days.

This so-called "Fact-Finding" committee on page 131 says
that my father took me to Detroit, where I attended the public
schools until reaching the third grade, at which point I left home
at the age of 16 and wandered from city to city serving various
jail terms for vagrancy and other minor offenses, except for a
term of 4-years in the Federal Penitentiary.

The truth is, I was born in Georgia, went to the public
school in Georgia and was never out of the State of Georgia,
until I was 25 years of age. I married and had two children
and moved to Detroit in April, 1923, from Macon, Georgia,
where I worked for the Southern Railroad Company and the
Cherokee Brick Company, the latter as a tramroad foreman and
builder.

I never was arrested and served no jail terms on any charge or charges until 1934.

Then I committed myself to the jail in Detroit after learning that the Michigan State Board of Education had arrested the Muslim Teachers of the School of Islam and the secretary of the Temple on false charges of contributing to the delinquency of minors.

This false charge was dropped, and the teachers were freed. I was at that time given 6 months' probation to put our Muslim children back in the public schools under Christian teachers.

This I did not do, and I moved in September of that same year to Chicago.

The next time I was arrested was May 8, 1942, in Washington, D.C., by the F.B.I. for not registering for the draft. When the call was made for all males between 18 and 44, I refused (NOT EVADING) on the grounds that, first, I was a Muslim and would not take part in war and especially not on the side with the infidels. Second, I was 45 years of age and was NOT according to the law required to register.

The above can be verified from the court records in Detroit and Washington D.C.

The name "Poole" was never my name, nor was it my father's name. It was the name the white slave-master of my grandfather after the so-called freedom of my fathers. They, being robbed of the knowledge of self and kind, for the past 300 years did not know what deadly harm the slave-master's name would do to them in the way of TRUE freedom and recognition among the free and independent nations of our own and the spiritual nonacceptance by Allah (God) on the Day of Resurrection from the devil's names.

They allowed themselves to continue to be called by the devil slave-master's name.

But on the coming and appearance of Allah in 1930—who taught me a thorough knowledge of the devils, the time, the resurrection and end and the judgment of the devils and their followers and the danger of being called by devil names and believing what they teach as religion—He (Allah) gave me His Name.

Later my father and all our family accepted His Name (Muhammad).

Other believers in Detroit and Chicago accepted many other

of His Names, (called attributes) and His true religion and only religion of God, Islam.

The religion Islam is universally recognized as the true religion of God, even by many of the disbelievers and infidels and Hindus.

Over 3 million white Americans recognize it (in secret). We want to know just what is characterized as un-American? What is characterized as TRUE American?

Is being Muslims and righteously trying to obey and observe all the Divine Laws of God (that even you the Christian preach, but do not obey) and trying to obey your civil laws what you call un-American?

You and the world know that we seek to do no evil to any one. We carry no weapons of evil, we are trying to be respected and we respect you as the rulers of the land.

You printed my Twelve-Point program for my people on pages 132 and 133. Is there anything wrong with any of the words mentioned in it for my people. They are:

1. Separate ourselves from the slave-master. You had us segregated for 400 years and now say that we are free, is it being un-American to leave you or separate from you, a people who have enslaved and destroyed us as human beings? Have not you separated yourselves from us?

2. Is pooling our resources, education and qualifications for self-independence, as you and other nations have done and since you say we are free, what do you call un-American?

3. Should we not stop forcing ourselves, our presence, on you in places of yours where you forbid us and tell us we are not wanted? Is this what you call un-American—keeping away from that of yours that you forbade us?

4. Making our own neighborhoods a decent place to live and seeking a place in your neighborhood just because yours looks better and cleaner; making wherever we live a nice and clean place to live and making a decent life among ourselves if you and yours can do it, so can we! Is this what you call un-American?

5. If we want to rid ourselves of the lust of wine and other intoxicating drinks and learn to love ourselves first BEFORE loving you or others, is this what you call un-American?

6. Uniting and creating for ourselves. Have you given us anything in the way of your past and present treatment of us that we can believe that it will not be "hell" on "hell?"

7. Is it un-American for us to build our own homes, and schools, hospitals and factories while we are suffering and being turned away from many of yours?

8. Is it un-American for us to want to keep our blood pure from being mixed with yours, our enemies?

9. Is it un-American for us to stop wasting our money in trying to buy your finest cars, clothes, shoes before being able to live in a nice home?

10. Is it un-American for us to spend our money among ourselves (what little we have to spend)?

11. Is it un-American for us to build up an economic system among ourselves?

12. Is it un-American for us to protect our women, as you and other nations protect women? Is it un-American for us to try to set up a clean respectful society among ourselves as other nations? And should we not, as well as you, set officers over our society who will see to it that the rules and laws are obeyed?

You know it is absolutely false to accuse us of violence or preparing for violence. Allah (God) forbids us to do such a thing. He is the One who will do our fighting for us against you, as Jehovah did for Moses and Israel; only Allah is a little more angry with you for the evils done to us than Jehovah was with Pharaoh, as Jehovah only wanted to set a sign for you of what you may expect today, and Israel was not the real people of Allah.

Your evil and false accusations of me and my followers are only to frighten already frightened so-called Negroes from coming to Allah, that they may inherit the earth. You frighten especially the proud so-called Negroes whom you have made like yourself, thinking that they might be of some help to us. But Allah is sufficient as a Helper.

You will not be able to help yourself pretty soon, let alone make poison-proud Negroes to help you against us.

We want to be ourselves, and we are going to. have some of this earth that we can call our own, with the help of Allah, as He has promised us through the mouth of His prophets from

Moses to Muhammad.

It is up to you to mistreat us, or treat us well. Do as you like; we will not follow you any more.

The United States of America calls all so-called Negroes who want to live as decent civilized men or women un-American. We want to live in peace. We are they who want to be treated like human beings. We are they who want freedom, justice and equality. We are they who want a moral reformation of our people as well as a spiritual reformation. We are they who love unity among the so-called Negroes. We are they who want to do for ourselves. We are they who want a home on this earth that we can call our own. We are they who want deliverance from the midst of our 400-year enemies who keep us subjected to the status of servants and subjected to every brutality and murder known to civilized men. We are they who seek to rid ourselves of such an inhuman race of devils and live to ourselves in peace from the fear of such human beasts attacking and killing us night and day—and they call us un-American!

The entire Federal Government is against Freedom, Justice and Equality and total separation of the so-called Negroes in a state or states to ourselves. We want not only physical and moral freedom but even spiritual freedom—if it is the true religion of God called ISLAM. The Federal Government's agents follow us everywhere we go.

They question the new converts, seeking to pull them away by fear. They threaten them with the loss of jobs and persecution if there be the slightest grounds for it.

They call the truth and salvation of Allah, that He has brought to us, false and "trouble making." They call in both men and women who believe for questioning just for the sole purpose of trying to frighten them away.

They are trying to frighten them from that which they know is their so-called Negroes' salvation and universal recognition, friendship in all walks of life, money and good homes. The United States does not like to see us enjoying these things.

The only way is for us to accept Allah and His religion, Islam, and unite and leave such devil race of people. REMEMBER, Allah is with us to the end. He will give us this whole earth to rule forever. Accept and do my Twelve-Point Program. The white race is destroying itself and wishes to take you and I into its own destruction. BEWARE OF THEIR TRICKS, AS

THEY ARE NOW PLAYING THEM ON YOU 100 PER CENT.

According to the dictionary's definition of un-American, it means, "One that is not American, not characteristic of or proper to America, foreign or opposed to the American character, usages, standards, etc."

As you know, any or all Negroes who seek freedom, justice and equality are charged or accused of being un-American. They are accused with seeking to overthrow the government of America by force. (We, Muslims, prohibit the carrying of arms but yet are accused of planning to overthrow the government by force.) No Negro leader has been successful in helping his people to freedom, Justice and equality who was not opposed by both his own people and the merciless, wicked white Americans. And also by those "poison" intellectual so-called Negroes who love and worship the devils and hate self and kind.

Today, the Americans hope to unite all educated so-called Negroes along with their already poisoned Negro Christian preachers against us, the Muslims, who preach freedom, justice and equality for the Black Nation.

They are united against my followers and me. Thanks be to Allah you are a little too late to win. Allah (God) knew the tricks you would use to try deceiving the Black Man before you were created.

Un-American: I wish to prove, according to the English language, that every so-called Negro, Indian and all nonwhite Europeans are un-American according to the dictionary's definition of an American. An American according to the dictionary "is a citizen of the United States or of the earlier British Colonies; one not belonging to one of the aboriginal races." We belong to the aboriginal nation of the earth; the white or European race is not aboriginal.

Native or inhabitants of the Western Hemisphere. The above explanation makes it clear that we are not members of the white Europeans or descendants of that race. We are the aboriginal un-Americans. The above explanation also makes it clear that we (so-called Negroes) are not and cannot be American citizens, since we are not American by nature or race.

A true American is one other than the aboriginal race or races that inhabited the Western Hemisphere or the Whole Planet Earth before the coming of the white man from Europe.

We, the so-called Negroes (members of the aboriginal Black

Nation of the Earth and of the tribe of Shabazz), were kidnapped from our native land and people by the white Englishman and Americans.

We were brought here not to be made Americans or American citizens but rather to be slaves or servants for the true American citizens, whites who originally came from Europe.

We, descendants of the Asiatic nation from the continent of Africa after 100 years of so-called freedom, cannot claim by the law of justice to be Americans or American citizens. Nor can we expect anything like equal justice under the law of true American courts.

The government with its great standing armies cannot even force equal justice for the so-called Negroes. Why? Because we are not real American citizens. We are "un-American," and by nature we are different. Know from this day on that if you are a so-called Negro or red, or black or an Indian or any member of the aboriginal Black Nation you are an un-American. Even though you may have been born in the United States of America you CANNOT be an American.

USED FOR CRIMINAL PURPOSES: What or why are we called un-American? It is to classify us as criminals or with crimes that we are not guilty of. They make the truth God has given to us an untruth; they use it to conceal our true intentions. But at the same time, they claim freedom of speech, freedom of the press and religious freedom, lawful under the constitution.

Again, it is abundantly clear to you that have eyes that America never intended freedom for her so-called Negroes.

She stands in the way and opposes true freedom, justice and equality from coming to the poor black man and woman in the Western Hemisphere.

She is pleased with the foolish and ignorant worship of the so-called Negroes. She does not ever want the Negroes to accept the true religion, which is Islam. WHY?

Here, in Islam, the Negroes have a true God and true friends on their side, and that means help to the poor Negroes against their open enemies the white race.

So you can, or you will see why they do not want a so-called Negro Muslim people in America. It means independence, friendship, Divine guidance and help against the devils. As it is written in the Holy Qur-an, "Know that Allah is with Muslims."

TRICK THE NEGROES TO STAY IN DEVIL'S NAMES: For the first time, the so-called Negroes are awakening to just why white Americans still like to call their much-hated and despised once Negro slaves after their names or make the Negroes think names do not mean anything and that they should remain in them.

The devils have knowledge of the time. They know you will not be accepted by God or your own nation if represented under their names—which are not names of God— and will not see the hereafter.

The intellectual so-called Negroes think it is a disgrace to them to not be called by the slave-master's name. Even a doctor once tried to make me change my name and be called by the slave-master's name and said if I wanted to be called "Muhammad" I should go to the court and have my named changed legally.

I laughed and said that I was sorry, but I had my legal name, and there is no law to make me pay to be called by that name.

I have been called by an illegal name. Now I have gotten rid of that illegal slave name for a legal and Holy name of God.

Again, we must remember that the white race never intended anything like good for you. They are not seeking good for you today; death is really their aim for you. Why do they oppose our struggle for justice and freedom if they want to see all people free and enjoying justice and equality?

They are not referring to you; you are not people in their eye. It is their people they are referring to.

Why do they oppose segregation of us into a state or territory of our own, since we cannot live in peace with them? When we read of the evils done to us and to our fathers by this race of devils, we cannot foresee anything in them but evil, hatred and murder for us and our unborn children.

Read some of their books as to what was done against our slave parents by the fathers of these modern murderers of ours. For instance, the book entitled "Brown Americans," by Edwin R. Embree, printed in 1946, page 54, tells the story of law against education for the so-called Negroes.

He quotes a devil, Henry Berry, as saying while speaking in the Virginia House of Delegates in 1832 and describing the situation as existed at that time in many parts of the South:

"We have as far as possible, closed every avenue by which light may enter the slaves' mind. (The avenue of the light of Allah you are unable to shut out from coming to us.) If we could extinguish the capacity to see the light, our work would be complete; they would then be on a level with the beast of the field and we should be safe. I am not certain that we would not do it, if we could find out the process and that on the plea of necessity."

The above words, desires and works against you are still in the hearts of their evil, bloodthirsty children against you.

Today they go around in large cities like Chicago at night in cars loaded with baseball bats, guns, iron pipes and knives to pounce upon and kill poor, harmless, so-called Negroes. We are living under the very shadow of death in such a place as America.

Unity under the guidance and protection of Allah will bring an end to this horrible situation. What do you see as a future in them for you and your children? Nothing but hell.

Remember, if you are black or a member of the Black Nation you are un-American. If you want equal justice and a decent way of life to live, or have love for the black people, you are un-American. The American is the only one that can sing "The Land of Freedom"—it is for white Americans.

MISUNDERSTANDING AND MISINTERPRETATION

In the Name of Almighty Allah, The Most Merciful Savior, Our Deliverer, Master of the Day of Judgment. To Allah alone do I submit and seek refuge.

My dear, original Black people of North America and the world, there is much talk—both good and bad—going these days about the ending of the world that we now live in (the world of the white man). The people of the white race are losing their divine power to rule the world of the original man. It is very easy for us to see and understand that throughout the world there is unrest among the original black people, who are working at a boiling pitch trying to get to themselves and for themselves as never before, not even since the white race has been placed on the planet, even more so than in the time of Muhammad of 1,400 years ago. (May the peace and blessings of Allah be upon him.)

From the seventh century to the eleventh century, we had a much smaller world than we have today. Islam did not conquer the whole world—only Africa, the Near East and part of Europe as far as Vienna. She did not conquer Italy, China, Japan and the Islands. But today, Islam for the first time has nearly completed her march throughout the world.

She has not converted Europe or Christian Americans and never will. But, as far as the Original Black People in America, the Pacific Islands, the Southern realm of America, Argentina and South America, you will find a small population of Islam. America is the last place that Islam was to reach.

Not by the missionaries of Asia and Africa, but America was left for the divine Supreme Being who is referred to by the Name of Allah.

In this country, Allah desired to make Himself known as He did (for example) in Egypt, only this time it is universal, coming first to the lost and found members of the Black Nation of America. That prophecy of the Bible from Moses to Jesus must be fulfilled. There is much taught against the divine work that is going on here in America by Orthodox Muslims and Black Christians of America.

Many of the Orthodox Muslims do not want to believe that Allah has appeared in the Person of Master Fard Muhammad or that He has made manifest the truth that has been hidden from their religious scientists—the truth of God and of the devil as revealed to me. Though they do have the Holy Qur-an, many of them do not understand the meaning of it, and some of them believe everything that is prophesied in the Bible and Holy Qur-an about a last Messenger or Prophet being or referring to Muhammad of 1,400 years ago.

They even take all of the people prophesied from Moses to Jesus, who received a prophet coming after Moses and like Moses to the people of Muhammad of 1,400 years ago. This is very wrong. It must be understood that the prophesies are referring to God and a Messenger in the resurrection of the dead in the last years of this world ruled by the Caucasian people.

Moses and Jesus were both examples of what was to come at the end of this world, not the end of Moses' and Jesus' world. Moses' and Jesus' lives were examples of what would take place among the so-called Negro in America—that lost and found people mentioned so much by Jesus in Revelations where it is shown that the Messenger becomes a lamb.

In Revelations, the symbolic lamb is in the midst of four symbolic beasts. All of the scholars and scientists of the white race know this is not referring to Muhammad of 1,400 years ago.

The anger of the beast refers to a dragon against the Messenger who is referred to as a lamb or as a woman pregnant with child. This is one of the clearest prophecies of the opposition against him in the last days and the type of people to whom the revelator refused to give credit for being not human beings but beasts who desire to destroy the woman and her child.

This only means the Messenger and his followers of Islam.

All Messengers were attacked by disbelievers and governments of their time, according to the Qur-an. As an example of what the last Messenger and his followers would face, Pharaoh openly confessed that he desired to slay Moses and did not believe that God (Allah) would be able to protect Moses from his evil plans.

But the Holy Qur-an says that Allah made him an example, for in the last days both Moses and the symbolic lamb are declared to be victorious.

Revelations states that the lamb and his followers, after escaping the evil plans of the beast, sang the song of Moses, which was of the victory over Pharaoh.

Let us remember that the scholars and scientists have not understood the true interpretations of the Bible and Holy Qur-an concerning the last Messenger. They should meet and confer on this most important of all scriptures and come to the correct interpretation.

Both of you, Christians and Orthodox Muslims, are absolutely wrong to believe all of this prophecy refers to Jesus or Moses and a prophet like himself and to believe that the symbolic lamb in Revelation refers to Jesus or, as the Orthodox Muslims believe, that it refers to Muhammad of 1,400 years ago. How gravely you must interpret your Bible and Holy Qur-an. This important understanding is causing a lot of divisions.

Some of the well-read scholars among the Orthodox Muslims are grieved to hear from America that I call myself a Messenger of Allah, though not one of them has been able to do the work that I have done in resurrecting my people in America. They could not do it. It was not for them to do what I am doing (the resurrecting of the dead). Their own Holy Qur-an teaches them that Allah teaches a Messenger from every people that he intends to warn or destroy. It tells them in plain words that an Arab and an Arabic Holy Qur-an could not be the instrument sent to the people who must be resurrected because they would have the excuse that they could not read Arabic and therefore exercise their disbelief by saying that this was an Arab and an Arabic Qur-an.

The Qur-an teaches that they must have the Qur-an in their own language and they must not have a foreigner but someone from among themselves who could speak their language.

He could not be one who could speak Arabic until Allah taught him Arabic. Therefore the Messenger is not an Arab or an Arabic speaker in the resurrection of the dead, not the people who must be resurrected, according to the Qur-an. But later Allah taught him Arabic, and then He said in His Qur-an that now I give to thee a Holy Qur-an in the language of the people (whom he is among who did not speak Arabic). and now I give thee an Arabic Holy Qur-an that I may warn the Mother city.

This means that he received two books. One in a foreign language to Arabs and another in the original language. Both called Holy Qur-an. There must be something that is wrong about the Mother city which all the scholars agree is Mecca. Those are the last days, not in the days of Moses—only his work of correcting the ills of the Arabs in Mecca where he was born.

This was an example of what was to come or what will come. He, not Jesus, referred to the old truth which was given to either one, though the Holy Qur-an is without a doubt a true book, but it only takes us up to the resurrection of the dead not beyond. It does not give you a real knowledge of Allah and the Devil because it refers to the coming of Allah as the Bible refers to the coming of Allah.

The Holy Qur-an refers to the days of Allah, meaning in the

years of the resurrection, and it often repeats that the people will meet with Allah in person, not in visions. He will return to them or give them a knowledge of that which they have done, good or evil.

He will not allow the good ones to enter into everlasting goodness without knowing of their good. It says that on that day Allah will give every man a book so that he can read his own account in the resurrection of the dead, especially the so-called American Negro.

They will receive these accounts literally because they are a people who must be separated, and these books will verify their actual worth. Of course, they have a knowledge of the chastisement of the wicked and disbelievers' rejections of the truth, and the righteous will have a knowledge of their right by being separated by Allah from evil doers and hypocrites.

The jealousy of the last Messenger is written of and mentioned throughout the Qur-an and the Bible. All prophets had people among them who were hypocrites who were jealous of them and wanted their place.

But they were not fit or chosen by Allah for that high place, as they probably could not go through the punishment or persecution of the wicked. There are religious scientists in Islam who know these things to be true that I am saying, and there are those who do not understand their Holy Qur-an and the prophecy of Muhammad being last among the dead, for the Bible teaches that God will use him to make Himself known in the last days. The people will probably fall for everything evil.

I will not acknowledge the hypocrites' charges against me by going and contending with them before my enemies. I am not sent to accuse my people. I am sent to clear them of the charges of the accusers—the devils.

This is the divine problem. God, Himself, will liberate the Negro. Africa is trying to liberate herself from the same enemy.

These prophecies concerning the Resurrection and Freedom of the so-called American Negro cannot be cast aside as false, especially today, for you can see the fulfillment.

The so-called Negro must be delivered by God and God only. He will use a Messenger who is symbolically referred to as the Lamb of God in the Resurrection to spiritually liberate the American Negro.

They must be taught a thorough knowledge of their people

and the devil. They must be Muslims to be liberated. They must have the Name of God, which means one of the 99 names that comprise the Name of God. The names are now being given.

The foolish hypocrites do not know the scriptures or prophecies, but they desire recognition by the people as great leaders without any followers.

There are many Africans and Egyptians who are now giving me credit for what I have said. They are actually surprised when they come into the knowledge of Allah's work in America and me, His chosen Messenger, sent to my people here in America.

I will accomplish the mission Allah has given to me to raise my people here in America, both spiritually and physically, above the nations of the earth, if it pleases Him.

ECONOMIC PROGRAM

TO HELP FIGHT
AGAINST POVERTY AND WANT!

I appeal to all Muslims, and to all the members of the original Black Nation in America, to sacrifice at least five cents from each day's pay to create an "Economic Savings Program" to help fight unemployment, abominable housing, hunger, and nakedness of the 22 million black people here in America who continue to face these problems.

This will not interfere with, the government's program for better housing conditions at all; it will only aid those who have never known anything in the way of help and those who do not even know that there is a government housing act to help dependent people. There are thousands of our people living in worse conditions than dogs and pigs. At least dogs are not bothered with too many rats and roaches in their houses because they kill them to keep out the uncleanliness and filth which dominate and create bad housing conditions.

We hope to set up a committee to teach and force our people to be clean: The Committee of Cleanliness. We already have such a committee in effect among the Muslims. It compels our people to clean their bodies as well as their houses. If you have only one suit of clothing, you should wash it and press it each night so that you can wear it the next day. If you are not able to have your hair trimmed at the barbershop, you should take turns and trim each other's hair. You must shave yourselves and look like men.

And our women should clean up. You do not have to have a dozen dresses. Just keep the one you have clean and pressed. Until we enforce cleanliness among the people of our Nation and get them into the spirit of self-respect and the spirit of making themselves the equal of other civilized nations of the earth we will never be recognized as being fit members of any decent society of those nations.

Send your quarters every week to Muhammad's Temple No. 2 in Chicago, Illinois. These quarters will be banked until we have a million dollars to begin building a banking system.

We have wasted too much money trying to be the equal of the millionaires of America. We like sport and play, but we suffer the pains of hunger because of the millions of dollars lost paying notes for luxuries we could do without--such as fine automobiles, fine clothes, whiskey, beer, wine, cigarettes, tobacco and drugs.

Let the entire nation sacrifice for three years. Confine ourselves to buy not more than three suits of clothes a year, never exceeding $65 in cost. Buy the minimum amount of shoes, never paying over $16 a pair, as long as current prices for the abovementioned merchandise remain the same. (Of course, inflation can run prices up until money has no value.) We should cut down on waste in high-priced food. Eat pure and wholesome food without being extravagant. Let us cut our extravagances.

As soon as we have enough money in our banks to purchase lands sufficient to feed the 22 million black people, we will build storage warehouses to store our supplies of the necessities of life for our people.

I believe that if we make these sacrifices throughout the nation for three years, as all our nations are doing or have done, we will soon rid our people of poverty and want. Russia did it on a five-year plan. Pakistan and other nations did it and are today on top. We must sacrifice for three years. I will not ask you to try a five-year plan: I am afraid that you, with your short patience, will not agree. But try three years on an "Economic Savings Program" to fight against poverty among our people here in America. I know you will become a happier and more recognized people and have the spirit of independence which is the glory of any nation.

Please respond and help yourself. Each and every one of you will be sent a receipt which will be recorded in our books for the Muslims' Three-Year Economic Program for the Black Nation in America. You will get a receipt for every penny you send to this office, which you will keep as your record.

You can mail the money directly to the Muslims' Three-Year Economic Program Department, Muhammad's Temple No. 2, 7351 Stony Island Avenue, Chicago Illinois 60649. You can send 25 cents each week or $1 per month. Send postal or personal money orders. No personal checks will be accepted unless your financial savings are verified by the bank.

We, the Muslims, will support this program and hope that every member of the working class of our people throughout the country will join us. We will show the world that we can build an independent nation· out of those who have been a dependent people for 400 years.

We are asking you to help us enlarge our educational system so that our people can be educated. This we refer to as re-education into the knowledge of self, our history and the knowledge of the good things of life, of which we have been deprived. You can also aid us by subscribing to the *Muhammad Speaks Newspaper.*

May Allah bless our poor dependent people in America with better homes more money and better friendships among the nations of earth.

A SOUND ECONOMIC PLAN I

The economic plight of the black people of this land has so long been neglected by so-called leaders that even our own people have forgotten it's basic importance.

Our economic position remains at the bottom of the ladder because of this ineffective leadership and because so many of our people ignore the basic rules of a healthy economic life. We fail to develop self-leadership in economics.

We are in the midst of the so-called civil rights struggle and ferment among the black and oppressed reaches new heights. I shall list, critically, but constructively, the guide and outline which must be followed if this black nation of 22 million is ever to achieve true independence and equality.

We shall begin with these four points.

No. 1. Our knowledge of self, others, and the time should force us to become more prudent in our spending. Unnecessary spending by trying to keep pace with the wealthy of this country has done more to put us on the path of the "prodigal son" than anything else. Let us be taught how to spend and save by those of us who desire to see us out of poverty and want.

No. 2. Do not be too proud to meet together as leaders and teachers to discuss the solution of "How to stop this reckless, down-hill fall of our people."

No. 3. Not one so-called Negro leader seems to want a meeting with me to discuss the plight of our poor people in North America.

No. 4. I have set before you a program, according to the Divine Supreme Being and His Prophets. You have neither produced a better program nor anything to equal it. Your present plans are involved in one of the most disgraceful programs—especially you who boast that you are free and want freedom, Justice and equality with your slave-masters by sitting, standing and begging to be accepted as the brothers of those who, for 400 years, have brought you into your present condition, and have made you a people unwanted by the civilized nations of the earth.

No one wants foolish people who love everyone but themselves and their own kind; who would rather beg than go for self, or even ask the slave-masters to help them go for self. Such people, numbering into the millions, are on the road to destruction if their down-hill speed is not checked by Allah (God) and His Messenger.

HOW TO MAKE AN ECONOMIC PROGRAM SUCCESSFUL: It is very hard for an economist to plan a wise program and see his plans carried out, because the so-called American Negroes' economics are controlled by the white man. The white man owns the country and the industry. He is manufacturer and producer of everything. Now, it is difficult to plan an economic program for a dependent people who, for all their lives, have tried to live like the white man.

The first step the so-called Negro wage-earners should take is to spend only when necessary and according to their income. They should save as much of their salaries as possible--weekly, biweekly or monthly. We, as wage earners, should always plan to save something from whatever we are paid. Do not become extravagant spenders like the rich, who own the country and everything in it. It is sheer ignorance for us to try to compete in luxury with the owners.

If we can save just five cents a day from our wages, 25 cents a week, $1 a month—that would mean $13 a year we could save in a national savings bank. We number around 22 million and approximately five million are wage-earners. If five million wage-earners saved $13 a year, this would mean $65 million saved out of our wages. At the rate of 25 cents per week, it would be painless. But the so-called Negroes do not have that in a national bank.

Let us see how much money we spend unnecessarily: Suppose we spent the same amount (25 cents a week) in tobacco (cigarettes, cigars, chewing or snuff dipping). But, of course, you will spend far more than that. Some people spend 25 cents per day for cigarettes alone. Let us say we spent the same amount (25 cents a week) on beer. Again the actual amount would be more. This means $65 million a year spent for beer and the same spent for whiskey, wine, cigarettes and cigars. We also spend unnecessarily on sports. You average the same on sports ($65 million). Another $65 million is spent in gambling—averaging five cents a day, 25 cents a week. This is just the minimum.

If five million wage earners saved just $47 per year, they could save $235 million dollars a year. And this figure would be far greater if we included extravagant buying of clothes, furniture and cars. Eating the hog, the Divinely forbidden flesh which keeps us filled with arthritis, rheumatism, high blood pressure and fever makes unnecessary doctor and drug bills. All of this wasteful spending should be checked and you will see within a one-year period that you have not saved one billion dollars, but several billions.

The economical way to use the money you save is first to buy farm land and produce your own food. You can raise enough cattle, sheep, cows and chickens by the thousands if you try following our program. We could cut down on our clothing bills —some of us by about 30 per cent—and yet be well-dressed. Again in this way we could build a national savings bank from deposits for ourselves, and invest our money in the purchase of necessary things for our nation. Then, you could cut down your present high cost of living.

Purchase real estate, buy farm and timberland. Convert the timber into lumber and build homes for yourselves as the white man is doing. Of course, he will have the authority over whether or not to sell the land to you. Get clay land. With marsh clay land and hill clay, you can make your own bricks. Bricks are inexpensive to make once you get your kiln built and tracks laid. The greatest expense would be coal or gas to fire your bricks. Build brick homes for your own people and sell them to your people at a very reasonable price.

Try and save your people from unnecessary high-price buying. Take your cotton to the mills and have it converted into lint. And take the lint to the textile mills and have it converted into cloth. You are very smart. We have many technicians among us who are about as smart as they come. Why shouldn't we get together and produce something for ourselves?

Ask the government to help us go for ourselves. And if the government will not help us, although we and our fathers have been loyal and helped them to become and remain independent, then appeal to your own people to allow you to move in among them. I am sure that if you are a Muslim you can find a place anywhere on the earth.

We are the righteous and it should not be hard for us to do something for self if we unite. We do not need to unite and then go fight some other nations to get their country. No! That will not be necessary. Come follow me and I will show you how to do this without having to shed a drop of blood. Shedding blood for something that you are Divinely justified in having is not necessary.

It is a disgrace for us to have all this present trouble--standing around begging, quarreling and fighting with slave-masters over something that we can do for ourselves if only given a chance. This chance can be had if you go about it in the right way.

THE ECONOMIC PROGRAM II

As I noted previously, on matters of economics there is entirely too much distrust among us. We trust everyone but ourselves. We, therefore, have to build or produce trust in ourselves in order to do something for self and kind. We cannot depend upon the white man to continue to care for us and build a future of good for us and our children.

We can see every hour and every day how the white man's world is narrowing and how his time is growing shorter. This narrowing of his world power teaches us that we must strike out for ourselves or be left behind helpless and without a future.

If you would accept Allah for your God and His religion, Islam--which means entire submission to His will--it would produce quality leadership that you could trust; a leadership capable and willing, with a heart of love for one's people.

Christianity has never been able to produce the right leadership for our people—and never will. It is disheartening to a wise leader of the so-called American Negro to see how foolish he has been made to think and act.

The black man in America as well as the black man abroad has never been able to provide good leadership for himself under Christianity, because Christianity is not the true religion of God. It is a division of religions and uses a division of God which makes it impossible to establish true love and unity of brotherhood.

As I wrote previously, it is difficult to plan an economic system for a people who are subjected to the whim of another people. You are limited in your jobs, salaries and incomes by the white man. But you still can learn not to be reckless and wasteful spenders and happy-go-lucky people with nothing of your own. Every sport the white man—with bulging banks of money—enjoys, you try to imitate him.

Take what he gives you and learn to save some of it. The hardest times are before those of you who will not accept this program and follow the way of Allah and Islam, guide you and set you in heaven at once, with money, good homes and friendships in all walks of life.

Begging and praying to the white man to accept you (his once abject slave, and now willing slave) and give you the things he is giving himself and his kind is really out of place today.

The white man claims he has given you freedom. He feels that he is not responsible for your poverty—since you have had 100 years on your own. He believes that if you did not like him, you should have left him, and if you do not like him today, you should leave him. You do not want to leave him because of your great desire for his wealth. This classified you as being lazy; a people who do not want to accept their own responsibility. Think it over, my friends.

We could save money by walking instead of riding in luxury. If we can purchase an automobile, we should not try to get the most luxurious model unless we can afford it.

You have read in previous articles on economics how you can save hundreds of millions of dollars—even billions—if you would accept the right economic program and stop using things which destroy your health, such as tobacco, which doctors warn us can cause cancer. X-rays are known also to be dangerous and produce cancer. While X-rays aid doctors in finding the source of an ailment, they are not good for our bodies. Scientists now warn you against gazing into TV sets for any long length of time, because this can produce cancer in the body. This is especially true of children, who prop themselves in front of TV sets and gaze for hours at close range.

We must remember that the new inventions are still in the experimental stage. None of the new inventions in this great modern world are completely safe. Look at TV only when you know there is something of importance to be seen; not for foolishness and sport.

Beware of the national elections, my black brothers and sisters. There is no salvation in them for you—only false promises. The only salvation for you and me now is in unity and being under the guidance of Allah through His Messenger and His program for us all.

Do not follow those self-made leaders who are seeking only the praise of the people and have no good in mind for you and will lead you back into becoming more of a slave than ever. Our problem is to be solved by a divine solution given to Allah's Messenger.

Follow me and live. Reject me and die as people without the help of God and friend.

UP! YOU CAN ACCOMPLISH
AS YOU WILL!

I am asking that we (the whole nation) sacrifice for the next three years and when we get enough in our bank, we will put it to work to make more money. We do not mean to let it lie idly for three years; we could invest in anything to help the Nation improve our economic condition.

Heretofore our distrust in each other has kept us down. We have to trust each other as other nations trust each other in order to do something constructive for the original Black people of this country.

We would like to raise at least $500 million in the next three years. If all would contribute willingly and honestly all that they

could to this economic plan we would soon have billions and
enough money to have something for ourselves, other than begging
at the gate, door, and floor of the white man's business places
for that which we--if united--could get for ourselves.

I am sure that the white people would have more respect for
us after giving us a job and salary, if we would try saving some
of that salary to help ourselves in that which we could do for
ourselves. If they give us jobs and pay us living wages, we
should do more for ourselves than we are doing with high wages
and salary that we are receiving today. If the wages were rightly
distributed, they would prevent our begging for food and shelter.

No nation will ever respect us as long as we beg for that
which we can do for ourselves. There has never been a leader
of our people who went all-out to set up an economic plan for
our people. I use the saying of Jesus, "All before me were
thieves and robbers."

There are millions of your dollars lying in the white man's
banks doing nothing for anyone. Put these millions of dollars
to work buying farm land, since this is the basis of independence. Raise cotton, corn, wheat, rye, rice, chicken, cattle, and
sheep. The sheep would clothe us with its wool and feed us
with its flesh. The cow would also serve as food for us, as well
as his hide being used in making shoes, belts, jackets, coats and
hats. The cotton could be woven into cloth. Remember how
America once had to spin its yarn to make clothes by a spin-
ning wheel?

Today, if you have the money, you can buy machines which
will weave and print thousands of yards of cotton goods per
day. Do you say that you cannot do it?

The white man is not preventing you from doing these things.

He has many textile mills: he will help you and even weave
your clothes at his own mills for a price. We can cobble our
own shoes: the white man will sell us the machines. In fact, he
will sell us almost anything to help us manufacture what we
need.

However, you must first go to the farms, till the earth, and
produce your own food. Build stores and warehouses to preserve your food throughout the seasons. We just are not trying to do anything for self. As I have repeated until my throat
is dry, one day America (the white man) will not be able to
carry this entire nation of 22 million black people on her back.

Their world is getting very small and if you are dependent upon this world, yours too, is getting very small. Self-preservation is the first law of nature. Everyone tries to provide a future of his own but the American so-called Negro.

Turn your millions of dollars over to our National Three-Year Economic Savings Plan and I will show you how you can do all of these things overnight and be a happy people right here in America. This will bring about peace between the two people because you will not have to fight, or beg the white man for that which you can get for yourself (if you were only united). You most certainly should be tired of being beaten and killed.

I am appealing to you—each and everyone of the 22 million black people of America—to send every penny, nickel, dime, dollar, hundreds of dollars and millions of dollars that you can spare to the "Three-Year Economic Plan" MUHAMMAD'S TEMPLE NO. 2—7351 South Stony Island Avenue, Chicago, Illinois 60649.

Russia did it and became independent. Pakistan did it and became independent and you can also do it and become independent. As soon as your money is received, it is banked in the Continental Bank of America and other federal banks until we reach the mark of $1 million. When our mark of $1 million is accomplished, we are going to build a national reserve bank for the black people of America.

Thank you again and again for your contributions. We will prove to you that we are honest people and only want to see you out of the mud of dependency and on a rock of independence.

We can help accomplish this task by asking the government to do her once-slave a favor for the next ten years--by exempting us from tax.

THE WORLD HAILS
THE NEW ECONOMIC PLAN

Our Three-Year Economic Savings Plan is receiving great response. Those able to give who are giving, are giving far more than I expected and this includes all of the Muslims. Those unable to give are in sympathy with our cause. We thank and praise Allah for His coming and blessing those who have neglected their duty to Allah and self, because of ignorance and fear of those who put fear in us, and prevent us from uniting for a common cause. If Allah continues to bless us--and He will —with the progress that we are now making, the set goal will be accomplished at the end of the three years.

We, the Muslims, have responded nearly 100 per cent for the past month. This savings plan is intended for all of our people in America who are from slave parents. It was not meant solely for the Muslims, but for the entire 22 million of our kind. Let it be remembered that what is good for the Muslims is good for all of our people here in America, because you are the ones we are trying to reach with good. A national savings plan for us (22 million original black people) is one of the greatest steps towards financial help against poverty ever set before us since our so-called 100 years of freedom from slavery.

The black man or woman refusing to give our Three-Year Savings Plan credit as mentioned above and who will not contribute to it, cannot be considered a man or woman who wants to see his or her people out of the chains of want and suffering. We can do nothing constructive until we unite in a constructive plan for the entire 22 million of our people here in America. Jealousy, envy and suspicion in and against good planning for us, will always keep us down as a Nation and will always keep us serving the god of poverty and want.

If our forefathers had the power of life, to speak from their graves, they would condemn you for wasting your time and life —after being freed and not availing yourself of this freedom. They were forced into slavery against their will, but you are now forcing yourself to remain in slavery by trying to force the white man to allow you to remain with him and provide for you as he has always done.

You must admit that "White America" envies the success and prosperity coming to us (especially the poor devils in the South). This is why they will not give us an equal chance with them in that which will bring us progress and success. Since that is true, I am appealing to you to seek separation from such people on some of this earth that we can call our own, away from a people who openly show and tell you that they hate you and any or all good that may come to you.

Join us (the Muslims) and our program for a united Black Nation, so that we may free ourselves from our oppressors with whom we cannot get along in peace. Spend only when it is a "must" and contribute — all of you — all you can to this Three-Year Economic Plan.

We will not, however, be responsible for contributions given or sent other than directly to the Three-Year Economic Savings Plan, Temple No. 2, 7351 South Stony Island Avenue, Chicago, Illinois 60649.

SEPARATION!
INDEPENDENCE!

With the right understanding and with business unity we can turn the great flow of millions of dollars that leave black communities and go into the hands of white businessmen back into the pockets of the poor black men and women who would benefit most by it. HOW CAN WE DO THIS?

First we must stop being so foolish as to spend our few hard earned dollars with the rich of this land.

Those of us who are wealthy or rich should help set up independent businesses which our people need and which could add wealth to our communities. With such cooperation our own businessmen could actually help lower prices and provide employment for the multitude of unemployed.

But to be successful, WE MUST HAVE SOME OF THIS EARTH TO PRODUCE OUR PEOPLE'S NEEDS.

For example, in Chicago, Illinois, as well as in other communities, throughout the country, the Black Man is robbed through giant cut-rate stores, owned exclusively by white men who make it almost impossible for independent stores owned by black people to survive.

We cannot compete in business unless we unite and get some of this earth so that we can produce our own people's needs.

It is the right time that we seek SEPARATION AND INDEPENDENCE for our nation from the evils of our open enemies, and not the foolish things other organizations are doing. They want our people integrated into our open enemies to be destroyed as a people.

They seek that (recognition) which demands better qualifications: education, the knowledge of self and others, manners
and self-respect and the respect of others.

But our people just do not have these qualifications until
they first come to Islam and bear witness to what Allah (God)
has revealed to me. No intelligent and refined society will accept
us until we have the above stated qualifications.

We, once slaves, have grown to be a nation of twenty million
or more in a nation that enslaved our fathers and to this day
has deprived us of equal justice under their own laws. No equal
civil rights—most of us are treated by white citizens of America
as animals. It is common to see and hear of white mobs attacking, beating, and shooting down poor blacks whose fathers' and
mothers' labor, sweat and blood helped make America the rich-
est government on earth; nevertheless, we are yet the most hated
and mistreated people.

Allah (God) wants to make a great nation out of us (so-called Negroes). But if we desire to remain the slave of servants
for our slave-masters, it is all right with Allah. Do we love ourselves and our children? If so, why not build a future for ourselves rather than beg the same slave-masters for jobs and equal
shares in whatever they have—even to equal membership in their
society and families (intermarriage).

This is definitely not a wise thing to do, but a very foolish
and destructive thing for the once-slave and his master to do.
By the help and guidance of Allah (God), I have put before you
the wise and best thing for your future.

Firstly, some of this earth that we can call our own. Without
some of this earth that we can call our own, we cannot hope
to even become a free nation out of the nation of the slave
master. IT IS FAR MORE IMPORTANT TO TEACH SEP-
ARATION OF THE BLACKS AND WHITES IN AMERICA
THAN PRAYER. Teach and train the blacks to do something
for self in the way of uniting and seeking a home on this earth
that they can call their own!

There is no such thing as living in peace with white Americans.
You and I have tried without success. Look what white Americans did to my followers in Los Angeles, California, on April
27, 1962.

They know that we, the Muslims, are a peaceful people and

do not carry arms, but the heartless enemy devils care not for peace, they were created and made to hate peace.

Night and day they are out seeking a chance to beat and kill you, while at the same time you are out seeking to show them HOW MUCH YOU LOVE THEM. A very foolish people you are. How can anyone, other than you (so-called Negroes) love an open enemy?

THE PERSECUTION
OF THE RIGHTEOUS

PROTECTION
OF THE FAITHFUL

"None dispute concerning Message of Allah but those who disbelieve. So let not their control in the land deceive them." Holy Qur-an 40:4

The preceding verse is very clear. According to the Holy Qur-an, the truth must always be rejected and classified as foolishness by the rejectors. It is always those who consider themselves to be in the seat of authority and power in the land who reject the truth. They desire to lead others in their rejection of the truth, especially the poor man in the mud, because he is the one whom they exploit.

Their rejective behavior is similar to that of the people in the land of America today. The white man is in control and he seeks to deceive the so-called Negro just as Pharaoh deceived the Israelites. Pharaoh had control and power over Egypt. He made a mockery of Moses saying that Moses could not speak plainly, and he criticized Allah's offer to Israel. Pharaoh did not give the Israelites that promised land of milk and honey (fertility and riches).

The white man in America is like Pharaoh in Egypt. He, the modern Pharaoh, is trying to control the 22 million so-called American Negroes as Pharaoh did the Israelites in Egypt. The white man's control over the so-called Negro makes them helpless in trying to follow Allah and His servant into a land they call their own and where they can rule themselves as other nations are doing.

The so-called Negroes are deceived in thinking their future

in America will be a great one. They should accept their own
(Islam) and try to do something for themselves as other nations
are doing, on land they can call their own. They have intelligence but do not have the desire to do for themselves. Conse-
quently, the white man of America is helping them to continue
to have such foolish desires. He wants to keep the so-called Negro looking up to the white American for what he wants.

The so-called Negroes are disgracing themselves lying at the
feet of the white man and begging him to accept them as equals
in sharing the wealth of America. It is against the very nature
and disposition of the slave-master to accept his once slave as
his equal, or to share equally with slave in his wealth. Therefore, the ignorant so-called Negro who has never gone to school
is now showing himself to be wiser in his acceptance of Allah
and His true religion of Islam than the learned of our people.

The poor among our people desire to be white through intermixing with the white man and sharing in his wealth. They prove
to be even more ignorant than the learned in their fascination
with gaining the enemy's wealth and power and their desire to
trust the white man's power and wealth instead of acquiring
permanent houses and wealth that Allah has offered. This makes
them look very ignorant in the eyes of the civilized world.

What is going on in the South against our people is their
own fault since they have heard the truth. The so-called Negroes
have gone back to the slave-master who said they were free 100
years ago. As a result, they are beaten, trampled and attacked
by police dogs as though they were again living 300 years ago
under slavery.

These incidents only occur because of our people's great love
for and desire to remain under their slave-masters' children.

If our people in the South are permitted to vote, for whom
are they going to vote? They will vote for none but the white
man whether the black man's vote outnumber the white man's
or not. The fact that you can vote does not mean that the
white man will allow you to put men in Washington of your
kind who would love to give you justice, nor does it mean that
you will be voted in as President of the country. You can never
hope to attain this.

If you think because Kennedy said in 40 years a Negro man
would become President of the country, he will become just that,
then you misunderstood. Never will a black man be able to rule

a white man in America. He was only referring to the so-called American Negroes' unity with his brothers. This will make him strong enough to put a President in office, but not over white people.

Forty years from now, there may not be a white man in the Western Hemisphere. In addition, the President is aware of the shameful, humiliating and disgraceful acts by our people trying to be recognized and justified in the South as an equal of the white man. This is due to the poor leadership of our people. The leaders do not know that this is the time of separation and not the time of integration. The time for us to separate has come. The God of justice is bringing this about Himself by making us see the enemy clearly as he really is.

It is Allah who taught me that this is a race of devils, and those of you who think yourselves to be theologians know they are a race of devils according to the scriptures. Some of you may argue that you do not believe the scriptures where they teach the knowledge of this race of people, but this is written in both the Holy Qur-an and Bible several times. You will be punished for ignoring this truth as were the Israelites. They were in love with the Egyptians who were jealous and envious of Moses. The wisdom of Jehovah was communicated through Moses to the Israelite. The Egyptians opposed Moses, and Allah became angry as the Bible teaches you. He, therefore, sent fiery and angry serpents to fight and kill those who were rebelling against Moses' leadership. So it is with you today.

"Before them, the people of Noah and the parties after them rejected [prophets] and every nation purposed against its messengers to destroy him, and disputed by means of falsehood to render null thereby the truth, so I seized them; how [terrible] was then my retribution!" Holy Qur-an 40:05

The fifth verse is a warning to us today. It speaks of a people God has marked for destruction. Your actions are the same as disbelievers before you. They made mockery of Allah's Messenger and designed plans against him. They planned to destroy him, just as the present day disbelievers plan against my life. They desire to destroy me (the present Messenger).

How terrible was Allah's disapproval of their actions against His Messenger; so it is today.

WE SEEK TRUTH AND JUSTICE

America knows that under her flag we have received nothing but hell, beatings and killings without due process of the law, day and night, not only in the past but in the present.

She wants to make some so-called Negroes believe that the religion of Islam can be thrown out the window if they turn hypocrites themselves in trying to make democracy work. This is done only to deceive the so-called American Negroes.

But I say to every one who reads this book that Islam is here among these black people of America to stay as long as their life is in their bodies. The God of Islam (Allah) is with me and will back me and others who are working hard to deliver people from such an evil and merciless race of devils.

What glory and honor does a so-called Negro get under the Stars and Stripes? No honor, no glory—only hell. We have proof of this by their so-called courts of justice. There is no justice for you—and this America knows. She would like to hurt every one of you and make you like it. It pleases her to do you evil.

But not us Muslims. We will declare the truth and die for it. Thanks to Allah for removing fear from us, and I pray He puts it in them and they may fear and tremble every day until they are taken out of the way.

The Monroe, Louisiana, Southern Courts with their southern judges of hatred are thirsty to take their own law of justice, twist it up and throw it back upon the shelf. And when they look they see a poor, innocent so-called Negro begging for justice, as his grandparents and their grandparents before as far back as 400 years ago, who receive nothing but the spitting of anger and threats of murder from the judges throughout the Courts of America. Just to mention "justice" for a so-called Negro in the South is an insult to the judge, who is supposed to be the judge of right and wrong between the state and opposing attorneys.

He becomes a more vicious enemy against the poor so-called Negro than the prosecuting attorney when he sees a so-called Negro before him.

The so-called Negroes do not have justice under the law, not only in the South, but anywhere in America. As I plainly stated in Washington, D.C., in 1959, in the Uline Arena before 10,000 people, everything has failed us as far as justice is concerned—The Justice Department in Washington, the churches, the priests and the preachers have all failed the so-called Negroes.

We, the Muslims, were and are still being persecuted in Monroe, Louisiana, and throughout North America for what we teach of these two flags (Islamic and American) and especially because of the following words that you will find on a blackboard in most of our regular meetings: "Which Flag will survive the War of Armageddon?" (Armageddon is the final war of Judgment and separation of the righteous from the wicked, of which I am sent to teach.)

This is a question that is asked the mentally dead of my people in America, the so-called Negroes. This question is to show the answerer that he fully agrees that the Sun, Moon and Stars will survive the Cross, or the flag of America known as the Stars and Stripes. Everyone who is asked this question answers that the Crescent will survive America's flag and the emblem of Christianity, which is the Cross. A fool knows that the sun, moon and stars will survive any nation.

Then comes the next question. Since you believe that the Crescent will survive, why not accept Islam and the flag and Crescent emblem which represents the Sun, Moon and the Stars?

We are doing work that is well known among all the learned whites and blacks—the resurrecting of the mentally dead so-called Negroes to give them Divine knowledge of self, of Allah (God) and of the devil. In the past, we have been taught that God and the devil were something other than human, while the truth from Almighty God, Allah, who is now among us in Person, makes it clear that these two characters are human beings. I am not referring to the wise, who already know these things, but to the ignorant and foolish. If you read your Bible for understanding of the reality of God and the devil, you also will agree that they are human beings and not spirits or nonexisting beings—they exist! I have not the time or space to go into details.

That it is a crime, or that these words (which one—meaning the American flag or the Islamic flag—will survive the War of Armageddon, or Holy War, or the war to end wars) are considered a crime or a teaching to incite insurrection or revolution to take America by force, cannot be proven to be truth by anyone who may read this or may have attended one of our meetings.

If Troy X. Cade is guilty of teaching insurrection against the government, then I am guilty, because I am Troy's teacher. I would rather go to prison in place of Troy if this is the justice for the truth Allah gave me.

By the help of Allah, and by the blood of the original man, whose father is the originator, I, Elijah Muhammad, will fight for this cause to get our people justice in America—and by the help and power of Allah, the power that is in the Universe, the power that is in the Nation of Islam, and the power of every atom that is bound in the Planet Earth and that is bound in other planets.

What angers America is just the idea of her 400-year-old slave now wanting to go over to the paradise of freedom justice and equality under the Crescent of the Divine religion of Islam, where they will have sincere brotherhood and friends throughout the civilized world.

WERE MUSLIMS FRAMED
TO WHITEWASH
THE GUILTY?

You may know of the incident that took place on April 27, 1962, in Los Angeles, California, between the Los Angeles Policemen and my followers; one of my followers Ronald T. X. Stokes was killed out-right while his hands were raised and with nothing on him to do anyone harm.

Every one of the Brothers was unarmed when nearly one hundred policemen swooped down upon them, well-armed, out of the darkness of the night to kill the Believers of Allah and His religion (Islam) and to stop the spread of Islam.

On that fateful night, one of the policemen's bullets paralyzed one brother for life and others received serious wounds in the chest and private areas. They were all shot down for no reason other than that the devils wanted to kill the righteous as they have done in the past to the Prophets and followers, from Moses to Muhammad.

And after shooting down six unarmed worshipers of Allah and with one dead, they felt happy to boast that they had killed one of my followers. The same devil policeman who killed that follower said he shot the others and was trying to kill them all.

Again, this same devil was not wounded or even scratched by any of the Muslims, who were not armed and had nothing with which to retaliate against such a sudden attack by the murderers of our fathers and mothers and now the murderers of us.

For thirty-two years I have been trying to teach my people, the so-called American Negroes, the way of peace, and I have a record just that long in trying to live in peace with our open enemies. I have even warned my followers never to be the aggressors, as the religion of Islam teaches us that we cannot teach peace and then be the first to break peace with carnal weapons. I know who the fight belongs to. It belongs to Allah (God).

Allah wants to make Himself known in the Western Hemisphere that He is our God and has come to save us from the hands of our enemies and place us again in our own country and among our own people. He has said that He would do this job of delivering us and destroying those who have destroyed us. This is prophesied almost throughout the Bible.

He further said that there is no way of getting along with the white race in peace. They have been found by the Scientists of Islam to be disagreeable to live with in peace. The twelve Scientists met to confer over the possibility of returning us, the lost-founds in the wilderness of North America, to our own.

This can and will be done or the Prophets could be called liars, and liars they cannot be made, for they deliver the words of Almighty Allah (God) or his message, and that message is from the Lord of the Worlds (Allah) who cannot lie.

In Detroit, Michigan, where we were first attacked outright by the Police Department in April, 1934, we were also unarmed. There were no deaths on the part of the Believers, however. They fought back against the policemen who attacked them for no just cause whatsoever but that they wanted our Muslim children to go to their schools. We refused to let the children take their first courses in the public schools, although the high school children in their upper teens could do so. But let us shape our children first.

This was the cause of the attack at that time and Allah was with us and we had been peaceful there all the while. However, it was said after the battle with my followers who had nothing to fight with but their hands, that there was hospitalization on both sides.

There was no loss of lives on the side of the Muslims and not a gun was fired by them. The Lieutenant of police, the Captain and Commissioner of Police, had warned them to not use firearms against us because we were not armed--this was true. But when the battle was over there were more of them hospitalized than there were of us.

One year later, here in Chicago, Illinois, in the Police Court on 11th and State Streets, there was a complaint made against one of my followers, concerning his children going to our school, the University of Islam. As the courtroom began to fill with spectators, two court deputies showed disrespect for the Muslim women. They started, pushing them around and the Muslim brothers resented this harsh handling of the women. The police officers then began beating the men and almost within seconds the entire courtroom was in confusion and fight.

When the battle was over, the Police Captain lay dead from a heart attack and others were wounded by their own gun fire. They opened fire upon my followers point blank in the courtroom because of their (Muslims) seeking justice in the charge made against us and our school as in Detroit, Michigan, the previous year.

In Detroit, Michigan, the Police Department charged us with "contributing to the delinquency of minors," involving one of our students, Sally Allah, who had left the public school and had come over to the University of Islam. They charged us with going around to the various school grounds, begging our poor black children to leave the white schools and come over to their own.

This is when they made the charge of contributing to the delinquency of minors. The records are in Chicago to date for anyone to read. Now one year later (1935) here in Chicago, Illinois, they attack us on nearly the same charge. They wanted to school our children, they wanted them to go to their public schools.

We know that kindergarten children and first graders once in Islam cannot be taken into Christian schools without having to suffer mockery and attack from the Christian children and from the Christian teachers who hate Islam, the God of Islam, and the Prophets of Islam.

Therefore, we believe that to keep peace with the Christians, we must teach our children in their own schools although they may study the same textbooks. And this will prevent clashes between the Muslims and Christians over the truth of the history of the people and the spiritual guidance and message that Allah has revealed to me.

The message of Islam is bringing about one of the greatest reforms, for a better life to the American so-called Negroes, greater than it did ever to the Arabs fourteen hundred years ago. I would compare this reform here with that of the Israelites under Moses four thousand years ago, to prove the teachings of Almighty Allah (God) of the white race being made the devils from the beginning and that they are not ones who seek peace. They only use the word peace to deceive the black people, to get a chance at making mischief among them, and causing bloodshed.

Know that by nature the black people are for peace and know by nature that the white people are for war, bloodshed and are destroyers of high morals. They refuse to show any respect to their peaceful, free slaves in America today. They know that we are not armed—in thirty-two years they have learned that my followers are not armed. They have learned that the God of peace is with us by watching great mass meetings of ours and never seeing even a dispute arise.

If the white race were for peace they would thank God for raising up in their midst a peaceful people who do not desire to make any mischief among them. Here we have the NAACP, CORE and various other organizations before our eyes, who attempt to try achieving their aims of asking for freedom, justice and equality with the slave-masters' children without weapons, without anything harmful. They lie down at the feet of the vicious, weakened, human-like beast only to be kicked and stamped upon and have dogs sicked upon them to rip their flesh apart and poison them with rabid teeth.

They have no respect for people who want to be at peace with them. They have no respect for the laws of justice. They have made trouble all over the world with people who were at peace among themselves until the white shadows of the trouble-makers spread out over them.

We have history that they, themselves, have written of self, bearing witness to what I am teaching today. What must be done since we cannot get along with them in peace?

RIGHT TO PEACEFUL ASSEMBLY DENIED TO SO-CALLED AMERICAN NEGROES

Dear Brothers in the Nation of Islam, and especially my people here in America, where live the worst enemies of Islam and of the peace of the world.

It should now be clear to you after the attacks that have been made upon us and are still being made by the brutal American police forces with FBI harassment and persecution, that Allah has manifested the white race of America to be nothing but a race of devils.

We are forbidden by Allah to carry weapons. It is well known that this is our rule. No armed person is to sit in our meetings, and because of this rule we have been successful in enjoying a peaceful assemblage wherever we have gone.

But it has again been made clear by the hostile act of the Flint, Michigan, police department against our peaceful assemblage, the devils do not respect anyone's peace.

Because of this we shall never again permit white people to sit in our meeting—armed or unarmed. This does not include the Turkish people, Chinese, Japanese, Filipinos, those of Pakistan, Arabs, Latin Americans, Egyptians and those of other Asiatic Muslims and non-Muslim nations.

All black Americans or non-whites are welcomed to our mass meetings. We will soon make a try at converting and uniting all the originals of this Western Hemisphere.

All black Americans, even those who have a few drops of black blood in them, must unite under the crescent to try and save ourselves from the doom of the enemies who have ruled and killed us for the past 4,000 years and especially during the last 400 years.

For they have covered the earth and sea with their death-dealing rule over the aboriginals of the earth since they left the confines of Europe.

And now to their latest outrage in Flint, Michigan. There on October 27, 1963, the police department harassed us for three hours in order to enter our meeting, fully armed inside an auditorium filled with peaceful unarmed people.

This proves beyond a shadow of doubt that there is no justice nor peace for our black people in America, whether they be Christians or Muslims.

We had rented this public auditorium in Flint to teach the so-called Negro of the presence of Allah, of the judgment of the devils, and of the separation of the two peoples (black and white).

Approximately 6,000 people, including 200 or 300 devils, had submitted to being searched for arms and other possessions that might be against the peaceful assembly. A black policeman had entered but had surrendered his arms.

Later on, however, two white officials appeared claiming that their law compels them to go into all public meetings armed and that their weapons were not to be given up.

They insisted on coming in with their arms, and upon the right to overrule those who would oppose their entering, I left in the midst of my lecture; I went to the door to speak with the haters of so-called Negroes. I told them, that if they wanted to come in, to do as their white brothers had done. That is, give up their weapons until dismissal. And if anyone acted other than peacefully in our meeting we would surely let them know and they could arrest them.

But this was not enough. They continued to demand entrance without being disarmed.

I, therefore, dismissed the meeting. I could have called their bluff, but there were too many women and children in the audience.

Their record of unprovoked, evil attacks against our people is a long and vicious one. The attacks began in Detroit, Michigan, in 1932, '33 and '34 and from there to Chicago, Illinois, April, 1935, and down to the attack on and murder of the

Muslims in Los Angeles, California, April 27, 1962.

Even under the laws of America brutal police forces beat black people and deprive them of simple justice, including those who are in prison at the present time and those who are being sent to prison throughout the country. Untold thousands are being held in prison unjustly.

Muslim prisoners are making court appeals against false charges in Monroe, Rochester, New Orleans, Attica, Dannamora and Baton Rouge, Louisiana, and against unjust court rulings. In upper-state New York and Massachusetts, the Muslims, unjustly charged with attacking the police department in a peaceful assemblage, have appealed.

THE RIGHT OF SELF-DEFENSE

The so-called Negroes of Birmingham, Alabama, would have been justified by the law of justice if they had killed every dog sicked upon them by the hired, tax-paid policemen, for the tax-payers did not hire dogs to police their lives and property.

And if the policemen had fired upon those who defended themselves against the bites of savage dogs that the Police Department trained expressly for the purpose of attacking so-called Negroes, they would have been justified by God and the Divine law of self-defense to fight and defend themselves against such savage dog and human attack.

Surely the American so-called Negroes would have God and world sympathy on their side if they would take the right steps or actions. The present actions being taken by them are wrong, for this action consists of demanding that the slave-masters accept their slaves (so-called Negroes) as their equals and as equal sharers in whatever the master has, such as social respect (which will destroy both as a people), an equal share in the government, decent housing conditions, and equal employment (not that they do not deserve it).

No master of anything can accept an unequal as his equal. This law of nature is divinely respected. If they (Martin Luther King and his followers) would accept the right way, which is the belief in Allah as God and Islam as a religion, and demand a place on this earth for our 20 million or more people that they can call their own, I would demand that every one of my followers join forces in a minute!

And if what they are asking for would be granted them, it would only be short-lived; nothing permanent is in it for the so-called Negroes. It would be very foolish for a leader of 22 million once-slaves to ask for temporary employment from their slave-masters' children, who now use the 22 million for sport. (Sicking dogs on the so-called Negroes was done only for sport to see the frightened so-called Negroes run for their lives.)

But as soon as the so-called Negroes turned upon the dogs and policemen with stones, Washington, D.C., ordered the Army to intervene—not to help the so-called Negroes against the white southerners, but to help the white devils against the so-called Negroes if they tried to defend themselves. But as long as the dogs and policemen were biting and clubbing black so-called Negroes, it was all right.

This clearly shows how much we are in dire need of unity, but the unity must be backed by a power superior to the power of our enemies. This power is in Allah and the Nation of Islam whose arms are outstretched if we would only accept them.

It is ignorant to look for heaven from the devils who only seek to take you to their doom (hell fire). They (Reverend King and followers) want the rights that the constitution offers to white citizens, but they are learning the hard way that the constitution does not apply to the black slaves with respect to the right to vote. Certainly there is power in voting if there is justice for the so-called Negroes. But the crooked political machine of America can always keep the once-slaves, free slaves.

Who prepares and teaches politics? Is it not the white man (the enemy of so-called Negroes)? Who will the poor so-called Negroes vote for? Would it not be for a white man or a black man whom the white would back? We could not hope for anything but more bloodshed at the polls in seeking justice from crooked politicians.

We are a Nation in a nation! Why not use these 22 million people's power for their eternal salvation instead of temporary enjoyment with the same wicked people who murder our people? (Let us build our own political machine.) Unite with me and with the help of Allah I will get you what you want. And I know what you want for I am your brother.

"...IT IS NOW TIME THAT YOU AND I TAKE COUNSEL

Of this grief you and I must suffer, all of these burdens we must bear. It is beyond comprehension that the American government—Mistress of the Seas, Lord of the Air, Conqueror of Outer Space, Squire of the Land, and Prowler of the Deep Bottoms of the Oceans—is unable to defend us from assault and murder on the streets of these concrete jungles....

The lynchers live right next door, down the street, up the alley, yet they are not brought to justice. What sane man can deny that it is now time that you and I take counsel among ourselves to the end of finding justice for ourselves?

When you stand up and speak a word in behalf of your own people, you are classified as a troublemaker, you are classified as a Communist, as a race-hater, as everything but good.

If God has revealed to me the truth of this race of people and yourself and I tell you of it and that is the truth, then don't say that I am teaching race hatred, just say I teach the truth.

The message I bring is not for the cowards. Those of you who follow me must be ready to withstand the barbs and insults of those who come to investigate, pry, and claim that our ultimate aim is to undermine the American way of life. We have no such intentions and our critics know it.

How ironic it is that the very people who charge us with disturbing the status quo themselves go around raping, lynching, denying citizens the right to vote and talking in the halls of Congress to call you and me everything from a beast to an amoral entity.

I have no alternative than to tell you that there is not any life beyond the grave. There is no justice in the sweet bye and bye. Immortality is NOW, HERE. We are the blessed of God and we must exert every means to protect ourselves.

LAND OF OUR OWN AND QUALIFICATIONS
THE UNITY OF 22 MILLION

The unity of 22 million so-called Negroes up from slavery is the answer to our salvation.

We are suffering untold torture and murder at the hands of our enemies (the children of our slave-master) because of the lack of unity. The cause of this lack of unity among us is due to the work and teaching of our enemies, the slave-masters' children. Our slave-masters' children have reared our fathers and mothers to be enemies of each other. They have destroyed our love of self and kind. They have educated us to hate and refuse all that goes for black people.

This lack of love for self and kind keeps us divided, and being divided we are a nation of prey at the hands of our ever open enemies. Whatever the amount of education we receive from our enemies we are still the slaves of our enemies due to this lack of knowledge of self, God and the devil; the true religion; self-pride; self-interest; and self-independence and the desire of a country and of a government of our own under the law of justice and righteousness for every one of our poor black people throughout the earth.

But let us start first here in America where we are the victims of no freedom, justice and equality, and we know the pains of being divided.

At present, we have hundreds of clubs and organizations; thousands of teachers; hundreds of educators, scholars, scientists, technicians, doctors, lawyers, judges, congressmen, ambassadors, professors, tradesmen of all kinds and engineers of most every kind. We have all kinds of religious believers, teachers, preachers by the thousands, agriculturists, herdsmen and cattlemen and fisherman and hundreds of hunters of wild game.

What more do we need but unity of the whole for the whole? What actually is preventing this unity of 22 million or more of us is the ignorance and foolish love and fear of our enemies in the professional and leadership class of this nation of 22 million black people up from slavery.

These are disgraceful "Uncle Toms" in a world of freedom, learning an advanced science in every branch of study. How long shall we seek the white men's education to become their servants instead of becoming builders of a progressive nation of our own on some of this earth that we can call our own?

Why are you so foolish to think it cannot be done? I have Allah (God) and the world of the righteous on my side to accomplish this.

There is no hope for us in Christianity; it is a religion organized by the enemies (the white race) of the Black Nation to enslave us to the white race's rule. But our unity under the crescent with our Allah's guidance can get us anything we desire in the way of help and some of this earth that we can call our own.

By the help of Allah, I have and I will still prove to you that Allah (God) has given me the only solution to our problem here under this race of merciless devils. If you can prove to me that you have a better solution for the future of our Nation I will bring my followers and myself and join you. And if the solution given to me from Almighty Allah is best, come you and your followers and join with me.

HOW CAN WE UNITE?

So you say that we cannot unite and produce our own necessities? We are 22 million or more people depending on the white American citizens to produce food, clothes, shelter, transportation, employment and our educational training.

And if they (white Americans) do not share equally with us, we charge them with discriminating; some of us will go to the extreme of disgracing ourselves in trying to force the white American citizens to give equal respect. The love of self and self-respect along with the will to do something for self, if given a chance, will get you the respect of all civilized nations.

It is a shame and disgrace to the intelligence of any people to lie at the feet and doorsteps of another nation, asking, praying to be cared for. Love and unity of self and kind is the key to our salvation.

If you say we cannot unite, you are wrong. We can unite! Before your very eyes you see the Believers in Allah (God) and his religion. Islam uniting and this Divine power from Allah working among us, uniting us into a nation of brotherly love, disapproves the lie of that "old saying" that the Negroes cannot unite.

I agree with you who are in the Christian churches, lovers and followers of white Christians, that you cannot enjoy love and unity among yourselves. The basic aim and purposes of the religion, Christianity, was to deceive other races, namely, the black, brown, yellow and red, to make an easy prey for the white race.

But today, you and I both see the powerless forces of Christianity unable to bring about peace among those who profess it.

Since Christian Europe and America cannot bring peace to their troubled world with all their satellite nations as helpers, what kind of peace can they make for us?

Their religion divides one against the other. This I am sure we all can agree upon. We must know self to gain self-respect. This will remove that old slave idea that the so-called Negroes cannot unite and build an independent nation on some of this good earth that we can call our own. Stop looking for others to help you in that in which you can help yourself.

The white man has made the black man lazy that he may rule and enslave him by producing and selling to him that which he can produce himself. But the white man knows that he has destroyed the black man's unity, and as long as the black man thinks he cannot love and unite with black, the white man knows that he has a permanent slave.

Come and let us unite under the crescent and do something for ourselves in the way of supporting our own needs. Go after some of this earth for our nation of 22 million here in North America. If it cannot be had here, there is plenty of earth elsewhere.

We want nothing short of a home on this earth that we can call our own—not to be servants and slaves for other free nations.

Let us capture the market of our people by producing their needs. We cannot produce our needs on the soil of another.

OF LAND AND A NATION

What we must understand today is the importance of acquiring land of our own. We are no longer a mere handful of people. We are a little better than 22 million in population and still increasing.

We cannot forever continue to depend upon America to give us a job, send us to school, build our houses and sell us her food and give nothing in return.

America was not established and chartered with constitutional guarantees for the Black man but for the white man.

America was not founded to guarantee the freedom and equality of the Black man and woman, and, indeed, she is not seeking to grant these privileges to our people today.

In what other country on this earth will you find 22 million people within the framework of another people's government seeking to become qualified citizens joyously singing the song of integration? Our people are the fools of the nations. Integration means self-destruction, and the means to this end is exactly that— death and nothing less.

The Black people throughout the earth are seeking independence for their own, not integration into white society. What do we look like trying to integrate with our 400-year-old enemies? The average so-called Negro wants to change his own flesh color and blood for a strange blood and flesh.

In order to build a nation you must first have some land. From our first generation of slaves to the present generation of our people, we have been unable to unite and acquire some land of our own due to the mental poisoning of our former slave-masters, who destroyed in us the desire to think and do for self and kind.

Do you as educated and professional men and women desire to be recognized forever as the mental slaves, beggars of white America?

Today, the international conception of honor, pride and dignity is not concerned with individuals within a country but is rather concerned with your work and value as a part of an established nation.

In order to be recognized today you must represent your nation. We must understand the importance of land to our nation.

The first and most important reason that the individual countries of Europe, Africa and Asia are recognized as nations is because they occupy a specific area of the earth. Second, they are recognized because of the effectiveness of their internal unity and policies and then by their enactment of international policies and agreements with other established nations. The black man has been actually worthless when it comes to exercising the rights as human beings in an ever-advancing civilization. So remember, we cannot demand recognition until we have some land that we can call our own.

You might argue that this is impossible, but I say to you, with Almighty Allah (God) on my side this is not only possible but is in the working for our people and will manifest itself soon!

A HOUSE OF OUR OWN

We cannot be successful in the house of our enemies; we should be in our own house. That which is other than our own is for those who are other than our own. "Our own" is unlimited physically and spiritually.

There are those who think that our lack of freedom, justice and equality can be solved in the white man's crooked and corrupt politics. But these so-called leaders who think this political strategy will solve our problem are as far wrong as the distance from the East to the West.

I have said many times that the solution to our problem is divine. There are so many who would—just for self-praise or exaltation—like to lead you astray under the false claim that they can solve the problem by ways other than divine. You should never listen to these leaders because they will lead you into the fisherman's net. Such leaders show no respect for Allah and His power to solve our problem of freeing us from our enemies and raising us into a state of independence like other independent nations.

Independence, to you, is strange. You have given up the hope of ever being independent, but this is just what Allah (God) wants to do for you. Don't you think it is time, after 400 years as servants to strangers? It is hopeless to think that these strangers will ever be other than what they now are to you. Please do not think that they can be conquered by brickbats, shotguns, a few arms or homemade bombs. It takes the forces of nature and the confusion of minds and thoughts, which are controlled by the power of Allah. Be wise and submit to Allah, who has the power to defend you and destroy your enemies who are too powerful for you.

Much is being done in attempting to stop Elijah Muhammad's deliverance of Allah's message of life and salvation to his people here in America who have been used as merchandise, cattle and animals.

The hypocrites and devils are now united against me and my followers, and wish to make a concerted attack on us with many false charges as well as planning actual death for us. But Allah, too, has planned.

I say to my followers, fear not! If you are with me, Allah is with you, and the more they attack us, the more Allah is attacking and will attack them. The truth of Allah will be universally and permanently established. I have Allah on my side, while the hypocrites have the devils, and they cannot defend the followers on their side who are against Allah. I knew that the enemies and hypocrites were going to do this long ago, because Allah had told me of them and the evil, deceitful plans they would try to carry out. He will bring them to naught before your very eyes. As you see, their efforts in trying to oppose me are being counteracted by Allah with the conversion of more people everywhere.

The hypocrites will never find true friends and will never enjoy the light and guidance of Allah. They are confused and cannot claim Allah because they have not believed in Him by forsaking His Messenger.

May He (Allah) give them the chastisement that He promised them in His Holy Qur-an and give those who believe in Him and His truth the joy of fearlessness, lack of grief and peace of mind and contentment.

DO WE HAVE THE QUALIFIED MEN AND WOMEN FOR SELF-GOVERNMENT?

The answer to the above question is YES! We do not have to be equal in knowledge with every nation to be successful in operating our own government. Were those whites who first came to this country seeking self-government equal with England's Parliamentary Lords?

There are probably many independent people who do not have among them many who have the "know how" of the American educated class of so-called Negroes. We have enough technicians, such as mathematicians, construction engineers, civil engineers, mechanical engineers, electrical engineers, physicists, chemists, educators, agriculturists, navigators and aeronauts, among the 22 million or more of us. You will find scholars or scientists whom we can use in every branch of government; then there are our own independent people outside of this country who would be glad to help us get going in a country or state for ourselves. We do not expect to build, nor do we desire to build a government patterned after the order of the white race. Naturally we would need help for the next 20 or 25 years. After that, we would be self-supporting! The spirit of "doing for self" is now fast coming into our people. They only need a new education of self and others.

WORLD'S GREATEST PEOPLE

Unity under the crescent of Islam is all that is necessary for you and me to become the world's greatest people. The lying and slavery teachings of the white man's Christianity that has crucified our people all over the earth must be given up! We must accept the true religion (Islam) of Jesus and the Prophets before and after Him before we can be successful in doing anything.

SEPARATE AND BE SAVED

The unwillingness of the slaves to leave their masters is due to their great love for the slave-masters. If America is unwilling to grant her 22 million ex-slaves freedom to go for self today, it is the same unwillingness of white America's forefathers in dealing with our parents less than 100 years ago.

During the time of the Emancipation Proclamation we were scattered to the winds without any knowledge or ability to undertake the responsibilities of a half freedom. Our fathers, lacking the skills and the training needed to provide for themselves, were forced to remain with the masters in order to receive even the barest necessities of life.

Our former slave-masters, knowing of our dependence upon them, maliciously and hatefully adopted attitudes and social and educational systems that have deprived us of the opportunity to become free and independent right up to the present day.

But we, the black slaves of this soil of bondage, were not deprived of the freedom to fight in America's wars, but we are deprived of the right to fight for our own freedom.

The opposition met by our foreparents who fought for their freedom is a chilled memory that history will not forget. The black people are given the freedom to give their lives for the American cause of tyranny but are not free to fight for their own freedom and independence.

As long as my people are the blind lovers of their enemies, they will seek to forever return to the bosom of their masters in no better status or position than that of a slave.

Our foreparents desire was to see us free indeed, and not only are some of our people willing to betray those of our blood and kindred who died before us, but they are now willing to betray the fruition of freedom of our generations to come. Allah will help us to get this freedom, justice and equality and some of this earth that we can call our own.

I say to the American white citizens who are in a position to oppose us to hasten the separation of the two or suffer the consequences as did the Egyptians opposing Jehovah and His Servant Moses.

We must have some of this earth that we can call our own! We and our fathers have been robbed of all that we originally possessed. And now we are left without anything to use for self like wealth and modern instruments to start a civilization as you have, though we helped you to get what you have. We now must have justice and some of this earth and its wealth that we can call our own.

WE MUST HAVE
SOME EARTH AND SOON!

Let the foolish educators and teachers think not that we have a future in white America's promises. For they themselves do not have a future, unless they are willing to divide this country between our people (the so-called Negroes) and the Indians, whom they robbed nearly 500 years ago. However, we must have some of this earth that we can call our own and soon! We, also the Indians, deserve justice in this matter! We can no longer think in the slavery-time terms as we used to think.

The preachers need and must be taught the true religion of God and stop enslaving our people into that lying and slavery teaching of the devils (white race).

Believe it or not, we have been serving and worshiping the REAL DEVILS! STOP preaching that old lie that God loves all human beings. He most certainly DOES NOT love the devils (the white race). He set a day for their doom the day they were grafted and given 6,000 years to rule us—rule of lying and murdering us day and night and deceiving nearly the entire nation of black, brown, yellow and red people. I possess a letter that is suppose to be authentic on how the devils boast that they have murdered (killed) 100 million black Africans since they have contacted them with their lying Christianity. Do we not love our black brother's blood regardless of where spilled?

In 1898, a devil by the name of Lacroex, representing Belgium's "big business," admitted he had murdered 160 million so-called Negro men, women and children. He also admitted he had tortured some and crucified women and children. THE CONGO: In 1880, Belgium estimated a population of 30 million. By 1911 the population was reduced 8½ million. In 1894, an English traveler, E. J. Glave, reported: "Twenty-one heads of black men were brought to Stanley Falls and used as decoration around a flower bed in one of the homes of a high-ranking army officer." Missionaries reported that white Christians forced the so-called Negroes into slavery producing rubber. And if the rubber was bad quality, the poor black slaves were made to eat it. And you are fools enough to preach their deadly poisoned religion, Christianity, to the suffering of self and kind. Are you in love with your open enemies and murderers of all black people, God and His prophets? Then stick around and see where you will end up!

A NATION OF OUR OWN

The poor slave. After his masters let him go free, his first problem to solve was securing a home of his own for the first time. He must now do for self. Master is no longer responsible for him, he must solve his own problems.

He must now realize that he must work hard to be equal of other nations. He must also remember that justice and righteousness is his defense and wickedness his enemy and the downfall of his government and his people.

He must learn to make friends and to protect himself against enemies. He must dig into the earth for her rich treasures. He must now seek the friendship of other nations to do business with them and trade product for product.

But if the slave is lazy, he will always be the slave for another. No nation respects a beggar.

We, the members of the original Black Nation of the earth, who were once lost from our own kind, are supposed to be free. It absolutely does not make sense for us to be seeking integration with our slave-masters' children instead of seeking unity among our own kind.

There is not any EARTH offered to us in integrating—how can we and our children build an independent nation of this earth without some of it that we call our own.

Do not we look ignorant begging white America to accept us as equal members of their society without having one square foot of earth that we can call our own?

We are like hunter dogs whom the hunter is tired of and wishes that they would go and hunt food for themselves. But the poor, foolish dog is there whenever his master sits down to eat, standing in the door begging with his tongue hanging out and wagging his tail, while at the same time, had he gone into the woods looking for a meal, he would not have had to suffer the hatred, kicks and curses of his master.

Without some of this earth for a home that we can call our

own, rest assured we will forever be 22 million begging slaves at the door of some nation. We, the black people of America, should be ashamed of ourselves to go sit in the white businesses to force them to serve us.

Let us unite and serve ourselves! If the spiritual leaders could understand the Bible's prophecy, they would see how foolish they are in doing the things they are now doing.

We should seek a permanent home for our nation—not by begging others for what is theirs—and stop acting foolish and unite. Do for self before you will have it to do!

The white race's days are drawing to a close; their rule over the darker nations must end, according to Allah (God) and His prophets. This wicked world must give way for a world of righteousness.

A NATION WITHIN A NATION

From a few comes a great nation. The Lord God of Islam taught me that in 1555 a devil by the name of John Hawkins, or Hopkins, of England brought the first of our parents here for slave purposes. We were not to be citizens, not to be represented as human or to be given equal justice under the American laws.

In 300 years of slavery, we were lashed, beaten and killed; given no education; and reared and cared for like the slave-master's stock (horses, cows and other domestic animals). Our children were separated to different plantation owners. For the last approximately 100 years of so-called freedom, the so-called Negroes have been subjected to the worst inhuman treatment of any people who have ever lived on the earth. They (the devils) have lynched and burned the so-called Negroes during the past century as sport for their wives and children to enjoy!

Edwin R. Embree states in his book, "Brown Americans," page 169, that "The burning of Henry Lowry in Arkansas, proceeded by inches. Leaves soaked in gasoline were heaped about in small bundles so that torture would be dragged out. Ralph Roddy, a reporter, described the entire orgy in the Memphis press of January 27, 1921. He was able to cover the story because plans for the lynching had been made well in advance. The newspapers were notified to be ready to issue extras. When

Henry Smith was burned at the stake in Texas, excursion trains were run for the event. Many women and children were in the throng that gloated over the suffering of the victim." This is something the teachers and leaders of the so-called Negroes should teach their children—the evil and murder of their people by these blue-eyed white devils. Instead, because of their fear of the white blue-eyed devils, the so-called Negro parents teach their children just the opposite. Their doctrine is "love your enemies" and "do not hate those who mistreat you." That is, if it is a white person! But if he is a Negro, kill or beat the hell out of him!

The so-called Negro leaders know the white devils do not care about a Negro killing another Negro.

How can we keep our younger people of the present day from loving their open enemies, the devils? The Lord, God of Righteousness, dislikes any one of us who loves these white blue-eyed devils. He threatens to send every one of us to hell with the devils who show love for them, love to be called by the devil's names or worship their images. Read your Bible and Holy Qur-an.

Edwin Embree, also on the same page, mentions what Walter White, deceased secretary of the NAACP, said he heard and saw in Florida. In his book, "Rope and Faggot," White recounts the gruesome tale of lynching in this country. While investigating an atrocious riot in Florida, White was met, he says, by three clean healthy children (white) headed for school. None were over 9 years of age. They gleefully described the event and "the fun we had burning the niggers."

Do thank Allah for revealing this evil deceitful open enemy, "the devil!" The devil has deceived most of the world of black people. They have nearly nine-tenths of the black people headed to their doom with them. Curse be to the black man or woman who loves this open enemy, the devil, and hates his own black skin and kind! May the chastisement of Allah choke you until you submit that: There is no God but Allah and that Muhammad in the wilderness of North America is His Messeger! After all of the evil we have suffered at the very hands of these devils, we have become a Nation in a Nation. We must now be separated from them and given a place on this earth that we can call our own!

They, the white race, cannot treat you and me with justice

and equality. They cannot do so among themselves. Even though they are against us. This does not mean that they have love and peace for each other. No! They war against each other all the time. They are devils. No heart of love and mercy are in them as you may think. Nature did not give them such a heart.

The Bible warns us against the love and worship of these devils. Psalms 106:37, says "Yea, they sacrificed their sons and their daughters unto devils." In another place it states, "And I would not that you should have fellowship with devils. Ye cannot drink the cup of the Lord, and the cup of the devils: ye cannot be partakers of the Lord's table and of the table of the devils. (I Cor. 10:-21). "They should not worship up devils" (Rev. 9:20).

The so-called Negroes, because of their fear and ignorance of this real open enemy devil, will fall victim to them if we do not constantly warn them of the consequences.

I am willing to die for the so-called Negro that they may see and understand the truth of self, God and this race of devils.

We have served them well through ignorance and blindness because of being without a teacher. Allah (God) has given you one. I, Elijah Muhammad am from God, Himself! Why not believe and follow me? Are you afraid of being persecuted for the sake of truth to this 22 million blind, deaf and dumb lost-found Nation of Islam? In that case, your life is already doomed.

FOR FREEDOM, JUSTICE, EQUALITY!

With the fight going on in the South between the slaves and their masters, the slaves (in mind) have become home-born slaves as it is written (Jer. 2:14). They love their master and desire to be their master's kin in the line of true brotherhood. This is the truth which cannot be hidden in these modern times.

The intelligent people and the college university graduates are poisoned 100 per cent more in mind and into the love of the enemy than the uneducated. It is no wonder that the scriptures say the poor gladly receive the truth after being offered heaven at once from Almighty Allah (God) Himself.

According to black men's actions and rejection of Allah and the true religion, Islam, which means entire submission to the will of Allah, they will take all kinds of humiliation. They are beaten and killed by the white man (the real citizen and owner of the land) while trying to force him to admit them (the once slaves) as equals to the white race.

I have taught for years that you cannot demand the white man accept you as his equal or as his brother, because he is intelligent enough to know that you are not his equal and that you are not his brother. Even if you go back to Adam—he is not the black man's father. We are not all compatible. Adam is the father of the white man. This is known.

The suffering of my people in trying to force themselves on the white man in the South and elsewhere as their brothers and sisters is to be pitied. I, for one, have true love for them, and I pity them. But I cannot help them when they deliberately walk away from God. By their deeds and acts they indicate they would rather help the enemy, the murderer and those who hate them than help God Almighty, Whose proper name is Allah and who came in the person of Master Fard Muhammad and to whom praises are due forever.

The best and most intelligent way is to give Caesar what is Caesar's and let us go for ourselves on some of this earth that we can call our own, just as did the white people. When Europe was overpopulated, they found expansion in the Western Hemisphere.

If we want freedom, justice and equality, we must look for it among ourselves and our kind, not among the people who have destroyed and robbed us of even the knowledge of ourselves, themselves, our God and our religion.

We have a world of Muslims under Allah and His religion, Islam. The white people do not teach you this because it points the way to your freedom and equality. It is a shame that our people are beaten and killed because of their ignorance in wanting to be white people, while there are billions of people on the face of this earth who look like them but only 400 million white people on our planet earth.

Our population runs into billions, and the earth belongs to us. We are the original owners of the earth and will take it and rule it again. This is the time.

OUR DAY IS NEAR AT HAND

Jesus did not teach in his time what today we call Christianity. He knew nothing about Christianity in those days. He had never heard of such. Jesus taught in his times the same religion that Moses taught—Islam.

We must be separated, whether we like it or not. I say we must be separated. I do not know why they want to hold on to us unless Allah is forcing them to do it so that he can get a better chance to punish them as he has wanted to do—as he did Pharaoh.

I do not know why the white people want to deceive you, trick you, try to court you and make sweethearts of you and marry you in order to get you to stay with them. I would be telling you to go, and when they see what is after them, they will say go. They won't tell you to stay.

I want to tell you who think that you are inferior, who think that you are nothing, who think that the white race is superior and the wisest people there ever were—that you are mistaken.

I want to satisfy your minds, my friends, my brothers, my sisters, that you fear not that the white world will destroy us. They cannot do it. We have a Savior with us.

We have a Savior that is born. I do not think any white ruler is silly enough to destroy the Muslims. I do not think that the white government of America would try to force us to our knees by not giving us employment. If they do so, come to me.

We have a Savior today. He is with me. He is able to feed you. He is able to clothe you. He is able to shelter you.

I say to you who think that I am begging for some of these states, as I read in the papers, I am not begging for states. It is immaterial to me. If the white government of America does not want to give us anything, just let us go. We will make a way. Our God will make a way for us.

I am not going to start a war with them to take land, because all of it belongs to us. I say to the government that if they cannot agree on giving us justice and agree on giving us a chance to make a living for ourselves as they are for themselves, with freedom, justice and equality as they have, then let us go. Let us go back to our native land and people. Every Muslim can go. We, the Muslims, are the true owners of the heavens and the earth.

I give the white people credit. They do the best they can in some instances, but, at the same time, I cannot say that they are angels. They have jailed us and bound us up among them. They should take care of us, give us a chance. If not, they should let us go.

Do not tell me that we are equal. We are not equal. We cannot be equal. How can we be equal when they own everything and we own nothing?

We have enough educated black men and women in this government to start a government big enough to take care of the world.

War is due. War is inevitable. There can be no showdown here in America until your problem is solved. He (Allah) has made me a door. If you get out, you will come by me, and if you reject me, you will not go. I have been given the keys to heaven.

This white government has ruled us and given us plenty of hell, but the time has come that you shall taste a little of your own hell. The only way that America could have an extension of time. I guess you think I am acting like a judge, but I heard what the Judge said.

If America attacks any nation, she will herself be shot to pieces. For centuries she has boasted that she has made other nations bow at her feet. Now God wants to show the others that He will make you bow. It would be wise for you if you want to get an extension of time to treat us right. And if you want to hasten your time—shoot us. Shoot Elijah. Kill us all. Kill all of my followers, and Elijah will go down laughing and knowing that this is the end of you.

All of my followers have been questioned by the FBI. Just what are you trying to do? You want to find out just how weak or how strong we are?

We want the FBI to know what we are teaching. We are not teaching what we do not want you to know, FBI. We want the government to know we have no secrets. The thing that you should do is to keep it a secret yourself, when you can.

Do you think that I am happy knowing that you are behind me trying to keep my followers from following me? I am not happy about you trying to take my followers—carrying them with you because I KNOW where you're going.

Now the white people want to marry Negroes. Negroes who

have no knowledge of themselves want to marry white folks. It is like a frog wanting to marry a rattlesnake because the rattlesnake is so full of frogs he cannot swallow another one.

The whole world is angry. We must have a showdown. We have to have it. We want to live in peace.

Every day of our lives we are at your mercy. An army of policemen throughout the country with clubs in their hands set out to beat the "nigger" and to shoot the "nigger" if they feel like it.

Nothing is hindering him. He is not going to go to prison for doing it. All he has to do is to tell the judge that he shot that old "nigger" and the judge will wink his eye at him and say "Wish I had a chance to shoot him myself." This is the kind of people we are living with. With murderers, not friends, but murderers.

Look at the Southern Senators saying that they will sit down and stay there night and day before they will ever agree to give the Negro civil rights.

There are many of my poor black ignorant brothers and even preachers preaching the ignorant and lying stuff that you should love your enemy. What fool can love his enemy?

Martin Luther calls himself a preacher and has written a book to try to fool you, to make you love the devil himself. How can Martin Luther, being the minister of God, he claims, teach his people to love their enemy, when God Himself said he had set a day to deal with his enemies. And he said himself, according to the Bible that Martin Luther reads, that there were two brothers—I loved one and hated the other.

I want to know from you why so much about hate teachings? It is hate teachings, you say. It is race teachings. I want to know if you were born in America as I was. All your life you have been hated by white people and you are hated by them today. Here comes the truth of the white man making you know that he cannot love—that he is the devil himself.

Now you say, no, no, he is not the devil. God said he was. They say we teach that he is the blue-eyed devil. I did not make him. They say that I am teaching you all to hate the devil. But when did they ever love our people? I will most certainly not teach you to love the devil.

They are doing everything they possibly can, and I do not

care if the entire white race hears me say this. They are doing everything they possibly can do to deceive the poor old Negro.

We are happy, we the Muslims. We know we have a Savior.

In 1877 a Savior was born—to go after that particular people that was lost and swallowed up by Israel seeking something that did not belong to Israel—not seeking any but His own particular people.

A Savior is born, not to save the Jews but to save the poor Negro.

I am here to teach the way back to the truth, back to the author of Truth.

A Savior has come to save you from sin, not because you are by nature a sinner but because you have followed a sinner. You have been taught by a sinner.

I want to say to you again that this truth has come to you to separate you from the devil. I am taught by Almighty God, Allah, that he is going to destroy this world. You should try to get out of it, not integrate into it.

THE FLAG OF

U.S.A. AND ISLAM

In the Name of Allah who came in the person of Master W.F. Muhammad to whom praises are due forever, the Finder and Lifegiver to us, the so-called Negroes, who have been lost from our own Nation, God and religion for the past 400 years:

The teachings on the significance of the American Flag and the Islamic flag were given to me by Master W. F. Muhammad (Allah-God in Person). The meanings are essential in teaching a people who have become spiritually or mentally dead. These two flags represent the emblems of the two great religious forces and religion and government can be read in the science of this flag.

Of course, the great cross is the sign or emblem of the Christian religion. The flag of this country is designed for and according to the wishes of those who are called Christians.

There is a much broader science or significance when it comes to the flag of Islam. Here, the flag of Islam is the recognized emblem of both the government and the religion, while the American flag, according to their teaching, stands more for the people and their conquering power or bravery than for religion. On the other hand, the science of the Islamic flag does not come under the spirit of conquering and bravery.

The nature of its science is the greatness of the unlimited wisdom of its designer, the great source of goodness for all that is under and in the flag of Islam; the freedom, the justice, the equality that is freely exercised by both believer and non-believer under the flag of Islam, which is revealed for the sole purpose of teaching the great unlimited source of mercy and love that the Designer has for His creatures.

They all enjoy equally the natural benefits of the Sun, Moon and Stars (the Islamic flag), which are essential for our existence regardless of religious beliefs.

To lead the American so-called Negroes back into their own religion of Islam they must know how strong and powerful the religion of Islam is while they are now under the emblem (cross and flag) of religion of the citizens and owners (white) of the United States of America.

The religion, Christianity, and the true history and science of their flag must be taught to the American so-called Negroes before they can see their way in returning to their own God and religion to become an independent people.

I do not see why the southern white citizens of America and Louisiana are trying to make it a crime to teach the meaning of these two flags, when they know how necessary it is. Any person who is a citizen of any country should have a thorough knowledge of the flag which he claims to be his own and that he is willing to give his life to maintain.

I have heard it said that we teach that under the flag of America we receive suffering, slavery and finally death. Why, this is as true as the existence of the American flag on our part, according to their own history written concerning our welfare under their flag. Today, the government is trying to force the recognition of the so-called Negroes equally with the true white citizens of America. This the South objects to, which makes it again abundantly true that the poor, once slaves have actually suffered slavery and death under the stars and stripes of America and numerous other cruelties and deaths which hardly be put into writing.

Just why does the South want to make it a crime for her so-called freed slaves to say they have suffered slavery and death under the American flag? Why does the South want to twist it and claim that it is to "excite war and the taking of America by force" when the so-called freed slaves are yet shackled and tied to their power, which makes it impossible for them to take America by force.

This is absolutely a willful and knowingly false charge made for the purpose of inciting more hatred and more abuses and more deaths for the once slaves of America. The abundantly clear signs of freedom, justice and equality that await the converts to the religion of Islam must also have something to do with the anger and false charges and the ignoring of their own law of justice in the South when it comes to the so-called Negroes.

The teaching of the true history of the so-called Negroes under the American flag is a crime in the state of Louisiana and is not a crime in Michigan, Illinois, New York and other states of the Union; the Federal Government should be the sole judge and the only independent and rightful party to say whether it is a crime or not. If the Federal government allows Louisiana to send so-called Negroes who believe in Islam to prison for 3, 5 and more years for teaching the truth of his history under the flag of America and of the very scientific meanings of the design of it, then the Federal Government should make it clear whether or not it ignores its own duty of protecting what is known to be the Federal law of the land.

Just because it is a so-called Negro involved, the decision is left to the southern courts as to whether it is their rightful part and duty to exercise this law. This means there is no Federal Law that can be relied upon for protection in America if certain white citizens do not like it.

Could the science of the colors of the flag be the secret that has caused the rise of anger of the Louisiana white citizens against the Muslims? The Islamic flag consists of an all red color with a crescent of white placed in it. The red represents the Sun, which is truthfully a red ball of fire that lights up and warns the planetary worlds in her circle. This is the physical meaning, that we receive freedom of light and warm from this mighty red ball of fire whether Muslim, Christian, Buddhist or any disbeliever—even atheists.

The American flag has red in it. The American flag has stars in it, but no moon. It is not necessary for the science of a moon in her flag because it would not correspond with the nature and government of the people who own the American flag. But in our flag, that of the Nation of Islam, the moon's physical work is that of equalizing. And the Star on the Islamic flag is put there for the purpose of showing her physical help in guidance for man as well as to beautify the universe. According to science, the stars are without number. Allah (God) said, "They put one star in our flag which serves to represent all of the stars."

The now 50 stars in the American flag physically represent the 50 states which make up what they call a United States. The spiritual side, however, is never mentioned in the teaching of the American flag.

THE TRUE SOLUTION

Will Civil Rights solve the so-called Negroes' problem? By no means will it, or anything else except Allah, solve our problem. Civil Rights, according to the English dictionary, means the equal rights of a human being on a level with any other human being. These rights are limited here in America. First and foremost, the so-called Negro needs human rights which will warrant his recognition as a human being by his slave-masters. This also gives him universal rights—the same equal rights as any other human being.

Will the so-called Negro enjoy the equal rights that the American white citizens enjoy? Or, will he continue to wait patiently for Civil Rights to come within 100 years from now? I am convinced that neither a white nor a Negro government will be here 100 years from now to witness what will take place. There is nothing good coming from the white man for the so-called Negroes' future. I have repeatedly warned you that there is no justice for you in the white man. This Civil Rights Bill was made up by white people and passed by white people. Even at this late date, there is no indication that the white man will—or even desires to—treat the so-called Negroes equally. It is not his nature to treat you or even his kind right; it cannot be done.

Reverend Martin Luther King, Jr., the 1964 Nobel Peace Prize winner, would have honored himself and his people if he had refused the medal. The money could have been accepted, since his people need it. Even if he did not need it himself, there are poor among his followers who really need financial help. He won neither peace nor justice for his people.

Reverend Martin Luther King, Jr., wants brotherhood with white America for himself and his followers. As reported here, the Nobel Peace Prize was conferred on him in Norway. Reverend King sharply warned in St. Paul's Cathedral that "A doctrine of black supremacy was as great a danger as one of white supremacy." He followed up with the words, "Unless men and nations live together they will perish together."

Then came the statement according to the paper, "Too many of our white brothers are only concerned with their economical problems, their social status, their political powers and their so-called way of life." Of his own people he said, "We must not seek to rise from a position of disadvantage to one of advantage substituting injustice of one type for that of another."

I have never heard of any such talk coming from a leader's mouth in all of my life. If a man is NOT going to rise from a position of disadvantage why is he preaching for the passage of the Civil Rights Bill for his people? No wonder he had the privilege of going into a cathedral where no so-called Negro had ever stood in the pulpit. He is ignorant, preaching for brotherhood of white people and destruction of his own people, because brotherhood with the white people means the destruction of the black people. According to the Bible—he preaches from it—you should not make friends or have friendship with the wicked if you are the righteous, and you should not worship the devils. Most certainly, the white man is the devil—his own Bible teaches him that.

He said, "God is not interested in the freedom of white, black or yellow man, but in the freedom of the whole human race." Here, again the Reverend shows that he has not studied the scripture, for it surely teaches you that the world has been under the rule of satan (the devil) for 6,000 years, and now separation must come between God's people and the devil so that the righteous can survive. This kind of talk coming from a theological college graduate is almost unbelievable. How many American so-called Negroes would like to follow a man who speaks like one who cares nothing about them?

Reverend King has made it clear that he never wants the black man to rule, because he knows it will be "just as dangerous as white supremacy." This shows that all black people should disregard anything that a man like that says. He disagreed that his people should ever rise from the level of a subjected people of slavery. I would like to ask the Reverend under whom he would like to live, since he condemns the ability of both for the supreme character of ruling the nations of the earth, as the white man has done and enjoyed for the last 4,000 years.

He wants to be a brother to the white man and wants the black man to be like the white man. This is continued enslavement. I am just wondering how many followers he has after his last statements.

I heard the Rev. King say on television that he wanted white people to be his brothers and not his brothers-in-law. He loves our enemies. Any black person who believes in himself should not go near or even listen to this type of teaching. It is really awful to hear a man say such things when he has been beaten and thrown into jail seeking the right to exercise the rights of a member of his own black nation.

So, in view of such statements, Rev. King is of no good among black people. What are you going to do? Are you going to follow such teachings, or will you turn around and join your own kind? I cannot see, nor can I understand, why the so-called American Negro is so blind, deaf and dumb. We have the right to live and do for ourselves and our children. We do not want any more promises, and we cannot get along in peace with a universally known enemy of black men.

Since Allah has revealed the very nature of the Caucasian race—that they are devils—there is no way of changing them to be anything other than that which they are.

A RULE WE MUST LIVE BY

Almighty God, Allah, who appeared in the person of Master Fard Muhammad, has given us the knowledge of self and others, and we are now spreading it. Allah chose me to teach you this particular subject: "Accept your Own and be Yourself." This was His first and foremost teaching for us. This is the teaching and these are the words of Almighty God, Allah, to us in the Person of Master Fard Muhammad, to whom praises are due forever and ever.

Is it true that you have rejected your own? Is it true that you do not want your own and reject the truth that the Almighty God of Truth has brought to you? Is it true that you would rather be other than yourself?

Let us examine our thoughts to see what we are actually thinking about and just what we would like to be. Let us present ourselves to the world as we really are. I do not think that God could have taken a better subject to teach us than the one He has: "Accept Your Own and Be Yourself."

The so-called Negroes, of which I am a member, are the lost and found members of the tribe of Shabazz, from that great aboriginal people of the earth—the Black Nation. Remember this, we are the aboriginals of the earth and are called the black people, and we are the Black Nation.

Living under the rule of other than our own kind and self for the past 6,000 years has brought much misunderstanding, much not knowing and many theories that have been used in many places and the people have taken theories that have been used in many places. A theory is not true until it has been proved to be true.

We today, 6,000 years from the beginning of this world, are disputing with one another on who is who and what is what. But the wisest step taken to put an end to this disputing was taken by God, Himself, in these same words: "Accept Your Own and Be Yourself."

For the past 6,000 years we have not been ourselves. This is true. For the past 400 years, we, the lost and found members of our kind here in the Western Hemisphere, especially in the part called the United States of America, have been actually made more ignorant to the knowledge of ourselves than any other people on the earth.

Though our black brothers in Africa, and Asia too, have to learn the knowledge of self, they are a little step ahead of us because they have not been deprived of their way of life or their desire to live their own lives; that is, for the past few centuries. The coming of the white European race into their countries interfered with their own. And to this day this has caused great confusion among the African original people, so much so until today they, too, are a long way from having the true knowledge of self.

We can take the examine the knowledge of all the people as far as races are concerned, such as the white, brown, yellow and red races, and find that they, too, are really off the knowledge of their real selves, according to the teachings and truth of Almighty God, Allah, Who has revealed it to me.

Let us take a look at some of what Allah has revealed to me on this subject. Spiritually He says that your own self (referring to you) is a righteous Muslim. Physically, He says that we are the first and the last and that there were no people before us.

We are not from a father of another people. We are the father of all human beings, regardless of color or language. This covers the brown, yellow, red and white. Originally, all of these races—and they are truthfully named by the word races—were begun by the Black Man. They all came from him, and there are some white scientist who know this and will agree, and there are probably scientists of the darker races who will also agree. But there are only a few who actually know these truths, and these few have not felt that they should reveal it to the masses because they feel that this is something they should hold for their own interest.

TRUTHS TO SET YOU FREE

What should you know, what should you do, and what is your place in this change of worlds, governments and people? You have the best offer; better than that of any other human beings who have ever lived.

You have been taught for the past 34 years from the mouth of Almighty God, Allah, through His Messenger that you are and first and the last and that you have been loose in what He (Allah) calls a wilderness—a place of sin and evil doings opposed to a civilization of righteousness and the doings of good. For the past 400 years you have been robbed completely of the knowledge of self and kind and of Almighty God—the Creator and Maker of the heavens and the earth. We are the direct descendants of God, while those who have mistreated us and still do are the direct offspring of a rebellious scientist of God.

A scientist who grafted and made the white man an enemy to us. From the rebellious spirit of their creator, they have deceived, murdered and ruled the righteous, who are of the original Black Nation of the earth. This has been made very clear. Being born and nursed by the enemy of righteousness, you have fallen in love with them.

The history of the life of your fathers reveals an evil, murderous condition that they had to undergo. The treatment you are receiving now and have received should bear enough witness to the truth. Your love for this unalike people and their wealth which they have robbed you of and the majority of your people now makes you want to be one of them and desire to intermarry with such people, while history has recorded them as burning your actual living flesh at the stake out of the law of justice.

We live in a government that has always yielded and sided with the murderers and those who slay us and our people at home and abroad—anywhere the black man may be on the earth. You should realize that your black brother is your black brother wherever he is on the face of the earth. Look at your brother in Africa who has been dominated by the Europeans and other white races of the earth. He is fighting for a chance to shake off the shackles of the open enemies, while you here in America profess to be their friends. Are not you ashamed of yourselves, seeking love and intermarriage with them?

Your brother is trying to regain the power of his own country. You are playing the part of a hypocrite to yourself and your kind—wherever they live—by appealing to the murderers to accept you as one of them, as their sons-in-law. What a fool you are making of yourself without the knowledge of self and the time in which you are living.

This is the time that justice has come to you to settle the injustice done to you by your enemies and separate you from such evil people and give you a place somewhere on this earth that you can call your own. But you do not want a place of your own; you want to continue to live in a place with the murderers and crushers. What a silly people you are.

At the same time, he is shooting and killing you in the open eyes of the world, showing that he is your worst enemy and hated you from the very beginning and will always hate you as long as he is a human being made in nature which he is.

The Prophets were, unable from Moses to Muhammad, to reform him into a God-like person to deal justly. He cannot be reformed unless you graft him back into that which he was grafted from. As Jesus said to Nicodemus, "By no means can you see the kingdom of heaven unless you be born again." This refers to the whole Caucasian race. They must be born again. Not just a change, but a change in the very nature of them.

You are lying at their gates and footsteps begging, fighting and bleeding and falling from their blows and gunshots. You are trying to get them to accept you as their equal and as a free person. There is no way that you can settle the price of justice between you and your open enemy but by your entire submission of will to Allah who came in the person of Master Fard Muhammad; come follow me, your brother Elijah Muhammad.

ON SPORT AND PLAY

How can we say that we are the civilized people of the world when to be civilized, as Allah has taught me, one must have knowledge, wisdom, understanding, culture and refinement and not be savage. America, more than any other country, offers our people opportunities to engage in sports and play which cause delinquency, murder, theft and other forms of wicked and immoral crimes. This is due to this country's display of filthy temptations in this world of sport and play.

Great sums of money are spent in sport and play, in games of chance and gambling, in the operation of sporting houses. Millions are spent on horse racing and numbers rackets and are a disgraceful publicity of indecent sport.

Hundreds of millions of dollars change hands for the benefit of a few to the hurt of millions of poor people in the bread lines, and suffering from the lack of good education, with their last few pennies they help the already helped to try winning with these gambling "scientists" who have prepared a game of chance that the poor suckers have only one chance out of nine hundred to win. Therefore, the world of sports is causing tremendous evils.

Think over the destruction of homes and families, the disgrace, the shame, the filling up of jails—state and federal—with victims of sports and play, the loss of friendship, the loss of beautiful wives and husbands, the loss of sons and daughters to these penal institutions. From dope, knives and guns, this evil is practiced under Christianity.

The poor so-called Negroes are the worst victims in this world of sport and play because they are trying to learn the white man's games of civilization. Sport and play (games of chance) take away the remembrance of Allah (God) and the doing of good, says the Holy Qur-an. Think over what I am teaching, my people, and judge according to justice and righteousness.

Almighty Allah, to whom all praises are due, did not raise me as a Messenger like the Prophets of old, but he raised me as a Messenger, a Warner and a Reminder to the Nations of that which was prophesied to take place in these last days.

We have come to the end of the Prophets and the end of the old wicked world. I am missioned by the Supreme Being to awaken my people (so-called Negroes) to the times in which we are now living.

It is my people who are more ignorant to the truth than any other people on the planet earth. It is my people, furthermore, who are in the house of their enemies whom Allah is ready to destroy by fire. And they must be warned.

Finally, I must warn you against the devil's temptations, for they are seeking to make you unfit for acceptance into Allah's New World of peace, happiness and unlimited progress.

They have made you drunkards from their wine, whiskey and beer and other intoxicating. They have made prostitutes of our women. They have caused some of our women to love other women and men to love men and practice sex relations with their own sex. They have our people addicted to the worst kind of filth. They have made you dependent upon filth and vulgarity for survival.

They have made us eaters of the forbidden and poisoned swine. They have made us to have wicked, swearing mouths against the Most High God, Allah. But Allah knows the guilty ones, and you shall soon see the reality about which I have been warning you for the past 31 years made manifest in this rich, wicked world of Satan.

HYPOCRITES, DISBELIEVERS AND OBEDIENCE

WE NEED NOT HAVE FEAR FOR THE FUTURE

These above words are those of disbelievers and hypocrites. The disbelievers and hypocrites of prophets and messengers of God never want to give them credit and honor and bear witness with them in saying that the message they are delivering to the people is from the Lord of the Worlds (God).

They always wish to give the lie to what a Divine Messenger or warner brings to the people from God. They say he has forged it or it is of his own making. It is not what God said, it is his saying. These are the words of disbelievers, hypocrites and proud ones against the truth and the bearers of truth.

The above verse says to the Messenger that he is to warn a people to whom no warner has come before him. Many of the writers on the history of Muhammad (may the peace and blessings of Allah be upon him) of nearly 1,400 years ago, write that Muhammad was the first prophet that Mecca had ever seen. Even Maulana Muhammad Ali, who translated the Holy Qur-an in English, says in his footnotes on this verse that Muhammad was the first prophet that Mecca had ever seen and that he was raised among the descendants of Ishmael.

How do the scholars and writers of Islam say such when, if they make Muhammad a descendant of Ishmael they are condemning their own sayings that he was the first prophet of Mecca, when both Abraham and Ishmael were prophets according to the Holy Qur-an. Even the Bible and all religious people recognize Abraham as being a prophet.

Therefore, Muhammad could not have been the first prophet,

because the very significance of the signs that Abraham and Ishmael built in Mecca tells us much about the type of prophet and people that would be raised up in the last days. So how can they say that this revelation refers to Mecca, the Meccans and Muhammad.

It reads: "Thou mayest warn a people to whom no warner has come before that they may walk aright." This condemns the very fundamental teaching of the origination of the Prophets and Guides for the people coming from that direction, from the East. Mecca has been a sacred place. God, Himself, has protected its sacredness ever since time immemorial.

How then could this be a savage and unknown of the righteous and of even a righteous warner if there were not the will of God to keep that city sacred and deserving as a sign of righteousness?

Then how can the scholars say that it has not even seen a prophet or a warner from Allah? Would Abraham and Ishmael have chosen a more wicked place to set up a sign of the last warner and his people, which the Kaaba and black stone represents?

The very words, "to whom no warner has come before," that they put in a book that is called the last revelation of Allah to the people could not mean Mecca. The last warner and the last people to whom prophets and the truth have never come to are the same people that the Bible and Holy Qur-an refer to as being blind, deaf, dumb and (mentally) dead, who must be resurrected before there can be a judgment of the wicked.

No people answer this description better than the American so-called Negroes. And there is no country that better represents that description of where no prophets have been sent than America. As far back as history takes us in reference to America, we find no prophet of Allah preaching Islam or warning the people in the Western Hemisphere of a coming judgment and to submit to the will of Allah that they may be saved from the destruction of that day. It is America.

The prayer of Abraham does not refer to the raising up of a prophet in Arabia, but of a prophet among that particular seed or people of his, who must be searched for, located and found, a teacher must be given to them from Allah to teach and warn them of the purpose of Allah and the purpose of the Messenger being raised among them.

The Bible gives us a very clear prophecy and knowledge of this particular last messenger in many places. It is that he is the first and the last who will be among the people, because they would be the only and last people who would be without the guidance of Allah at the end of the world and must be guided into the path of Allah if they are to be saved from the destruction of the enemies of Allah who had deceived and now hold that people in bondage—the true descendants of Ishmael of whom Ishmael himself was a prototype and his mother the outcast.

There are many erroneous mistakes made by the scholars and scientists that have caused much misunderstanding of the truth. There are many Arabs throughout the world who cannot bear witness to anyone that another messenger would rise up after Muhammad, who was here nearly 1,400 years ago. This is due to their misunderstanding of the Holy Qur-an and the scriptures of the Prophets Abraham, Moses, Jesus and even Muhammad, himself.

They forget that the Bible prophesies of a lost member of the nation of the original· people of the earth, who would be lost somewhere on the earth. But neither the Bible nor the the Holy Qur-an specifies the place. The nearest the Bible comes to it is that they would be lost in the wilderness. That fits America.

And Moses says that God told him (Deut. 18:18) "I will raise them up a prophet from among thy brethern like unto thee and will put my words in his mouth and shall speak unto them all that I command him."

This is an answer or a prophecy that compares with the prayer of Abraham—that God raised up a messenger from among them and taught him the wisdom and the book, because his people would not have knowledge of the book and were only guessing at its meaning. This book is referring to the Bible—that they were guessing at its meaning.

This is true! Thousands of preachers here are preaching the Bible and do not understand the true meaning of it. They only guess at its meaning.

It is not true that the Bible was being taught and preached by the Arab people before Muhammad. The Torah was used among the Jewish people but not in the vicinity of Mecca and its inhabitants. A prophet would be raised among a people and that this man would be like Moses, but the Holy Qur-an and

Bible do not give the direct place where this people would be. Moses was raised among his brethren to warn and guide them, and they were the ones who rejected him at first. And it was Moses that God spoke to that a last messenger would be like him.

Moses' people had not had a prophet to come to them from God before the raising up of Moses, and they did not know the scripture because Pharaoh had them worshiping in his false religion. Therefore, Moses had to preach a new God and a new religion to the Hebrews and give them a new concept of God and His religion.

So shall it be with the last messenger. His people must be taught about the true God and that God's true religion which the slave-masters did not teach them. The Holy Qur-an backs up the truth of Allah, that He always raises an apostle from among a people whom He would warn.

If Allah would warn America and the poor slaves who have been blinded and made deaf and dumb by their masters, should not that messenger be one of the so-called Negroes instead of a so-called Negro trying to learn from what Muhammad said to the Arabs nearly 1,400 years ago. This is a guide for us today? It does not stop there.

We have to have something more; therefore, the Holy Qur-an prophesies of another scripture being given, and the Bible also prophesies of another scripture being given in the time of the judgment, because the Holy Qur-an takes us up to the resurrection of the dead but not beyond that.

"Warning a people whom no warner has come before that they may walk aright." It is directed at the American so-called Negroes in North America. As Jesus comes close to revealing the whereabouts of the lost members of a great nation in these words, "that he was sent to the lost sheep of the house of Israel, or in the house of Israel." He did not say that he was sent to the lost Israel, but to the lost sheep in the house of Israel. The lost sheep are not Israel. The lost sheep were in the house or government of Israel and were swallowed up by Israel so thoroughly that they were always overlooked.

But we just cannot overlook the prophecy of Ezekiel wherein he prophesies that God said, "Even I will go and search for them, and I will bring them again and settle them in their own land and among their own people."

This is referring to the so-called Negroes. And Isaiah says in his prophecy concerning us that God said He would call them by a new name that He, Himself, would give them, one of His own names, and would take away the names of the enemy and would slay the enemy.

Let us remember that we must understand the truth of prophecy, the sayings of the Holy Qur-an and Bible on this subject, and then place them where they belong and not try to fit them in some place where they do not belong.

BEWARE OF FALSE PROPHETS

A hypocrite is a person who is disliked by everyone—whether it be a hypocritical wife, husband, parent, son or daughter, the hypocrite is unwanted. You can never trust hypocrites. They are liars. They are worse than disbelievers, because a disbeliever has not lied, saying that he believed and then turned back. This makes hypocrites the most hated of all people.

The Holy Qur-an repeatedly warns the believers against hypocrites. Let us quote the 9th Verse of Chapter 2 of the Holy Qur-an, which reads like this:

"They seek to deceive Allah and those who believe and they deceive only themselves and they perceive not."

When they come in, they hope to make Allah think that they are believers and on their leaving sincerely seek to deceive the true believers so that they may turn them against Allah, the Messenger, and the truth that he has brought. They are mockers of the believers and say that they believe, but yet they are mockers of true believers. The 15th Verse of Chapter 2 says of them:

"Allah will pay them back their mockery, and He leaves them alone in their inordinacy, blindly wandering on."

The Holy Qur-an (63:1) reads: *"When the hypocrites come to thee, they say: We bear witness that thou art indeed Allah's Messenger. And Allah knows thou art indeed His Messenger. And Allah bears witness that the hypocrites are surely liars [63:2]. They take shelter under their oaths, thus turning [men] from Allah's way. Surely evil is that which they do [63:3]. That is because they believed, then disbelieved; thus their hearts are sealed, so they understand not."*

They desire to make the Messenger think that they are true believers by saying that they believe that he is the Messenger of Allah, while in their hearts they do not believe that he is the Messenger, and Allah knows what is in their hearts—that they are liars. They come in believing and then disbelieve. After their disbelief, Allah seals their hearts so that they cannot understand or believe. In the 150th verse of the 4th Chapter, they are warned against trying to deceive Allah and His Messenger. They say that they believe in one and disbelieve in the other. But disbelief in God or His Apostle means a disbelief in both.

This Verse (4:150) reads like this: *"Those who disbelieve in Allah and His Messengers and desire to make a distinction between Allah and His Messengers and say, We believe in some and disbelieve in others; and desire to take a course in between [4:151]. These are truly disbelievers; and We have prepared for the disbelievers an abasing chastisement."*

Holy Qur-an [4:152] reads: "And those who believe in Allah and His Messengers and make no distinction between any of them, to them He will grant their rewards. And Allah is ever Forgiving, Merciful."

This is going on today among my followers. Many of the hypocrites who go out from me will still say to you that they believe in Allah but do not believe that I am the Messenger of Allah. This is as if they said that they do not believe in either one of us. You cannot get to Allah unless you come through a Messenger, Apostle or Prophet of Allah. When a hypocrite begins disbelieving, the light is taken from him, and he is not able to see that he is actually a disbeliever. It is like someone wandering around in darkness but claiming that he sees his way, while the person in the light, looking on the dark, knows that he is not able to see his way around.

The Prophet is warned to strive hard against the hypocrites and disbelievers and be unyielding to them, for their abode is the "Fire of Hell." The relation between the hypocrites and the believers is cut off. They are not allowed to go around the Muslims. Not even charity is accepted from hypocrites by the believers. They seek friendship with the enemies of Islam. Read Chapter 5, Verse 53 (Holy Qur-an), and also Chapter 4 Verses 144 and 145. There is no help for the hypocrites. They practice deceit. Read Chapter 47, Verse 23, and also verses 25 through 28.

This particular group (hypocrites) should always be watched by the believers. They are very deceitful and must be opposed by all means. They are not to be killed, for Allah desires to make them examples for others by chastising them like a parent does a child. He chastises one with the strap to warn the other not to disobey. After a divine chastisement of the hypocrites, they are turned into the doom of the real enemies (the devils). That is why the Holy Qur-an speaks of them as inmates of the "Fire of Hell."

The Messenger is warned not to be easy with hypocrites but to be hard against them. Read Chapter 66, Verse 10, as well as Chapter 66, Verse 9, which even warns the Messenger that there were prophets who had hypocritical wives. This makes it clear to us that not only the common people can have a hypocrite in the family, but also the families of prophets.

Because of this, some people will think you are weak. They will say: "Oh, if his wife does not believe in him, he must not be the Messenger of God." If his sons and daughters do not believe in him, they say: "They should know more about him than we do. He must not be the Messenger."

But this does not mean that the Messenger is not the true one. Jesus prophesied that the truth will cause separation in the family. Mothers and fathers believing with children disbelieving. And children believing with mothers and fathers disbelieving.

This is going on now. There are many who come to us saying that they believe and want to join with us who believe in Allah and His truth and His Messenger, but many times their parent and/or children do not believe. This is the Judgment Day which you have been warned will come. The truth of Almighty God that I preach to you is not denied by scholars or scientists who understand. And if they do not understand, send them to me, and when they leave me, they will understand that it is the truth.

Chapter 104 of the Holy Qur-an is entitled the Slanderer. Please read it and the footnote (#2794), which fits very well with the slander I am now receiving from the chief hypocrites.

ON HYPOCRITES

A hypocrite, regardless to where he appears or regardless to what organization he may be a member of—whether a governmental hypocrite, an industrial hypocrite, a business hypocrite or a religious hypocrite—is the most unwanted and hated of all the people concerned. They are also the most hated by God. They are double-crossers; they come in claiming belief and then go out disbelieving.

I quote several passages of the Holy Qur-an on hypocrites of which the average leader or searcher of the scripture has not known, because the scripture teachers here in America have never studied the Holy Qur-an. If they had, they would not be hard to awaken or be united with their own kind.

"Those who disbelieve—it being alike to them whether thou warn them or warn them not—they will not believe" (Holy Qur-an 2:6). Allah has sealed their hearts and their hearing; and there is a covering on their eyes, and for them is a grievous chastisement (Holy Qur-an 2:7).

This is not for people who have not known the truth of Allah and His true religion, it is for those who have known and then disbelieve after their believing. The 8th verse of the same chapter reads like this: "And there are some people who say: We believe in Allah and the Last Day, and they are not believers." Verse 9: "They seek to deceive Allah and those who believe, and they deceive only themselves and they perceive not." Verse 10: "In their hearts is a disease, so Allah increased their disease, and for them is a painful chastisement because they lie." Verse 11: "And when it is said to them, Make not mischief in the land, they say: We are but peacemakers." Verse 12: "Now surely they are the mischiefmakers, but they perceive not." Verse 14: "And when they meet those who believe, they say: We believe; and when they are along with their devils, they say: Surely we are with you, we were only mocking." Verse 15: "Allah will pay them back their mockery, and He leaves them alone in their inordinacy, blindly wandering on."

In Section 16, entitled "Hypocrites are Dishonest," the Muslims are warned not to try to defend them or contend in behalf of those who act unfaithfully to their souls. "Surely Allah loves not him who is treacherous, sinful" (4:107).

"Behold! You are they who may contend on their behalf in this world's life, but who will contend with Allah on their behalf on the Resurrection Day, or who will have charge of their affairs!" (Holy Quran 4:109).

In Section 17, entitled "Secret Counsels of the Hypocrites:" "And were it not for Allah's grace upon thee and his mercy, a party of them had certainly designed to ruin thee. And they ruin only themselves, and they cannot harm thee in any way. And Allah has revealed to thee the Book and the Wisdom and taught thee what thou knewest not, and Allah's grace on thee is very great" (Holy Qur-an 4:113).

"There is no good in most of their secret counsels except (in) him who enjoins charity or goodness or reconciliation between people. And whoever does this, seeking Allah's pleasure, We shall give him a mighty reward" (Holy Qur-an 4:114).

"And whoever acts hostilely to the Messenger after guidance has become manifest to him and follows other than the way of the believers, We turn him to that to which he (himself) turns and make him enter hell; and it is an evil resort" (Holy Qur-an 4:115).

I have followers who are now fulfilling these verses of the Holy Qur-an; they are true and they are very easy to understand. Allah warns them that He will not aid them against His Messenger but will let them be manifest and bring to a naught their evil plans to destroy the Messenger and the truth which he preaches and even to take his very life and those who are with him.

"And thus have we made in every town the reader of its guilty ones, that they may make plans therein. And they plan not but against themselves and they perceive no" (Holy Qur-an 6:124).

Allah allows the wicked and the leaders of opposition to the Messenger to make their plans therein. And they plan not but against themselves and they perceive not.

Allah allows the wicked and the leaders of opposition to the Messenger to make their plans and try to carry them out against the Messenger. And then Allah makes them to about-face, and the planners of the evil receive the evil results that they wished for the Messenger. (Holy Qur-an 8:46).

"O, Prophet, strive hard against the disbelievers and the hypocrites and be firm against them. And their abode is hell, and evil is the destination, " (Holy Qur-an 9:73; read 9:74).

I do not beg anyone to believe, because it is not allowed by Allah for a Messenger to beg people to believe in Allah and His word of truth, neither to take him for an angel or for a Prophet. This is absolutely immaterial on a Prophet's part.

They seek to judge the Messenger of God and (as the Bible teaches) they seek to bring him into courts of the infidels to be judged by them while the Bible and the Holy Qur-an warn you against trying to be the judge of a Messenger of God, in these words: Who is he that judges another man's servant?

The Holy Qur-an repeatedly warns the disbelievers and hypocrites that Allah is sufficient as a judge of His Messenger, and by no means will He let those who molest and seek to destroy His Messenger with their tongues and their hands for no good reason.

There is no excuse for their deviation, only that they were actually hypocrites, eating and feasting with us (as the Bible says), and we did not know they were such people. Allah makes them know whenever he pleases, and I warn you who read this article that these are the days of Judgment, and I am your little brother missioned by God to try to save you from going to the doom of the devil and disbelievers.

Allah is a friend, and I am a friend that He has caused to rise among you, the poor black people of America who have suffered every injustice that man could suffer and are still suffering today.

The enemy cannot be but a hypocrite who will now try to change to offer you friendship. The same enemy who fought and killed you yesterday cannot turn overnight and become your friend.

Be warned and be careful of how you deviate and follow such evil-tongued people as you see now appearing, for in a few days, God will destroy them all with those whom destruction and justice is due.

May Allah pour upon the hypocrites the chastisement that He poured upon my Mother's son, my own brother who rose up against me in 1935 and joined himself with those who were bent upon taking life away. This was for no cause other than jealousy and envy of my mission. May Allah strike them with terror and grief that they may not have rest day or night for they return to me evil for good. I have been better to them than they were to themselves. Let Allah judge between me and the hypocrites and disbelievers who take Allah and His Messenger and religion for mockery.

BEWARE OF FALSE PROMISES

The government only wants to pacify her once slaves with fancy false promises that she knows she cannot fulfill without the loss of friendship and bloodshed among her own people. But there is nothing like a good future in these rosy promises for the so-called Negroes. Why should the government hinder us?

We want some of this earth and its treasures of raw materials to build us an independent nation as you and other nations have done. We want to live in peace. It is impossible to get along with you in peace while you cannot even get along with each other in peace! We were created of the essence of peace, while you were created of the essence of evilness, and evilness you will always do to either self or others.

That awful day of yours will surely come—the appointed hour you are hasting by your evil intentions and doings to us, the poor black people. We who have given our sweat and blood all our lives today we cry for justice, and you send your armed forces with trained wild dogs to kill us as it is written of you. "Ye have condemned and killed the just, and he doth not resist you" (James 5:6).

You send armies of heavily armed policemen to slay the unarmed so-called Negroes. Does this act of murder of unarmed people show that you are brave or cowards? You, like your fathers, hate and despise your slaves, and you beat and murder them daily. And after such inhuman treatment you want them to love you so that you may carry out your evil doings on them without resistance.

The beating and killing of those among us who say they are Muslims is most surely hasting your doom. You hate them because Allah has revealed the truth of you to them and you are angry and seek to take revenge on them for what Allah has made known to them of truth.

There is no solution to the problem between the slave-masters and their slaves other than the once slaves are going for self, for they have become a nation in a nation. One or the other must leave the other or suffer death.

It is the will of Allah (God) that the two be separated. Both books, the Bible and Holy Qur-an, prophesy of a separation between the two people. A temporary solution will only increase the trouble of finding a peaceful solution between the two people.

It is the government that is hindering a peaceful solution to this problem. It is true that the government does not want her once slaves, but it is equally true that she does not want her once slaves to go from here where they can become independent.

We, the Muslims, are sure of help from Him (Allah) who has visited us in the name of Master Fard Muhammad (God in Person), the long-awaited Mahdi who was to come and has come to slay the enemies of the righteous.

He (Allah) has power over everything—small or great. He will let you kill a few of us that He may be justified in killing all of you for the murder of all the righteous you and your people have slain since you were created.

We will, by the help of Allah, unite. We will get some of this earth, by the help of Allah, that we can call our own!

THE TEACHINGS OF THE HOLY QUR-AN ON OBEDIENCE

Say: Obey Allah and the Messenger; but if they turn back, Allah Surely loves not the disbelievers" (Holy Qur-an 3:31).

The religion of Islam demands strict obedience to Allah and His Messenger. The word "Islam" means submission "obedience." Obedience to God (Allah) is not accepted if one is disobedient to the Messenger.

"The Messenger believes in what has been revealed to him from his Lord, and (so do) the believers" (Holy Qur-an 2:285).

A true follower of the Messenger believes as the Messenger believes, but a hypocrite pretends he believes but is not at all a believer. There are those who claim they are believers but are sympathizers of the hypocrites; those are the ones who will never say anything one way or the other, fearing that they will show their sympathy for the hypocrite. Such ones are warned in the Holy Qur-an:

*"Behold, you are they who may contend on their
behalf in this world's life, but who will contend
with Allah on their behalf on the resurrection day"*
(Holy Qur-an 4:109).

There are those who like to dispute and act hostile toward
the Messenger of Allah. They are also warned in the same
chapter:

*"And whoever acts hostilely to the Messenger
after guidance has become manifest to him and
follows other than the way of the believers, we
turn him to that to which he himself turns and
make him enter hell: And it is an evil resort"*
(Holy Qur-an 4:115).

This refers to those whom the Messenger has guided to Allah
on the right path, and who have tasted the blessings of Allah
and then turn back to that which they had been brought out of.
And here Allah causes them to meet with a worse condition
than they left. This is tasted by such ones in this life. Allah
does not spare a Messenger's nearest of kin or their wives and
children. (See Holy Qur-an 66:1-11.)

Allah will chastise Messengers if they disobey Him, but Allah
does not allow us to be the judge of His Messengers, nor does
He make a second choice in choosing a Messenger for another.
Read the histories of the Prophets of God.

"O you who believe, obey Allah and obey His Messenger and
make not your deeds vain."

"Surely those who disbelieve and hinder men from Allah's
way then die disbelievers, Allah will not forgive them" (Holy
Qur-an 47:33, 34).

God is very hard on those who disobey His Messenger. He
warns in His Holy Qur-an not to quarrel and dispute or raise
our voices above the Messenger's voice. Strict respect and honor
is demanded for His Messengers. We should not take them
lightly, we may underestimate them without knowledge.

VICTORY OF THE APOSTLE

THE HYPOCRITES

*"Announce to the hypocrites that they shall
have a painful chastisement.*

"Allah will gather together the hypocrites and

the unbelievers all in hell.

"Surely the hypocrites strive to deceive Allah, and He shall requite their deceit to them.

"Surely the hypocrites are in the lowest stage of the fire and you shall not find a helper for them except those who repent and amend and hold fast to Allah and are sincere in their obedience to Allah. These are with believers and Allah will grant the believers a mighty reward" (Holy Qur-an 4:140, 142, 145 and 138).

The Holy Qur-an has the same announcement for all disbelievers and hypocrites of the Messenger. It is also the same given to Noah and his followers. It is the same given to all disbelieving foes and hypocrites. The hypocrites around Moses, Jesus and Muhammad were given the same warnings. And, they (the hypocrites) are prophesied in the Holy Qur-an (which is a very true book), to be the same type of hypocrites and to be saying the same words to the last Apostle and his true followers today as they did to the former prophets and their followers.

My followers here in America—and the hypocrites among them--are now being manifested to be the same as all others in the past. The hypocrites utter the same words, make mockery of the Messenger and his followers, and plan to do harm to us just as the hypocrites of the past did all other Messengers and their followers.

The Holy Qur-an says to the last Apostle: "All Apostles before you were mocked and called liars, but Allah reminds the last Apostle to think of His disapproval of other hypocrites and disbelievers."

He destroyed them and some of the hypocrites returned after they had tasted of the chastisement. We have, today, such a perfect fulfillment of the prophecy of the Qur-an in the recent outbreak of hypocrisy among my followers. The chief hypocrite of them all—and the worst of them all—has never stopped in his attempt to do harm to my mission.

The Holy Qur-an teaches: they will fight you with their tongues and even with their hands. So their tongues were not sufficient; they wanted quick action. So, the chief hypocrite resorted to arming his followers, as well as himself, with .30 caliber weapons. Knowing that my followers and I had not resorted to such weapons, they intended to spring a surprise attack by mowing us down. What happened? He and his ignorant followers had forgotten that God was with me and my followers. They did not know they could not stop us with weapons. The hypocrites always will be the losers.

This chief hypocrite took a group with him to build a "Mosque in opposition" to me and filled it with all types of wickedness and disbelievers like himself. He wished the praise of the people and not of God. He has said everything imaginable against me, which likely will hurt him and those who follow him more than he thinks. He wants the world to recognize him as a qualified leader. He should seek the recognition of Allah. Allah is the One who makes a leader for his people.

This chief hypocrite is not with Allah; if he were with Allah, he would be with me. Since he is not with Allah, he cannot claim guidance from Allah. He has admitted that he cannot trust a religion and cannot trust a God who teaches when to act. He wants to act when he is ready to act, rather than depend upon a God who will act in His own good time.

He does not wait on a God like that. Many other such fools passed away in great dishonor and shame long before this chief hypocrite. No weapons (as it is written) formed against me will prosper as long as Allah is with me and I am with Allah, because the twain will never break. We always shall be together against the enemy and together for the believers. Some of the hypocrites have come to know all of these things, but they must be punished.

A hypocrite is one who first says he believes in Islam and then disbelieves and seeks to oppose the Messenger and those who believe in him and his God. Their punishment—says the Holy Qur-an in several places—is grief, regret, shame and disgrace. I will never forget this hypocrite's hateful acts against me.

If he is the last of the 22 million, I shall remind him of his evil and wicked acts done to me in return for the good that I did for him. He could not have risen up against me if I had not given him so much knowledge of Allah and His religion. When I made him a leader and a teacher among the people, he felt proud. He now thinks that he should be elected top man, but I am sure that he will be appointed the lowest man.

He went, first, on the side of the Muslims, and then on the side of the devils, and again on the side of the Muslims and against the devils. He is—as the Holy Qur-an says—neither this nor that. His greatest desire is for someone to declare him as their leader. He is insane for leadership and disgraces himself for that office. As I have repeatedly taught—and the scholars and scientists will agree with me—the so-called Negro must have divine leadership today. The leader must be divinely appointed, not self-made or made by the people. This is universally known; I am that man, divinely appointed by Allah.

According to the Bible and Holy Qur-an, punishment is sure to overtake hypocrites and those who seek to oppose Allah and His Apostle. I quote here a verse from the Holy Qur-an.

"Do they not know that whoever acts in opposition to Allah and His Apostle, he shall surely have the fire of hell to abide in it, that is the grievous abasement" (Holy Qur-an 9:63).

That is the hell that the hypocrites and disbelievers will suffer, and it begins with their feeling of fear and excitement—fear that someone is going to do harm to them (as they plan to harm those they oppose). There is no fear for a true believer, nor shall he grieve. This grief of the hypocrites, according to the Holy Qur-an, prostrates them and makes them wish that they were dead. They even wish for someone to kill them.

But Allah, the Holy Qur-an says, will not permit anyone to kill them, because death would take them out of their chastisement and grief. They will not bow in submission to the will of Allah and obedience in following His Messenger, and after a year or so under this condition, they are classified with the devil, to be destroyed in hell-fire—the final end to both.

The Bible's last book, under the title of the Revelation of John, prophesies a grief falling upon the followers (the so-called American Negro) of the symbolic beast (the white man) who are in the beast's names and who worship and believe in the white man's religion, called Christianity. They worship the white man as though he were God above the Supreme God of heaven and earth. They also worship the white man's leader of the Christian religion, the Pope in Rome. This is mentioned in Revelation 14:4.

The grief of the hypocrites is such that even the victim is not able to say his prayers. In the first place, God has closed the door and does not hear the prayers of the hypocrites when He sends chastisement upon them. This is in store for my hypocrites and shall befall them at any time—just as it did the hypocrites of 1935. We actually witnessed this type of chastisement that fell upon those hypocrites in 1935. One of the hypocrites then was my own brother, and another was a minister by the name of Augustus Muhammad, my top assistant at that time in the Chicago Mosque No. 2. They felt proud after they had acquired a little wisdom and thought that they were more powerful than the teacher.

I have been told directly by some of the hypocrites that they think it is time for a change and that a younger man should take my place. And they even go so far as to designate a person whom they think should take my place.

I look at them and say within myself, "What a fool you are! How can you appoint someone to take my place when I did not appoint myself? God, Almighty appointed me. You are foolish to play with God's mission and His messenger to the mentally dead nation. You take it lightly that you can vote out, put down or shoot down God's Messenger and set up another of your choice. What will you do with the next group of hypocrites who may not like the man of your choice? They may shoot both you and your man down and take over."

Let the hypocrites be aware that there is a great chastisement in store for them—and their aims, purposes and wishes will never materialize. The Holy Qur-an teaches that their grief will be so severe that it will prostrate them and they will be unable even to blink their eyes—and that which they feared will come to pass. What they actually feared is:

> Exposure as the losers who had lied.
> Punishment for wishing their grief upon the Messenger and those with him.
> Victory of the Messenger over them.

They shall suffer the loss of true friendship, and they are not helped. They go to the devil for friendship, and he turns them down because he knows that they will not be able to help him against Allah and the Apostle, because Allah and His Apostle are considered submerged into one.

The Apostle is considered one in Allah and Allah is one in the Apostle. So, when you look at óne, you see both; when you hear one speak, you hear both, because they both are as one in their agreement for the right and against the disbeliever. Therefore, Allah brings this to pass. As it was in Noah's day, so shall it be in the day of the last Apostle, whom God raises from the mentally dead Negroes in North America.

THE JUDGMENT

ON UNIVERSAL CORRUPTION

*Corruption has appeared in the land and the sea on
account of that which men's hands have wrought,
that He may make them taste a part of that which
they have done, so that they may return.*
[Holy Qur-an 30:41].

Allah, the All Wise, the Best Knower, who has knowledge
of the past, the present and the future revealed this above prophecy to Muhammad (May the peace and blessing of Allah be
upon him) nearly 1,400 years ago, as though it were taking place
during that time. However, it was referring to these days, and
we see the manifestation and fulfillment of the above verse.

There is no doubt in anyone's mind today that the condition
of the nations is such that needs a ruler who is not involved in
the present world of corruption to bring about peace and good
will among the people of the earth. There cannot be peace for
the lovers who seek after peace until the peace breakers have
been removed from authority and their activities of mischief
making, causing bloodshed, grief, sorrow and trouble among
peace-loving nations.

There is not a civilized government of people at this writing
that is not in trouble and trying to find a solution to the cause.
All the nations of the earth are so corrupt with other than good
that they cannot come to any agreement on peace with each
other, then carry it into practice. The disagreement and corruption today is seen not only in the Christian world of Europe and
America but also in the very heart of the Holy Land in Africa
and Asia.

Corruption started in Europe, and it has now spread over
nine-tenths of the population of the Planet Earth. It has caused
the dissatisfaction of nearly 100 per cent of the civilized nations.

Dissatisfaction has reached such a percentage that it is bound to bring about universal war, since the corruption is universal. The continuing disagreement between the heads of the nations is referred to as CONFUSION and CONFLICT in the Bible and Holy Qur-an. In this world of universal corruption and crises and the ever-growing threat of universal war, we, the so-called American Negroes, the Lost-Found members of the tribe of Shabazz, should unite and take our stand on the side of Allah (God), His religion of Peace (Islam) and our own nation (the Black People).

THE BREAK-UP OF THE OLD WORLD!

According to the changes of civilization by Allah and His Messengers from Moses to this day and the last Messenger, the resurrection and return of the lost and found mentally dead members of the aboriginal people of earth (the Black Nation) is now.

Today, we live at the end of the world of people who have ruled the black man and his various colors between black and white for the last 6,000 years. The world of disbelievers and hypocrites know these are the days and the end of the rule of the white man.

I am referring to the rule of the people mentioned by Jesus, Allah and the Holy Qur-an as being a people who were created (grafted) so that they might be tried at ruling the righteous for the past 6,000 years. Their first 2,000 years were spent in the caves and hillsides of Europe (the only appointed continent of Allah for that people).

They suffered divine chastisement for the first 2,000 years on this continent for their trouble-making and for causing war and bloodshed among the original black people, who had not suffered from wars, exploitation and enslavement before the creation (grafting) of this people by their father, Yakub.

Today, they have filled the earth with their wickedness, and there is 100 per cent dissatisfaction against their continued rule over the nations black people.

Allah now has put it in the hearts of the original people to forsake them and to separate them from living to themselves as they did before the grafting of this race of people by Yakub. We find it as hard to separate from them as it was 600 years after they were grafted from us. In those days, they fought back to remove them from among the righteous (the original black people of Arabia).

In that war, Allah was successful, driving them (most of them) out into what is known today as Europe: EU stands for hills and cavesides of that continent and ROPE means a place where that people were bound in.

Since 1492, the people of the white race have been allowed to spread over the face of the earth (to have the freedom of deceiving all that they could). To learn more about them, let us read and study their history. Read in the Bible the Revelation of John, under the title of "The Beast and the Dragon."

Their history shows trouble-making, murder and death to all darker people from the far-off islands and mainlands of Asia as well as the South Seas and the Pacific and Atlantic Oceans. All have been touched by their destructive hand and evil way of civilization and finally the bringing of my people to make their destruction sure.

Actually it was suicide for them to have brought our fathers in slavery. This act was charged to them by the Divine Supreme Being as being the most wicked people on the earth. Now we see the results in the fight of the ignorant among our people to gain sincere love from a people who have no sincere love among themselves.

They have never practiced sincere love, according to their own history of war making, robbery, murder and exploitation among themselves. This is clear to you who see and understand.

The so-called Negro has been made so blind, deaf and dumb by them that even the intellectual blacks now are blind and seek to make love and friendship with the people of the devil and satan. The day of decision between the dark races or nations was begun by God Himself in the Person of Master Fard Muhammad, to Whom be praised forever, as is prophesied in the

Bible: "Multitudes in the valley of decision, for the day [before or by 1970] of the Lord is near in the valley of decision" (Joel 3:14).

It is clear that the armies of the nations of the earth have geared themselves for a showdown between their forces and Allah and the Nation of Islam. We, the so-called American Negroes, the lost and found members of our Nation, are in this decision. The second and third verses of this same chapter (Chapter 3) read like this: "I will also gather all nations and will bring them down into the valley of Jehoshaphat [Europe and Asia—between black and white] and will plead with them there for my people and for my heritage [the lost and found, so-called Negroes], Israel whom they have scattered among the nations and parted my land [between the European white race] and they have casted lots for my people and have given a boy for a harlot and sold a girl for wine that they might drink" (Joel 3:2, 3).

America has fulfilled this to the very letter and spirit with her slaves (the so-called Negroes) under the type of Israel. The Egyptians did nothing of the kind to Israel when they were in bondage to them. In fact, and as God taught me, the Bible is not referring to those people as His People, it is referring to the so-called Negro and his enemy (the white race). The seventh verse also gives us a hint in this way:

"Behold, I will raise them out of the place where you have sold them and will return your recompence upon your own head" (Joel 3:7).

The slave-masters of our fathers must reap what they have sown. Allah calls them to war in the ninth verse of the same chapter.

"Proclaim you among the Gentiles, prepare war, wake up the mighty men, let all of the men of war draw near, let them come up" (Joel 3:9).

All the mighty men of science and modern warfare have been called in an effort to devise instruments and weapons against God and the armies of heaven. The nations of the earth are angry. The disbelievers and hypocrites of my people also are angry over the change of the old world to a new world of justice and righteousness, causing much spiritual darkness and misunderstanding to fall upon them. They want to judge the person Allah should choose for His Messenger.

Believers, be aware of this chief hypocrite who has, for the past year, stepped beyond the limits in trying to keep people from following me (see Holy Qur-an 68:10-16).

I am no more to suffer the evil and slanderous talk of the disbelievers (as though they are the judges of Allah's Messenger) as did the Messenger before me. Not one of you of the 22 million who do not believe in the truth that I am teaching will harm me in the very least; you are harming only yourselves. As I have said, Allah has given me the key to your mental death here in America (hell). I am not allowed by Him to even beg you to believe, because the truth is plain enough for a fool to see and say that it is the truth.

THE DAY OF
AMERICA'S DOWNFALL

Allah manifests the fall of America. He desires to make Amercia fall as a warning to her brothers in Europe. White Americans and Germans—Allah has taught me—are the most wicked of the white race. The wicked deeds that have been performed and are still being performed by white Americans upon the so-called Negroes (their slaves) are the worst in the annals of history.

They have been clever enough in their wickedness to make the so-called Negro slaves love them, though they are their open enemies and murderers. Allah in the person of Master Fard Muhammad, to whom be praised forever, now judges the American whites and is causing America's fall and total destruction. Egypt under Pharaoh is an example. It fulfills the signs and other prophecies of the doom of this people as foretold by the prophets from Noah to Jesus.

Moses and Jesus are the most outstanding prophets in the history of the Caucasian race for the past 4,000 years. There are several other contemporaries, but Moses and Jesus are the major prophets of the white race's history. The whole of the civilized world today, as prophesied in Isaiah, is against the white man of America. Allah hates the wicked American whites and threatens to remove them from the face of the earth.

Since white Americans and the white race in general have deceived the entire world of black people and their brethren (brown, red and yellow), Allah now is causing these people to wake up and see the white race as it really is, the created enemy of the darker people. As we see today, there is a general awakening of the darker people into the knowledge of self and the knowledge of their age-old (6,000 years) enemies all over the earth. The American white race cannot sincerely give the so-called Negroes (their slaves) a square deal. She only desires to deceive them.

Today, America is trying, against her will, to give the so-called Negro civil rights (which is against the very nature and will of the white race) for the first time since the black man has been here. America falsely offers him social equality in certain parts of the country. This social equality consists mostly of permitting the American black race to mix openly with the white man and his woman (the devils). The actual idea, however, is to grant the so-called Negro social equality among the lower class of whites. This is done so that the scriptures, wherein the prophecy that the white man tempts and corrupts the so-called Negroes with his women, might be fulfilled.

God has taught me that the white race was grafted unalike, and, being unalike, it is able to attract the black man and black woman, getting them to do all the evil and indecency known to the white race.

The years 1965 and 1966 are going to be fateful for America, bringing in the "Fall of America." As one of the prophets of the Bible prophesied in regard to her, "As the morning spreads abroad upon the mountains a great and strong people set in battle array" (Joel 2:2). This is the setting of the nations for a showdown to determine who will live on earth. The survivor is to build a nation of peace to rule the people of the earth forever under the guidance of Almighty God, Allah. With the nations setting forth for a final war at this time, God pleads for His people (the inheritors of the earth, the so-called Negroes).

The so-called Negro is the prey of the white man of America, being held firmly in the white man's power, along with 2 million Indians who must be redeemed at this time and will be, if the so-called Negro turns to His Redeemer. The problem of the American black man is his unwillingness to be separated from his 400-year-old enemies. The problem, therefore, is harder to solve, especially with the enemy trying to fascinate the Negro with his lower class girls and women arraying them partly nude before the Negroes in every public news medium (cheap daily newspapers and magazines, radio and TV) and the Negro is quick to imitate.

The problem between these two people, separating and dignifying the so-called Negroes so they may be accepted and respected as equals or superiors to other nations, must be solved. This is God's promise to the so-called Negro (the lost and found members of the original Black Nation of the earth). This promise was made through the mouths of His prophets (Bible and Qur-an), that He would separate us from our enemies, dignify us and make us the masters after this wicked race has been judged and destroyed for its own evils.

But, as I said, the solving of this problem, which means the redemption of the Negro, is hard to do, since he loves his enemies (See Bible; Deut. 18:15, 18; Psalms; Isaiah; Matthew 25:32; and Revelations, Chapter 14).

The manifestation of Allah and judgment between the so-called Negro and the enemy of God and Nation of Islam will make the so-called Negro see and know his enemy and himself, his people, his God and his religion.

We hear the statements of black educational, political and Christian classes, which express their love for the white man, publicly asking to be his brothers, if not his brothers-in-law. Now, this class wants to make it clear to the world that they really love the white race and not the black race. This means they want to be white instead of black. The devils have made them hate black. They reject the thought of black ever being the ruler or equal with the ruler. They ask boldly for inferiority, not only for themselves, but for their people.

They want to absorb themselves and their kind (especially the so-called American Negro) into the race of white people, thus ending the black race. It is just the opposite with Allah (God), myself and my followers. We "want out completely." We want no claim to kinship with a people who, by nature, are not our kin. Read from Genesis to the Revelation in the Bible and from Sura 2 to Sura 114 of the Holy Qur-an.

By no means are the so-called Negroes and the whites kin. God did not create them to ever become brothers. One is created an enemy against the other, and since the righteous are more powerful than the wicked, Allah, the God of righteous, set a time of reckoning for the enemy (the white man) of the righteous.

We want separation. We want a home on this earth we can call our own. We want to go for self and leave the enemy who has been sentenced to death by Allah (Rev. 20:10-14) from the day he was created (See this subject in the Bible and Qur-an). No one, white, black, brown, yellow or red can prove to me by any scriptures of Allah (God) sent by one of the prophets of Allah (God) that we should not be separated from the white race, that we should believe and follow the religion dictated, shaped and formed by the theologians of the white race.

The coming Allah and the judgment of the wicked world is made clear by the prophetic sayings of the Prophets. The so-called reverends and the proud intellectual class are doomed to destruction with the enemy, if they remain with him instead of joining onto Allah, Who loves them and Who will deliver them and the Nation of Islam.

The so-called Negro masses must be warned of the grave mistake they make in following the leadership of those who love and befriend their murderers. This will not get them freedom or civil rights.

America is falling. Her doom has come, and none said the prophets shall help her in the day of her downfall. In the Bible, God pleads with you to fly out of her (America) and seek refuge in Him (Rev. 18:4). What is going to happen in 1973 and 1974? It certainly will change your minds about following a doomed people, a people who hate you and your kind and who call one who teaches the truth about them a hater. They are the producers of hatred of us. We are with God and the righteous.

AMERICA IS FALLING
HER DOOM IS SEALED

I compare the fall of America with the fall of ancient Babylon. Her wickedness (sins), is the same as history shows of ancient Babylon. "Babylon is suddenly fallen and the destroyed howl for her; take balm for her pains, if so she may be healed" (Jer. 51:81). What were the sins of ancient Babylon? According to history she was rich; she was proud and her riches increased her corruption. She had every merchandise that the nations wanted or demanded; her ships carried her merchandise to the ports of every nation.

She was a drunkard; wine and strong drinks were in her daily practice. She was filled with adultery and murder; she persecuted and killed the people of God. She killed the saints and prophets of Allah (God). Hate and filthiness, gambling, sports of every evil as you practice in America were practiced in Babylon. Only America is modern and much worse. Ancient Babylon was destroyed by her neighboring nations.

I warn you to let their destruction serve as a warning for America. This people has gone to the limit in doing evil; as God dealt with ancient people, so will He deal with the modern Babylon (America). As God says: "Son of Man, when the land (people) sinneth against Me by trespassing grievously, then will I stretch out Mine hand upon it, and will break the staff of bread thereof, and will send famine upon it, and will cut off man and beast from it" (Ezekiel 14:13).

We see with our own eyes — but, the wicked Americans are too proud to confess that they see the bread of America gradually being cut off. Take a look into the Southwest and Middle West, see the hand of Allah (God) at work against modern Babylon—to break the whole staff of her bread for her evils done against His people (the so-called Negroes).

Texas and Kansas were once two of the nation's proudest

states. Kansas, known for its wheat and Texas, for its cattle, cotton, corn and many other vegetables and fruits. They are today in the grip of a drought, continuous raging dust storms; their river beds lie bare, their fish stinking on the banks in dry parched mud. When the rain comes, it brings very little relief and does more damage than good. Snow comes – it brings not joy, but death and destruction. After the snow comes more dust storms. With the rain come hail stones, very large stones. America has not seen the large hail stones; she will see hail stones the size of small blocks of ice breaking down crops, trees, the roofs of homes, killing cattle and fowl. Behind this terrific earthquake, the people – frightened, killed, much sickness, and death will be widespread. You are getting a token of it now. On the outside, a threat of an atomic war between the nations of the earth. Yet you have your eyes closed at the manifest judgment of Allah (God), going on in your midst to bring this country to naught.

Allah (God) has found His people (the so-called Negroes), and is angry with the slave-masters for the evil done by them to His people (the so-called Negroes). Allah (God) is going to repay them according to their doings.

My poor people who have turned to their own God and religion (Allah and Islam), are being tracked down and watched as though they are about to rob a bank. This is done to try and put fear in them – so that they might stay away from their God (Allah) and His true religion (Islam), as the devil knows – their salvation and defense.

They (the devils) watch the steps of the righteous (the Negroes) and seek to slay them (Psalms 37:32). The so-called Negroes live under the very shadow of death in America. There is no justice for them in the courts of their slave-masters. Why should not America be chastised for her evils done to the so-called Negroes? If God destroyed ancient Babylon for the mockery made of the sacred vessels taken from the Temple in Jerusalem, what do you think Allah (God) should do for America's mockery of the so-called Negroes – that she took from their native land and people and filled them with wine and whiskey.

Now she (America) puts on a show of temptation with their women (white women) in newspapers, magazines, in the streets half nude, and posing in the so-called Negroes' faces in the most indecent manner that is known to mankind -- to trick them (so-called Negroes) to death and hell along with them. Be wise, my people, and shut your eyes to them -- do not look at them in such an indecent way. Clean your homes of white people's pictures -- put your own on the walls. The only so-called Negroes' pictures you will see in their homes are one they have lynched, one they want to kill, or one who has betrayed his own people for them.

America is falling; she is a habitation of devils and every uncleanness and hateful people of the righteous. Forsake her and fly to your own before it is too late.

THE DECLINE OF THE DOLLAR

The stronghold of the American Government is falling to pieces. She has lost her prestige among the nations of the earth. One of the greatest powers of America was her dollar. The loss of such power will bring any nation to weakness, for this is the media of exchange between nations. The English pound and the American dollar have been the power and beckoning light of these two great powers. But when the world went off the gold and silver standard, the financial doom of England and America was sealed.

The pound has lost 50 per cent of its value. America's dollar has lost everything now as power backing for her currency, which was once backed by gold for every $5.00 note and up. All of her currency was backed by silver from a $1.00 note and up.

Today, the currency of America is not backed by any sound value, silver or gold. The note today is something that the government declares it will give you the value in return but does not name that value. They definitely are not backing their currency with silver or gold.

This is the number one fall, and it is very clear that the loss of the power of the American dollar means the loss of the financial power of America. What will happen, since there is no sound backing for her notes, we do not know.

What should we expect even in the next 12 months under the fall of the power of America's dollar? This means that we have 100 per cent inflation. What could happen under 100 per cent inflation? Your guess is as good as mine. The power of gold and silver was once abundant in America. But the touch of the finger of God against the power of so mighty a nation has now caused the crumbling and fall of America.

We can easily and truthfully liken the fall of America to the prophetic symbolic picture given in the (Bible) Revelation of John (18:2). The name Babylon used there does not really say whether it is ancient Babylon or a picture of some future Babylon.

The description it gives is as follows: *"And he [angel] cried mightly with a strong voice [with authority] saying, Babylon the great is fallen, is fallen and is become the habitation of devils [Allah has declared the people to be a race of devils], and the hole of every foul spirit and a cage of every unclean and hateful bird."* The description here given to the Babylon by the Prophets compares with the present history and people of America and their fall.

The picture shows the cause of her fall. First, she had become the habitation of devils, making her a haven for every people that love the works and doings of the devil. Here the Prophet refers to them symbolically, as being a hole of every foul spirit and a cage of every unclean and hateful bird.

People are referred to as birds, snakes, beasts, fish and other animals to tell or represent the characteristics of that person. It is universally known that the very beginning of the American people was from the lower class of European people. Their first ruler (President Washington) was a fugitive from England. The common, dissatisfied and lower grade of European people followed and boosted his authority. This filled and inhabited America with a very low-class and low-based people.

Then this type of people went into Africa and purchased slaves from among our people, who were also uneducated, most of them, but there were a few who were highly educated. All of these begin to mix with the low-based, evil-minded, real citizens of the Western Hemisphere (whites). When America began to get strong in power, she opened her doors to the underprivileged (laborers) in overpopulated countries, such as China, Japan and other European states, to seek citizenship in America.

This brought America into being one of the most mixed people who were granted the freedom to live any kind of life they chose. They were not forced to serve the God of the Universe who made heaven and earth, or any religion. They had freedom to worship. This made America a haven for any people who wished to be free of the compelling aspects of religious and just rule and authority. This people for the past 500 years has put into practice every evil that is imaginable.

The freedom of uncleanliness is granted and is worshiped. The percentage of sexual worship of the same sex is greater than in any other government on the face of the earth. Little children are being taught sex almost from the cradle, making the whole nation, as one man put it, nearly 90 per cent freaks of nature.

On the streets of any metropolitan city in America, it is common to see men sweethearting with men and women sweethearting with women. Little boys with boys and little girls with girls.

It is so common that a decent family is puzzled as to where to send their children for schooling. There are no all-girl schools as there once were. They are all-girl schools of sweethearts. The same sex falling upon their own. Boys' colleges are breeding such filthy practices, the jails, prisons, and the Federal Penitentiaries are all breeding dens of homosexuals.

As the Prophet says in the 18th chapter: "She is a cage of every unclean and hateful bird." There are types of hateful birds. This is why a symbolic name is given. It means human beings. There are birds of prey and birds that are unclean, such as crows, owls, buzzards and ravens, who live and thrive off the carcasses of others. And there are unclean people living and thriving off the unclean.

It is time that God intervenes to bring about an end of such people as the wicked of America. She offers the same filth to all of the civilized people of the earth, and she hates you if you are against her way of life and will threaten you with death as the Sodomites did Lot and his followers. But I say to you, as the 4th verse of Chapter 18 says: You that want to be a better people than this, "come out of her."

The so-called American Negroes are referred to here in the 4th verse as being God's people (My People): "Come out of her that ye be not partakers of her sins and that you receive not of her plagues."

This is a call to the American so-called Negroes to give up a doomed, wicked people that have destroyed them from being a people worthy of recognition and who have now become lovers of their enemies and destroyers.

The 5th verse tells us that "Her sins have reached into heaven and God has remembered her iniquities and is ready to destroy her." Her destruction cometh quickly according to the 8th verse, that plagues of death, mourning and famines which cometh in one day (one year) and then after that she shall be destroyed by fire, utterly burned.

This is backed up in these words: "Strong is the Lord God who judge her." Here it gives us a knowledge that He who judges is well able with power, with wisdom and with deliberate and careful maneuvering to give judgment against her.

THE RESURRECTION
OF OUR PEOPLE

The old world must be removed to make way for the new world. There is a universal struggle being waged by the old world against the beginning of the new world. Will the old world's opposition prevent the establishment of the new world? According to recorded history the efforts being made by the old world against the beginning of a new world will fail, as did former opponents of Allah.

According to the history of Noah, the people ridiculed the very thought of Allah bringing a flood to drown them. Noah was laughed at and scorned for preaching such a doctrine. According to the Bible and Holy Qur-an, he was called a liar and looked upon as a crazy person. Some of the members of Noah's family joined the mockers and disbelievers of Allah and His Messenger who was Noah. They also met the same fate of the others who disbelieved.

The opposition of that world to the advent of a better world was a total failure. So shall it be with those today who oppose the beginning of a new world of righteousness (Islam). In the time of Abraham and his nephew (Lot), before the birth of Ismael and Isaac, Abraham's two sons, the people, mockers, and haters of truth and righteousness in that part of the world (the cities of Sodom and Gomorrah) had become victimized by every imaginable evil.

They even threatened the life of the preacher of righteousness, Lot, disregarding the strangers (angels) visiting Lot, until it was too late. So it is with the opponents of the Messenger of Allah today in America.

The wicked always believe they are mightier than Allah, and they make a supreme effort to thwart the plan and purpose of Allah to bring about a better world. They always love to attack the Messenger to try to condemn him as a liar. Trying to prove the Messenger a liar means calling Allah a liar. The Holy Quran repeatedly prophesies a miserable, shameful and disgraceful defeat for the disbelievers and hypocrites in their campaign against the last Messenger of Allah whom Allah would raise in the time of the resurrection of the dead people.

Messengers are never sent. They always are raised in the midst of those whom Allah would warn so they cannot claim that they did not understand the language of the Messenger or say that he was a foreigner or stranger. The Messenger is one from them.

For over 40 years I have served you, just as Allah's warners of old served a hard-hearted and hard-headed disbelieving people, who were great lovers of the enemies of Allah and the true religion, Islam (which means entire submission to Allah's will). There is mockery, and evil plans are made against my life by the wicked, just as they were made against Noah and subsequent prophets.

The powerful, rich world of Christianity, especially America, is made to seem as immovable as the mountains. But it is not impossible to remove mountains; they can be removed by high explosives. So wealth and power also can be reduced to nothing.

We are now living in the judgment or doom of the white man's world. Preparations have been made to meet every effort by the white man to oppose the beginning and setting up of Allah's new world of righteousness (Islam). The government (U.S.A.) today watches my followers with an evil eye, seeking to deceive anyone who would enter the fold to help further the cause of truth and the upliftment and the mourning heads and grieving hearts of the American so-called Negroes to help them make a nation of righteousness and justice to serve as a star for the nations of their own kind forever. The U.S. government is active in its deceitful work of trying to slow the progress of resurrection of our people.

American whites want us to reject Allah and the true religion, Islam and believe in their false religion and false god, whom they cannot make manifest to you. They cannot prove to you in this day and time that Christianity is a defense for you as well as for themselves against their doom.

America must be taken and destroyed according to the prophets, at the time and end of the wicked world, where the lost and found members of the ancient and aboriginal people are found, America hates and mistreats her slaves to the extent that it has reached the heart of Allah and the righteousness of the people of the earth (the Nation of Islam).

We read where our black brothers refer to the American so-called Negroes as their brothers, while according to the preachings of some of these lost and found members of the aboriginal nation of the earth they would rather have themselves referred to as the brothers of their enemies.

The extent to which the enemy has poisoned the minds and hearts of my people here in America is shameful. They wilfully do anything to deceive the so-called Negroes into going to their doom with them. There is no way for the enemy of Allah, His Messenger and His people (the darker people of the earth) to find strength, power and wisdom enough to win in a war against Allah. As it is written in the Christian Bible and many other

places: "But the day of the Lord will come as a thief in the
night; in thee, which the heavens shall pass away with a great
noise and the elements shall melt with fervent heat, the earth
also and the works that are therein shall be burned up" (Peter
3:10).

The earth shall not be burned; it will be here for many
thousands of years to come. Only that on the earth (the devils)
which has sinned against Allah and His laws will be destroyed.
The earth, the sun, the moon and the stars have never disobeyed
Allah since their creation.

MAKE AMERICA
KNOW HER SINS

The doom of America approaches, and there are many people
who do not really know why. There are also many who would
not like to know. As I have always said, truth hurts—especially
the guilty. It is the expressed purpose of the coming of God,
whose proper name is Allah, to make manifest the sins of a
people who He would destroy, justifying His destruction of that
people.

America represents herself as a Christian nation. This means
that they are followers of Jesus, whom they call the Christ and
say that they are crystallized into him and God and have become
one. As they say, God the Father, Jesus the son and the Holy
Ghost.

They profess to be a friend and defenders of all peace-loving
and freedom-loving people. The only people we really see that
they want to be friends of are themselves and their kind. They
are really sincere when they say that they are freedom-loving
people. Above all, the white man the world over wants to be
free to rule and dominate the aboriginal people.

Today America's doom is set like a die. She cannot escape;
it is impossible. For her to escape would classify the prophets
of God and God Himself as predicting lies. When God appeared
to me in the person of Master Fard Muhammad, to whom
praises are due forever, in 1931 in Detroit, He said that America was His number one enemy on His list for destruction.

While He mentioned other European whites as getting a little extension of time, He singled America and Germany out as being the two worst vicious, evil, destructive trouble-makers of the entire nation earth. And that America had mistreated us (the so-called Negroes) so much that she cannot be equally paid back for the evils she has done to the poor black slaves.

There are thousands and tens of thousands of American so-called Negroes and in those tens of thousand are such professional and educated class of people as preachers, ministers of the white man's Christianity, even scientists, scholars of many kinds and technicians of all kinds who have become submerged into the love and worship of the white race because of advantages.

Today they preach the gospel of being an American citizen and worship equally their intermarriage with white Americans who used the black women from the time they were brought here 400 years ago until this very day, as they would their stock and cattle.

It is a perfect shame and disgrace to see men of the black nation professing themselves to be spiritual guides of God and His people, endorsing and backing the rule of enemies who have spoiled and exploited them to the extent that they are not recognized even among their own kind outside America. These ignorant black people will oppose anyone who preaches freedom, Justice and equality and some of this earth that we can call our own.

It is clear that such a spiritual leader as this is more an enemy to his people than the real devil (Caucasian). They want to please the enemy at the expense and destruction of their own people. They are more upset (the clergy) over the preaching of justice for our people and a home on this earth that we can call our own than the white man himself.

They hope, as I said, to always say, preach, teach, pray, sing and act in a way which pleases the slave-master of their fathers and his children. They are a class of "Uncle Toms" and "Stool Pigeons."

They are the first to go to the policemen and F.B.I. seeking persecution for those who stand for freedom, justice and equality and independence for the black man of America by their admired and worshiped enemy (the white race). They will accuse them of trying to overthrow the government or even of causing trouble.

The white man has looked into their faces many times as into their children's faces and cursed them and called them Black Negroes and told us to our faces that they hate us and should kill us.

All of my life I have heard this, and all of their lives they have heard the same from the mouths of these people. But today they wish to save their skin by sacrificing their poor, blind, deaf and dumb people to the destroyer for their own selfish gains.

I have begged and begged for many years for just a conference with them, but they will not come near. But they will go to the white man and beg him to drive Elijah and his followers out and even kill them. This is the enemy, but Elijah Muhammad is laid as a stumbling stone. That stone that has been rejected by the builders. Whosoever falls on that stone will be broken to pieces, and whosoever the stone falls upon will be ground into powder.

No wonder the Bible says, woe, woe unto such professional class that stand in the way of those who would enter the Kingdom of Heaven. They refuse to go in themselves and seek to prevent those who are trying to enter.

I am sorry for my poor people who should be helping in the right way to get a permanent future of freedom, justice and equality and who now, due to fear, are doing everything to oppose it. They are dumb enough to the knowledge of the scripture of what God has prophesied He would do in this day and time, and they make mockery even of the Messenger of God because God did not choose one of them or one of their proud politicians. They make mockery of him as being too ignorant to lead them.

But let them tell you what type of an Apostle or prophet God promised them. Was it a man from some of the enemy colleges and universities with an arm full of degrees coming from these institutions of learning of the enemy?

Let them read their scriptures and see what type of man God promised to choose for a last messenger. How many of the prophets in the past were educated men of the civilization in which they were born before the call of God?

The sins of America are terrible. She has risen up in this part of the earth which was wilderness forsaken by all our people for thousands and thousands of years and was used for a kind of exile continent. The white man came out of Europe in desperation seeking a place to expand and began to kill the aboriginals of this continent (the Red Indian) and take their homes. This was one of her great sins.

The white man has left a remnant of that people for the sake of mockery and for his children to see the people their fathers conquered in taking this land of the Indians for their own land (as they call it today). God never intended that the people of the earth go about killing each other to rob each other of their homes. It was never done by anyone but the white race.

He was not satisfied in killing all the aboriginals here to take their homes but went back into the old world of Africa and Asia and deceived and brought our fathers here for no other purpose than to make them slaves and to experiment on them.

They have never been a friend to us, nor do they ever intend to be. They cannot be a friend because they were not created in any such nature to be a true friend to anyone, not even to themselves. Today she is being upset with wars, little scrimmages breaking out here and there over the earth keeping her busy running from one fire to the other trying to prevent the fire from spreading into a national or international fire.

She must get a taste of what she has put upon other people. Therefore, Almighty God Himself is stirring up the nations of the earth against her. And, as it is written, they shall come against her as she has gone against other people and taken away their wealth and brought it and poured it into her treasuries, so shall it be done to her.

A HOUSE DOOMED TO FALL

We cannot deny the fact that the Christian West is responsible for this universal corruption in the land and sea.

From the same corruption that their own hands have wrought will come their doom.

The Christians preach that which they do not do and cannot do. Such as "Love thy neighbor." I have as yet to meet one who loved his neighbor as he did himself. "Thou shall not kill." I have as yet to meet such a Christian.

They even fight against each other, rob and kill each other, but yet represent themselves as World peacemakers—with whom?

The great deceivers of the World will reap what they have sown. Have they not corrupted many people and Nations under the false disguise of good peaceful loving Christians?

The Christian West is full of the worst crimes, practicing evils and indecencies to the fullest and seeking to practice them on other Nations as well.

Universal tempters ever parading before the world their bold half-nude girls and women. They are before your eyes in almost everything, regardless. Murder, gambling, robbery, drunkenness, drugs, adultery, lying—there is hardly any end to it.

Their land and seas are filled with deadly weapons of war; their islands of the sea are filled with corruption by all the Nations of earth, for they are proud and boastful and are now hated and despised according to their wishes.

Their religion (Christianity) is a curse to us (the Black Man) and is full of slavery teaching. They have poisoned the Bible with their adding to and taking from the truth. Now their doom is in sight. It is their own work.

They rule the sea with powerful deadly ships, parking them off the shores of the homes of other Nations. They secure air bases on foreign soils to park deadly bomb-carrying planes within striking distances of those whom they think to be their enemies. Is this not the easy way to make enemies?

Is this the act of a real Christian, the followers of Jesus whom they preach came for the peace of mankind and to teach the sheathing of the sword and the turning of the other cheek?

Where is a good Christian among this race?

They love meddling in other people's affairs. They are in every fight or war regardless of with whom or where, but yet crying "peace, peace" with every deadly weapon of war, brandishing them before the Nation as a dare.

Shall not the God of Peace and Justice deal with such troublemaking people as He did with those before you of old?

I warn everyone of you, my people, fly to Allah with me! As I warned you, the judgment of this world has arrived! Get out of the church and get into the Mosques and join onto your own kind, the Nation of Islam! The house you are in shall surely fall and never rise again.

THE FULFILLMENT
OF PROPHECIES SEEN

*The Signs of the Coming of God—"And Jesus
said unto them see ye not these things? Verily I
say unto you, There shall not be left here one
stone upon another, that shall not be torn down"*
[*Matt. 24*].

This chapter refers to the signs of the judgment of the wicked
world. Jesus pointed out examples of the destruction of the Jewish Temple or synagogue, and the historians wrote that the
Romans came about 70 years later—after the death of Jesus—
and sacked Jerusalem. Really, this was not the end of Jesus'
prophecy of the destruction of Jerusalem by the Romans for all
the stones were not overthrown by Rome.

This had reference to the end of the whole world of the
wicked. Let us take note of his words in the fourth and fifth
verses: "Take heed that no man deceive you for many shall
come in my name saying I am Christ and shall deceive many."

This did not happen before the destruction of Jerusalem by
the Romans. This refers to the entire period of 2,000 years after
his (Jesus) death. It is referring to the many who would come
and try to imitate him and shall deceive many, especially the
very ignorant people who are given to superstition, who can be
easily deceived, and they will sometimes add to a leaders title
whom they are not serving.

For instance, the ancient Romans were so ignorant and superstitious of the Divine Supreme Being that they made Gods for
themselves out of stones, wood, bulls and the stars of heaven,
such as Venus. They still have in the Vatican, so I am told,
an image of a calf made of pure gold.

It is the Pope of Rome today whom the church accepts as
its intercessor between and Christians and God. And all Cath-
olics, such as priests and cardinals profess to have the power
to pray the soul out of purgatory.

All of this is completely out of line with the true worship
of God. The Pope takes his place as the head of the Christian
church, while the church at the same time claims Jesus Christ

to be its head. But in reality, they recognize the Pope (Father) as being their head.

Of course, this is more true, because Jesus was not the head of any church. The church was organized by the Romans. According to history, and not by Jesus. And the truth of this is that it (the church) does not have any Divine power for anyone. If the Christians were not backed by the white man's money, guns, power and bombs, the church would have no power at all. Here many are deceived by the millions in bowing to the head of the church—the Pope of Rome.

The late Pope who recently died, according to history used to be a soldier and then a general. He fought in wars and did many other acts of unrighteousness before taking his place as the head of the church.

"Many shall come in my name." This does not mean every little local fellow. It means people who get national and world fame by claiming themselves to be Jesus Christ or God.

There have been many who have risen up in Islam in the past who went in the name of the Mahdi but were not the true Mahdi. Even to the late Maulana Muhammad Ali, who also claimed himself to have been Christ, the Messiah, when he was among the Christians, the Jews, Hindu, and among the Muslims, their Mahdi.

Today, that has all been hushed up and passed. The world does not look to him as having been their Mahdi or the Christian's Messiah. Old Orthodox Christians, like old orthodox Hebrews have expected a return of their once great spiritual leaders or prophets, Moses and Jesus, who taught, as the Christians teach today, a return of the Jesus at the end of the world.

Old Orthodox Muslims preach a return of Muhammad of 1,400 years ago, or that there will be no need of another prophet after him, for he settled everything. They do not take the slightest thought that these prophets could not have been the last who would usher in the Judgment. There have been so many things that have come to pass since that time that someone is needed to enlighten the people as to these latest events and to serve as a guide for the people into the presence of God.

What the Prophets brought to the people 4,000 years ago was for that people for the next 2,000 years to the birth of Jesus. And what Jesus brought (the Injil or New Testament) was to last until the end of the world—that is, the time and destruction of the wicked world ruled by satan and the setting up a new universal government under the guidance of Allah or Mahdi, sometimes called the Great Mahdi, to make a distinction from the many others who would be called by such name, as there are many Muslims who have adopted "Mahdi," like the many Italians who have adopted "Jesus" for their names.

The next verse (six) tells us that Jesus had in mind the end of the entire world and not Jerusalem. It reads like this: "And ye shall hear of wars and rumors of wars, see that ye be not troubled, for all these things must come to pass, but the end is not yet."

The wars mentioned in the sixth verse, the nations rising against nations, kingdoms against kingdoms, the famines and pestilence and earthquakes mentioned in the seventh verse, are what we must expect to take place before the end.

RISE AND FALL
OF THE CHRISTIAN WEST

The fall of America is now visible and understandable, not only in the eyes of scholars and scientists but even in the eyes and understanding of the ignorant. Long has Allah (God) been gradually removing the power of the great and mighty America while few have noticed it. This has been done by degrees, and they do not perceive it.

The Holy Qur-an says, "He brings powerful nations to a naught," and when it is discovered, it is like a growth of cancer that has been eating at the body for many years while the patient was unaware of it.

Today, it is visibly understood that the fall of America cannot be checked, for the foundation has been removed. The 1914 war, which involved all of the white race, crushed the power of Turkey in Europe and pushed that power back across the Bosporus (or pushed Islam out of Europe as nearly as possible). An old prophetic saying is that when Turkey has been pushed out of Europe (across the Bosporus), setting her capital away from the once Constantinople, this would mark the end of the white world.

I can say truthfully, and the scientists will agree, that the 1914 war marked the fall of the white world as a power over the black world (the aboriginal people). That was some 50 years ago.

In another prophecy, the war of 1914 is referred to as the War of the Anti-Christs, or what we today call Christian Europe and America. They are referred to as anti-Christs because they are against the government of the true God of the black people. Christ here means God in Person in the last days or end of the Caucasian world. The name, Christ, spiritually means "One Who is coming at the end to crush the power of the infidel or the race of devils."

It is easy for you to understand that they are against the real Christ by their persecution, jailing, beating and killing of the prophets and their followers of Allah (God).

Now they openly tell you of their plans to kill me, the Last Messenger of God and resurrector of the mentally dead of my people. At the present hour, they hold hundreds and thousands of my followers in prison, threatening them with the worst treatment because they are Muslims.

You can also see how, at the present time, no Muslim followers of mine can get justice in the lily-white courts of America. Of course, these same conditions prevail for most of the so-called American Negroes. There is no justice for any of us in the courts of white people.

They have been made manifest to the world as being a race of devils, wherein we cannot expect any justice or sincere friendship unless we are everything that they are in wickedness. Righteousness is hated by them. We have given you an example of ones who are trying to be righteous and peaceful in their midst, and yet we are the most hated of all. They even teach my own people to hate me and then charge me with teaching hate.

I warn my people to beware of such an evil race of people. Beware of their deceitful plans to trick black Americans into going to their doom with them. They are so afraid that Allah will give the so-called American Negro wisdom and a grand kingdom on some of this earth that we can call our own under the beautiful crescent of Islam (entire submission to the will of Allah—God) that they are even teaching the so-called American Negro soldiers (as I have learned) against accepting Islam. The truth is worrying them. This should teach the so-called

American Negro that the white man has never wanted him to
be free, never wanted him to leave them and never wanted to
exercise the God-given freedom, justice and equality that even
nature offer.

BATTLE IN THE SKY IS NEAR

The vision of Ezekiel's wheel in a wheel in the sky is true if
carefully understood. There is a similar wheel in the sky today
which very well answers the description of Ezekiel's vision. This
wheel corresponds in a way with the sphere of spheres called
the universe. The Maker of the universe is Allah (God) the
Father of the black nation which includes the brown, yellow,
and red people. The Great Wheel which many of us see in the
sky today is not so much a wheel as one may think in such
terms, but rather a place made like a wheel. The like of this
wheel-like plane was never seen before. You cannot build one
like it and get the same results. Your brains are limited. If you
would make one to look like it, you could not get it up off
the earth into outer space. The similar Ezekiel's wheel is a
masterpiece of mechanics. Maybe I should not say the wheel
is similar to Ezekiel's vision of a wheel, but that Ezekiel's vision
has become a reality. His vision of the wheel included hints on
the Great Wisdom of Almighty God (Allah); that really He is
the Maker of the universe, and reveals just where and how the
decisive battle would take place (in the sky).

When guns and shells took the place of the sword, man's
best defense against such weapons was a trench (ditch). Poison
gas and liquid fire brought him out. Today, he has left the surface for the sky to destroy his enemy by dropping and exploding
bombs on each other. All this was known in the days of Ezekiel,
and God revealed it to him, that through Ezekiel we might
know what to expect at the end of this world.

The Originator and his people (the original black people) are
supremely wise. Today, we see the white race preparing for the
sky battle to determine who shall remain and rule this earth,
black or white. In the battle between God and the disbelievers
in the days of Noah, the victor's weapon was water. He used
fire in the case of Sodom and Gomorrah. In the battle against
Pharaoh, He used ten different weapons, which included fire and

water, hail stones and great armies of the insect world and droughts and finally plagued them with death.

The Holy Qur-an says: "The chastisement of Pharaoh was like that which God would use against His enemies in the last days."

Throughout the Bible and Holy Qur-an teachings on the judgment and destruction of the enemies, fire will be used as the last weapon. The earth's greatest arms are fire and water. The whole of its atmosphere is made up of fire and water and gases. It serves as a protected coat of arms against any falling fragments from her neighbors. Ezekiel saw wheels in the middle of a wheel. This is true (the universe in the universe; it is made up of revolving spheres). There are wheels in the wheel.

The present wheel-shaped plane known as the Mother of Planes, is one-half mile by a half mile and is the largest mechanical man-made object in the sky. It is a small human planet made for the purpose of destroying the present world of the enemies of Allah. The cost to build such a plane is staggering! The finest brains were used to build it. It is capable of staying in outer space six to twelve months at a time without coming into the earth's gravity. It carried fifteen hundred bombing planes with most deadliest explosives—the type used in bringing up mountains on the earth. The very same method is to be used in the destruction of this world.

The bombs are equipped with motors and the toughest of steel was used in making them. This steel drills and takes the bombs into the earth at a depth of one mile and is timed not to explode until it reaches one mile into the earth. This explosion produces a mountain one mile high; not one bomb will fall into water. They will all fall on cities. As Ezekiel saw and heard in his vision of it (Chapter 10:2) the plane is terrible. It is seen but do not think of trying to attack it. That would be suicide!

The small circular-made planes called flying saucers, which are so much talked of being seen, could be from this Mother Plane. This is only one of the things in store for the white man's evil world. Believe it or believe it not! This is to warn you and me to fly to our own God and people.

THE GREAT DECISIVE
BATTLE IN THE SKY

And there shall be signs in the sun and in the moon and in the stars, and upon the earth distress of nations with perplexity; the sea and the waves roaring; men's hearts failing them for looking after those things which are coming on the earth: for the powers of heaven shall be shaken. They see the Son of Man coming in a cloud with power and great glory" (St. Luke 21: 25-27).

You will bear me witness that we are living in such time as mentioned in the above prophecy -- signs in the sun and in the moon. The phenomena going on in the sun and its family of planets testify to the truth that something of the greatest magnitude is about to take place. The final war or battle between God and the devils in the sky.

Allah (God), who has power over all things, is bringing the powers of the sun, moon and stars into display against His enemies. The fire of the sun to scorch and burn men and the vegetation and dry up the waters. The moon will eclipse her light to bring darkness upon man and upon all living things, to disrupt with her waves all air communications. The magnetic powers of the moon will bring about such tidal waves of seas and oceans as man has never witnessed before: the sea and the waves roaring.

As men's hearts fail them with fear at the sea, looking upon great tidal waves coming toward them like mountains, they also shall see such a great display of power from Allah (God) in the sky that their hearts will fail. Great earthquakes never felt before since man was upon the earth will take place, say the Bible and the Holy Qur-an. The Holy Qur-an says: "There will not be one city left that will not be leveled to the ground." Using this force against the enemies of Allah will make it impossible for them to survive.

This is all known to this world, but why are they trying to build up a defense against God. It is useless. America has it coming. Look how she has been and still is mistreating her freed slaves (so-called Negroes). The foolish (so-called) Negro preachers and leaders want social equality with these, their enemies.

The great distress of nations spoken or prophesied of coming in the above chapter and verses is now going on. Confusion, confusion all over the Western world today.

They (devils) see the end of their world and they see the signs of the Son of Man coming in the sky with power and great glory (the great Ezekiel's wheel and the unity of the Muslim world and the distress of nations).

The so-called Negro must awaken before it is too late. They think the white man's Christianity will save them regardless of what happens, and they are gravely mistaken. They must know that the white man's religion is not from God nor from Jesus or any other of the prophets. It is controlled by the white race and not by Almighty Allah (God).

"The near event draws nigh, there shall be none besides Allah to remove it. Do you wonder at this announcement? And will you laugh and not weep? While you sport and play, so make obesiance to Allah and serve Him" (Holy Qur-an 53:57,58,59, 60). Let us remember another Qur-an saying: "None disputes concerning the communications of Allah (God) but those who disbelieve, therefore let not their going to and fro in the cities deceive you. The people of Noah and the parties after them rejected prophets before them, and every nation purposed against their Apostle to destroy him, and they disputed by means of the falsehood that they might thereby render null the truth. Therefore I destroyed them: how was then my retribution and thus did the word of your Lord prove true against those who disbelieved that they are the inmates of the fire" (Holy Qur-an 40:4-6).

THE BATTLE IN THE SKY

The final war between Allah (God) and the devils is dangerously close. The very least amount of friction can bring it into action within minutes. There is no such thing as getting ready for this most terrible and dreadful war; they are ready. Preparation for the battle between man and man or nations has been made and carried out on land and water for the past 6,000 years. Man has now become very wise and has learned many of the secrets of nature which make the old battles with swords and bows and arrows look like child's play.

Since 1914 which was the end of the time given to the devils (white race) to rule the original people (Black Nation), man has been preparing for a final showdown in the skies. He has made a remarkable advancement in everything pertaining to a deadly destructive war in the sky, but Allah, the Best of Planners, having a perfect knowledge of His enemies, prepared for their destruction long ago even before they were created. Thanks to Allah, to whom eternal praise is due, who came in the flesh and the blood: He has been for more than seventy years making Himself ready for the final war.

Allah, whom we praise, comes in the person of Master W. F. Muhammad, the Great Mahdi, expected by the Muslims, and the anti-Christs (the devils) under the names: Son of Man, Jesus Christ, Messiah, God, Lord, Jehovah, the Last (Jehovah) and the Christ. These meanings are good and befitting as titles, but the meaning of His name "Mahdi," as mentioned in the Holy Qur-an Sharrieff 22:54, is better. All of these names refer to Him. His name, Fard Muhammad, is beautiful in its meaning. He must bring an end to war, and the only way to end war between man and man is to destroy the war-maker (the trouble-maker).

According to the history of the white race (devils) they are guilty of making trouble, causing war among the people and themselves ever since they have been on our planet Earth. So the God of the righteous has found them disagreeable to live with in peace, and has decided to remove them from the face of the Earth. God does not have to tell us that they are disagreeable to live with in peace; we already know it, for we are the victims of these troublemakers. Allah will fight this war for the sake of His people (the black people), and especially for the American so-called Negroes. As I have said time and again, we the so-called American Negroes, will be the lucky ones. We are Allah's choice to give life and we will be put on top of civilization.

REGRETS OF THE DOUBTERS

"And on the day when the wrongdoer will bite his hands, saying, would that I had taken a way with the Messenger!" (Holy Qur-an 25:27)

According to the histories of the prophets of the past, all of their rejected enemies and mockers of the people had this same regret when the truth of the message that these prophets delivered was made manifest.

And the disbelieves hated themselves for rejecting those warners and prophets of old. The people of Noah showed regret when they saw the flood coming upon them. The people of Sodom and Gomorrah regretted their ignorant acts of disbelieving the truth of Abraham and Lot and wished that they had followed Lot out of the city and that they had believed before the fire came so that their cities and their lives would not have been destroyed.

It was also the regret of Pharaoh and his people for not believing the warning that Moses brought to them from Allah. When these rejecters of the prophets saw their doom approaching, they said, as the disbelievers said in the twenty-seventh verse, that they wished they had followed the prophet.

And so it will be, according to the Bible and Qur-an, with those whom this particular twenty-fifth chapter refers to who reject the last one in the time we are now living in (the resurrection and the judgment). Those of my people and the weak Orthodox Muslims who reject the plain truth and warning that Allah has revealed to me and that I am teaching (to fly to Allah and His true religion of entire submission and submit to His will), do so because of their love for the enemies of Allah, His Prophets and His religion, Islam. They reject this truth to me, the bearer of this truth.

They love the wealth and riches of this people who love not God, the giver of the wealth and riches that they have been so abundantly blessed with. They wish to remain and enjoy the wealth with these people as well as with intermarriage and their sport and play.

They will say what the formal rejectors said, when they see the chastisement of Allah coming upon them and all of their wickedness, evilness and murder. The so-called Negroes of America will also wish they had followed me to Allah.

The biting of their hands, as mentioned in this verse, shows intense grief for their mistake of accepting the false friendship of this evil and murderous race. The white American citizens and the Negroes who are today preaching friendship and intermarriage with their 400-year-old enemies will say these same words, "O woe is me, would that I had not taken such a one for a friend" (28th verse).

And they will confess that certainly he leads me astray from the messenger after he had come to me with clear warning and with plain truth (29th verse) and will admit that the devil's promises were all false and he only deceived them in the words given in that same twenty-ninth verse, "And the devil ever deserts man."

What should we set our hearts and minds on today? Finding the right path and walking therein to our God, Allah, and His religion, Islam, that He may make a way for us on some of this earth that we can call our own and deliver us from our open enemies, our deceivers and from evil and filthy doings.

The God of Islam demands us to forsake our enemies and their names and religion and all that goes with them and to completely submit to Him. He, Allah has said to me that He will set us in heaven at once.

Allah's promise is ever true. He fails not in His promise, but this race of devils will promise you and will fail to fulfill it, especially if it is a promise of good. I beg you as a brother and sister of mine, fly to Allah. For the days of the resurrection are not coming, they are here now and the dead are rising as it is written. Let us repeat this prayer:

"O Allah, guide me among those whom Thou hast guided aright and preserve me among those whom Thou has preserved and befriended and bless me in whatever Thou doest; grant me and deliver me from the evils of what Thou has judged. Surely Thou judgest and none can judge against Thee and He whom Thou befriendest is not disgraced."

TIME IS AT HAND

Know that Allah is with us (the believers) and Allah has promised, in the Bible and in the Holy Qur-an, that if we believe and put our trust in Him, He is sufficient as a Protector, that no weapons formed against the true believers will prosper.

We are the true believers of Allah. As the Holy Qur-an teaches, they planned against us, but Allah also has plans, and He is the best of planners. I warn all of you that the devils, hypocrites and disbelievers will continue trying to turn you away from truth so you will have to suffer hellfire with them.

The so-called American Negroes (my people) are now in a time when they must decide on life or death. The world we have known is on its way out, and it wishes to carry you and me with it. But, it will not; this is the right path—believe in Allah and come follow me.

We are the last members of the original Black Nation and have been found and chosen by Allah to make a great nation—a nation under His guidance to excel the nations of the past.

Study the parable of Jesus and the lost sheep, the prodigal son (Luke 15:11, 21,22), the stone that the builders rejected, the garden taken from the wicked husband and given to another and the mustard seed becoming a tree under which the beast found shade and in which the birds found rest.

Know that you, the so-called American Negroes, are divinely promised the Kingdom of Heaven (as it is called) after the destruction of this world. The people of this world will stop at nothing in trying to seduce you to follow them and remain with them so that you, too, will share in their doom. They ask you to take part in their doom, and you accept. When accepting the call to their false friendship you are accepting death.

I hope you remember what I said to you concerning the prepared destruction by Allah for this people and you who take part with them. Since they already have a head start, they believe they will deceive you in going along with them, ignoring the call of Allah and your own salvation and heaven at once while you live.

The consequence of this rejection of His call will get you a disgraceful year's punishment or chastisement (night and day). You will wish that you were dead. When night comes, you will wish it were day, and when day comes, you will wish it night. You can find this chastisement mentioned in Revelation (Rev. 9:6; 19:20; 20:10, 14, 15, and 21:8).

Salvation has come to the black men of America, but their fear of losing the hate—I cannot say the love because they do not love you—of their enemies causes them to reject it.

In the coming years every one of you who is now a disbeliever in Allah and the great brotherhood of Islam will be suffering the punishments that have been mentioned in the above chapters and verses.

America is the first country and people that Allah wishes to destroy, but he will not destroy them until you have heard the truth of her and of yourself. I shall continue to warn you of the divine penalty that awaits you who reject your God and my Saviour, Master Fard Muhammad. In this world of crisis and destruction of nations, the only escape you have is in Allah and following me.

WILL YOU BE THE WINNER?

The non-Muslim world cannot win in a war against Allah the Great Mahdi, with outer space weapons or inner space weapons. It does not matter, for He has power over everything—the forces of nature and even our brains. He turns them to thinking and doing that which pleases Him. The great waste of money to build your defense against Him or the third World War is useless.

You don't need Navys, ground forces, air forces, standing armies to fight this last war. What America needs to win is to give freedom and equal justice to her slaves (the so-called Negroes). This injustice to her slaves is the real cause of this final war. Give them up to return to their own or divide with them the country that you took from their people (the Indians), which they have helped you to build up and maintain with their sweat and blood for 400 years. They even gave all of their brain power to you. They helped you kill anyone that you said was your enemy; even if it was their own brother or your own brother. What have you given them for their labor and lives?

It is just a job to labor for you. You hunt them and shoot them down like wild game, burn them and castrate them, and they are counted as sheep for the slaughter—all who seek justice. You have continuously persecuted me and my poor followers for 25 years. Both fathers and sons are sent to prison. Just because we believe in justice and teach our brethren the same. We are imprisoned and forced to eat the poison and divinely prohibited flesh of the fifthy swine as our food, to your joy.

You set your agents and guards around and about our meeting places, where we are trying to serve the God of our fathers, to frighten our poor, blind, deaf and dumb people away from hearing and believing the truth. With 50 states, which equal approximately 6 million square miles with billions of dollars in gold buried and rusting, which we helped to get for you, yet none is ours—not the tiniest or the worthless state of yours have you offered your loyal slaves. Not even one square mile for their 400 years of labor and lives.

Shall you be the winner in the third World War? The God of Justice (The Son of Man, the Great Mahdi) shall be the winner. He is on the side of the so-called Negroes, to free them from you, their killers. As it is written: "Shall the prey be taken from the mighty or the lawful captives delivered? But thus saith the Lord, even the captives of the mighty shall be taken away and the prey of the terrible shall be delivered; for I will contend with him that contendeth with thee. I will feed them that oppress thee with their own flesh; and they shall be drunken with their own blood. As with sweet wine and all flesh shall know that I, the Lord, am thy Savior and thy Redeemer" (Isa. 49:24-26).

We, the so-called Negroes, are the prey. Thou are the Mighty, the terrible ones, thanks to Allah, the Greatest, who is with us, to save and deliver us, His people—20 million members of the Tribe of Shabazz—who must have some of this earth, that they can call their own. Their God will give it to them. But woe unto you, the unjust judges, for the Son of Man shall destroy thee and give the kingdom to the slave. He is not to come. He is here! Believe it or not, I seek refuge in Him from your evil plannings.

You have been so busy trying to keep your slaves (the so-called Negroes) under your foot, sitting, watching, spying on them to prevent them from knowing the truth of this day of our salvation, that you have failed to see and learn the strength and power of your enemies.

You have boasted that you could police the world and have come pretty near doing so but have failed to the "Bear" behind the tree and the "Lion" in the thicket. The sky over you is being filled with your enemy's arms which can be seen with the naked eye.

Your scientists are troubled and at their wits' end to find time to make ready, as it is written: "I have set the point of the sword against all their gates; that their heart may faint, and their ruins be multiplied. Ah! it is made bright, it is wrapped up fór the slaughter" (Ezekiel 21:15). Answer: "For the tidings; because it cometh and every heart shall melt, and all hands shall be feeble and every spirit shall faint, and all knees shall be weak as water" (Ezekiel 21:7).

The Holy Qur-an also says: "And you shall see every nation kneeling down. Every nation shall be called to its book. Do you think that you want to be called to yours? Today, you shall be rewarded for what you did. This is our book that speaks against you with justice. Surely we wrote what you did" (45:28,29).

Woe, woe to America! Her day is near, and she shall be visited. Your enemies warn you that the third and final World War will be decided in your own country and not in theirs. Remember the old Bible's sayings: "Wheresoever the carcass is, there will be eagles gathered together" (Matt. 25:28). You must understand and know to whom the parable is directed.

BUILD OUR OWN SOCIETY

When I speak of the time and what must be done, I am not referring to the time of the solar system but to the time of a people whose existence and rule of the original people of the earth is limited to 6 thousand years. This time of 6 thousand years was divinely given to this world—the time of being under the rule of a completely new and strange people whose nature is foreign to our nature. A strange and new civilization—a deceiving people to us—with its strange practices which include doing evil and murdering the people.

According to the teachings of Allah, this is the first and the last time we will ever have a trouble-making people on our planet. There is no doubt about it, we, who were brought here to the Western Hemisphere by the white slave-masters of our fathers, can bear witness that this is the most evil people that we have ever experienced.

Today, the wickedness of this civilization has become so great and fair-seeming to the original people of the earth. He said that twelve leaders from Islam from all over the planet earth have conferred in the root of civilization at Mecca and have found this people disagreeable to live with in peace, and they decided that they must be removed from the planet earth. And the main obstacle that stands in the way of this removal is the so-called Negroes in America who have been lost of the knowledge of self, their God, their religion and the knowledge of the enemy who has robbed them. They must return to their own.

A Messenger has been sent to teach them the knowledge of self that will qualify them to return to their own. The time of this spreading of the true knowledge of self, God, and devil is the important mission that I have. As it is written, the life of this world has been made so fair-seeming to you that you cannot conceive of another world that might be better. This is where you are making a fatal mistake.

Let us use some of the times that were limited for similar wicked governments and of people of the past. For instance, the people of Noah, Abraham, Lot and Moses and Jesus. All of these had a limited time. The Prophets who were sent to them had opponents who rose up against them, near the end of their time, to do the worst of evil against them.

What must be done? You must start thinking and working in the way of independence, as other dependent nations had to do and are still doing, when once free of those who hold you in bondage. Get away from that childish way of thinking that the white man forever owes it to you to provide for you the necessities of life. Should you not be too proud of yourself in this modern time to be thinking in the way of dependence instead of independence?

Why are you talking freedom, justice and equality if you do not like to be separated from the people on whom you and your fathers are dependent? Do you think that an independent nation is going to make you its equal while you will not accept your own responsibility to provide for your own? Can you blame America for rejecting you as her equal when you are going to the extreme of trying to force her to accept you instead of forcing self and your people to be independent?

You have disgraced yourself and still are in trying to force yourself upon your slave-masters' children so that they will continue to support you in the necessities for your existence. In this way, you are telling the world that you are too lazy to go for self. Allah and I want you to be freed of such childish thinking like men and accept responsibility.

You can never boast of being equal while still a subjected people. You are even laughing at me and my followers for preaching and striving for freedom to go for self on some of this earth that we can call our own. Which is the most intelligent, a man who seeks to earn his living by working for his needs or a man who depends on begging others for the things he could get by working for self? Today, you are beaten in city after city like an old lazy horse being whipped by his driver because he won't pull the plow to prepare the land to grow corn, oats and hay so that his master may eat the better food.

You are trying to force yourself into white society rather than take the responsibility of building your own society. This is your shame and disgrace as a people in this modern time. Allah and the Nation of Islam will help you build one of the finest and best societies the world of man has ever seen if you will only be yourself and get off of your knees, praying to be other than yourself—a member of the white race.

Just why do you want to be like the people who have robbed, spoiled and slained you and your fathers? Is it not an act of intelligence and honor to desire to look and be like a member of your own nation, speaking the same language and seeking and building the culture of your kind? The white race wants to stay a white race and maintain its way of life. Why should we not want to do the same?

You may say, what is our nation's way of life? I will admit that for the past few centuries you have been lost to the knowledge of self and kind. Allah has raised me to teach you the knowledge of your own self and kind and to join you onto your own kind, not as a subjected people, for superior wisdom cannot be subjected to inferior wisdom. And, a people guided by Allah, Himself, cannot be enslaved.

You must know the outlook and what must be done. America is in for much trouble, as the Holy Qur-an says: "One calamity followed by another until she is destroyed for her evils done to her slaves."

These calamities consist of all sorts of confusion and disagreements between the people and the heads of governments. In the Bible and Holy Qur-an, revolutions and wars are mentioned as being forces to break the power of resistance. The Bible says: "Sword without and sword within. The forces of nature against a terrific drought prophecied." In the Holy Qur-an it says: "Therefore, keep waiting for the day when the heaven shall bring a clear drought, that shall overtake men. This is a painful chastisement." (44:10).

THE HEREAFTER

After what?" may be the question asked. The hereafter means after the destruction of the present world, its power and authority to rule. The Bible and Holy Qur-an Sharrieff are filled with readings on the hereafter which I will leave to you to read for proof. This subject wouldn't be necessary if it were not for that man of sin being permitted to rule.

Since he (they) was given ruling authority to try him (them) for 6,000 years, the word "hereafter is used, meaning: After the present rule of the man of sin, because his (their) time is limited to 6,000 years. Some say: after the judgment, after the man when the man of sin and all who follow him were made. "Whoever of them will follow you, I will certainly fill hell with you all" (Holy Qur-an 7:18). The Bible says: "These both were cast alive into a lake of fire" (Rev. 19:20). The Man of sin and his people deceived the righteous by making them believe that he (they) also is one of the righteous. He (they) claims one father is the father of all, but that is not true.

We all look forward to a hereafter, to seeing and living under a ruler and a government of righteousness, after the destruction of unrighteousness. Even the people of the man of sin (the devils) are worried, disgusted, dissatisfied with their own world and wish to see a change to a better world; but they desire to be the ruler in that better world. The hereafter, some believe will be after the great War of Armageddon or Holy War.

A religious war between the two great religions of the earth and their believers, namely, Islam and Christianity; of course Buddism will also be involved. The hereafter: there the righteous will make unlimited progress; peace, joy and happiness will have no end. War will be forgotten; disagreement will have no place in the hereafter. The present brotherhood of Islam is typical of the life in the hereafter, the difference is that the brotherhood in the hereafter will enjoy the spirit of gladness and happiness forever in the presence of Allah. The earth, the general atmosphere will produce such a change that the people will think it is a new earth. It will be the heaven of the righteous forever! No sickness, no hospitals, no insane asylums, no gambling, no cursing, or swearing will be seen or heard in that life. Fear, grief and sorrow will stop on this side as a proof. Everyone of us who accepts the religion of Islam and follows what God has revealed to me, will begin enjoying the above life here.

I never felt the like before. Islam is heaven for my people. They will see their God in truth, the righteous will meet and embrace them with peace.

The life in the hereafter is an image of the spiritual state in this life. Just think how good you feel when in the Divine Spirit for awhile. You are so happy that you don't feel even the pain of sickness, no trouble or sorrow, and that is the way you will feel always in the next life.

We, the so-called Negroes who accept Allah and Islam will reap this glorious joy and happiness. You will be clothed in silk interwoven with gold and eat the best of food that you desire. This is the time when you enter such life, for your God is here in person, and you will never be that which you cannot be any more, after believing in Him. My people have been deceived by the archdeceiver with regard to the hereafter. They think the hereafter is a life of spirits up somewhere in the sky, while it is only on the earth, and you won't change to any spirit beings. The life in the hereafter is only a continuation of the present life. You will be flesh and blood. You won't see spooks coming up out of graves to meet God.

No already physically dead person will be in the hereafter; that is slavery belief, taught to slaves to keep them under control. This is taught also so that they won't be thinking about the wealth of their slave-masters while under the slave-master. The slave is made to believe his will come after death, and his master knows that death settles all, and that you can't return to tell him whether he lied or told the truth.

Read the Scriptures carefully on the life in the hereafter, and try to understand it; you will find that it doesn't actually mean what you have been believing. No one is going to leave this planet to live on another. You can't, even if you try. You can't reach the moon and live on it, so be satisfied and believe in Allah, live where you are on this good earth, but be righteous.

I must quote these beautiful verses of the Holy Qur-an: "O soul that is at rest, return to your Lord, well pleased with Him, well pleasing. So, enter among my servants, and enter into my Paradise" (89:27-30).

ANSWER TO CRITICS

MY MISSION IS TO GIVE LIFE

The following is an excerpt from an interview granted to the National Educational Television Network. The series of interviews took place in Phoenix, Arizona, and were conducted over a period of several days, by the staff of San Francisco station KQED.

QUESTION: How would you describe your mission?

ANSWER: My mission is to give life to the dead. What I teach brings them out of death and into life. My mission, as the Messenger, is to bring the truth to the world before the world is destroyed. There will be no other Messenger. I am the last and after me will come God Himself. I do not say I will live so long as that, but when God comes, if it pleases Him, I may be with Him. However, if I am not with Him, this is the final. This truth I bring will give you the knowledge of yourself and of God.

QUESTION: Earlier, when we spoke of defections, you mentioned something about the fact that Jesus has similar defections —would you explain?

ANSWER: Yes. Such defections are nothing. The public should not think it's strange, this time in which we live. We have the actual spirit of God moving among the people.

QUESTION: Well, now if in time, sir, your grandson, Sharrieff or your son, Wallace or Malcolm, ever expressed the desire to return to follow you again, would you accept them?

ANSWER: There is nothing unforgivable, the Holy Qur-an teaches you. The only thing that is unforgivable is this: that you will not accept Allah as God and not accept His Messenger as His Messenger. These two things are one, we say, the belief in Allah is the belief in the Messenger of the Prophet of Allah.

The belief in the Messenger or the Prophet of Allah is a belief in Allah, if you disbelieve in one you disbelieve in both.

You cannot believe in one and disbelieve in the other. This is the knowledge the world has not realized, and this is what God wants the world to know.

When God chooses His representative for the people, He speaks to the people through that representative, and if the people will accept that representative (we call them prophets, apostles or messengers), then they are accepting Allah.

But if they reject him and still say they believe in Allah, they are considered enemies of Allah and disbelievers. Because that is Allah in that representative and you cannot accept one without accepting the other. You have got to accept both.

You cannot get the blessings of Allah if you reject His Messenger. Now, these boys that you were referring to, they do not worry me; I do not give my time arguing with them or talking about why they believe or disbelieve.

I do not even argue with them because I knew these things in the beginning. I knew they would act like this, some of them. I was told about this 34 years ago. But they did not know these things, and I am not excited, as the public would be, or as the public would like to see.

In some cases, if the son disbelieves in his father, his father must be wrong. But that is not so when it comes to a Messenger of God.

If we say that is true, then it stands true in the common life of the family.

There are some children who never sincerely accept their father as they should. There are some fathers who never accept their children as they should. So this is the nature of the human family of the earth, and when it comes to spiritual teachings, it is also the same. Not all of the family of a Messenger are such as Noah and Lot.

They do not always have true believers, but that did not detract one atom from his messengership.

You do not take advantage of that unless you get into war or trouble with God.

You do not say, "I do not believe in him because his own wife or his own son does not. Why should I follow him?"

You would be getting yourself in trouble, because that is given. I do not care anything about those who fall away from me after I have pointed out the truth to them and despite this they get wrong and go away from that truth.

I am not responsible for this, for whatever they say against me, it is against themselves. What they preach and tell the people in order to get the people to disbelieve in me is much like Absolom and his father, David.

Absolom stole the affection of the people because he thought he looked better and younger than David. He thought, therefore, the people would follow, that he could steal the people over to himself and get rid of his father as king and be king himself. But he was not to be king. The man that was to be king had yet to be known; that was Solomon.

These facts are all put there to deepen our knowledge, and time repeats these things over again and again.

And so this is what we face today, and I am not surprised the public is surprised, some of them at the deviation of Malcolm or my son Wallace. I am not surprised. But they cannot yet say that I am not the Messenger of Allah. They cannot take that away from me.

QUESTION: Mr. Muhammad, would you make some statements about Dr. Martin Luther King and the Civil Rights Movement?

ANSWER: Yes, I think Rev. King has been doing a good job according to his knowledge. He has been trying to do his best to get our people some justice in the way of civil rights. I believe that he means well, and I believe he would have done better if he had known more about the time and the people and the history and what must be done in such times.

He has the desire to see his people dealt with according to justice and not according to injustice. But he does not know that he is living in the time when justice is bound to come to his people. However, it is only through Divine and not through civil government. And that goes for most of the groups who are trying to do something for the betterment of our people.

They, most of these leaders, have good intentions, but they just don't have the right instruments to work with, and they do not know how to use the instruments, since they were not appointed to do the job.

But all of our people today have the desire to do something for themselves and, first of all, to see injustice removed from the whole.

We have suffered injustice at the hands of the white people for 400 years, and today some want to be called "Citizens of America," but all of this without the qualities that go along with freedom. We are today, I repeat, imbued with the spirit of justice for our people, and something must be done. This oppression cannot go on forever.

What the civil rights movement is trying to do is just another effort to bring home to our people a better life. But this is the time when our people should and will get a better life on a permanent scale. NOT on a TEMPORARY scale.

The political administration may change every 4 years. The Constitution gives to the people of America. And if we understand it well, it was not written with the so-called Negro in mind. It was written for the white citizens of America and not the slaves.

The slave is not mentioned there and it was not in the mind of these lawmakers that he should share equal justice with the master. No, he was considered to be the property of the master. Therefore, the servant or the slave cannot get justice—equal justice—with the master unless the master wants to give up his position as master.

If the master gave up his position as master, the slave would soon become his equal, and the slave would probably vote for equal justice, go to the White House or become the ruler of the country, if the equal justice were obtained all the way through as it should be. But the Constitution was written by white people for white people and not for you and me.

We were under the slave-masters at that time, and again I would like to make clear: I am not fighting those leaders who are trying to do something good for our people, or get something better for them. But I do oppose them in their way of opposing that which is good and which would be just and permanent for our people. For we now have come to the time when we want justice and equality. We want freedom equal with other people. They have never made us citizens, and under their law we cannot be made citizens. We could never be citizens as stated in their first slavery courts.

If we want to go into the facts about it, we are not the equal of the American white man, nor are we citizens with him here. We are in alien country. We are aliens and not citizens.

And this is proof that we have to admit and not to try to hide to make some black brother feel good. To tell a black brother that he is a citizen and has equal rights is like telling a child to go to sleep on the 24th night of December and on the next morning awaken and Santa Claus will have left a present in your stocking when THAT is Santa Claus talking. And the child, when he grows up, learns that. Well it is the same thing with us. We have had a lot of Santa Claus teaching, and now we are growing up because we know that a lot of these Santa Claus teachings were nothing but a lot of pacifiers. We are no longer satisfied to be pacified. We want something permanent.

QUESTION: Mr. Muhammad, even though the Economic Plan was only introduced in August of this year, (1964) what has been the response?

ANSWER: We are really surprised at the response we have received. In fact, it is increasing daily, and we have to set up more secretaries to take care of the donations that are coming.

QUESTION: Is this coming from all over the country?

ANSWER: Yes, sir, from everywhere. For 3 years, we want to see what we can do.

We're going to put the donations in banks that have already been established. We are not going to build one until we have need to do so By the end of the 3 years, we can tell what we can do. It costs perhaps a million dollars or more to set up a bank, and the government has much to say about how this is done. Those who understand banking systems will be called in by us to help set up such a system for our people.

QUESTION: Are any of your aims perhaps similar to the middle-class aims of acquisition of properties and material goods? Do you think the objectives of this plan are similar to those of the white middle-class?

ANSWER: What are white middle-class aims? Will you tell me that?

QUESTION: Ordinarily I would say it is the acquisition of property, of material things. Now do you think in the savings plan idea there will be a number of Negroes who will submit monies to save for those particular white middle-class idea which seem to be unimportant at the the moment?

ANSWER: Well, the purpose of the Economic Plan is to fight poverty and want, as I have said; this includes material things. We need better housing, for instance. We also need farms to grow our food.

QUESTION: Do you think Johnson's War on Poverty Bill will be any assistance at this time?

ANSWER: I do not know the details of his plans. But I would

say this, as a subject people who have given all they had for the independence of the white man, whoever is President should do something to aid the so-called Negro of America, to protect him from brutal treatment, from poverty and from want. America is able to feed Europe and part of Africa and is able to finance them. Yet, the poor slave who helped her build up her country and establish her banks that are bursting with money, he has nothing to say about this.

She should do more to aid her so-called Negro in the way of putting him out for self. She should make him independent and not dependent. She should put a stop to police brutality, which is absolutely condoned by the government. The police are free to beat and kill us at will, and they are not punished for this.

This should be done by whoever is in the White House as the ruler for the next four years. They should stop injustice. The time is now when a stop will be put to it if America herself does not cease mistreating the so-called Negro.

The Negro is going to get his freedom because he is not the forsaken race he was a few years ago. There are definite divine plans being made to help him. He will be divinely helped from now on.

The government can help the so-called Negro in many ways. I do not say the government should take us and set us down and make us lazy so we will not want to work for ourselves. I do not condone that sort of thing. No, help us to get a chance of doing something for ourselves. We are no more a people who can be classified as a necessary people for use only as servants. We are too many. We are 22 million people; no nation needs that many just for servants.

I was born in the South. I married and went to Detroit with my two children in 1923. I know the South and the Southern white people. They are actually a people who envy any success that comes to the so-called Negro in any way. If you own a little more than the white man there, why he's against you; he may even kill you. He may bomb you or destroy your property. He just doesn't like the fact of your having anything. Whether in court, in justice or in any way. This is naturally in their blood.

They want the black man to have nothing but hell, excuse the expression, that's all they desire and they are tickled to death to see you in a hell of a condition. They are angry when they see you trying to live prosperously.

They will make trouble with you if they think that you are trying to be at peace.

QUESTION: Is that only the white man in the South?

ANSWER: No, he's up here in the North, too, but he is not as numerous in the North as he is in the South. This is almost dominant in the South.

The North has a fair share of the evil. That's why the Negro cannot get any place, because he is in a race of people whom they do not intend to ever see prosper too much.

So, therefore, we should look forward and try to get the government to agree to let us go somewhere by ourselves and build a nation of our own and on some of this land that we helped get.

When we were brought here as slaves they didn't have 50 states, but now they have 50 states and they have offered the so-called Negro, who numbers in the millions, not the tiniest state in the union. Nor have they offered to give him anything like revenue coming from countries they have conquered. We helped them to conquer the Philippines. We helped them conquer Japan.

All right, what have we gotten from this? What commerce have we gotten from this?

We got nothing, as revenue, for our deaths. Only they gave us death when we returned back home.

If we were given any credit for it back, we would feel that we did something good, perhaps, for the people. But we were hated when we got home. We were cast out and shot down on the streets and highways, just for the fun of it. They were innocent people.

They would kick a black man and push him around and try to force him to say something that they could claim as the reason why he was killed. Therefore, the people just don't want you, and why should we say, today, after 400 years, "Let's try to plan to live with the white American people and get along with them in peace" when we have not been able to live with them in peace for 400 years.

THE GREAT DECEIVERS

Arthur R. Gottschalk, state senator, 8th district, Park Forest (Ill.), wrote our National Secretary, John Ali, asking him and my followers to disavow and repudiate publicly the truth Allah has revealed to me of the Caucasian race, the truth of them being REAL DEVILS and our (the Black Nation's) open enemies.

Part of this letter was printed and published in the *Chicago Tribune,* June 15, 1962. Gottschalk failed to include in his letter to Secretary Ali proof of material proving that the truth Allah has given me of them being real devils is false. This leaves my secretary and followers helpless to deny the truth.

I am surprised at the intelligent senator writing a letter before first making an attempt to consult me as to what Allah has revealed to me. The senator's letter is a perfect insult to my followers. Without showing proof that what I am teaching IS NOT the truth, he is asking my followers not to believe it and tell the public that they do not believe.

What the Senator does not like is that my followers BELIEVE Caucasian (the white European Race) are the real devils, as Allah has said. Also, the true history and the Teachings of the Prophets and their scriptures (Bible and Holy Qur-an) bear witness.

I think the Senator has attacked something that may surprise him and his race because of his intentions of making my followers disbelieve the truth of Allah as taught me.

One of the characteristics of the devil is to deceive. In the last two paragraphs of his letter to our Secretary, John Ali, Gottschalk hoped to deceive him with the following words:

"At this time when men of good will of all races are working hard to promote harmonious human relations and eliminate the social and economic conditions which have produced injustices, it is tragic that men like Elijah Muhammad are attempting to tear down their good work and accentuate racial tension and misunderstanding."

Mr. Gottschalk, we are not your slaves any more, therefore do not misunderstand us. We care very little about you or any person or race who would think after knowing you that a promise promoting harmonious human relations, social equality with you will solve our problem. You are mistaken! We want nothing less than freedom to build our economy and society and on some of this earth that we can call our own!

We want to be independent, as you and other nations are, to do what we think is best for our own selves. What kind of future can you prepare for us other than as subjected slaves to you and your kind? I am not attempting to tear down anything good, for I have not found anything of good that you or your kind have set up that was for the good of my people. Allah and I are the only ones I know who are setting up any good work for our people.

Since your government declares us to be free, why let us go and enjoy this freedom for ourselves on some of this earth that we can call our own? The language used in your letter is that of a deceiver who knows that he has laid hands upon a great value and hopes to deceive him to believe that which he has been given or found is of no value and what you have is the best.

The entire 20 million of my people here should learn a lesson from your letter and be careful of you and your kind erupted promises of social equality without some of this earth we can call our own!

Your dogs enjoy honor in your society. They are seen eating from the table and riding in the same seat in some of your best transportation.

We do not desire any such place and level with all the evil you have done to us for the past 400 years and as you continue to mistreat us.

Do you think we will be satisfied to settle for less than some of this earth we can call our own? I think you are in for a great surprise. The Senator is outright asking my followers to recant and make it publicly known that they disbelieve in the Truth Allah has revealed to me in the closing lines of his letter to Secretary Ali in the following words:

"I call upon you (John Ali) as National Secretary of your organization to disavow and repudiate publicly all of the above statements (that the Caucasian race is a race of devils says Allah to me) by your leader, Elijah Muhammad.

"Failure to do so would be a clear admission that the statements of Elijah Muhammad accurately represents the policy of your organization which sponsors and operates the University of Islam."

For nearly 32 years, the students of our school had knowledge of you and your kind and have a very good record of being at peace in your midst. This comes from having the knowledge of you. If you fear this true knowledge of yourself will cause your mistreated once slaves to hate you, then your argument is with Almighty Allah who has revealed it. It is surely not with brother John Ali and my followers, for you will not be able to give up the truth about you, their God, Allah and their Leader and Teacher.

CLARIFICATION OF CONFUSION SURROUNDING MUSLIMS

In order to clarify some of the confusion surrounding Muslim outlooks and objectives, I will confront the rumors and false allegations of Muslim 'threats of violence' with a direct statement which answers the implied question 'Will the Black Muslims Attack America?' in a direct and forthright manner.' These are some statements I gave in an interview to the *New York Herald Tribune* Newspaper.

ON HATE AND VIOLENCE

"We are not going to take part in any violence whatsoever. We're not going to do anything other than what we are doing. That is trying to deliver the truth to our people and teach them that they are supposed to be Muslims, and that means they are supposed to be righteous people and that we have shed all things that pertain to wickedness.

"We have stripped ourselves of arms to let you know that we are not people of violence. We don't intend to attack you. We have no idea or knowledge of anything like that coming in the future.

"Because if we attacked you, we would have to have superior weapons to attack you with, and we don't have factories nor earth to dig metals to manufacture tools or weapons such as you have.

"All this is your creation, and, therefore, if we would get some of this, you would have to let us have it—and you would

not give me a gun to shoot you with. Therefore, God forbid
us even to accept weapons and even to carry anything like weapons to fight with. Because to fight is with Him, and you are
not with us."

ON ISLAM IN AMERICA

The aim and purpose of Islam here among my people is to
give them a knowledge of self and a knowledge of God, knowledge of their religion, Islam and to separate them in time, that
these 17 or 20 million American dark people should go for themselves.

"This is the basis of the whole, it is to separate our people
and put them by themselves."

ON NONBELIEVERS

"We have respect for them and their professions, and we try
to treat them as we treat ourselves, for that matter. We know
they are not believers as we are. We know that.

"But as long as they tolerate our faith, we tolerate theirs,
and we treat them as brothers."

ON POLITICAL ENDORSEMENT

"He would have to be in sympathy with us and he would
have to have some knowledge of the aims and purposes of Islam
in America."

ON WHITES AND NEGROES

"This is the real trouble: the whites oppose us, the black
people of America, who were their slaves once upon a time,
from ever becoming anything like self-independent. They want
to keep them subject to themselves in a more educational and
scientific way, other than their fathers.

"Their fathers only used the common knowledge of enslaving
our people. But, today their children can use one of the smartest
scientific ways against our people to keep them subjected to them
that ever were invented by a race of people since time was.

"We want what you want today, and that is independence.
We want peace, and, whether you want peace or not, we want
peace and security from you. You are our worst enemy. We
have no other people who are an enemy to us but you, because
we don't live in the country of other people.

"We live only with you, and we have been here for 400
years, and you say now that we are free, but yet you are doing
everything to keep us from exercising the rights as equals or
of a free people.

"This is what I want you to understand. We are tired of suffering, brutality, beatings, killings, just because you don't like us, and just hate us, and absolutely knowing that we are powerless to resist because you have all the odds against us.

"You are absolutely the boss, and we have nothing. And we are asking to leave you, that's all we're asking. We can't get along with you in peace; you don't want us in peace.

"If we sit over there in that house across the street, peaceful all day and all night, after a while that worries you. You will send someone around to see what is going on over there in that house.

"It's the white man's way of starting trouble—breaking the peace of people by interfering with their peace. We're not sitting over there in that house planning anything but are trying to plan peace for the house."

ON SEPARATE TERRITORY

"The American white man is not going to move out of his estate to give to the so-called Negroes. We are not asking you to do any such thing.

"No, only unless you prevent our going to our own. If you are going to prevent us from going to our own, or back where we came from, where you found us, then give us a place here to ourselves.

"There has been too much talk about separation and about our acting or demanding a territory here. We're not demanding territory in America. No, sir, we're asking America only if they don't allow us to go back to our own people and to the country from which we came.

"Then give us a place to ourselves; as you know and we have learned through experience for 400 years, we can't get along in peace together. You're not going to accept us as your equals, and we know you're not going to do so. We disregard your promises because you are not going to live up to them; because 100 per cent of your people will not agree with such. And we have proof today in the South."

ON "BLACK SUPREMACY"

"Allah has revealed that the black is the original Man, and that's what I teach. Now, where this supremacy teaching comes in that is charged by the disbelievers—that I teach it in order to suit their particular purpose of charging us with being an aggressive movement, or intending to become such, because of the teachings of one being superior over the other.

"We say that the black man is the first man in the sun, and then they take this and just change it around—that he is teaching supremacy. And that we are not doing. We already know that we are inferior to you here in America.

"We cannot say physically or even mentally that we are equal, nor say your superior, when it comes to actual physical or educational ability."

INTEGRATION IN THE SOUTH

The head of this movement, Mr. King, is trying to force the white men in the South to do that which is against his will and nature, because some of the Northern parties of the white people, maybe in Washington, have said to him that this should be done and should have this in the Constitution and, therefore, you should enforce it and, therefore, have it enforced by the government.

"But Mr. King has not learned as yet that the white man in the South is brethren to the white man in Washington and the Washington white man is a brother to the Southern white man—that they are not going to go to war over the Negro and kill each other for the sake of the unlearned Negro—of the knowledge of self and others—to integrate into that which they don't master, give me a piece of your meat that you have there in your house.

"Therefore, Mr. King is making a fool of himself in the South and acting like a dog around the house, where the master stands at the door and the dog wants something to eat and he just waddles all around the door, around the master's feet, whipping his tail on the ground and grinning and leaning his ears back on his neck to show that he is a good, peaceful dog, and master, give me a piece of your meat that you have there in your house.

"And this while there is plenty of meat for the dog in the bushes out there, if he would go out and hunt for it."
ON JAMES MEREDITH
"Poor fellow, trying to force himself into a school where it is 100 per cent white and they're telling him they don't want him. And then the Army is standing around trying to force him in there—that's their crazy idea.

"I wouldn't want the Army to think about coming to help me against a white man, to allow me to come into his house or in the school or his restaurant, or anything else that he owns.

"If you tell me, I don't want you here, that's sufficient. I'm gone."

ON SELF DEFENSE

"In a case where the person.....wants to fight and he pounces upon us, sometimes without even warning us, we want our own men and women and our girls to learn to try to protect themselves the best they can in case of attack.

"But in the case of the so-called American Negro, we have nothing to fight back with. If you come to the door shooting, we have no guns here to shoot back with, so, therefore, the right is with God, as it is written in the Book.

"He will defend us if we believe in Him and trust Him, and we're not going to start fighting with anyone to have Him to defend us. But if we are attacked, we depend on Him to defend us because He has stripped us."

ON INTEGRATION

"What are we going to integrate for? What do we want to marry a white woman for, when we are black men? That is going to ruin our family. We will spot up our family. What does she want a black man for? Or what does the black man want the white one for?

"This is ignorant on both parts to want to intermarry with each other. The very desire there is ignorant and evil. It's against divine law for either side to integrate in such a way.

"God made all of us as we are. We have black nations, brown nations, red, yellow, and white. We have all these five major colors in races or nations. Why should they not remain like that? Why should they be thrown in like bones or birds into a pot to make soup out of?

"I don't blame the white man in the South for not wanting my people to marry with them. But I blame the South for mistreating him."

"You see, I am between life and death, and I have to say these things in the way I see them. There was a time when I had no knowledge of them. But they have been revealed to me, and now Allah would punish me if I did not say them."

ON CRIME IN SOCIETY

Incidents on criminal insanity are now news, and the religion of Islam is no more responsible for one of its subjects succumbing to insanity than the Christian religion is responsible for the steady multitudes of their members becoming so afflicted.

Christianity has long taught "Thou Shall Not Kill," but for centuries the most devastating killings have occurred constantly by Christians killing Christians, killing Buddhists, killing Moslems, killing Jews and killing members of their own family or the families of friends or associates.

In the case of the recent Los Angeles family killing involving a Muslim, all Muslims throughout our nation have been deeply grieved and angered by the accounts of the alleged crimes committed by Melvin E. Jackson. This man had been accepted into Islam in January of 1961, and his wife had joined in May of that same year.

No one can foretell the future or anyone who joins this religious body any more than any other religion can predict the future of all of its individual converts. For such acts of madness alleged to have been perpetrated by Jackson, institutions for the deranged have been built by federal governments. If this man is found insane—and his act would suggest that of one insane—he should be committed to such an institution.

In so far as the law of Islam is concerned, the penalty for such acts by a sane person against innocent human beings is death. And if the courts would give us permission to execute such criminals we would do so ourselves. For we desire to put a stop to such crimes—including thefts—and we feel that the courts should turn over such criminals to be executed under the real Islamic law. It is our desire to put a stop once and for all to such crimes being committed among our people.

ON "UNCLE TOMS"

"That doesn't mean that we are in any way aggressive toward them and seek an aggressive act. We only just criticize them for being like that.

"I love all my people, and I believe one day they all will believe as I believe. If they don't the prophets have lied, and we just can't make liars out of them."

ON WHITES AS "DEVILS"

"It's what He revealed, and what He revealed is what I am teaching and believe in, and this term "devil," or name "devil," is applied to wicked people, people who are by nature wicked.

"They were made white, or different color, because they had

been grafted out of the darker people, and, therefore, they have that color."

ON FRUIT OF ISLAM

"The Fruit of Islam means the first converts to Islam here in America and the first people to be cleaned and made fit to be called Muslims.

"And their training is on this basis, as being Muslims, to keep in practice, not just say it is their faith or belief. You must put into practice the principles of Islam that you believe in and serve as an example for others who would accept Islam.

"They take physical training and exercises in many ways to keep physically fit and healthy and to try to get away from many of the physical ailments that they have suffered long before coming into the knowledge of Islam.

"And trained into the knowledge of what the aims and purpose of Islam are, They are to clean up a people who are not clean, morally as well as spiritually, in America and to make them fit to become good members of the society."

REPLY TO A JUDGE

On November 8, 1963, according to the *Chicago Tribune* newspaper, Federal Judge F. Ryan Duffy ruled that the Black Muslim "sect" is not a religion but is rather racist and has for its objective the overthrow of the white race. He further charged the believers of Islam inside prison walls as having a impressive history of inciting riots and violence.

I asked Judge Duffy to prove his charges. This is not true. In 1943, I was sent to the Federal Penitentiary in Milan, Michigan, for nothing other than to be kept out of the public and from teaching my people the truth during the war between America, Germany, and Japan. This war came to a halt in 1945 when America dropped an atomic bomb on Japan. And the following year, in August, 1946, I was released on what the institution called "good time" for being a model prisoner who was obedient to the prison rules and laws.

In the year 1942-43, according to reports, there were nearly a hundred of my followers sentenced to prison terms of from 1 to 5 years for refusing to take part in the war between America, Japan and Germany because of our peaceful stand and the principle belief and practice in Islam, which is peace.

The very dominant idea in Islam is the making of peace and not war; our refusing to go armed is our proof that we want peace. We felt that we had no right to take part in a war with nonbelievers of Islam who have always denied us justice and equal rights; and if we were going to be examples of peace and righteousness (as Allah has chosen us to be), we felt we had no right to join hands with the murderers of people or to help murder those who have done us no wrong. What would justify such actions? Let the truth answer.

Judge Duffy listened to an appeal made by a new convert to Islam who is serving a 200-year sentence, charged with slaying two Chicago men in 1951. (He should be given credit for his desire to be a Muslim). The appeal was asking for the freedom of obtaining publications and reading material distributed by the Black Muslims, including the Holy Qur-an.

According to the rules and laws of the prison—before we Muslims began to be imprisoned—all religious believers, regardless to their religion and God, were permitted access to their books and visits by their religious teachers. This freedom is written in the Constitution for everyone, but when we were imprisoned that freedom was denied us and us alone. And this is the freedom that is guaranteed in the American Constitution. A person is free to criticize anyone he wants, even if it is the Congress or President of the United States of America.

But while the Constitution of America was being written, our fathers were slaves, and we, today, are merely free slaves who do not have the knowledge of self and have not registered with Allah and His religion, the Nation of Islam.

When I was admitted into Cook County jail in Chicago, I wanted the Holy Qur-an, too, but I was denied having it, though it is not a "sect's Bible." It is the religious scriptures and guide for the Muslim world, recognized universally as the last revelation given to the world. And the Holy Qur-an has been the Holy book and scripture for all Muslims for the past 1,381 years.

We are not an organization; we are a world. I use the same Holy Qur-an that all Muslims use; the book that is universally recognized as being 100 per cent true. And such scholar and U.S. Judge as F. Ryan Duffy calls it a "sect's book."

One of the officers, who was a very fine man, tried in vain to persuade the warden in the Cook County jail to allow me to have my Holy Qur-an as other religious believers were receiving theirs in prison. But this same officer came back and told me that the warden said "That is what we put them in prison for, and to let us read the Bible, ha,ha,ha."

They do not even want to hear the truth of the Bible; for there is no paradise in it for them. According to their own Bible that they wish all black people to read, when carefully understood, Genesis to Revelation teaches that they were an appointed people for hell fire from the beginning of their creation. I am ready to prove this with any scholar or scientist. They hated Judge Rutherford for his interpretation of the Bible which condemned the church and its father, the Pope of Rome.

The *Chicago Tribune* also quoted Judge Duffy as saying that a social study showed that the Black Muslim movement, despite its pretext of a religious facade, is an organization that has for its objective the overthrow of the white race. But when have the so-called Negroes in America been classified as social members in the white American society; even in Christianity, not to think of social equality and human relationship?

The so-called Negroes have never been equally recognized members in anything in America as far as the white man is concerned. Nor even in their prisons are they recognized equally with the white race.

How can he or anyone put us under social study when there is no social equality between whites and so-called Negroes? This gradually brewing revolution is to reclaim our respect as human beings and equal members in the civilized society of the nations of earth. Isn't it true that this is what the fight going on in the South today is for; where poor, so-called Negroes are being beaten, shot down and bombed in even those churches that the white man permits them to have because they want to be recognized as equal members in the society or order of the American white people?

We have turned to our God, Allah, and His religion, Islam, and our own people, where there is no such thing as distinction. We want to be separated from our open enemies, the slave-masters' children, who desire nothing more than to mistreat us.

When have we, the Muslims, ever received justice under the Constitution of America? Not one time in the courts of America, a country and people that hate the religion of Islam because it demands freedom, justice and equality for black people.

The greatest racists that have ever lived on our Planet Earth are the white people. We only ask for the privilege of being ourselves, seeking to restore brotherly love and respect among our people who have been divided, robbed and spoiled by the American whites.

Judge Duffy has now openly spoken his hatred for any justice coming to us who have turned to do righteousness, which is the fulfillment of the prophecy which reads: "Ye, truth faileth; and judgment is turned away backward and justice standeth afar off [for the so-called Negroes] for truth is fallen in the streets and equity cannot enter. He that departed from evil maketh himself a prey: and the Lord [Master Fard Muhammad] saw it and it displeased Him that there was no judgment [justice]" (Isa. 59:15).

Blessed are the so-called Negroes that depart from the evil and filthy doings of this American white man. How happy they are who seek refuge in Allah and are believers.

WHAT THE MUSLIMS TEACH: FATHER TO A SON

My son had been questioned concerning my teachings and had been asked to sign an unprecedented qualifying statement, completely contrary to his teachings and principle. My son, refused to sign the letter.

After months of an adoption preceding in Chicago Cook County Court which appeared definitely prejudiced against the religion of Islam, the right to adopt a Muslim baby girl was granted to my son and wife, Mr. and Mrs. Elijah Muhammad, Jr.

Instead, he referred the matter to me, and presented to the court a letter written in direct reply to him by me, authorizing him to show the message to the Judge so "that he may have a better understanding of what I am teaching."

Because the message expounds on many aspects of what the Muslims believe and teach and because it answers many historic questions, the full text is herein presented."

Dear Son:

In regard to the letter that the court gave you to sign, I think it was given only to try you at answering to the good of self and the truth.

To bear witness to the truth is the fundamental principle of the teachings of truth of those who believe. I am sure the Judge was not expecting you to agree with such answers as written in the letter you are supposed to sign; for it will be giving the lie to the truth and making you an absolute hypocrite to your own religion and its teachings. I laughed after reading the words that you are supposed to put your signature to, which would affirm all that is written in the letter.

The coming of Allah, in the Person of Master Fard Muhammad, with truth which means life and light to us, the mentally dead of the civilized world, cannot be denied and condemned as false. I have taught you from your cradle of what Almighty God, Allah, revealed to me who appeared in the Great Person of Master Fard Muhammad.

He taught me there is no birth record of the black man but that there is a birth record for the white race. He referred to the Black Nation as being the original people of the earth, which means the first.

He said that the beginning of the white race came through graftage of the white race from the original people—this is universally agreed upon by the scholars and scientists of the white people, both religious and non-religious. That which comes by grafting cannot be the equal of the original. This is also universally approved, as in the horse and the mule; the orange-grapefruit and the lemon. The mule is not the equal with the horse and is not the same; the grapefruit is not like the lemon or like the orange, although it is grafted from them it looks more luscious. It is not as good as either however.

It is impossible for us to agree that all men are created equally. There is superiority even in the animal world. Some animals are created strong, and some are created weak; some are vicious, and some are harmless. God has created two kinds of everything, so teaches the Holy Qur-an and we have these things in reality to study for our own education. The universe was not equally created. There are lesser and greater in the whole of the creations. When I have the chance to visit you I will go into details on all of this with you.

I am quite sure the court will not be objecting to the truth of what has been said in this letter, and this is universally known.

The white race, we must remember, was given superiority or

supremacy over us for a limited time in wisdom. The God who grafted them gave them a superior wisdom to qualify them to 6 thousand years.

To be equally created is to be of the same; one is self-created, the second one is made from the first. It would be foolish to say that God made all men from one man and then say that all are equal with that first one in the creation; because if they are made from one, then everyone who is made from that one must be totally the same. And the children who are produced by the original, who have not been changed by graftage into a different race, are the same as the original.

We do not teach superiority of races in the sense that I think the court is trying to get you to answer to. They seek an answer to charge us with aggressive teachings of superiority of the races, while we know that they have made us inferior. I shall be glad to clarify to the court any misunderstanding on what I am teaching.

Now concerning the child, she already belongs to us as far as religion is concerned and as far as the legal giving up of her by her mother, who is also a Muslim. Actually, I do not know why the court has such power over the child. I do not see just what the court is arguing about, since the baby has been legally given and under the same faith.

The child was not born a Catholic, nor is her mother a Catholic. It is universally approved that no black person is born a Catholic by nature. But by nature, all darker people are of the religion of Islam—this the Holy Qur-an teaches. So since the child's mother is not of any faith other than Islam, I do not see why the question of religion comes up in court at all. Our religion of Islam is universal.

If I had been teaching hate for the past 32 years in Chicago, I do not suppose I would have been able to live there—not to think of my followers! I have been teaching the truth, and if they call truth hate, it is up to them and God to settle.

As far as the hatred of groups and races, as your letter mentioned, that is a misunderstanding. It is just the plain truth that Allah has revealed to me that I teach. It is natural that the white race would not want to be known as the real devils. But who am I to prevent it if it is the will of Allah (God), while His Prophets have foretold of it (John 8:44)? Shall I not teach and bear witness to the truth of Allah?

You may give this letter to the judge that he may have a better understanding of what I am teaching. Thirty-two years in Chicago have not produced any insurrection against the white people from what I teach. In fact, we have lived more peacefully among the whites since having the knowledge of them.

May the peace and blessings of Allah be upon you, my son, and all the Believers.

As-Salaam-Aliakum

Your father,

Elijah Muhammad,

Messenger of Allah

AUTHORITY FROM ALLAH, NONE OTHER

The incredible upsurgence of Muhammad's Temples of Islam in North America has brought forth not only popular acclaim and acceptance, but also occasional unfounded attempts to discredit my mission.

In response to alleged statements made by an Eastern Muslim leader and printed recently in a white newspaper purporting criticism of the teachings of the Muslims in America, I gave the following reply to this widely circulated story in the interest of clarity.

"We do not have any authentic proof that the Muslims in Jeddah, Arabia, said anything of the kind to the white American newspaper reporters. Be it known that the white Americans and their newspapers will be printing much propaganda against the truth that Allah (God) has given to me to deliver to my people, the American so-called Negroes.

"We are the brother of the Muslims not only of Arabia but from all over the entire world, wherever one is found. This I have proved time and time again.

They know me and I know them; we are not enemies of each other, and the time will come when the white Americans and Black Americans (so-called Negroes) will know.

"There have been a few things said here of the Orthodox Muslims as not agreeing with me on the white race being the race of devils, as God has revealed them. But from wherever this was picked up, it is only from those who wish continuous socialization with the American whites. But as time goes on you will not find them in any such pictures as being my enemies.

"They, too, are gradually coming over with me in the understanding for the first time in their history; the realization of the devils. It is in the Holy Qur-an that these people are the devils, and the scholars of Islam know it.

"This is the last and final truth to be delivered to the world; the knowledge of God and the devils.

"I will not dare accuse the Secretary General of Mecca as speaking the exact words these reporters have given.

"You should ask yourself why are Americans so worried over the spread of Islam to the black man in America. It is because this truth of them, and of the slaves and true religion of Allah, must first come to them before there can be a final resurrection of the mentally dead slaves and judgment upon their cruel masters.

"Be not deceived by this deceiving and crooked enemy of black mankind. They are going like life and death to deceive you against accepting the truth which is written in the scriptures of truth (Bible and Holy Qur-an).

"And again in their race to try and deceive and hold you in what they have taught to mislead you in the knowledge of the truth there should also be a proof that they actually do not intend you any good.

"If they had freed you in deeds 100 years ago, why should they now be trying to force you under a lot of propaganda and empty promises to remain with them in that which has enslaved you and continue to hold you subjected to them?

"White America does not want you to be free; they want you to be subjected to them forever on the pretense that they will give you work to do and pay you for that work but never offer you freedom to acquire some of this earth that you can call your own.

"And they have killed off the original owners and have taken their homes and call it their home today. And many other countries of the Black Nations they have taken and master under false claims and promises and under superior power of arms.

"The American so-called Negroes are now a prey in the hands of the children of their once slave-masters. And the salve-masters' children have the same minds as their fathers had toward the so-called Negroes; that is, keep him under their power and never let him go free for himself.

"So today, they treat the so-called Negro as a child that is crying for a more comfortable place in the house, by sticking a little piece of candy in his hand or in his mouth to suck under the pretense that you are going to give him a more comfortable place in the house.

"But when he begins to nurse on that candy he goes to sleep and you can lay him down anywhere, whether comfortable or uncomfortable, because that baby is asleep.

"Now this is not an answer to the Muslims of Saudi, Arabia, because I do not know the truth of what they have said; this is an answer to the *Chicago's American* newspaper and its correspondents.

"There is no such thing as that you will see coming from the Muslim world a representative to tell me and my followers in America to stop teaching what we are teaching. To stop the teaching that I have received from Allah to give to the American so-called Negroes is not in the power of any Orthodox Muslim or non-believer.

"But in answer to such attempt, I will say that neither Jeddah nor Mecca have sent me! I am sent from Allah and not from the Secretary General of the Muslim League. There is no Muslim in Arabia that has authority to stop me from delivering this message that I have been assigned to by Allah, anymore than they had authority to stop Noah, Abraham, Moses, Jesus and Muhammad.

"I am not taking orders from them, I am taking orders from Allah (God) Himself.

ANSWER TO
CHRISTIAN KNIGHTS OF
THE KU KLUX KLAN

J. B. Stoner, the Archleader and Imperial Wizard of the Christian Knights of the Ku Klux Klan addressed a letter to a gathering of Muslims in Convention in Chicago during February 1957.

1 Thessalonians 2:14-16   St. John 8:44-48
CHRISTIAN KNIGHTS
of the
KU KLUX KLAN
Archleader, J. B. Stoner,   P.O. Box 48
    Imperial Wizard   Atlanta, Ga.

"Infidels:

"Repent of Mohammedanism or burn in hell forever, throughout eternity.

"The Lord Jesus Christ is the only begotten Son of God and He is the only One Who can save your infidelic souls and lead you into Heaven. Read the Holy Bible. St. John 6:35—"And Jesus said unto them, I am the bread of life. He that cometh to me shall never hunger; and he that believeth on me shall never thirst." St. John 6:47—"Verily, verily, I say unto you. He that believeth on me hath everlasting life" St. John 8:12—"Then spake Jesus again unto them, saying, I am the light of the world; he that followeth me shall not walk in darkness, but shall have the light of life." Acts 16:31—"And they said, Believe on the Lord Jesus Christ and thou shall be saved and thy house." Acts 4:12—"Neither is there salvation is any other: for there is none other name under heaven, whereby we must be saved." Therefore, Muhammad can do you no good.

"It does not surprise me to hear that Islam is growing among the Africans of America. It is easy to understand because Islam is a nigger religion. It has only been successful among Africans and mix-breeds and never among the white people never. As you probably know, Christianity was well established throughout North Africa by white people before Mohammed was born. As time went on more and more people in North Africa became mongrelized with African blood. Therefore, they were no longer able or willing to stand up and fight for Christianity when persecution came upon them from Arabia. Their faith in Christ was shallow and weak. Then came the bloody Islamic conquerors from Arabia who slaughtered the white Christian leaders but spared the black people and mix-breeds. The Africans quickly forgot Christ, the true religion, and became Mohammedans. Some scholars have wondered why, but not me. I know why. Islam is a product of the colored race. Islam is a dark religion for dark people. I don't know why Africans would support Islam for any other reason except of race. There are several reasons why niggers should oppose it. One reason is that the Qur-an forbids Muslims to drink intoxicating drinks, whereas most niggers like to get drunk. It says also that thieves should have their hands cut off. How many niggers would be left with hands?

Christianity, the one and only true religion, has only been successful in white nations among white people, as recognized in the literature of The Christian Party. Christianity prevails in every white nation, even when outlawed, but does not appear to have roots in any colored nation that could withstand tribulation. Therefore on a racial group basis, it would appear that only the superior white race is capable of appreciating Christianity and that the dark inferior races prefer a heathen religion like Islam. Therefore, it is obvious that we Christians should work hard to preserve the great white race. Not only will we benefit; but by keeping the white race alive we will be able to do more missionary work and be instrumental in saving the individual souls of millions of colored people in spite of their racial weakness and racial inferiority. We white Christians love the souls of all men, with all due respect to the racial differences that God Himself created. If GOD had only wanted one race, He would have created one race.

"To every place it has spread, Islam has been a blight and brought darkness. Islam's armies conquered much of Asia and Africa and even of Europe and caused darkness in every country that it entered and it decayed their civilizations that the great white race had built.

"Muslims, in their efforts to conquer the world, occupied most of Spain and even invaded ancient France. Fortunately, there was a great white Christian leader, Charles Martel. He saved Civilization and the white race by defeating the Moham- medans at the Battle of Tours in the year of our Lord 732 thus stopping the Islamic invasion of Europe. Later the Islamic Turks invaded white Christian Europe from the East. The Turks, under Suleiman the Magnificent, got as far into the heart of Europe as the gates of Vienna before they were stopped in 1529 A.D. In 1683 A.D., during the reign of Mohammed IV, they besieged Vienna again, but were soundly defeated by the great King John Sobieski in Poland, the hero of white Christiandom and perserver of civilization.

"One of the main purposes of Mohammedan invasion of white Europe was to capture white women. Only white women are beautiful. When ruling over white sections of Europe, part of the tribute required of the conquered people was the regular giving of beautiful white women to the Muslims as slaves. They didn't like their own dark women. The African race has never produced a beautiful woman, so the Muslims were naturally not satisfied with their own black women. If the Africans were as good as whites, they would be happy with their own women in- stead of lusting for our white women. Your desire for white women is an admission of your own racial inferiority. One reason why we whites will never accept you into our white society is because a nigger's chief ambition in life is to sleep with a white woman, thereby polluting her. Everytime a demented white wom- an marries a nigger, your newspapers brag about the sin. The day will come when no nigger will be allowed to even look at a white woman or a white woman's picture. That will be a sad day for the men of your race who have no respect for their own women, won't it? For your information, nigger is the Latin word for black, so why are you ashamed of it?

"Yes, Africans in America are ashamed of their own race. They regret that they are what they are. As proof, look at the nigger newspaper that advertise skin whiteners, and so-called hair straighteners. If blacks are as good as whites why aren't they proud of their black skins and the kinky wool on top of their heads? If you aren't ashamed of your race, why don't you strive to keep it pure and preserve it and its characteristics.

"You blacks have a lower opinion of your own race than we whites have. You hate, yes hate your own African race so much that you want to destroy it by mixing your blood with white blood. You want white blood pumped into your race because you think white blood is better and will improve you and make you less negroid, less African. You are trying to forget what you are. You blacks are sick of each other and want to forget your heritage and your race by associating with your white superiors.

"If you were as good as whites and equal to us, you would not be trying to force yourselves into white society. You would be happy with the company of your fellow Africans. Or, is the odor too much for you? Since you niggers don't respect your own race and don't love your race enough to preserve it, how can you expect white people to respect it? I have more respect for an African who believes in Black Supremecy and racial purity than I do for an African who hates his own race and tries vainly to disown it. I admire the African who says that no white man is good enough to shake hands with him.

"I hope you will appreciate the fact that I am not a hypocrite like some Yankees who preach race-mixing and practice segregation. I actually express the sentiments and feelings that are in the hearts of most white people everywhere when I tell you that I believe in white supremacy and the inferiority of all dark races.

"Why should we whites let Africans infiltrate our civilization when Africans have never been able to build or maintain a civilization of their own? You Africans are afraid to do it alone. You are afraid that you would get lost without the white man to guide you and help you. Yet, with your mania for mongrelization, you are trying to destroy the white race that has given you civilization on a silver platter. You are striving to kill the white goose that laid the golden egg of civilization. If you succeed, you will not be able to get more golden eggs because the white goose will be dead.

"A new independent African nation will be born in a few days on March 6th, 1957. Now known as the rich Gold Coast, it will become known as Ghana. Blacks will run it from top to bottom. Do you think they are capable of success or does their black blood doom them to their failure? The black Prime Minister graduated from Lincoln University here in America. Many of Ghana officials have studied in America. English is a common language in Ghana. If the Africans had self-respect and ability, they would go to Ghana in Africa and prove their racial ability by helping to build a great African nation. They won't go because they have no confidence in themselves.

"They know that their race is a lower form of humanity and cannot stand on its own feet. The Africans of America are afraid to be without the white man, and thus, admit their own inferiority.

"The British West Indies that lie off the coast of the United States will also become a new independent black nation soon. They speak English there. However, America's black people won't even go that short distance to help build a black nation because there won't be enough whites to control them and lead them around. The Africans of America are convinced that they would perish without the white race to help and protect them. Blacks even claim that white teachers are superior to black teachers. Inferiors always demand the right to associate with their superiors. When the black man cries against segregation, he is actually singing praises to the white race.

They never intended for America to fall into the possession of a dark race. Many of the founders of this nation owned blacks as slaves, such as Washington, Jefferson, and the great Patrick Henry who said: "Give me liberty or give me death."

America is a white Christian nation and no infedelic religion such as Islam, has a right to exist under the American sun. Your Islam, your Mohammedanism is not a white religion. Mohammedanism is a nigger religion. The white race will never accept it, so take it back to Africa with you. It is like the Holy Bible says about GOD'S plan for the nations of men in Acts 16:31— "And hath determined the times before appointed, and the bounds of their habitation." Therefore you have no place in America with your African race or your Islamic African arligion.

"The Christian Party becomes stronger every day. When we are elected to power we will legally drive you out. Remember 1492 A.D. when those two great white Christian monarchs, King Ferdinand and Queen Isabella, expelled the Muslims from Spain. The Christian Party will be even more ruthless. We will not tolerate your infidelic Christ-hating religion on American soil. We will drive Islam into the ocean. America isn't big enough for the Christian Party and Black Islam, so Islam must go.

"You Muslims should be ashamed of yourselves for trying

to lead the poor darkies of America into your Mohammedam
hell. If they are smart, they will shun Mohammed and follow the
Lord Jesus Christ, the Son of God, into Heaven and a happy
and everlasting life.

Repent and confess the Lord Jesus Christ or you will burn in
hell forever, you infidels. Your false religion is an insult to the
true living GOD.

"May God have mercy upon your heathen souls.

"With many wishes for the failure of Islam in America, I am,
Yours for Christ, Country and Race,
(signed)

> J. B. Stoner
> Archleader of the Christian Party
> P. O. Box 48
> Atlanta, Georgia

My answer to Mr. J. B. Stoner and his Christian Knights of the
Ku Klux Klan is as follows:

Sir:

The only so-called Negroes who love you (the whites) and
desire you are those who are ignorant of the knowledge of you
(this you do not know). And as soon as they awaken, as they
will, to the knowledge of you being the real devils (their open
enemies), they too will not shake your hands, nor want to look
at your or even your shadow. The Truth of you will make all
black mankind hate you, regardless of their color—black, brown,
yellow or red. This Truth of you is part of that secret that was
withheld by Allah, to allow you to live your Time (6000 years).
(I admit that the so-called Negroes are not only ignorant of
self and you but they are actually mentally dead). Your time
is up and you are now being revealed, and you will by no means
be able to hide yourself or deceive my people any longer.

Who is to blame for this mixing—black Africans or the white
European devils? Did the black Africans go seeking your white
women in Europe or did you carry her to them in Africa? Isn't
it true that black Africans are today asking your kind to leave

them and their country, and that you won't leave without war? (They will one day throw you out!)

"How did the so-called Negroes get into America? Did they come here of their own desire for America and for your women, or did YOU go after them in their country and bring them here against their will?"

"Did your Negro slaves ever try making sexual love with their slave-masters' wives and daughters while you held and still hold complete power over them? Which of your houses and families show that the black and white males have been, and are still visiting--yours or the Negroes? We see you day and night after the so-called Negro women whistling and winking your eyes and blowing your car horns at them; making advances to every Negro woman that walks, rides, flies or works for you in your homes, offices and factories. Not in America alone but all over the earth wherever you go among the black, brown, yellow and red people, we see that you are after our women, whom you say to be "ugly." If your women are so beautiful why then do our "ugly" women attract you and your kind? You and your kind, according to history, have been after our women ever since being on our planet. We drove you out of Asia six thousand years ago, to keep you away from our women and from mixing your wicked blood in ours. We veiled and locked our women in, to keep your adulterous blue eyes from feasting on her beauty. And the only solution to this mixture of your devil blood in our homes is that Allah remove you completely off our Planet, also those of our own who love and desire mixing with you! This is the Resurrection and Separation of us all; little do you and the so-called Negroes know or believe it!

Your concern for the protection of your white women should have been prepared by your fathers, and self, by staying away from our women. YOUR race is still white, so what are you afraid of?

"I have been risen to raise my people here, and to help them into knowledge of self and their God Allah (who is in Person among them) and you their open enemies (the devils). Therefore, the so-called Negroes are your own product as far as teachings and training are concerned. If you have taught them (my people the so-called Negroes) the TRUTH why are you so afraid of them believing that which you didn't teach them?

"You said in your letter, "The Muslims should be ashamed

of themselves for trying to lead the poor darkies of America into your Mohammedan hell." Have you the Christian Party, led
the so-called Negroes into heaven? Wasn't John Hawkins (the
slave trader) a member of your Christian Party (race)? He didn't
sit them (the so-called Negroes) in heaven.

"The Muslims make the so-called Negroes who believe in
Allah and his religion, Islam, equal in the brotherhood of our
Nation. Have you done or are you doing it now: making the
Christian believing Negroes your equal brothers? You say, "Con-
fess the Lord Jesus Christ or you will burn in hell forever."
That hell must not be so hot, that one can burn in it forever
and never burn up.

"Isn't it true that your Christian Party lynches and burns
your black Christian believers there in your own state (Georgia)?
Have you ever seen or heard of us Muslims lynching and burning Negroes who believe or don't believe in Islam?

"You said we are 'Christ-hating'. You have used the name of
Jesus for a bait to deceive the Negroes, while at the same time
you are not a doer of the teachings of Jesus, nor of the Prophets
before Jesus.

"Your Bible teaches against the doing of evil. It also warns
you to do unto others as you would have done unto yourself,
and to love thy brother as thyself. Not any of these teachings
have you or your kind ever practiced. You do not care enough
for a Negro Christian believer to call him your brother Christian.
And you do not think of doing unto him as you would have done
unto yourself. You beat and kill them (Negro Christian believers)
day and night and bomb their churches, where in reality they
worship YOU, not Jesus. You even burn your own Christian Sign
(the Cross) when you plan to kill or burn your poor black Christian slaves.

"You acknowledge in your letter that 'Islam was the Negroes'
religion,' and that 'Christianity was a white peoples' religion.'
Then why don't you leave the Negroes alone or help them get
back to their OWN religion (Islam)? And why do you insult
men and the whole Nation of Islam and threaten to drive us into
the ocean for teaching the Negroes their own religion, since YOU
won't dare teach it to them? You further say that America is
a white Christian nation, that it was founded by 'white men for
white men,' and that they (the founders) never intended for America to fall into the possession of a dark race. Just why then are

you hindering the Negroes from going back to their OWN religion and people, especially since YOU are not going to divide this country with them and not going to treat them as your equal?

"Your Bible teaches that the 'Day' will come when every man will turn and go to his own. Did YOU originally own this part of our Planet? Aren't the red Indians the original owners, who are brothers of the dark Nation (of Islam)? There is no part of our Planet that was ever given to the white race. The Planet belongs to US—the Nation of Islam! And I am afraid that you might fall backwards into a lake of fire when you attempt to drive Islam into the ocean. If the ocean is ours, so is the land that you claim to be yours. Your Bible teaches you that it belongs to us. You shall soon come to know.

You accuse the so-called Negroes, who are really members of the Holy Tribe of Shabazz, of being drunkards and thieves, and suggest that they should oppose Islam because it forbids Muslims to drink intoxicating drinks whereas most so-called Negroes (or as you said niggers) like to get drunk.' Who makes the intoxicating drinks? Do YOU make it or do the so-called Negroes make it? And doesn't your Government legalize the sale of intoxicating drinks? Since you say that you are Christians and followers of Jesus, did Jesus teach and legalize the sale and drinking of strong drinks? And did you find that my people were thieves and drunkards in their Native Land four hundred years ago when they were kidnapped by John Hawkins and brought over here into slavery? And haven't YOU been their master and teacher ever since? The whatever they are today, YOU (the Christian race) made them that.

"You admit that Islam doesn't allow such evils, but still you call Islam 'infidelic'. The Christian religion permits every evil practice that is known to mankind and legalizes them. Such religion and people you call to be of Jesus!

"We know who YOU are, and who the so-called Negroes really are. The God of the Universe and the Right Religion are not asking you, nor thank you, for trying to tell us or our people (whom you call niggers) anything of God and His religion. When we get through opening the Negroes' eyes, you will take your hats off to them.

"Your letter is headed with 1 Thessalonians 3:14-16 and St. John 8:44-48. Why not 2 Thessalonians 2:3,4,7-12; also 1 Corinthians 10:21. All these as well as St. John 8:44 refer to you and

your race as the real devils, who even killed Jesus and the Prophets before Him, and who persecute us who believe and preach
go to hell with you for believing and following you and our
your own Bible to pick that which condemns your own self! I
am real happy to have received such open confessions of your
evil self, as I am doing all I can to make the Negroes see that
you and your religion are their open enemies, and to prove to
them that they will never be anything but your slaves and finally
go to hell with you for believing and following you and your
kind.

"I hope the world of black mankind will read your letter to
me. For you have many of them fooled. Some Arab Muslims
think that you (the whites) can be made Muslims, but not me
unless you are really born again. And it is too late for a rebirth.

"I say all so-called Negroes should give up the white race's
religion and come into their own (Nation of Islam). In Islam
alone they will enjoy brotherly love, peace of mind and contentment.

I will admit the so-called Negroes educated and trained by
you and your kind will never be able to maintain self-rule. But
they are now reaching out for Allah and Islam, and for training
from others of the OWN Nation who are and have been independent long before you were even created. We all know that you
hold back the very key of knowledge that would make the so-
called Negroes, that you school, from ever being capable of self-
government. But they will get it in Islam. And when they have
finished their courses, they won't even think of building a government on your basis. The world that you have built is nothing
compared to that which Allah will build with your slaves (the
so-called Negroes).

"You make it clear why you doubt Ghana's success in main-
taining independence; because Ghana's Prime Minister graduated
from one of your schools (Lincoln University) and because its
your language (English) that is the common language in Ghana.
But now they are studying their own, (Arabic), language, and
soon they will return to their own religion (Islam).

"You said that if the Africans of America had self-respect
and ability they would go to Ghana and help build a great
African Nation. But not with your schooling! If you would stop
interfering with those who are trying to qualify themselves for
a return to their Native people and country, within a few years

they all would leave you and your evil doings. But nay! You don't want them to leave your country. No! Not any more than Pharaoh wanted to see his slaves leave Egypt. But Allah is going to take yours as He took Pharaoh's slaves, believe it or not.

"You like to make fun of your slaves whom YOU have taught and trained. But they ARE your product.

"You make the so-called Negroes do for you everything that a real citizen does and yet you will not give them equal rights as a citizen. You make them fight to keep you free to rule them and their kind.

"They (so-called Negroes) pay equal taxes, but are paid the lowest wages. Even in your own state (Georgia) they aren't allowed to use your highway filling station's rest-rooms (but will be arrested if they are seen relieving themselves in public). They are not allowed to eat in your public eating places, though they may purchase the food and eat it on the outside. Yet when your country's future is at stake you tell them that this is their country and that they are citizens of it! You know that they are fools for believing what you say knowing that you have told them the same old false story many times and many of them believe you. But not me, or my followers.

"If there was any good in you (which there isn't) you would exempt all the so-called Negroes from paying taxes, since they are your free slaves. You don't intend to divide your 48 states with them, not even one state, nor the spoils of war that they so willingly help gain for you.

"The so-called Negroes do not demand anything from you, except that you stop killing them unjustly and give them equal justice under your laws as you do for yourself, and equal WAGES as you do for your kind and for the same labor. No, not land for themselves, nor instruments and money to go elsewhere which you have acquired from their labor, sweat and blood. No real civilized people would be asking for such small pay in return for four hundred years of free labor, free blood, life and for the use (misuse) of their women by you at your will--only a foolish people without knowledge of you and their own kind would accept that.

"Thanks, thanks to Allah, our God, in the person of Master Fard Muhammad, The Great Mahdi, who was to come and has come, to restore--"we", who were lost from our Own--the Kingdom of Islam--and to destroy those who have destroyed us.

"Thou art our God, O Allah, and we are Thy people. Deliver us from our murderers and we will serve and obey Thee all the days of our life and we will teach our children Thy Praises and to submit to Thee for Thy Unequaled Love and Mercy for us.

"And thanks to You, O Allah, for making manifest our enemy (the devil), and help us, O Allah, to die the death of a Muslim."

Signed: Elijah Muhammad

A GUIDE TO UNDERSTANDING THE BIBLE

The Bible referred to unless otherwise noted is the one commonly known as The Authorized (King James) Version.

GUIDE TO UNDERSTANDING THE HOLY QURAN

The Holy Qur-an referred to unless otherwise noted is the
Arabic Text, translation and commentary (Revised Edition)
BY Maulana Muhammad Ali. 3rd or 4th Edition.

Acknowledgments

"Whoever brings a good deed will have tenfold like it . . ."
(Holy Qur-an 6:161)

"And judging on that day will be just; so as for those whose good deeds are heavy, they are the successful." (Holy Qur-an 7:8)

The making of this book was a task which was made much easier for me by the assistance given to me by Brother John Ali, National Secretary, The Nation of Islam. He went through articles which I had previously written and he gave general supervision to the editing, typing, typesetting and proof-reading. Thanks to Mr. Richard Durham and my son, Herbert Muhammad, who read first drafts and offered valuable comments. Much thanks must be given to Mrs. Maria Comeaux who did such an excellent job preparing the typewritten manuscript from very small newspaper type. Thanks to Midway Editorial Research, particularly, Mrs. Ruth Grodzins, who gave a professional reading of the manuscript and galley proofs. Thanks to Sis. Arlene and Sis. Novene Pasha who aided in typing, reading and corrections. Thanks to Bro. Roosevelt 4X who made at all hours, trips to the typesetters and printers. Greatly appreciated is the professional quality and workmanship turned out by the typesetters, Adwest Corp. under the able direction of Mr. Charles Porter.

I desire now, be The will of Allah, to write a book going into greater detail of the science covering the full extent of my mission from what Allah, Who came in the person of Master Fard Muhammad, has revealed and still reveals to me. I pray Allah that I have as competent help in preparing this more comprehensive book which I plan to write as I did with this which you read. My thanks to all who aided in preparing this book.

Elijah Muhammad
Messenger of Allah